DEVELOPING AN EDUCATIONALLY ACCOUNTABLE PROGRAM

Lesley H. Browder, Jr.
William A. Atkins, Jr.
Esin Kaya

School of Education, Hofstra University
Hempstead, Long Island, New York

McCutchan Publishing Corporation
2526 Grove Street
Berkeley, California 94704

ISBN: 0-8211-0121-8
LC: 72-83476

Manufactured in the United States of America
Typography by PBS, Berkeley, California

About the Authors

Lesley H. Browder, Jr. has served the public schools of four states from classroom teacher through the superintendency. A "magna cum laude," Phi Beta Kappan Bachelor of Arts from Lehigh University, he received his Master of Arts, Master of Education, and Doctor of Education degrees from Cornell University. Recognized in the field of educational administration as both scholar and practitioner, Ley is a member of numerous honorary and professional groups. One of Ley's major works in the area of accountability is his edited work, *Emerging Patterns of Administrative Accountability* (also published by the McCutchan Publishing Corporation). A past recipient of Stanford University's "Outstanding Teacher Award" of the School of Education, Ley is currently associate professor and chairman of the Department of Educational Administration, Hofstra University, Hempstead, New York.

William A. Atkins, Jr. began his career as an elementary school teacher and advanced to the position of superintendent of schools, during which time he had experience in five school districts. He holds a bachelor's degree from the University of Denver, a master's from Washington University, and a doctorate from Harvard University where he was a student in the Administrative Career Program. Recently he was with General Learning Corporation, first as director of a Job Corps Center, and then as manager of their Management and Training Services where he had responsibility for the operation of training programs throughout the country. A member of numerous professional associations, active in community affairs, Bill is also vice-president of International Training Systems, Inc. In addition to extensive consulting and a variety of teaching assignments, he is associate dean of the School of Education at Hofstra University.

Esin Kaya is a psychologist and a specialist in educational research and evaluation with experience in university teaching, in consulting to school systems, to the Ford Foundation and to industry on research and evaluation problems, and in directing a number of funded research projects. She has developed and directed the Bureau of Educational Evaluation at Hofstra University and has published a number of research articles. She holds a Bachelor of Arts degree from Barnard College, a Master of Arts from Teachers College, Columbia University, and received her Doctor of Philosophy degree from New York University. Currently, she is a professor of education and chairman of the Department of Educational Psychology, Hofstra University, Hempstead, New York.

Preface

Victor Hugo noted that an idea whose time has come is not to be resisted. The time has come for accountability—educational accountability. The notion of accountability itself is not new. It dates back to biblical times, and, up to 1898, showed traces of application to education in nineteenth century England. Its most recent application, to education, is freshly minted, adding a slightly different twist to a venerable concept. In oversimplified form, the idea is to hold schools answerable for their students' learning.

Still emerging in its application to education, the concept of accountability has a malleable quality. It is capable of being shaped in many ways. Definitions of educational accountability abound, and so do suggestions on its applications. Since the late 1960s, when Leon Lessinger gave national visibility to the idea from the associate commissioner's office in the U.S. Office of Education, no single work on the subject has been able to set down the concept in a way that etches it in stone tablets (a process known academically as producing a "definitive work"). If you like working with a concept that has a cutting edge, broad application, and is still in transition, it might be worth your time exploring more deeply. You too can shape its destiny.

Another quality of accountability is its stickiness—that is, many other concepts in the educational process (and some outside it) can be easily included in a process that attains accountability. In a sense, the accountability process may act to contain otherwise independent movements in education—needs assessment, performance objectives, participatory involvement in goal setting, management technology, program evaluation, etc. It is a versatile concept, as long as its conditions are heeded.

To date, reaction to applying accountability to education has been mixed. If remarks attributed to James Lade are correct, an idea passes through an evolutionary sequence of stages: (1) indignant rejection, (2) reasoned objection, (3) qualified opposition, (4) tentative acceptance, (5) qualified endorsement, (6) judicious modification, (7) cautious adoption, (8) impassioned espousal, (9) proud parenthood, and (10) dogmatic propagation. Some—frequently legislators, school boards, and a few commercial hucksters—have seemingly short-circuited the evolutionary sequence and reached a point of impassioned espousal rapidly. Others—usually those individuals who fear or otherwise detest the idea of being held accountable to anyone for results attained—cluster at the starting gate, indignantly rejecting the thought.

Serious observers of the movement, however, take a modified position, ranging from qualified opposition to tentative acceptance and qualified endorsement of the concept. No one rejects it as trivial; no one acclaims it as a panacea. All appear to recognize educational accountability as a potentially powerful concept, and most soberly view it as a natural culmination of many parallel activities, an intersection point captured in an idea—an idea whose time has come.

Under such conditions, the educational accountability movement can be expected to pick up a velocity of its own. At this point in history, it is too young a movement to assess well its likely impact on American education. Many observers feel its arrival is a necessary precondition to move public education to a new and higher level of performance, sophistication, and effectiveness.

This book is intended for those administrators and others who search for potential ways to improve educational programs. It offers an approach with some options for developing accountability. The book makes no pretense at representing either THE APPROACH or THE AUTHORITY on the subject. We recognize neither. If we are successful as authors, we will have performed an act as midwife between yourself and the exploration of an exciting concept.

The Plan of This Book

Part I, "About Educational Accountability," contains two chapters. Chapter 1, "Toward Accountability," provides a setting for understanding the accountability concept as it appears on education's changing scene. It defines accountability as a concept in transition, briefly traces its evolution, and discusses its expression in education.

The second chapter, "Developing an Educationally Accountable Program," presents a model for developing an educationally accountable program. It begins with a listing of preliminary imperatives believed to be useful in considering such a venture, and follows with a four-phase model and some suggestions for tailoring the accountability process to fit local situations. Some frank statements about its limitations are also included.

Part II, "Considerations in the Development of an Educationally Accountable Program," offers a series of chapters that, in part, represent elements in the model presented in chapter 2, but are not treated as integral parts of this model. Our intention is not to tie the reader to our model. Rather, we say: "Look, in Part I we tell you something about accountability and offer you what we hope is a useful way to develop your own program, and in Part II are some more items on things frequently associated with educationally accountable programs." Then, if the reader comes for example to chapter 5, "Community-Staff Involvement," and cares not a fig about involving community and staff in curriculum policy making, he can skip it (or conversely, maybe he will be more interested in our comments here and less—heaven forbid!—anywhere else). Accordingly, though we think of the chapters as loosely following one another, they need not be read strictly in order. As in considering a new car, you may not be interested in all the accessories offered. We hope they are worth at least a quick look.

Chapter 3, "Needs Assessment," describes a preliminary step in the accountability process. "Knowing where your schools are" educationally is requisite knowledge before suggesting changes that involve many people, and otherwise make large commitments of time and effort.

Once needs have been assessed, the question arises how a solution to meet these needs might be attained. Chapter 4, "Change Strategies," deliberates among strategies that might be used in bringing change into the picture.

One of the thorniest issues in education today, especially for administrators, is concerned with involving people in the setting of school goals. Chapter 5, "Community-Staff Involvement," deals with this critical topic in the area of curriculum policy-making. Closely related is chapter 6, "Performance Objectives," in which we illustrate how measurable goals and objectives might be created. Chapter 7, "Planning-Programming-Budgeting-Evaluating," illustrates another option in the plan to develop greater fiscal understanding and accountability for program effectiveness.

An indispensible part of the accountability process, as we view it, is the training of staff as a prerequisite to program implementation. Chapter 8, "Staff Development and Program Implementation," follows through with these vital steps while chapter 9, "Performance Contracting," portrays another option in the accountability process.

The final phase appears in chapter 10, "Program Evaluation," and chapter 11, "Rendering the Account," with these portions completing Phase 4, the standing-to-account part of our model.

With a little luck, a picture of the accountability process should grow in the reader's mind as its various parts unfold before him. He may even come to think of accountability as a broad process involving his total educational community in the search for agreement on specified goals and objectives for the school's program. He may see the process of program development as encompassing decision making on plans to meet the pressures of change, as well as determining those educational outputs to be accounted in a variety of ways. We hope so; it is our intention.

Several words of thanks are to be expressed, beginning with our dean, Jonathan Messerli, whose tolerance of our pursuits is greatly appreciated. A similar acknowledgment must be paid to John McCutchan, our publisher, for his willingness not to hold us rigidly accountable to a deadline we exceeded. We recognize a professional debt of gratitude to our many colleagues in the field whose thoughts and research efforts helped shape our own. These names appear in profusion among our footnotes. A special note of gratitude is also extended to Mrs. Josephine Sadowski, "super secretary" of the educational administration department, for her help.

But special thanks must be reserved for people who have had to live—if it could be called living—with the creation of a book; our spouses—Marilyn, Joan, and Aaron. For your patience, consideration, and encouragement, heartfelt thanks!

Naturally, for any difficulties a reader experiences with our efforts, we are accountable.

Table of Contents

Part I. About Educational Accountability

1. Toward Accountability

Change, Education, and the Schoolman

Think about change. Realize that it is hard to develop any multifaceted project today—especially an educational program combining men, money, and materials—without having to acknowledge change. Omnipresent and accelerating, change by itself is recognized as an elemental force in the twentieth century. Alvin Toffler coined the term "future shock" to describe the impact of the force of change—a force that produces a "shattering stress and disorientation" on people, caused by subjecting them to "too much change in too short a time."[1] Warns Toffler, "Unless man quickly learns to control the rate of change . . . , we are doomed to a massive adaptational breakdown."[2]

Whether or not Toffler's warnings and message are correct, he has much company.[3] B. F. Skinner's view of our civilization running away like a frightened horse, panic and speed feeding on each other, may be overdrawn,[4] but there can be little doubt that acceleration of the change rate continues. Declares Sir Geoffrey Vickers: "The rate of change increases at an accelerating speed, without a corresponding acceleration in the rate at which further responses can be made; and this brings us nearer the threshold beyond which control is lost."[5] It is with these thoughts that we shift our attention to education.

For most of the history of mankind, education, in one form or

Portions of this chapter originally appeared in the introductory essay to *Emerging Patterns of Administrative Accountability* (Berkeley: McCutchan Publishing Corp., 1971).

3

another, has concerned itself with transmitting society's values, cus-
toms, and knowledge. The past cast its shadow over the present and
extended indefinitely into the future. Earlier life-style patterns could
be taught with some concrete assurance of their values to the future
generation. The individual sought instruction from the past to know
and understand what he would do in the future. Without the prominent visibility of change, older civilizations understood the role of
education to be the instruction of the young on what had been done,
said, and thought yesterday as a guide for tomorrow—a tomorrow
that would be nearly identical to yesterday.

As change became more and more visible, the concept of educational transmittal from the past began to alter. As inventions like the
printing press multiplied, as dreams of new social orders emerged,
followed closely by massive social, political, economic, and technological revolutions, the thrust of education's concern changed. The
promise that past knowledge was a sufficient guide for the future
could no longer be kept in industrialized societies. Instead, educational transmission from the world of the present, because it had
become distinctly different from the past, became for many a better
guide. To be sure, transmission from earlier times will always be part
of the educational process, but its guidance in coping with future
problems seems less useful, less appropriate, less clear in many matters. An impatient youth might say it is less "relevant."

An ancient human behavior pattern suggests tendencies of men
at different stages of their life: older men look back to see where
they came from; men in their prime look around to see where they
are; and youth look ahead to see where they are going. Traditionally,
a man's age sorts out and establishes the values of these behaviors—
but never before has there been such a disparity of outlooks. The
man in his seventies knows a world that has gone; his son in his
forties sees a world changing faster in some ways than he is able to
respond; and the youngster in his early teens looks toward a world
where the only certainty is that it will be different. The older man's
wisdom and experience are less useful. The striving adult is a less
certain guide as the shifting present crowds in on him. The youth,
feeling a gap (a "generation gap"?) in the outlook and ability of
adults to help him, looks to his peers for comfort and guidance while
marching toward an "unreal" twenty-first century. For most American youth, education in the form of the public school will be the
major guide along the way.

But a paradox exists. On the one hand, the importance of education for the future is almost universally acknowledged. Some

would even seem to paraphrase the Twenty-Third Psalm to read: "Education is my shepherd . . . ." On the other hand, there is a widespread conviction that education in its present form is not geared for the task. Notes Kenneth Clark: "I do agree strongly that the public school in America is presently unresponsive to contemporary educational needs."[6] More boldly, Toffler states: "What passes for education today, even in our 'best' schools and colleges, is a hopeless anachronism."[7]

It might be said that change has pushed man faster and further than the institutions charged with his education can respond. It is toward making an institutional response to this condition that schoolmen are (or should be) concerned. How does the situation look to a school administrator?

Schoolmen, who handle the daily educational issues of our time, could reply, "Unsettling." The pressure for change—change here-and-now—dogs most administrators. A recent study of school superintendents conducted by their major professional association suggests that simply responding to current change pressures can be nearly all-consuming. Keeping pace with current school costs alone is a leading problem, followed by pressures for responding to "demands for innovation, greater visibility, changes in values and behavior, and the revolution in school staff relations."[8] They find these pressures at once pointed, differing, and tending to converge on them. The study notes that increasing "attacks" on administrators is listed as the major reason for them to consider leaving their posts.[9]

One way or another, the local school administrator comes to understand that the development and coordination of education's response to the pressures for change rests largely on his shoulders. Many participants share in the local educational enterprise—teachers, students, board members, parents, taxpayers, minority groups, and others. All face the experiencing of "future shock" as change continues to accelerate. If massive adaptational breakdown is to be avoided, if the "threshold beyond which control is lost" is not to be crossed, then *all* share an obligation to develop a rate and quality of institutional response that will enable our youth to make the transition to the twenty-first century. But above all the others, the schoolman stands accountable.

About Accountability

What is meant by "accountability"? A clear-cut definition of the term is complicated. For example, the term appears in the

literature frequently with three senses.[10] First is an uncritical usage
of the term as synonymous with "responsibility." A second usage
is more critical, suggesting an obligation to explain or account for
the disposition of tasks entrusted to an individual.[11] The third
sense appears in the form of a partially defined concept peculiar to
education—"educational accountability." This usage conveys the
notion that the schools and the educators who operate them be
"held to account" (i.e., held both responsible and answerable) for
what they produce as "educational outcomes" (i.e., what students
learn).

Before education borrowed the term and inflated it with its
own meanings, "accountability" expressed a relationship between
the occupants of roles that control institutions, the "holders of
power," and those who possess the formal power to displace them.[12]
The scope of this form of accountability includes everything—
everything—which those who hold formal powers of dismissal find
necessary in making their major decision. This decision is whether to
continue or to withdraw their confidence in those officeholders
"held to account." A simple definition of accountability follows
from this role relationship: "the requirement on the occupant of a
role, by those who authorize that role, to answer for the results of
work expected from him in the role."[13]

Accountability as a Concept in Transition

Few things remain simple. Change, that tenacious force of our
times, has been busy reshaping this simple idea. A more extended
modern version of the original concept might be rendered as follows:

1. Accountability is a process that occurs in a relationship
between those entrusted with the accomplishment of *specific* tasks
(stewards), and those having power of review (reviewers).

2. The heart of the process is for the party "standing to
account," the steward, to explain *as rationally as possible* the results
of efforts to achieve the *specific* task objectives of his stewardship.

3. Of major concern to the parties reviewing the stewardship of
the tasks performed is the matching of performance and attainment
levels against their expectations *as expressed in the task specifications*, and determining their level of confidence in the steward and
his efforts.

4. Of major concern to the steward standing to account is his
ability to accomplish the *specified* tasks as well as his ability to

explain attainment levels in a manner that maintains or builds the reviewers' confidence in his stewardship.

The italicized words and phrases above are intended to represent, in part, the newer modifications of the original concept, its newly emerging pattern.

In the new pattern, the relationship between an individual and an organization, for example, still exists, basically in the form of a contract. Each party to the relationship has power. The one party can offer or withdraw his services. The organization can also offer or withdraw the benefits it offers in return for services rendered. Under the traditional pattern of accountability, when the agreement was reached, the individual was then liable to have work assigned him. It was *generally* understood that he was accountable for the work assigned. Under the emerging pattern, however, a significant shift is noted, namely, that *at the point of agreement* both parties are fully aware of: the tasks to be assigned; the manner in which the account is to be rendered; the nature of the performance expectations; and the rewards and penalties to be levied from determinations (made in advance) of the levels of confidence accorded by results.

For purposes of illustration, it may be possible to highlight this change in the outline offered below. Admittedly, such an outline cannot be entrusted to represent much more than an idealized tendency, a shifting degree of emphasis:

1. Task definitions (specifying what work is to be done)

Traditional pattern: The work to be done is merely implied or stated generally; it may or may not be expressed in writing. The highest degree of task definition in this pattern is illustrated by the conventional contract and/or budget document.

Emerging pattern: The work to be done is highly specified, usually in written statements, "operationally" defined (i.e., defined as assignable, measurable units of responsibility to be fulfilled under certain conditions and within certain constraints). Emerging forms of these task definitions include Plan-Program-Budget Systems, management networks, etc.

2. Rendering the account (telling how well the work was done; what resulted)

Traditional pattern: Explaining or accounting is usually in accordance with the steward's understanding of the task. Accordingly it follows that a loosely stated and understood task (more typical of the traditional pattern) begets a loosely ordered explanation rendered by the steward.

Emerging pattern: The explanation is directed at accounting for the performance and attainment of levels designated in the specified task. Increasingly the clarity of this explanation is aided by advances in management technology and data collection.

3. Performance expectations (deciding how well the work is expected to be done; what should result)

Traditional pattern: Expectations on how well the work should be done—what should happen—are not clearly focused, particularly in public institutions. These expectations range from the vague and simplistic to the moderately complex and even to excessively impossible levels, hopelessly beyond attainment. Similarly, degrees of rationality run a gamut from the emotionally irrational gut-level to overly calculated forms of callous reason. Not infrequently, each party will have his own expectations (sometimes unexpressed), stemming in part from an unclarified consensus of the task's objectives prior to its undertaking. Many times these divergent expectations are not pressured to converge in order to avoid intense emotional-level trade-offs among the parties in reaching agreement.

Emerging pattern: The range of expectations is narrowed considerably by working out agreement and forming consensus on the task's objectives *prior* to its undertaking. Increasingly, this action is supplemented with the review of more comprehensive forms of task planning, offering alternative task approaches, and providing input-output models of what may be anticipated to happen. The major hurdle in this skewing of expectations toward rational, articulated, commonly understood levels of expected results is the development of a consensus supporting it. There is still no easy way to form such a consensus—particularly if the parties to it do not wish to be held responsible for operationally defined results. The usual approach, beyond offering token expectations at the outset (e.g., "a better _____ for _____"; "more _____ for _____"; "a hope that _____"; etc.), is to let "sleeping dogs lie" and allow the matter to resolve itself as the task progresses. The emerging approach is at the outset to "take the bull by the horns," determining operationally as fully as possible what is expected to happen as a result of the work before beginning the task.

4. The level-of-confidence issue (deciding whether the work results are good enough; is it acceptable)

From the reviewer's standpoint: Historically, when the reviewers have exercised their prerogative of holding stewards to account (i.e., determining progress toward task accomplishment and thereby making a decision about their level of confidence in the steward and his efforts), a wide range of rewards and penalties have resulted. Rewards have included such things as the creation of "divine" emperors, lifetime appointments (tenure), promotion, salary increases, contract renewals, bonuses, stock options, merit pay, gold watches, and kindly smiles of appreciation. Penalty samples include death, loss of position, demotion, salary cuts, withheld payments, contract terminations, curses, grumbles, and frowns.

From the steward's standpoint: Stewards too have their own level-of-confidence determinations. Without prolonging the list, they have "rewarded" their reviewers with such things as sacrificing their own lives in the performance of duty, giving service beyond reasonable expectation, and a host of other favorable things associated with the phrase, "dedicated service." Penalties include assassination, revolt, strike, "job action," high absenteeism, surly dispositions, etc.

Emerging pattern: Both reviewers and stewards will find that the emerging pattern makes the subject of rewards and penalties resulting from the level-of-confidence issue a part of the original task definitions and plan. Generally, rewards for meeting expectations may be expected to receive more emphasis than penalties (a kind of accentuating the positive and subduing the negative features). Many task plans are likely to omit the entire level-of-confidence issue from consideration because of its threatening implications and/or the difficulty of reaching initial agreement on it. Future task plans, however, are bound to be influenced by the level-of-confidence determinations made for the task at hand—a form of "Karma accountability" in which the delayed level-of-confidence determinations resulting from the consequences of the earlier action influence future agreements (e.g., "the last time we did this task, we failed to include ____").

Because the emerging form of accountability lends itself so readily to forms of contract negotiation, particularly in the public sector, it seems likely that someone will coin the phrase, "negotiable accountability." A definition of negotiable accountability might be: the requirement on the occupant of a role, as determined by a negotiated contract (defining assignable, measurable units of responsibility to be fulfilled under certain conditions and within certain constraints), to answer for the specified results of work expected from him in the role in return for specified benefits accorded by results.

About Education and Accountability

What has caused education to court accountability? A thorough explanation is beyond our intentions. However, it seems possible to point to two broad sources of support for attempting to link education with a more virile form of accountability. First, change pressures of our times—political, social, and economic change pressures—are demanding responsiveness to perceived problems. American education has its share of "perceived problems." Secondly, advances (usually technological in form), within education as well as outside it, have developed to a point where applications of emerging accountability patterns appear feasible—at least worthy of trying in the absence of other visible measures of success or suitable explanations for what is happening.

An analysis of the pressures of our times should not require much elaboration. Is it necessary to belabor, for example, the message of our news media ("telling it like it is," we are told) about the current happenings in American education? From the daily collage of recitations even a casual observer is likely to get an impression that:[14]

1. Vocal minority groups do not always find education appropriately responsive to their needs and occasionally feel it necessary to take matters into their own hands to get results;

2. Students do not always find "the Establishment" (i.e., adult authority exercised in governing the schools) responsive to their needs (real as well as manufactured) and find that some kinds of results can be obtained through violence;

3. Parents raise questions about what and how well their children are learning and, finding answers evasive, frequently band together in neighborhood groups, pressuring their schools for answers and results;

4. Taxpayers, witnessing a comparatively staggering increase in their taxes in recent years (most of it disappearing into the bottomless pit of staff salaries, frequently—as they view it—"extorted" from the public through a conspiracy among school boards, teachers, and administrators) with neither discernible evidence of improved results nor clear explanations for what the expenditures are intended to accomplish, increasingly reward this "lack of account" by rejecting school tax levies;

5. Local boards of education, feeling pressure mount from an aroused, diverse public demanding results and holding them respon-

sible, find themselves hard pressed (through red tape, legal con-straints, employee contracts, tenure issues, and, most irritatingly, the incredibly fuzzy mystique of the educational trade with its compet-ing philosophies, peculiar norms, and unproven assumptions) to get straightforward answers, let alone hold anyone accountable (beyond those few vulnerable administrators who are occasionally placed on sacrificial altars to reduce pressures);

6. Some teacher groups, finding pent-up feelings of powerless-ness released through collective action and state laws mandating negotiation of "working conditions" (construed by many of these teachers to mean any—*any!*—condition that influences their role in the schools), exhibit greater preoccupation with their "working con-ditions" than with a commitment to the teaching task, while at the same time advancing a position that as "professionals" they are ultimately accountable only to themselves for their actions;

7. Other teachers, desiring better teaching results and willing to risk change in developing "more relevant" educational programs, frequently run into difficulties and pressures for "status quo" (from other teachers, administrators, board members, and/or community groups) if the proposed change requires from others even small amounts of time, money, effort, and/or attitude accommodations;

8. Congressmen, legislators, and political leaders are frustrated by having expended millions of dollars for specifically designated educational programs and having received in return little intelligible information about the results obtained (e.g., "everyone agrees that it is a good program") beyond the fact that the funds are expended and a substantial increase is requested for next year's operation;

9. Finally, school administrators (especially superintendents and building principals), who are the most vulnerable to pressure (i.e., they lack legal authority—held by boards through state law and by teachers through contracts—and, being few and usually singular in number, are unable to force demands on any other parties without active support from another group), finding their powers of adminis-trative control being constantly negotiated by others into smaller amounts (a form of "administrative emasculation"), and having to rely increasingly upon "good will" and volunteered cooperation (a form of "democratic leadership" coming to mean the cajoling to act of persons not obliged to do anything not covered in the contract—and sometimes, then too), find that their position strategically places them at the convergence point of nearly all those pressures.

In sum, the pressures create a climate of opinion for change, within which the notion of accountability has strong appeal. As

Stephen Barro phrases it: "Under the accountability banner, other-wise diverse programs for educational reform coalesce and reinforce one another, each gaining strength and all, in turn, strengthening already powerful pressures for educational changes."[15]

A reform-minded line of reasoning is directing the emerging patterns of accountability into education. This effort can be traced to Washington as a sort of spillover from the launching of the Elementary and Secondary Education Act of 1965 and the continu-ing federal efforts since then in the field of compensatory education. Simply expressed, this reasoning holds that:[16]

1. The educational evaluation of the schools and their programs is most important (in fact, the belief holds that schools should be monitored regularly with the results critically assessed and made public knowledge);

2. A similar close reporting should be made on the cost inputs of educational programs and their resulting benefits as derived in measurable cost/effectiveness terms;

3. An old educational cliche should be put to the test and the schools should be held responsible for devising programs that "meet the needs" (operationally defined) of *all* students (from the most endowed to the least);

4. The people whose children are being educated in the schools should have a closer partnership and form of participation in this matter—a partnership with a hand not far from the controls.

This line of reasoning received its most forceful public expres-sion to date in President Richard Nixon's March 3, 1970, "Message on Education Reform," which opens with the flat statement: "Amer-ican education is in urgent need of reform." A few excerpts from this message illustrate the above points:

> What makes a good school? The old answer was a school that maintained high standards of plant and equipment, that had a reasonable number of children per classroom, whose teachers had good college and often graduate training, that kept up to date with new curriculum developments and was alert to new techniques of instruction. This was a fair enough definition so long as it was assumed that there was a direct connection between these school characteristics and the actual amount of learning that takes place in a school.
>
> Years of educational research, culminating in the Equal Education Oppor-tunity Survey of 1966, have, however, demonstrated that this direct, uncom-plicated relationship does not exist.
>
> Apart from the general public interest in providing teachers an honorable and well paid professional career, there is only one important question to be asked about education: What do the children learn?
>
> Unfortunately, it is simply not possible to make any confident deduction

from school characteristics as to what will be happening to the children in any particular school . . . .

One conclusion (however) is inescapable: We do not yet have equal educational opportunity in America.

To achieve this . . . reform it will be necessary to develop broader and more sensitive measurements of learning than we now have . . . new measurements of educational output . . . .

From these considerations, we derive another new concept: accountability. School administrators and school teachers alike are responsible for their performance, and it is in their interest as well as in the interests of their pupils that they be held accountable. Success should be measured not by some fixed national norm, but rather by the results achieved in relation to the actual situation of the particular school and the particular set of pupils.[17]

In total, from the pressures of the times in which we live, education has found the emerging patterns of accountability alluring. At the same time, the burgeoning of new technologies provides underpinnings for the application of accountability. Our source of this stream can be traced back to Washington. Faced with the tasks of solving so many problems stemming from national defense in World War II and the subsequent cold war race for increased armament capabilities and space ventures, a series of conceptual frameworks were necessary to permit many different disciplines to work together. This framework developed around the notion of "systems."

A system, simply defined, is "a set of objects together with relationships between the objects and between their attributes."[18] While that definition is too skeletal to offer much sustenance for initial understanding, it does express the common relationship between the more than forty terms used to express forms of its use. At the same time, its parallel to the accountability definition should be unmistakable.

In general, forms of the systems concept seek to explain "relationships between objects" in a manner that permits close scrutiny of the objects as well as how they fit together in a whole system or part of it. Usually this explication is done by building and analyzing abstract models of the empirical world representing the "necessary and sufficient" relationships of the items being considered. For Anatol Rapoport, it means that "general systems theory subsumes an outlook or a methodology rather than theory in the sense ascribed to this term in science."[19]

Thus the systems concept performs an integrative function in its application and appears able to fuse together for several purposes the contributions of many disciplines that would otherwise be strange bedfellows. The impact of these advances (under the "systems"

banner) on the school administrator, operating as a generalist in the
social-behavioral science milieu of an educational, organizational, and
administrative world, is powerful: "It can be used to counter the
trend toward myopic fractionalization of knowledge that renders the
generalist obsolete."[20]

Expressions of the systems concept have assumed many forms.
In the social sciences alone, multiple system conceptualizations have
emerged. For example, David Easton developed a framework for
analyzing political systems,[21] the field of economics generated a
whole series of systems analyses (including input-output analysis,
econometric models, and benefit-cost analysis),[22] sociology contributed theories of social systems through the writings of Talcott
Parsons and others.[23] Even management found uses for analytical
system techniques, spawning operations research (OR), management
information systems (MIS), program evaluation and review techniques (PERT), critical-path method (CPM), cost-effectiveness analysis (differing from the "economic" focus of benefit-cost analysis by
accounting for a variety of noneconomic objectives also), and plan-
program-budget systems (PPBS).[24] Explication of each of these
approaches falls beyond the scope of efforts here. Their significance
to us lies in that they provide a greater variety of ways to view
problems—alternative ways that are logical, systematic, comprehensive, and above all rational.

At its best, systems analysis represents an approach through
rational technology that seeks to clarify what is known, to isolate
what is unknown, to simulate future behavior, to handle fantastically
complex interrelationships, and, when different combinations of
inputs are introduced, to yield insights into the likeliness of future
outcomes from alternative approaches. As Harry Hartley summarized
it:

> It enables one to raise probing questions in a universal language. By cutting
> across academic fields of specialization with general systems theory, much
> needed interdisciplinary dialogue on problems, including those pertaining to
> schools, is encouraged. Systematic thinking is logical thinking. By expanding the
> options and reducing uncertainties, the systems analyst increases the probability
> in his favor. The range of potential application . . . is nearly unlimited . . . . Its
> major virtue is the enhancement of human judgment.[25]

Any technology that enhances human judgment is bound to be a
powerful tool in planning, negotiating, and rendering an account.

While new applications of systems concepts were evolving, the
field of education was at the same time developing a thrust vital to
any consideration of accounting for educational performance,

namely "behavioral objectives." Receiving a major impetus from the scholarly work of Benjamin Bloom and others in the *Taxonomy of Educational Objectives* handbooks,[26] and a popularized form of application in Robert Mager's *Preparing Instructional Objectives,*[27] the behavioral objective movement has made steady forward progress.

Behavioral objectivists are concerned with educational measurement, and hold that if a child learns his behavior will change. Changed behavior is possible to observe or otherwise measure through various means. Thus, if the child's behavior changes as he learns, it makes sense to develop educational goals and objectives in forms of the behaviors desired. The instructional program may be geared to developing these desired behavior changes.

While the behavioral objectivists were studying changes in learner outcomes and shifts in behavior, the educational field was increasingly receptive to this kind of thinking. Jerome Bruner's *Process of Education*[28] managed to capture the attention of practicing schoolmen while public concerns about public education, stemming from Sputnik, Rickover, Conant, and others, helped support an unprecedented era of innovation and change in elementary and secondary education. Many of these changes (e.g., continuous progress education, nongraded instruction, team teaching, individually prescribed instruction, computer assisted instruction, etc.) depend on knowing with some precision where the student is in his learning.[29] The methodology of drafting behavioral objectives aids this movement where teachers attempt to assess student needs and prescribe objectives that are appropriate (i.e., that reflect considerations of the nature and needs of the learner, his society, and the content to be learned).

From behavioral definitions of learner outcomes and increasing demands from teacher groups for greater rights in determining educational decisions, it is but a short step to one more conclusion: the responsibility for moving the learner from a state in which he cannot perform a desired behavior to one in which he can, belongs to the teacher. The teacher is accountable for the learning outcomes of the student.[30]

Although systems technologists and behavioral objectivists started their reform movements separately, it was, as Erick Lindman states, "inevitable that they should discover each other and find they had much in common."[31] Combined with the pressure of the times, the notion that accountability could and should be more rigorously applied to education has gained currency. Why should persons employed by the public to provide a service (and given considerable latitude in determining how and under what conditions that service will be rendered) be exempt from standing to account for the results of that service?

It is not likely that the premise of this argument will be seriously (or at least openly) challenged. The problem will lie in the manner of making accountability operational. The issue of "who is accountable for what to whom" in education is complex, but, argue the change pressures of the times, necessary, and, suggest the new technologies, possible.

Toward Developing Accountability in Education

A variety of approaches, singly or employed with others, have been proposed to make the schools more accountable. Some broad approaches may be noted.[32]

Developing Greater Management Sophistication among Educators

This approach depends upon acquainting educators generally (and administrators specifically) with the developments in the systems-based technologies—particularly those that stress management control. Presumably the schools could be made more accountable by making more critical and effective uses of their resources through employing these technologies (e.g., PPBS, PERT, etc.). In the foreword of a new book on educational project management, for example, an official of the U.S. Office of Education contends that demands for accountability can be helpfully accommodated with "the development of management sophistication among educators":

> Although the necessity for competent management is part of the conventional wisdom of business and industry, the concept of educator as manager . . . is just being accepted—gingerly. Although educators . . . may indeed have "functioned" as managers—manipulating resources and coping with multiple demands to meet certain ends—the tools devised by managers in other fields have not been available to them, nor has the relevance of such tools been immediately apparent.[33]

James observed: "More recently a newer priesthood of economists and political scientists has joined the engineers in advising government about improving schools, and schoolmen now have a new catechism to learn."[34] This catechism has "come a long way, baby!" At least that is what the new priesthood believes.

Use of Educational Program Auditing

This device stems from traditional public fears that they are not being given the full truth about the quality of their children's education. To help bridge this "credibility gap" and keep the schools honest in their labors, an "educational program auditor" (EPA) is employed, to "audit" or otherwise critically evaluate specified portions of the school program (from specifically designated programs, to building-level programs or even to the total district program). Although there are several obvious differences between the two roles, the EPA acts somewhat similarly to the role performed by a certified public accountant: both represent an independent external quality-control agency. Kruger notes:

> The Educational Program Auditor does not operate the evaluation system, as the fiscal auditor does not operate the accounting system—yet both use their expertise, objectivity, and perspectives to improve the quality of these performance-control systems, and thus indirectly influence the quality of overall program design and management without diluting the responsibility or authority of program management personnel.[35]

While variations may be expected (e.g., one variation is the "audit committee" composed of parents, teachers, students, community-at-large representatives, and administrators who work with the technical audit personnel to assure that they give sufficient attention to the "auditing" of program areas of particular concern to their individual interests), the general form for the movement and use of EPAs will probably come from Washington along the lines represented in internally circulating memoranda.[36]

Developing and Implementing Defined Levels of
Performance Expectations

The development of defined performance expectations is bound to be the most difficult, and probably the most significant, feature of the accountability movement. As one administrator remarked, "Getting any six people to agree on general things in education—let alone behavioral objectives—is God-awful." Almost fifteen years ago Paul Woodring raised a powerful set of questions: should the schools be responsible for the child's intellectual development only, or should they be responsible for his social, moral, religious, vocational, physical, and emotional development, as well as for his recreation? If the schools are to be responsible for everything, is everything of equal importance, and if not what is the order of priority?[37] Clear answers to these questions have never been resolved in most communities, and are likely never to be resolved. Accordingly, specific behavioral objectives will probably continue to be worked out by the staff and restricted to academic areas in application.

A more clearly defined general consensus on what the schools should be accomplishing will be necessary, however, if accounts are to be rendered, and arriving at a consensus is no easy task. One superintendent, describing his lack of success at building a working consensus in his community, noted: "There's a lack of good will. That's the problem. They come on as members of a political party to fight and they fight."[38]

Given the politicization of efforts to define performance expectations, the task may be too difficult for many public schools (but perhaps not for private schools). This difficulty makes it attractive to use a piecemeal approach to defining expectations where consensus can be obtained, trading off other expectations, and providing alternative forms of schooling for meeting differing forms of expectations. Even this approach is difficult. Writes a parent to a friend:

> Mr C [the Principal] in his chat did mention that he would like our school to offer a choice in "styles of teaching" with the traditional type on the one hand and the more experimental on the other—where the children learn by "inquiry." I didn't argue with him at the time, but why must they be mutually exclusive? I don't see why a good teacher can't use many approaches to learning in her classroom. I don't see why in one room all the children must rigidly sit at their desks all working on the same page in their workbook where in another they crawl around the room searching for knowledge, with the teacher handing a lantern as they crawl by. Billy [son] is lukewarm about school this year. This teacher is an older woman, nice if uninspired—a traditional type if we must apply a label. Joe [husband] went to visit on parents night and was not impressed with the reading program, so we started Billy at home . . . . Almost miraculously he began reading with competence.[39]

Many people do have expectations of their schools, are seldom neutral in their educational outlooks, and feel compelled to act if the school cannot meet their expectations.

The task is to form a general consensus of the major objectives spelled out to a point where progress can be assessed with meaning. Though difficult, it should not be impossible to develop some graduated acceptance of a goal such as "reading with competence," behaviorally defined. Perhaps the use of the Delphi Technique might be helpful in probing and developing such a consensus within a community school.[40]

Developing a consensus on defined levels of expectations is difficult; implementation also promises to be so. The school system is conventionally held accountable by the school board primarily for "staff performance" (i.e., the staff is held responsible in a generalized sense for knowing and doing things supposed to help educate the student). The entire system of teacher certification, school accrediting procedures, and similar structures buttress this generalized assessment of staff performance. The "system" is further reinforced by granting automatically a form of lifetime appointment, tenure, by length of undisputed service and within a reward structure based on the "unified salary schedule," with emphasis on length of service and graduate credits collected as the only significant variables. Accountability shifts the focus, however, to "pupil" (rather than "staff") performance; the emphasis is placed on results, or producing specified levels of student accomplishments. A commonly imagined way to implement this approach is the use of "incentive pay" for teachers. Plans for vertical differential staffing patterns linked with salaries that are based on levels of student achievement as well as staff performance may fit this pattern.[41]

Another approach, largely conceived by Leon Lessinger and focused directly on specified achievement test gains of students, is to use "performance contracting." Usually an outside independent agency or firm contracts with the school board to achieve specified levels of student achievement, to be paid in accordance with the measure of success obtained. The most publicized experiment to date is the Texarkana experiment. By fall 1970, the Office of Economic Opportunity had undertaken the funding direction of eighteen such experiments involving six educational technology companies.[42] How successful this approach will be is too early to conclude. The Office of Economic Opportunity has since abandoned further experimentation with performance contracting, however.

Even more promising perhaps is "internal performance contracting," another variation of accountability implementation. Local teacher teams submit bids to the board of education. Specifications include the instructional objectives, the targeted students, the time period, and the educational costs (i.e., salaries, overhead, materials, and subcontracting costs for teacher aids from the community or special consultants as needed). The degree of accountability is negotiated by representatives of the local teachers association. The bid awards are regular contracts for specified results. Plan-Program-Budget Systems and project management techniques work neatly into this approach. Interestingly, the various contracted teacher teams may—or may not—contract for administrative services from their own building principal and other central office personnel. Under a grant from the Education Professions Development Act (EPDA), the Mesa (Arizona) Public Schools are attempting such a plan. It is noted:

> The value of the internal educational performance contract is that it is regulated by teachers through their own professional organization. Governance through peer regulation and evaluation is meshed with the real reward structure. This, in turn, is rooted firmly in client growth. Such an approach may unite accountability and governance at the operational level.[43]

Internal performance contracting appears, on the surface, to be ripe with exciting possibilities.

Quickening Institutional Responsiveness through Increased
Local Participation and Semiautonomy

This avenue increases accountability by removing the major locus of power from the usually more centralized distant sources to the various participants on the scene. Increasing local participation makes the schools more responsive by shared decision-making powers between school authorities and the people whose lives are touched by the school. In a gross sense, it is accountability through political exercise. By concomitantly decentralizing the administrative structure, the local administrator is usually more "in harmony" (e.g., if it is a black neighborhood, the administrator is black, etc.) with the setting of the neighborhood school and, accordingly, beholden to it. His tenure in office depends upon it.[44]

The source of power lies generally in the informal structure of the local community itself. As a recent publication (subtitled "A Parent's Action Handbook on How to Fight the System") suggests, the ways in which local groups can bring pressure to bear on their schools are plentiful (if somewhat painful to those targeted for such action).[45]

At the same time, if local pressure is not sufficient, pressure for increased local participation is also coming from Washington. In an October 1970 memorandum sent to all chief state school officers, then Acting Educational Commissioner E.T. Bell pressed the issue of parental involvement in Elementary and Secondary Education Act

Title I projects. Specifically, the local educational agency is required to state how its parent councils:

1. Provide suggestions on improving projects or programs in operation;

2. Voice complaints about projects or programs and make recommendations for their improvement;

3. Participate in appraisals of the program; and

4. Promote the involvement of parents in the educational services provided under ESEA Title I.[46]

Further, a description is mandated of the means by which local people have an opportunity to inspect the Title I application and present their views prior to its submission. Reports must also be filed stating how complaints of parent councils on Title I projects have been handled. Such activities ought certainly to encourage the responsiveness of the accountability that comes through political exercise.

An Appeal to an Alternative Form of Education

Another means of accountability is based on a kind of "consumer's choice" logic. A parent can pay for the schooling of his choice through the use of "educational vouchers," assuming selection of schools is available and that the parent is sufficiently dissatisfied with the educational fare at the local school. Presumably, through competing forms of publicly financed educational systems (public and semiprivate), the parent can hold schools accountable by exercising alternative choices. While some individuals view the voucher plan as a form of accountability, it falls outside the scope of the emerging accountability patterns mentioned earlier. While alternative forms of education have special appeals of their own, it is not apparent what particular qualities they possess that increase accountability as the concept is used here.[47]

In brief, several avenues to increase accountability seem available, taken singly or in concert with others. How successful any or all of these approaches might be probably will have to be determined in measures of degree—a measurement difficult to obtain in instances of heretofore undefined or loosely held objectives.

Putting together all the elements for rendering a better account, what picture emerges? A picture of the full-blown pattern emerges in another U.S. Office of Education memorandum (with Technical Assistance Coordinator Stanley Kruger's name affixed at the end). According to the memo, the Division of Plans and Supplementary

Centers distributed it "in an effort to promote the implementation of accountability in DPSC programs to a greater extent than has been accomplished heretofore." Twelve factors are "identified as being critical to the process":[48]

1. Community involvement: utilizing members of concerned community groups in appropriate phases of program activity in order to facilitate program access to community resources, community understanding of the program's objectives, procedures, and accomplishments, and the discharge of program responsibilities to relevant community client, service, and support groups;

2. Technical assistance: providing adequate resources in program planning, implementation, operation, and evaluation by drawing upon community, business, industrial, labor, educational, scientific, artistic, social/welfare, and governmental agencies for expertise and services necessary to effective operations;

3. Needs assessment: identifying target-group and situational factors essential to the planning of a relevant program of action;

4. Change strategies: developing effective strategies for systematic change in the educational enterprise and incorporating the strategies into program operations;

5. Management systems: adaptation of the systems approach, through such techniques as Management by Objectives, PPBS, PERT, CPM, to educational program management at the local, state, and federal levels;

6. Performance objectives: specifying program objectives in a comprehensive, precise manner that indicates measures and means for assessing the degree of attainment of predetermined standards;

7. Performance budgeting: allocating fiscal resources in accordance with program objectives to be realized, rather than by objects or functions to be supported;

8. Performance contracting: arranging for technical assistance in program operations through (internal or external) contracts that condition compensation upon the accomplishment of specified performance objectives;

9. Staff development: determining the nature and extent of staff development needed for successful implementation of the accountability concept at local, state, and federal levels, and for the design and conduct of indicated development activities;

10. Comprehensive evaluation: establishing systems of performance control based on the continuous assessment of the program's operational and management processes and resultant products;

11. Cost effectiveness: analyzing unit results obtained in rela-

tion to unit resources consumed under alternative approaches to program operation, as a determinant in continued program planning;

12. Program auditing: setting up a performance control system based upon external reviews conducted by qualified outside technical assistance, designed to verify the results of the evaluation of an educational program and to assess the appropriateness of program operation and management.

The current range of ideas, practices, and definitions of educational accountability is broad and differs in rigorousness;[49] but the change pressures of our times and the advances of technology should be enough to ensure continuation of the search for new ways of implementation. Caught in this web of circumstance is the ubiquitous school administrator. His role—like those of the other participants in the educational enterprise—is likely to experience constant redefinition over time, particularly as education seeks to respond to change.

Toward the Twenty-first Century: Who Will Lead?

We are living in paradoxical times. On the one hand, it seems recognized that the multitude of problems in all areas of human life facing this fragile spacecraft, earth, are not likely to find workable solutions without direction, leadership, and some form of rational control over scarce resources. On the other, the current trend of antileadership has seldom seemed stronger. Too often an overnight antileader demagogue has opportunistically seized upon dramatic situations to make wild accusations and oversimplified half-truths before a closely focused public attention, sometimes reducing the image of a public statesman (who must explain highly complex situations and at the same time defend his own integrity) to that of a bumbling bureaucratic hack. Too often, the leadership role has been granted in default as the result of jealousies among competing groups voting *against* rather than *for* candidates, yielding a leader with no clear mandate of support and with many factions ready to "get together and give him hell."

Such occurrences have led Brock Brower to ask, "Where Have All The Leaders Gone?"[50] Within the field of education, Roald Campbell inquires, "Is the School Superintendent Obsolete?"[51] And Allan Talbot speaks of searching for a "new breed" of educational leader.[52]

So the leadership search continues, in all fields of public activity, for an individual who inspires confidence and trust in his followers, who embodies the hopes of many persons, and who, most importantly, is capable of establishing that critical bond that unites people and supports efforts.

It is this bond—a relationship—between leader and follower that the behavioral science literature identifies as being leadership's essential ingredient.[53] Where no tie exists—a tie that calls for obligations acceptable to all parties concerned—a leadership crisis results.[54] Chester Barnard in 1938 described what happens when a bond between individuals and organizations is broken; the same might characterize the bond between leaders and followers: "The most devoted adherents to an organization will quit it, if its system results in inadequate, contradictory, inept orders, so that they cannot know who is who, what is what, or have the sense of effective coordination."[55] When a bond is broken today, it is difficult to sustain significant organizational progress over periods of time. Short-term solutions and short-sighted compromises can be expected, yielding an organization with overextended commitments to everything and adequate support of nothing. As John Stuart Mill observed, responsibility is null when nobody knows who is responsible. Such an organization cannot be expected to cope successfully with the task of educating society's children for the twenty-first century, nor to encourage the presence of competent staff with other options or the sustained support and goodwill of a community. Leadership is vital. So is followership. Neither can operate a complex organization successfully in a democratic society without the consent of the other.

And here is our point: it is the potential for establishing that positive bond between leader and follower that carries the accountability movement beyond the pale of simply standing-to-account for learner outcomes via measurable criteria (as difficult and significant as this achievement is educationally). Through the process of establishing an agreement on accountability, leaders and followers of necessity interact—they cannot escape or ignore the other in the search for mutual consent. Their roles will be redefined at times, perhaps yielding following leaders and leading followers. In such instances the leader will know when to follow; the followers will not become scattered in the fog of dimly-lit responsibilities so that their leaders can never resume leadership. The individual follower will in turn have some notion where his leader *ought* to be headed and thus be better able to judge the amount of confidence he cares to entrust to his leader. In this process, new relationships between leader and follower will emerge—new points of terminal responsibility, terminal authority, and degrees of terminal decision-making powers.

There can be no guarantee that a bond of positive mutual respect and trust will grow out of this arrangement. That variable is left to the chemistry of the individuals as they define their roles. How all the participants in the process create a bond through accountability depends largely on the individuals themselves. Those pursuing a philosophy of "rights for me and responsibilities for you" might find the establishment of a balanced ledger of rights and responsibilities incompatible. But more real forms of freedom for all parties might be extracted from a negotiated settlement of accountability. If, as James Thompson asserts, "uncertainty appears as the fundamental problem for complex organizations and coping with uncertainty is the essence of the administrative process,"[56] then the new patterns of accountability should provide a sane propaedeutic condition for the appropriate growth of a leader-follower bond. Thomas Carlyle observed: "There is no act more moral between men than that of rule and obedience. Woe to him that claims obedience when it is not due; woe to him that refuses it when it is!"[57]

The presence of so many groups in public education with interests frequently at cross-purposes ensures that forging the bond will be difficult. Nevertheless, in the middle of the action, the school administrator is bound to discover himself. The probabilities are great that obligations of leadership will continue to rest on his shoulders—perhaps in slightly redistributed form. His best ally will be his own conviction of what needs to be done, hopefully forged with informed judgment and planned foresight, and expressed in technically rational terms that can be minted into accountability—his own accountability as well as others'. If he accepts the obligations of leadership in educating youth for the twenty-first century, he will probably find the words of a first-century religious leader useful in measuring his own career fulfillment as an educational leader: "I have fought a good fight, I have finished my course, I have kept the faith."[58] As he contends with change and looks toward the on-rushing century to come, he will find the attitude of a twentieth-century political leader even more helpful: "Some men see things as they are and say, 'Why?' I dream of things that never were and say, 'Why not?' "[59]

Notes for Chapter 1

1. Alvin Toffler, *Future Shock* (New York: Random House, 1970), p. 2.

2. Ibid.

3. For other selections of futuristic observers, see Daniel Bell, ed., *Toward the Year 2000* (Boston: Houghton Mifflin, 1968); Kenneth Boulding, *The Meaning of the 20th Century* (New York: Harper & Row, 1964); Harrison Brown, *The Challenge of Man's Future* (New York: Viking Press, 1954); Peter F. Drucker, *The Age of Discontinuity* (New York: Harper & Row, 1968); Donald N. Michael, *The Unprepared Society* (New York: Basic Books, 1968).

4. See B. F. Skinner, *Walden Two* (New York: Macmillan Co., 1948).

5. Sir Geoffrey Vickers, "Ecology, Planning and the American Dream," in *The Urban Condition*, ed. Leonard Duhl (New York: Basic Books, 1963), p. 374.

6. Kenneth B. Clark, "Foreword," in *New Models for American Education*, ed. James Guthrie and Edward Wynne (Englewood Cliffs, N.J.: Prentice-Hall, 1971), pp. ix-x.

7. Toffler, *Future Shock*, p. 398.

8. Commission on the Preparation of Professional School Administrators, *The American School Superintendent*, ed. Stephen Knezevich (Washington, D.C.: American Association of School Administrators, 1971), p. 12.

9. Ibid.

10. Tom James finds six senses for defining accountability; see H. Thomas James, "Public Expectations," in *Conferences on Educational Accountability* (Princeton, N.J.: Educational Testing Service, 1971).

11. An understanding of the more commonly used forms of "accountability" might become clearer if some closely related words are examined. These related terms include "answerable," "responsible," and "amenable."

The terms "answerable" and "responsible" exhibit a close relationship in sense (i.e., both refer to some kind of answering or responding action), there are some shades of difference between them in application, for example, a person is "answerable" for the tasks he himself undertakes, or for tasks left in his direct charge, or for the efforts of those who work closely with him whose work he is liable for (e.g., an executive is answerable for letters sent out of his office even if his secretary erred in sending them out). Being "responsible," on the other hand, carries a higher, more extended sense of obligation. A military general is "responsible" for the conduct of the men under him as a matter of trust, higher duty, and moral obligation (as implied in the commission he receives, stating that he is "an officer and a gentleman"). Similarly, public officials are "responsible" in the sense of carrying the obligation of responding to society as moral agents.

Both "answerable and responsible" carry implications of a pledge made for the performance of some act, a breach of which subjects the defaulter to punishment or penalties of some kind. To be "accountable," however, simply implies an explanation, an accounting, of what one has done or been doing. Whereas being answerable and responsible pertain to obligation only, "accountability" results from the relationship between parties. A subordinate is "accountable" to his superior for the manner in which he has handled any tasks entrusted to him. In most families, a child is "accountable" to his parents for all his actions while he is under their jurisdiction. In a legal sense, "amenability" is a form of accountability within a framework of policies and regulations binding upon a person. For example, one is "amenable" to the laws of society and to the rules of the organization in which he is employed.

12. For an excellent discussion see Sir Geoffrey Vickers, *The Art of Judgment* (New York: Basic Books, 1965), chapter 12.

13. A. D. Newman and R. W. Rowbottom, *Organization Analysis* (Carbondale, Ill.: Southern Illinois University Press, 1968), p. 26.

14. For interesting portraits of the pressures of our times, see Michael W. Kirst, ed., *The Politics of Education at the Local, State and Federal Levels* (Berkeley: McCutchan Publishing Corp., 1970); Luvern L. Cunningham, *Governing Schools: New Approaches to Old Issues* (Columbus, Ohio: Charles E. Merrill Publishing Co., 1971).

15. Stephen M. Barro, "An Approach to Developing Accountability Measures for the Public School," Report P-4464 (Santa Monica, Calif.: RAND Corporation, September 1970), p. 1.

16. Ibid., pp. 1-2.

17. Richard M. Nixon, "Message on Education Reform," *American Education* (April 1970): 30-34.

18. A. D. Hall and R. E. Fagen, "Definition of System," *General Systems* 1 (Yearbook of the Society for General Systems Research, 1956), p. 18.

19. Anatol Rapoport, "Mathematical Aspects of General Systems Analysis," *General Systems* 2 (Yearbook of the Society for General Systems Research, 1966), p. 3.

20. Harry J. Hartley, *Educational Planning-Programming-Budgeting: A Systems Approach* (Englewood Cliffs, N.J.: Prentice-Hall, 1968), p. 28.

21. David Easton, *A Framework for Political Analysis* (Englewood Cliffs, N.J.: Prentice-Hall, 1965).

22. For interesting readings and case studies, see Harley H. Hinrichs and Graeme M. Taylor, eds., *Program Budgeting and Benefit-Cost Analysis* (Pacific Palisades, Calif.: Goodyear Publishing Co., 1969).

23. A major comprehensive work is Talcott Parson et al., eds., *Theories of Society: Foundations of Modern Sociological Theory* (New York: Free Press, 1965). In the field of organization theory, see James G. March, ed., *Handbook of Organizations* (Chicago: Rand McNally, 1965).

24. For three well-conceived books of readings offering a sampling of these approaches, see: David Novick, ed., *Program Budgeting: Program Analysis and the Federal Budget* (Cambridge: Harvard University Press, 1967); Fremont J. Lyden and Ernest G. Miller, eds., *Planning-Programming-Budgeting: A Systems Approach to Management* (Chicago: Markham Publishing Co., 1968); David I. Cleland and William R. King. eds., *Systems, Organizations, Analysis, Management: A Book of Readings* (New York: McGraw-Hill, 1969).

25. Hartley, *Educational Planning-Programming-Budgeting*, p. 44.

26. Benjamin Bloom et al., eds., *Taxonomy of Educational Objectives, Handbook I; Cognitive Domain* (New York: David McKay, 1956); and D. R. Krathwohl et al., eds., *Taxonomy of Educational Objectives, Handbook II: Affective Domain* (New York: David McKay, 1956).

27. Robert Mager, *Preparing Instructional Objectives* (Palo Alto, Calif.: Fearon Publishers, 1962). For developing objectives in the "affective domain," see idem, *Developing Attitudes Toward Learning* (Palo Alto, Calif.: Fearon Publishers, 1968).

28. Jerome S. Bruner, *The Process of Education* (Cambridge: Harvard University Press, 1960).

29. For a good review of these changes, begun in the 1950s and continued

into the 1970s, see Maurie Hillson and Ronald Hymn, eds., *Change and Innovation in Elementary and Secondary Organization* (New York: Holt, Rinehart & Winston, 1971).

30. For a fuller treatment of this theme, see Ray Bernabi and Sam Leles, *Behavioral Objectives in Curriculum and Evaluation* (Dubuque, Iowa: Kendall/Hunt Publishing Co., 1970).

31. Erick L. Lindman, "Benefits and Costs of Education," unpublished report to the California Advisory Council on Educational Research, fall 1970, p. 2.

32. For an interesting and concise review of these areas defined in differing terms, see Barro, "An Approach to Developing Accountability Measures," pp. 3-7.

See also "Accountability in Education," *Educational Technology* (January 1971); Leon Lessinger, guest ed., "A Symposium on Accountability," *Journal of Secondary Education* (December 1970).

33. Howard J. Hjelm, "Foreword," in Desmond L. Cook, *Educational Project Management* (Columbus, Ohio: Charles E. Merrill Publishing Co., 1971), pp. iii-iv.

34. H. Thomas James, *The New Cult of Efficiency and Education* (Pittsburgh: Horace Mann Lecture Series, University of Pittsburgh Press, 1969), pp. 5-6.

35. W. Stanley Kruger, "Educational Accountability and the Educational Program Auditor" (unpublished report, January 6, 1970).

See also idem, "Program Auditor: New Breed on the Educational Scene," *American Education* (March 1970).

36. See for example, "Outline of Educational Auditing Procedures," memo (Washington, D.C.: U.S. Office of Education, April 3, 1970).

Under "Attachment B: Suggested Audit Report Content Areas," along with the usual summary statements, it is expected that the report will include:

• "Detailed critique of the product and process evaluation conducted for operation and management in each component, based on an assessment of the instruments used, data collection procedures, data analysis techniques, and data analysis presentation."

• "Description of the auditor's on-size visit findings and their correlation with the evaluator's data and reports, on a component by component basis; summary of consistencies and discrepancies, and interpretation of the discrepancies."

Recommendations and insights into problems are expected also, but these will be muted somewhat, recognizing that "specific corrective action is a local decision."

37. Paul Wooding, *A Fourth of a Nation* (New York: McGraw-Hill, 1957).

38. Christopher Weber, "Three 'Rs'—Rows, Rifts, Resignations," *Newsday*, February 1, 1971, p. 11.

39. Letter from a friend, January 20, 1971.

40. For an interesting application of the Delphi Technique to the ordering of goals, see Frederick Cyphert and Walter Gant, "The Delphi Technique: A Tool for Collecting Opinions in Teacher Education," *Journal of Teacher Education* 21, no. 3 (fall 1970): 417-25.

For a critique of the method, see W. Timothy Weaver, "The Delphi Forecasting Method," *Phi Delta Kappan* (January 1971): 267-72.

A classic work is Olaf Helmer, *Social Technology* (Santa Monica, Calif.: RAND Corporation, 1965).

41. For example, N. John Rand and Fenwick English, "Toward a Differentiated Teaching Staff," *Phi Delta Kappan* (January 1968): 264-68. For discussion on the pros and cons, see *Differentiated Staffing* (Special Report: Education U.S.A., 1970); Richard Miga, "Important Considerations in Program Management Evaluation" (Fredonia, N. Y.: Chautauqua Project Report, 1970); James Olivero, "The Meaning and Application of Differentiated Staffing in Teaching," *Phi Delta Kappan* (September 1970): 36-40.

42. For example, Stanley Elam, "The Age of Accountability Dawns in Texarkana," *Phi Delta Kappan* (June 1970): 509-14; "Performance Contracting as Catalyst for Reform," *Educational Technology* (August 1969): 5-9; Education Turnkey Systems, *Performance Contracting in Education: The Guaranteed Student Performance Approach to Public School System Reform* (Champaign, Ill.: Research Press, 1970); Leon Lessinger, *Every Kid a Winner* (Garden City, N. Y.: Doubleday, 1970); idem, "Accountability and the Controversial Role of the Performance Contractors" (White Plains, N. Y.: Knowledge Industry Publications, 1970).

Special recognition must be given to Leon Lessinger, referred to by many as the father of the current accountability movement. Congressman Roman Pucinski, chairman of the House Subcommittee on General Education, has declared: "Dr. Lessinger deserves the gratitude of the American people in having the foresight to encourage this experiment [Texarkana] and hopefully give overworked teachers in this country the assistance they can get from these major breakthroughs in education technology." *Congressional Record* (August 13, 1969), p. E 7021.

43. Fenwick English and James Zaharis, "Are Accountability and Governance Compatible?" *Phi Delta Kappan* (February 1971): 375.

See also idem, *International Educational Performance Contracting*, a report to the National Academy of School Executives, October 1970.

44. Several interesting discussions of this form of accountability are available, for example, Michael Usdan, "Citizen Participation: Learning from New York City's Mistakes," *The Urban Review* (September 1969); Marilyn Gittel, *Participants and Participation* (New York: Center for Urban Education, 1967); Luvern L. Cunningham, ed., "What Do All Those People Want?" special issue, *Theory into Practice* 8, no. 4 (October 1969).

45. Ellen Lurie, *How to Change the Schools* (New York: Random House, 1971).

46. T. H. Bell, "Advisory Statement on Development of Policy on Parental Involvement in Title I, ESEA Projects," memo to chief state school officers (Washington, D.C.: U.S. Office of Education, October 39, 1970).

47. A basic document to the voucher movement is *Education Vouchers: A Preliminary Report on Financing Education by Payments to Parents* (Cambridge: Center for the Study of Public Policy, March 1970). The report usually is referred to as the Jencks Report after one of its better known drafters.

For some interesting discussions, see Henry Dyer, "Accountability: Education Vouchers," *The United Teacher* (November 22, 1970): 12, 13, 18; Christopher Jencks, "Giving Parents Money for Schooling: Education Vouchers," *Phi Delta Kappan* (September 1970): 49-52; Ray Carr and Gerald Hayward, "Education by Chit: An Examination of Voucher Proposals," *Education and Urban Society* (February 1970): 169-91.

48. W. Stanley Kruger, "Accountability in DSPC Programs: Bureau of Elementary and Secondary Education," memo (Washington, D.C.: U.S. Office of Education, April 3, 1970).

49. Note, for instance, the range of implications and degree of rigorousness in these sample definitions of accountability:

Sample 1: "[Accountability is] the right to insure a good education for the children of a community and to sever from the school system those who do not contribute to that end." Robert Lovett's quote of Mrs. Blanche Lewis in "Professional Accountability in the Schools," *Record* (October 1970): 4.

Sample 2: "At a common sense level, there is accountability when resources and efforts are related to results in ways that are useful for policymaking, resource allocation, or compensation. It probably makes more sense to think in terms of degrees and kinds of accountability rather than to assume that accountability either does or does not characterize education." Myron Lieberman, "An Overview of Accountability," *Phi Delta Kappan* (December 1970): 194.

Sample 3: "The concept of educational accountability is a broad one, but is primarily concerned with those principles and techniques which may be utilized to assure a high level of attainment of the objectives of the educational enterprise, with an accompanying wise and efficient use of society's resources. The emphasis is upon performance. Although a central concern is the relationship of input to output, resources to results, the concept transcends mechanistic considerations for efficiency. The administrator is expected to place emphasis on planning *for* results as well as on assessment *of* results." W. Stanley Kruger, "Educational Accountability and the Educational Program Auditor," p. 1.

Sample 4: "Accountability . . . may be defined as an assignable, measurable responsibility to be fulfilled under certain conditions and within certain constraints." Russell B. Valaanderen and Arthur P. Ludka, "Evaluating Education in a Changing Society," in *Emerging State Responsibilities for Education*, ed. E. L. Morphet and D. L. Jessen (Denver, Colo.: Improving State Leadership in Education, 1970), p. 145.

50. Brock Brower, "Where Have All the Leaders Gone?" *Life*, October 8, 1971, pp. 68-80.

51. Roald Campbell, "Is The School Superintendent Obsolete?" *Phi Delta Kappan* (October 1966): 50-58.

52. Allan Talbot, "Needed: A New Breed Of School Superintendents," *Harper's Magazine*, February 1966, pp. 81-87.

53. For a comprehensive review of the literature on this topic, see Dorwin Cartwright, "Influence, Leadership, Control," in *Handbook of Organizations*, ed. James March (Chicago: Rand McNally, 1965), chapter 1.

54. For an excellent discussion on leadership and group change, see David Krech, Richard Crutchfield, and Egerton Ballachey, *Individual in Society* (New York: McGraw-Hill, 1962), chapter xii.

55. Chester Barnard, *Functions of the Executive* (Cambridge: Harvard University Press, 1938), p. 175.

56. James Thompson, *Organizations in Action* (New York: McGraw-Hill, 1967), p. 159.

57. As quoted in Brower, "Where Have All the Leaders Gone?" p. 80.

58. Paul the Apostle, 2 Tim. 4:7.

59. John F. Kennedy.

2. Developing an Educationally Accountable Program

Considering Some Imperatives for Program Design

Suppose you—YOU—want to develop an educational accountability program. What advice may we offer?

Probably our advice should be offered as a series of caveats expressed as "imperatives." The literature holds a variety of such imperatives. Lopez warns that your program must (1) pay attention to communicating with all parties; (2) have an organizational philosophy or plan of action that has the allegiance of everyone; (3) be based on ethical principles and on policies that work; (4) be specific about its purpose; (5) improve the performance of all persons involved; (6) be sensitive to human needs; and (7) have all persons touched by the program participate in its development from start through finish.[1]

Mazur joins Lopez in pointing out program pitfalls. You should avoid (1) making unrealistic administrative demands; (2) forcing accountability programs on unwilling and uncomprehending staffs; (3) perceiving accountability as an end rather than a means; (4) moving forward with a shallow understanding of accountability policy and procedures; (5) having too great expectations from minimal procedures and small resources; and (6) placing too much faith in the reliability of accountability measures (the "criterion problem").[2]

Mazur's own positive imperatives are brief: one must have a trained staff, opportunity to employ accountability procedures, and possess the capability for generating information appropriate to planning and development.[3]

Cunningham, writing about decentralization and community control, offers the following imperatives for program design: (1) responsiveness to the participation impulse in people; (2) movement toward demonstratably improved education; (3) recognition of the equality of opportunity mandate; (4) accommodation of lay-professional antagonisms; (5) financial feasibility; and (6) politically attainable goals.[4]

Without attempting to exhaust imperative listings, it might not be stretching too much to conclude there are nearly as many listings as authors—take your pick. At the same time, the listings are similar in many respects. It is also unfair merely to summarize imperatives and forego the closely written explanations with which the authors buttress their points. Our purpose, however, is to alert the reader that there are multiple and differing caveat emptor signs dotting the landscape, not to lead him by the hand to each one.[5]

What advice is the reader then to follow? His best advice is likely to come from his own judgment (seasoned, of course, by IBM's famous imperative: "Think"), but he is entitled to know what *we* think is critical in designing an accountability program under today's general conditions. Recall that accountability is a versatile concept; as long as its conditions are heeded, it can be attached to a number of current popular educational programs, as well as to any of the favored old ones. The advice we bestow upon our reader is given with an expectation that a sizeable commitment to accountability is being contemplated. All this advice giving looks ridiculous if you merely intend to apply "a little accountability" to Miss Johnson's third grade Bluebird group. With full awareness that our judgment is equally open to question, here are some hard-to-separate interrelated features we feel to be critical in developing an accountability program.[6]

One: The Program Must Have Knowledgeable Designers

Field experience with the births of new programs has demonstrated repeatedly that a certain level of knowledgeability and awareness on the part of program designers is necessary. How to specify when the program designer possesses the requisite range of information, awareness, and understanding to produce an appropriate program design is beyond our ability. Under varying circumstances, for example, a sick child may critically need the knowledge and skill of a highly trained team of surgeons, or a country doctor "making do", or even a desperate mother with a copy of Dr. Spock in hand. The level of knowledge necessary in each circumstance is determined by realizing that the child could die, or get better with or without the intervention of the would-be healers.

Chances of success appear greater when persons designing a new program have carefully considered critical variables in the proposed program's range and scope, have studied the program from start to finish, have thought deeply enough to anticipate problems before they arise, and are willing to develop the program around some theoretical design. This requires an individual who can assess needs and develop change strategies, who knows what technical assistance is available as well as alternative management systems, who can exercise that rarest of commodities, good judgment, and know whether it is all workable. Our guess is that not every administrator thinks he can do these things or is comfortable at the thought of learning how. Our advice however, is that he *ought* to possess knowledge and skill in this area—it is one of the ways the pressures for change are redefining his role. Too often educational programs have been slapped together in a manner not unlike a child putting together a complex toy model without bothering to read the directions. The nature of the accountability process requires more than a "read-and-apply" level of understanding. Figuring most of our readers to be in a position somewhat akin to the country doctor who has to "make do" with what he has on hand, we suggest that accountability programs are somewhat similar to the range of operations the country doctor might attempt—from the simple to the most complex, but always with a prerequisite level of knowledge and skill. In brief, the designer should have a fair notion of what he is doing before he starts. Toward this end, this book attempts to move at the most basic levels.[7]

Two: The Program Must Lead to Improved Education

There is little point in designing an accountability program in education unless it leads to real improvement. This statement is far easier to write than to do; the practitioner on the scene is likely to feel himself stymied at times. For example, because local educational programs are characteristically "loose," in that few attempt to reach behavioral objectives or specify learning outcomes, it may be difficult to locate where your program starts—rather like playing basketball when the score is only occasionally kept, it may be hard to know whether your game plan is an improvement over what has been happening prior. Once accountability has been put into effect, you should at least be able to know the score and whether you are getting better or worse results within the framework of your program.

A greater problem, however, is establishing a clear notion of where improvement is (or should be) directed. There are frequently differences of opinion about what needs to be "improved." Some educators are pleased if the student learns only to read and write, others want more. Deciding specifically what is to be improved and whether you are in fact improving on it is difficult, but necessary if you intend to operate an accountability program. Without an operationally defined set of objectives, you have neither a clear idea of where you are going nor an awareness of when you have arrived or succeeded with your program.

There is a further related problem—call it a "political reality." In our pluralistic society, clear resolution of goals and objectives is elusive, and goal declarations have generally been couched in terms of suggestive vagueness. Certainty of success, or of failure, has been correspondingly difficult to identify. Once objectives are specified and measurement of their accomplishment taken, accountability makes it a political necessity and an educational imperative that the program demonstrate improvement (or, at least, nothing less than a status quo ante-plan implementation). Wedded as our society is to the concepts of "progress" and "success," does any practitioner really feel he can ignore this imperative? That is, because of the greater visibility of results obtained and the near certainty that some people will be praised and others not (no matter how hard you desire to avoid it), the practitioner should be fairly certain that the program leads to improvement (i.e., is "doomed to success"). Failing educational experiments, especially where children are concerned, have never been popular. Like old soldiers, they "fade away," but it is doubtful that ineffectual programs producing highly visible results will be allowed to pass uncensured.

Three: The Program Must Recognize and Accommodate
Diverse Forms of Participation

Education, especially *public* education, is everybody's business, and in democratic societies everyone is expected to have a voice (from small peeps to howls) in the operation of the commonweal. Therefore any accountability design should recognize and accommodate diverse forms of participation in its development. As Getzels,

Lipham, and Campbell express it: "Whether he (the administrator) wishes to maintain or to alter the goals and operation of his school, he must begin by taking into account the relation between the structure of expectations of the school and the structure of values in the community."[8] Today, resolution of this issue has become a major dilemma for many administrators.

Schoolmen experience a daily existence made to order for aspirin ads—full of headaches, fevers, and mounting tensions. Pressures from the public, teachers, students, organized staff unions, vocal minority groups, and boards of education can be enormous. A leading contributor to this pressure is the touchy issue of expectations.

Not long ago, the expectations held by boards of education, their constituents, and school administrators seemed clearer. Schoolmen were expected to account for peace and order in the school community, maintaining and enforcing commonly accepted codes and policies, advancing certain educational "essentials" in the school program, and an annual budget that increased only imperceptibly. Achievement of these standards was assumed, and a degree of mutually shared confidence prevailed among boards, administrators, and the dominant community groups. In this climate an aura of semi-autonomy was permitted administrators.

But harmony between expectations and attainment is increasingly rare. The calmer waters of a relatively more stable era are rippled by the stirrings of newly articulate groups—teachers, students, and community minority groups. The advent of power politics and adversary forms of negotiation makes agreement on goals and objectives more elusive, more diffuse. Otherwise capable schoolmen find themselves unable to stand to account—that is, to meet the expectations of task obligations swollen far beyond the means of *any* administrator expected to cope with them. Frequently situations arise in which the various participants expect "more" without concern for how far their expectations could be met by *any* program or administrator.

In brief, we suggest that the designer seek to answer the pressure for participation. He should develop a strategy to clarify and resolve the diffuseness of expectations, to accommodate, where possible, the diversity of participants and their interests, but above all to seek clarification of the program's objectives. A supporting group consensus on behaviorally defined program objectives—if indeed possible—promises to be the most difficult variable in developing a program. Etzioni concludes: "Unless more and better

consensus building—in matters of substance, structure, and procedure—is added to more informed and less fragmented decision making, the schools—especially the public ones—will be increasingly more
out of step with a rapidly changing society and will suffer the
battering that ossified institutions take in stormy days."[9]

*Four: The Program Must Train Personnel before
and during Implementation*

It should not be necessary to advise administrators to train
personnel before and during implementation of any plans likely to
require them to change their manner of operation. Past experience,
however, suggests otherwise. Laments Hapgood about some reverses
experienced in the new American "open classroom" movement: we
cannot succeed in developing the open classroom "without fully
understanding the principle on which it is based, without going
through the necessary process of preparation, and without developing supportive methods to foster it."[10] Her illustration of the American pattern of program initiation is not unfamiliar: a teacher (or
administrator), excited by a quick workshop or even a book, returns
to work and attempts to create an instant open classroom, abandoning the concept as "impractical" as soon as she finds it difficult
to cope with the problems that arise. We tend to give training short
shrift, yielding an "I'm a professional just let me alone to teach"
attitude that assumes each person involved knows (in some mysteri-
ous way) exactly what to do. We should remind ourselves that it
took the English years to develop a few successful open classroom
programs, with heavy reliance on in-service weekend courses.

To illustrate further, compare the complex professional task of
educating children with that of winning professional football games
(with the easily understood goal of gaining more points than your
opponent). How many veteran professional football teams begin a
new season after an orientation day or two to draw equipment? How
many teams—even the poorest—fail to assess minutely what they did
last week at each position, man for man and objective by objective?
How often do they not scout and diagnose equally critically for their
next performance to determine their opponents' various strengths
and weaknesses? Do they not attempt to adjust and prescribe a game
plan that produces the necessary results and, if they find under field
conditions that their plan needs further adjusting, act accordingly?
How many hours and days of preparation for coaches and players go
into a single two or three hour performance, with the simple over-
riding goal to achieve a better result than their resisting opponents?

How long is a team of players and coaches permitted to fail at this task—a task that statistically guarantees that some will lose—before its personnel are assessed for the results produced and held to account?

The contrast is deliberately overdrawn, and we are not suggesting that educators ape professional football's manner of operation. We do advise that before and during any program undertaken, close attention be given to the aspect of training program personnel. We subscribe to the notion that little significant educational yardage is gained over time without serious preparation and continuous training. Spontaneous success from short off-the-cuff training programs is rare, fleeting, and usually trite. We are aware that it is often difficult to get staffs to respond willingly to such training requirements. The norms of individual autonomy in education, combined with a growing tendency for many persons to subordinate their work commitments to personal interests, as well as the increasing number of formal contracts that severely restrict time permitted for staff training, make this imperative a formidable one to achieve.

Five: The Program Must Fulfill the Conditions
of the Accountability Concept

An obvious ingredient of an accountability program design is that it fulfill the conditions of the concept. Fulfillment means that the design meets the following conditions:

1. The program's goals or objectives are specified operationally —that is, stated as assignable, measurable units of responsibility to be fulfilled under defined conditions and within defined constraints. If the proposed program focuses on student learning, the sought-after learner outcomes are designated in terms of behavioral objectives.

2. Periodically an account is rendered stating as clearly and accurately as possible what results are being attained toward reaching the program's specified goals. The use of various new components in management technology is expected to make such reporting easier and more accurate. The account is expected to be rendered to those who participated in formulating its objectives and certainly to those who hold legal authority for the operation of the district. If the program encompasses sizeable numbers of students (a matter of comparative judgment), there is an added expectation that the account be rendered as public knowledge. If a lay-professional credibility problem exists in a particular community, there is an option to use a third-party "educational program auditor."

3. The issue of what is expected from the program must be

resolved before it is put into operation—a prerequisite for stating the program's goals. In stable communities that hold their professional staffs in high regard, regularly support school tax elections, allow their staffs considerable professional autonomy, and appear to be getting "value received" for this kind of operation, there is likely to be less demand for direct participation from sources outside the school employ. This state of affairs, however, is not consistent with the trend. It is more likely that in order to get the program sufficiently supported and its objectives stated fairly to all parties, it will be necessary to involve many persons. Accordingly, some mechanism for community-staff involvement is deemed necessary as a step toward developing a consensus of expectations. Certainly those most affected by the proposed program should be represented in some manner. Some are likely to look upon this condition as one related to negotiating accountability. Political overtones are bound to be experienced in more volatile communities. At least attempts at meeting this condition should bring all parties face to face and, as they attempt to work out (negotiate?) their expectations as program objectives, cut through much of the standard rhetoric and dogma attached to interest groups.

4. An estimation of what an acceptable performance might be to maintain a high level of confidence in the program must also be resolved beforehand. Notice that we switched this condition from the program stewards to the program itself, believing it necessary to focus the level-of-confidence issue on the program rather than on the staff implementing it. This approach frankly subverts the full-blown accountability concept. The staff is more likely to be supportive of the initial idea and its implementation than if the rewards-and-punishment aspect is aimed at them. In an uncritical profession where it is not surprising to find 80 to 90 percent of the teaching staff self-rated "outstanding" in comparison with their peers, concern is more likely to be preoccupied with the punishment aspect of the level-of-confidence issue. At the same time, until the advent of militant, hard-nosed negotiation, the public concept of suitable rewards for teachers meeting generalized goals did not boggle the mind. This approach still gives us an accountability tiger, but he is admittedly missing a few teeth. As groups attempt to work out this issue (many probably abandoning the task), it may turn out to be a paper tiger involving professional ego only. Predictably then, the board of education will be handling the issue much as it was handled in the past. The accountability process should, however, make it a more rational and objective kind of decision making.

It should be kept in mind that the accountability concept is a process of relationships: it is a means rather than an end. As a process, it can be attached to any program the school desires—the standard curriculum, modern math, team teaching, nongraded instruction, the open classroom, differentiated staffing, etc. All that is required is that (1) the work to be done is specified operationally, (2) an accurate account of results achieved be rendered periodically, an appropriate group (3) decides what should be expected from the program, incorporating agreed-upon expectations into the program's task specifications, and (4) recognizes formally or informally that some party acts in authority to decide whether the results achieved are acceptable or not (with the option that this condition may be handled either in the initial agreement or, as is more common, as a matter of judgment applied after the account has been rendered).

Six: The Program Must Be Politically Attainable

The political climate today should be frankly recognized in your design. Politics—the schoolman's variety of it[11]—has always been a part of program decision making. "Will it work in this school district?" probably runs through the minds of most schoolmen before embarking on new programs. It is still a good question to ask—particularly before committing yourself publicly to the pursuit of a specific accountability program. If, after you have done some preliminary planning (i.e., assessed needs, considered several change strategies, reviewed possible resources, and thought through a plan far enough to anticipate what will be the major hurdles in your district), you cannot conclude a reasonable expectation for success, you should forget about it until more favorable conditions arise—unless various group pressures leave you no alternative.

Certainly, two key items in making your decision will be its financial feasibility and its ability to accommodate various group antagonisms. We have enough confidence in the nature of accountability to believe that, once in process, a truer picture of program finances will emerge. As it does, mapping out results achieved for time and money expended, as well as educational values received, is bound to add appeal for an accountability approach to decision making. Assuming that financial resources will remain scarce and that it will continue to be necessary to choose with limited resources among competing program alternatives, the financial and educational hard-data engendered by the process make it compelling.

There are no foolproof guidelines that we can offer for

accommodating group antagonisms—particularly when they are blatant. The nature of the administrator's role means that he is expected to work *rationally* toward *rational* solutions to problems. Many of the antagonisms among groups arise from frustration over achieving their aspirations as well as fears and suspicions of other parties. In working toward rational solutions to problems, the administrator is likely to have to design a mechanism that (1) tries to separate out what each group wants from what the data shows the educational program needs in more generic terms; (2) can make a data-referenced case for subverting portions of each group's antagonisms enough to permit mutually recognized needs to be treated as task objectives; and (3) attempts to maintain a critical balance of active support to assure legitimate program operation (i.e., "de facto" support rather than "de jure," in which parties are invited to attack unchecked any public servant). If such a mechanism is necessary in your district, if it can be fashioned, the man who applies it might do well to keep Kipling's lines in mind: "If you can keep your head when all about you are losing theirs and blaming it on you . . . ."

Given the opportunity, we guess most schoolmen will try an accountability program on a limited basis—perhaps either on the worst educational problems in the district (where people are willing to admit at least tacitly that things could not be much worse) or under the best conditions (where staff self-confidence is realistic, earned, and high; where the spirit of innovation is strong, and the parents understanding). Wherever it is applied—including across the entire district—as schoolmen become familiar with the components that support the extended treatment of the accountability process, they will cross a new threshold administratively, one that enables their institutions to respond more rapidly to change.

Developing Imperatives into an Educational Accountability Program

Forearmed with advice, what do you do now? It should be clear that, as we view it, there is no single "best" approach. The recent history of the accountability concept, a concept still in transition, applied to educational tasks is still too brief. It is impossible for us to prescribe minutely a single "best" approach that would hold for all cases, and doubtful that it will ever emerge. Accordingly, a blend of art, science, and good judgment (admittedly difficult terms to define rigorously) is expected to attend the pragmatic development of an educational accountability program designed to fit a particular situation. You must do your own tailoring. At the most basic level, a program may be earmarked an "accountability program" if it merely incorporates the conditions of the concept, whether it is applied to subjects learned (e.g., reading, math, and others) or organizational patterns studied. Successfully incorporating these conditions, however, is not likely to be casually performed, especially when the form of accountability is educational in nature and involves both the community and staff. Not being able to present you THE approach, therefore, we offer instead what we hope is a "reasonable" one.

Imagine yourself an administrative leader (one who, as the late Bill Odell would say, "calls for action on a problem toward which he is inevitably being shoved"). You are considering an educational change of some magnitude, for example, to make more accountable the educational program of many children in your jurisdiction. It would require a degree of change on the part of your professional staff as well as the involvement and support of the lay community concerned. We can imagine this pragmatic administrator to perceive the task of developing an educational accountability program in roughly four phases:

> Phase 1: Preliminary planning
> Phase 2: Formal planning
> Phase 3: Program implementation
> Phase 4: Rendering the account

Phase 1: Preliminary Planning

Characteristics of Phase 1. The aim of the preliminary planning phase is to determine informally whether it is feasible to consider some form of educational accountability program for the area under consideration (i.e., the particular area might cover the educational program of the entire district or only a single classroom). It represents a feasibility study seeking a decision whether to move into Phase 2 or to drop the matter from consideration for the present. Probably only a few key people need to be involved at this point. In framing an answer, it is expected that (1) each of the imperatives offered above will have been duly considered, and (2) a positive outcome to move ahead to Phase 2 is regarded as "tentative," allowing for an enlarged group involvement in the planning process, perhaps to repeat portions of the preliminary planning steps more formally before coming to a decision of its own to move further, or not to move at all.

Critical and optional considerations for Phase 1. To complete

Phase 1 two critical elements ("need assessment" and "change strategies") and one optional aspect ("technical assistance and management systems") must be considered.

One of the first steps for any administrator (or group) contemplating introducing a change into an organization is gathering data to understand its present condition. Knowing where your school are educationally is requisite knowledge for any school administrator. Aside from developing an accountability program for what *should* be done, having good data on what *is* being done (sometimes referred to as "informational power") (1) is capable of changing people's preconceived attitudes toward innovating change, (2) identifies and clarifies problems, (3) is indispensable to complex decision making, and (4) is a commonly shared expectation people have of those who would lead them (i.e., that the leader is "informed").[12] Making a "need assessment" is therefore a preliminary first step. It may be repeated in the second phase by a larger group, but the leader should have some notion beforehand where to lead such a group and be able to anticipate any "surprise" findings. (Chapter 3 deals specifically with needs assessment.)

Once the educational needs of the district or program under consideration are identified to a degree that an administrator feels he can speak with confidence about "where we are" educationally, the next step is to contemplate a preliminary change strategy to "take us where we want to be." A preliminary change strategy might aim at: (1) developing a general awareness—a "receptive climate"—of educational needs in a positive sense (e.g., "We think we have identified some areas that, with your help and cooperation, we can develop further"); (2) involving groups of persons directly concerned with the definition of tasks, particularly in setting program goals and performance objectives; and (3) leading the way to a formal change strategy (perhaps as already developed, or adopted from the preliminary or a new strategy) that embraces goal and objective setting (i.e., task specification), program planning, staff training and implementation, and program evaluation with the rendering of the account. As mentioned above, this preliminary change strategy development may be repeated as a process in Phase 2 to give thrust to the group's decision on what the specific goals of the program should be (chapter 4 deals with change strategy considerations).

End point of Phase 1. After the above considerations have been carried out, the remaining major decision for Phase 1 awaits: is it feasible for us to continue?

Every public school has limited resources in terms of time, men, and money. The problems calling for attention are typically numerous. Desmond Cook points out: "The organization, however, must recognize that if all available resources are allocated to a few projects, its ability to respond to new ideas is limited."[13] In relation to other needs, and for the future, does the project have sufficient merit to pursue as a priority? The answer for the administrator is plainly a matter of judgment; hopefully, if he has done his homework well in Phase 1, he will bring informed judgment to bear.[14]

Assuming that his judgment acknowledges the project's priority over other needs, assuming it merits further consideration, the imperatives offered previously call for review. Can he affirm that the proposed program:

- Has designers with the requisite knowledge?
- Leads to potentially improved education?
- Will recognize and accommodate diverse forms of participation?
- Will train program personnel before and during implementation?
- Will generally fulfill the conditions of the accountability concept?
- Is judged politically attainable?

If he feels satisfied with his answers to these questions, he is nearly ready to move into Phase 2. He has determined the program to be initially feasible. From this point on the program is likely to assume a momentum of its own. The administrator should recognize and be willing to accept this risk. If his homework was done well, we think the risk is worth taking. If you do not, consider the alternatives and ask: are they really viable today?

If the administrator takes the risk, he reports his recommendation to his superior (the school board or, if he is a lesser administrator, the superintendent and, with the superintendent's blessing, to the board). The school board, the state's legally empowered reviewer of local programs, should probably make the decision to move forward or not—especially if the preliminary plan calls for community involvement. Their decision—yes or no—completes Phase 1.

Phase 2: Formal Planning

Characteristics of Phase 2. The purpose of Phase 2 is twofold:
(1) To place before the community and staff two questions: what *does* our school do? and, what should it be doing?

(2) To bring together an appropriate group of persons to work on these questions by (a) examining the extant data (for what it says and, sometimes shockingly, for what it fails to say); (b) considering alternative ways to meet the questions; and, of major importance, (c) developing a consensus of the goals and objectives of an educational program.

At the same time, because much of Phase 2 is a closely related (but more refined and comprehensive) version of Phase 1, it also asks can and should we implement a particular accountability program? We hypothesize that if the judgments made in Phase 1 are accurate, the answers concerning feasibility for Phase 2 should be compellingly affirmative.

Critical and optional considerations for Phase 2. In the groundwork for Phase 2 two aspects appear critically important ("community-staff involvement" and "performance objectives") and a third consideration optional ("plan-program-budgeting").

The increased politicization of the schools makes community-staff involvement both more necessary and difficult. Many administrators are likely to seek to avoid this step because of its bothersome qualities. In his study for New York State's Fleischmann Commission, Dale Mann claims more than half (59 percent) of the representative cross-section of 165 administrators surveyed have a "trustee" role in their relationships with the community. These trustee administrators (principals and superintendents) "will substitute their own judgment for that of the communities they serve, even when those communities . . . have expressed wishes contrary to those of the administrators."[15] The study portrays a resulting downward spiral of confidence: the public, feeling unwanted, begins to withdraw its support (financial and spiritual); the educational quality of the school begins to show deterioration from a lack of interest and support; the public withdraws even further its confidence; and mistrust and disappointment fill the void between the school and the community. To build a healthy, viable educational accountability program, we argue against trustee administration, although we recognize that many communities willingly abdicate their responsibilities to the professional educator (in much the same way that many parents abdicate responsibility for their children, leaving other agencies such as the school to provide what absentee parental attention cannot). We believe time is running out on the trustee educator, however. With the pressure for change unabating, the chances increase that he will either succeed in building a cooperative relationship with interested citizens or fall victim to a political boss using blatant power tactics. We prefer that he take the initiative in building the former relationship.

In bringing together a diverse group of people the object is to raise an interrelated set of educational questions: what are we trying to accomplish? what should we be trying to accomplish? The data collected in the preliminary needs assessment will probably answer these questions only generally. Your task will be to help this group clarify its thinking. Educational goals need to be operationally defined with measurable results over a realistically long period of time. Their related objectives will be more specific, short-term, results oriented, and moving toward the achievement of a goal. (Chapter 5 discusses the workings of community-staff involvement, while chapter 6 handles the technical aspects of drafting performance objectives.)

As identifiable educational goals emerge, so does another option, that of developing a budget on a program-objective format as opposed to the traditional line-item organization. In that way it is also possible to chart and account for the financial costs of different approaches to learning achievements. (Chapter 7 explores further the option of plan-program-budgeting.)

End of Phase 2. Phase 2 is complete when:

An appropriate community-staff group has met and determined for an educational program (probably ultimately identified with the help of a needs assessment) its goals and objectives in operational terms.

It may have designed the specific program, although it is likely to leave this to the professional staff, subject to review before implementation.

It has some notion of who will render a progress report on the achievement of the specified goals and objectives, when the report might be rendered, and what information it should include.

Depending on the temper and earnestness of the group, it may even have designated or requested that those involved in the program are responsible for particular objective achievements (if the group's aim is to propose a formal contract—an option—it has committed its level-of-confidence decisions beforehand by stating the rewards and penalties awarded by the results achieved).

If the group has considered formal "performance contracting," it has reached a point at which it could post the RFP's (request for proposals); chapter 9 in Phase 3 takes a closer look at performance contracting.

Again, if the involved group has been able to realize this degree of accomplishment, the likelihood is strong that the checklist of imperatives will receive affirmative conclusions. If not, the group's attention should be focused on the problem area. If the problem cannot be resolved, either the project should be abandoned or salvaged where possible by redesigning it under some other label that presumably removes the obstacle.

Phase 3: Program Implementation

Characteristics of Phase 3. The major concern of Phase 3 centers on the task of further developing the staff and implementing the particular program. By now, the major dimensions of the program will have been formed: through needs assessment, specific problem areas have been identified; a preliminary and then formal change strategy to involve people in the review of needs, the framing of general goals and performance objectives, and the design of the program will have been employed; and, presumably, a generally supportive climate (in terms of attitudes, financial support, realistic time constraints, etc.) will have been established (negotiated?) through community and staff involvement. It now becomes necessary for the staff directly involved with implementing the project to come together to develop further the ways of achieving the program's objectives. Teaching strategies need to be considered, learners targeted, staff trained, and the program placed in operation.

Critical and optional considerations for Phase 3. Staff development is a critical component in successfully launching an educational accountability program. Most schoolmen believe that staff development is important. Unfortunately, a look at school budgets and practices too often reflects that, while it may be regarded as important, it is given low priority among competing needs. The combination of short funds, unfocused purposes, reluctant staffs, short-term time commitments, and off the cuff leadership has marked many "staff development" attempts. Our expectations are different. Remember, we want to avoid failure, not encourage it. Before the program is implemented, we expect that the staff:

(1) Clearly understands the purpose, goals, and objectives of the program;

(2) Knows exactly what measurable changes are expected in the identified learners and will be able to make this knowledge equally clear to the learners later;

(3) Holds a professional point of view—a "zero reject" conviction that no child will be abandoned or rejected as a learner[16]—if the

expected changes do not occur in the individual learner, and that the program and its manner of implementation as well as its appropriateness for that individual will be restudied with alternatives sought;[17]

(4) Understands the theory or model of instruction that buttresses the program being undertaken;[18]

(5) Attempts some mock-up or dry run pretesting of the program on themselves and then on a small group of students;

(6) Has devised procedures for monitoring the progress of the program sharp enough to pinpoint programming problems to permit necessary changes while the program is in progress;[19]

(7) Is knowledgeable about the manner in which the program is to be evaluated and the account rendered.

A desired secondary outcome of the staff development effort, an outcome that stems from involvement in the development process itself, is that a positive attitude will grow among the staff toward each other, the learners, and the program. For many localities, this secondary hope may be unrealistic. Some staffs may be closed, hardened, and cynical—perhaps with good reason. They may have worked in a world where seemingly no good deed goes unpunished. We are operating, perhaps naively, on Douglas McGregor's now classic assumption that most staffs would sincerely like to improve their performance.[20] Given the opportunity to become involved in the formative stages of the program, provided the tasks of sharpening their understanding and practices, noting the potential for better feedback of their teaching-learning impact, presenting a way for them to isolate learner difficulties more effectively, and allowing the emergence of some—to us—realistic standards of success in the discharge of their responsibilities, we believe most staffs should respond favorably. Frederick Herzberg holds that if a man has challenging work in which he can assume responsibility, he is likely to be favorably motivated.[21] This aspect of the staff development component is desired. The term *professional challenge* has been much abused over the past decade, but it remains critical to the success of the program that those involved perceive their work as both highly professional and challenging. (Chapter 8 deals with staff development and program implementation.)

Another optional approach may also be considered in Phase 3. It includes consideration of whether the program is to be shaped in the form of a performance contract (internal or external), spelling out all the clauses of the accountability process. (Chapter 9 reviews the characteristics of performance contracts.)

End of Phase 3. Phase 3 ends at some preestablished point according to the terms of the plan approved in Phase 2 (unless some further adjustment in the plan has been made in Phase 3). Usually a predetermined time is selected (the end of a semester, a year, two years, whatever) for making a critical judgment about the program. If the program is experimental (as most new programs tend to be viewed), this critical point will raise the question whether it should be certified as successful and continued (perhaps disseminating it to other programs or areas in the district), or as needing modifications, or as a failure. At any rate, in accountability programs there comes a time when its stewards are expected to reach a predetermined point in their work, to order their account formally, and to render it. For our purposes Phase 3 ends when that point is reached.

Phase 4: Rendering the Account

Characteristics of Phase 4. The final phase of the program deals with taking a close look at our efforts and reporting the results in accordance with the plan adopted in Phase 2. Did the students succeed in reaching the objectives stated for the program? What differences are there between the actual learner behaviors (what is) and those behaviors projected in the performance objectives (what should be)? Many other questions related to the program and the manner and effects of its functioning will be raised. But, after the account has been reached, learning achievements assessed, stated objectives compared with the data, the many facets of the program analyzed, the second task arises: presenting it to the reviewers.

Critical and optional considerations for Phase 4. The two critical functions very apparent in Phase 4 are the tasks of evaluating the program in terms of learner outcomes and rendering the account to the reviewers. Within both tasks are optional considerations and degrees of sophistication. At the simplest level, the task would be to collect, analyze, and report on the data that bears solely upon determining the degree to which the program's operation has met its stated objectives. This means that persons in Phase 2, when they established the goals and objectives of the program, also established the procedures and kinds of evidence used in evaluating and reporting it. Presumably the evaluation devices used are appropriate to the objectives. If standardized tests are used, for example, they are selected and used solely according to their ability to assess evidence on the particular objectives.[22]

The evaluation effort may go beyond this point. For example, it may consist of assessing: (1) both group and individual learner's aptitudes for the particular kinds of learning; (2) the general quality of instruction; (3) learner ability to understand that variety of instruction; (4) the degree of enthusiasm and perseverance shown by the learners in pursuing the instruction; and (5) the time needed by different students to attain their level of achievement.

It might include a cost-effectiveness analysis as well. For example, one very simple analysis uncovered a situation in which an exercise machine costing over $20,000 and operated by an athletic director (whose daily hours of time were prorated from an annual salary of $17,000), handling eighteen boys every twenty minutes (with another instructor working elsewhere with the remainder of the shuttling boys), achieved the same stated objectives as a student-run and faculty-advised twenty-minute calisthenic program. The latter program, in addition to costing only the faculty advisor's small $700 fee and $200 of the school doctor's time to okay the boys in the program (the same charge for the boys using the machine), had the added advantage of promoting leadership and record-keeping responsibilities among several of the boys.[23] In short, there are many ways and forms of evaluation. (Chapter 10 looks at evaluation.)

The task of rendering the account remains—a necessary condition of the accountability process itself. After the evaluation is completed (data collected, analyzed, and interpreted) it is incumbent on those responsible for the project's management to report the findings. From Phase 2, we will know (1) who will make the report, (2) how it will be made, (3) what it should contain, and (4) to whom it will be delivered. Another option toward rendering the account also might have been considered earlier: using an independent educational program audit. Perhaps either a special committee of community-staff persons or an independent educational program audit group from outside may have been selected to review the program and either corroborate or take issue with the findings. (Chapter 11 discusses the rendering of accounts.)

End of Phase 4. The program evaluated and the account rendered, the stewards stand ready for an expression of confidence from the reviewers. Will the stewards face "the slings and arrows of outrageous fortune" or, as suggested by Frank Lloyd Wright, bask in the glory of approval either in hypocritical humility or honest arrogance? More probably reality will place the reflection of confidence somewhere between arrows and exultation. If the early cards-on-the-table form of accountability was employed, the level-of-confidence issue was calculated in Phase 2, before undertaking the project. Reward (and penalties if they were included in the agreement) would be based on these preconditions. The level-of-confidence issue would be resolved then upon the degree of realization of the stated expectations and the positive or negative consequences to flow from it. If an independent program auditor was used, it is probable that stewards and reviewers have agreed to accept the auditor's report as the basis of decisions (with an appropriate pre-established mechanism to permit either the stewards or the reviewers to contest the auditor's report). Normally, it is the task of the reviewers to make the report public knowledge (unless it was decided earlier that the stewards would make this information public at the time of formally presenting their account to the reviewers). Presumably, the stewards have rendered periodic progress reports to the public. The reviewers have the tasks of: (1) receiving the stewards' report; (2) deciding whether the findings appear accurate and complete; (3) determining the degree of success with which the program may be certified; (4) settling the level-of-confidence issue in regard to the stewards; and (5) informing the general public of its action—the public exercising a level-of-confidence review of its own. But, for our purposes, the process of developing an educational accountability program is completed.

Two summary ways of viewing the accountability program's development may be expressed in figures 2.1 and 2.2.

Figure 2.1. A process for developing an accountability program

Phase 1: preliminary planning
  • Assess needs (critical)
  • Develop a preliminary change strategy (critical)
  • Consider use of technical assistance and management systems (optional)
  • Decision to move, or not to move, to Phase 2

Phase 2: formal planning
  • Community-staff involvement (critical)
    ---Repeat needs assessment (optional)
    ---Repeat change strategy development (optional)
  • Develop goal-consensus and performance objectives (critical)
  • Consider plan-program-budgeting systems (optional)
  • Decision to move, or not to move, to Phase 3

Phase 3: program implementation
  • Develop program staff (critical)
  • Implement program procedures (critical)
  • Consider
    ---Performance contracting (internal and/or external) (optional)
    ---Network monitoring (optional)
  • Predetermined completion points of program efforts reached

Phase 4: rendering the account
  • Program evaluation (critical)
  • Reporting the results (critical)
  • Using an educational program auditor (optional)
  • Determining level of confidence (critical)
  • Certifying the nature of results (critical)

Figure 2.2. A possible framework for

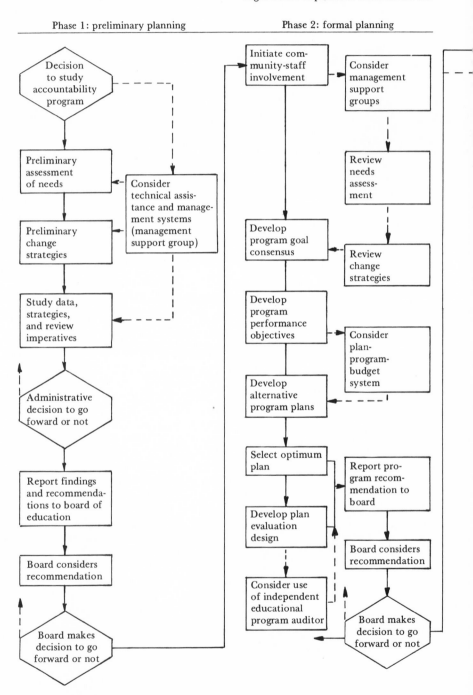

Phase 1: preliminary planning   Phase 2: formal planning

*Broken lines represent optional program aspects.

developing an educational accountability program*

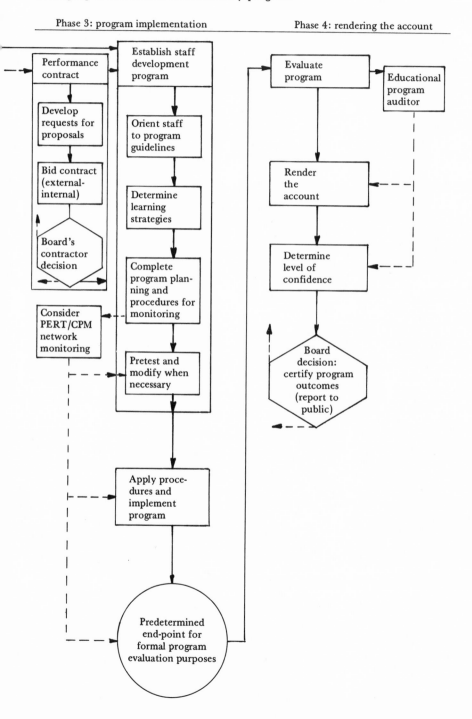

Phase 3: program implementation   Phase 4: rendering the account

Tailoring a Concept

It would be misleading for us to present only a single model for developing an accountability program. Certainly all the complexity and verification presented in our model can be considerably simplified. At the same time, there are degrees of accountability. Ray Bernabei, for example, has suggested it is possible to take a classic curriculum and instruction approach and, by degree, make it "more accountable." It may be accomplished simply by insisting that the criteria for validly evaluating the results be established prior to the operation of the program.[24]

From:

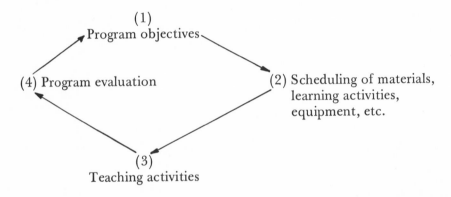

(1)
Program objectives

(4) Program evaluation

(2) Scheduling of materials, learning activities, equipment, etc.

(3)
Teaching activities

To:

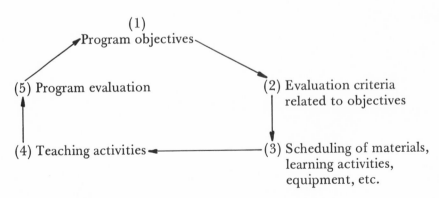

(1)
Program objectives

(5) Program evaluation

(2) Evaluation criteria related to objectives

(4) Teaching activities

(3) Scheduling of materials, learning activities, equipment, etc.

Several variations on the accountability theme are possible. For example, under the classification "flower" many kinds of plants grow. Some are hard to recognize and classify as flowers. Similarly, it is possible to conceive of many variations for program design. Some of these variations (sketched briefly as lines of thought) are offered in figure 2.3. No attempt has been made to exhaust the possibilities. Hopefully, the point is made that the accountability concept is generic and capable of breeding a garden full of hybrid program species.[25]

Figure 2.3. Some variations on the accountability theme

Elements of the basic theme

Clarify expectations into goals and measurable objectives

↓

Specify tasks/delineate conditions

↓

Render account of results achieved toward specified objectives

Variation 1

Someone (steward)

↓

Is answerable/responsible (account-able)

↓

To someone else (reviewer)

↓

For something (obtaining measurable results)

↓

Within certain contraints (specified goals, measurable objectives, deline-ated tasks)

Variation 2

Two parties (stewards and reviewers)

↓

Variation 2 (continued)

Negotiate agreement on
(1) tasks (goals, objectives)
(2) contraints (time, money, conditions)
(3) rewards/penalties based on results (predetermine level of confidence)

↓

Stewards do tasks

↓

Stewards render account of results

↓

Reviewers determine acceptability of stewards' account

↓

Account agreement settled on pre-determined levels of confidence, con-ditions to be accorded by results

Variation 3

Consensus sought by reviewers on goals and objectives (definition of re-viewer expectations)

↓

Stewards hired to fulfill measurable expectations

↓

Variation 3 *(continued)*

Stewards render account of measurable progress toward objectives

↓

Reviewers render a level-of-confidence judgment

Variation 4

Reviewers establish mission profile on goals/performance objectives

↓

Reviewers and stewards determine an accountability chart delineating responsibilities and conditions

↓

Reviewers and stewards develop an evaluation system that:
  (1) specifies performance criteria
  (2) identifies performance indicators
  (3) designs measuring instruments

↓

Stewards complete tasks

↓

Task performance evaluated (data gathered and interpreted)

↓

Reviewers determine their level of confidence in
  (1) the results
  (2) the stewards (optional)

Variation 5

The "accountability team" perhaps teachers and administrators)

↓

Clarify program objectives into specified, measurable outcomes

↓

Variation 5 *(continued)*

Delineate responsibilities (perhaps with an accountability chart)

↓

Develop alternative program means for achieving goals

↓

Selected optimum program plan

↓

Develop a supporting program evaluation system

↓

Implement program and its evaluation system

↓

Measure outcomes, performance, and program effectiveness

Variation 6

Teachers plan lesson unit using behavioral objectives

↓

Pretest and modify lesson unit

↓

Teach lesson unit

↓

Monitor teacher performance and learner behavior during instruction

Evaluate
  (1) learner outcomes
  (2) teaching performance
  (3) appropriateness of content and learning strategy
  (4) total effectiveness of lesson unit (student achievements, time, money, etc.)

↓

Replan lesson unit with review/modification goals, objectives, learning strategies, budget and administrative procedures

Variation 7

Student needs → Social values → Community expectations →

Order educational goals and priorities for district

↓

Hypothesize alternative approaches to meet district goals

↓

Establish program area task forces to develop appropriate programs

↓

Task force to develop program and instructional objectives

↓

Learning strategy formulated

↓

Program evaluation design created

↓

Program implemented

↓

Data feedback to reviewers

Variation 8

Student needs assessed

↓

Reviewer concerns and priorities assessed

↓

Goals established

↓

Alternative means reviewed

↓

Variation 8 *(continued)*

Selected means submitted to program and evaluation design

↓

In-service training provided program staff (pre- and during program operation)

↓

Program implemented

↓

Short-term monitoring feedback

↓

Formal program evaluation

↓

Rendering the account

Variation 9

Plan:
(1) define need
(2) establish objectives
(3) generate alternatives
(4) analyze and select among alternatives

↓

Program: assign resources (staff, time, materials, strategies)

↓

Budget: allocate resources to optimum plan

↓

Operate program

↓

Evaluate

It is also possible to alter further aspects of the program's design simply by choosing among the role combinations in establishing an "accountability team" (if you consciously strive to develop a "team approach" at all). This team approach brings specific combinations of persons together by design for purposes of involvement in program design, implementation, and review. It is presumed that once the program's goals and objectives are clarified and planning completed all the participants are members of a "team" moving in the same specific direction (i.e., no team member is supposed to hang back or criticize the program publicly while it passes through Phase 3. After the stewards have rendered the account (Phase 4) the team may dissolve). Figure 2.4 offers some possibilities; if nothing more, it should underline the variety of ways of combining people with tasks.

At the same time, many approaches used or considered by others tend to conform in varying degrees to the conditions of the accountability concept in terms of their own distinct procedures. Stretching some points, the degrees of accountability concept fulfillment can be illustrated as they are commonly understood procedurally. Figure 2.5 makes this attempt. Some approaches may appear to you more appealing than others in designing your program and may influence your selection of program tailoring choices. Most of these approaches carry literature of their own.

What to Expect: Some Limitations of Accountability Programs

What can you expect to happen if you embark on the accountability process suggested in our model? While the history of accountability in education is still too brief to supply many data-based conclusions, some limitations stand out. As in making any conscious choice, there are some advantages and disadvantages.

Let us begin by mentioning again that this form of accountability in education has had a short history. The brevity of its existence means at least that, (1) as a new concept to education, it must be acknowledged as an "innovation" and is therefore prone to all the maladies associated with educational innovations; and (2) because it is new, its workability and effectiveness cannot be abundantly demonstrated in terms of "research evidence." In education, these twin shortcomings (if you view them that way) are almost certain to be seized upon by critics. While we do not regard these items to be serious limitations, we do recognize them as being immediate.

What limitations might we expect from "innovation"? Because

education over the past fifteen years has been exposed to many ideas (e.g., what ever happened to bomb shelter plans?), many persons have assumed a sort of mechanical anti-innovation stance toward *any* proposal. This attitude may appear ludicrous to some, but it is administratively necessary to deal with it. Here are characteristics of educational innovations as they have appeared over the years that

Figure 2.4. Some possible "accountability team" combinations and roles

Sample accountability team combinations	Team participants identified by group	District level participation					Building unit level participation				
		Participates as reviewer	Participates as steward	Self-accountable	Mixed roles as steward-reviewer	Participates as adviser	Participates as reviewer	Participates as steward	Self-accountable	Mixed roles as steward-reviewer	Participates as adviser
1	Administrator(s) (Solo)	−	−	X	+	−	−	−	X	+	−
2	Teacher(s) (Solo)	−	−	0	−	−	0	0	X	+	0
3	Administrator(s)	X	0	+	+	+	X	0	+	+	+
	Teacher(s)	−	X	+	+	+	−	X	+	+	+
4	Board of Education	X	−	X	+	+	X	−	+	−	+
	Administrator(s)	0	X	−	−	+	+	+	+	+	+
	Teacher(s)	−	X	−	−	+	−	X	−	+	−
5	Administrator(s)	X	+	+	+	−	X	−	X	+	+
	Teacher(s)	−	X	+	0	+	−	X	+	+	0
	Students	−	−	+	−	X	−	−	−	−	X
6	Administrator(s)	X	0	0	+	0	X	0	+	+	0
	Teachers	−	X	0	+	0	−	X	−	+	−
	Community groups	0	−	0	−	X	0	−	−	−	X
7	Board of education	X	−	X	−	+	X	−	X	−	+
	Administrator(s)	0	X	−	+	+	+	X	−	+	+
	Teachers	0	X	−	+	+	0	X	−	+	+
	Community groups	+	−	+	−	X	+	−	+	−	X
8	Board of education	X	−	X	−	+	X	−	X	−	+
	Administrators	0	X	−	+	−	X	+	−	+	−
	Teachers	0	X	−	−	+	0	X	−	+	+
	Students	0	−	−	−	X	0	−	−	−	X
	Community groups	+	−	+	−	X	+	−	+	−	X

X: probable role
+: possible role
0: possible but not likely role
−: improbable role

Figure 2.5. Some approaches toward accountability concept fulfillment

| Form of approach | Conditions of the accountability concept | | | |
	Clarification of specific expectations	Tasks specified	Account rendered by specific results	Level of confidence
Educational program auditing	yes	yes	yes	Usually predetermined contractually and specified
Management by objectives	yes	yes	yes	Determined after review of results (unspecified)
Program evaluation review technique and/or critical path method (PERT/CPM)	yes	yes	yes	Not considered
Educational voucher system	no	no	no	Determined by consumer choice
Operations research	yes	maybe	yes	Not considered
Systems analysis	yes	maybe	yes	Not considered
Differentiated staffing	maybe	yes	maybe	Not considered
Criterion referenced instruction	yes	maybe	yes	Not considered

Plan-program-budget systems (PPBS)	yes	yes	yes	Determined after review of results
Programmed instruction	yes	yes	yes	Not considered
Community control	maybe	maybe	maybe	Determined by local community groups
Cost/effectiveness analysis	yes	maybe	yes	Not considered
Performance contracting:				
External	yes	yes	yes	Predetermined and specified
Internal	yes	yes	yes	May be either pre or postdetermined, specified or unspecified

seem applicable to our proposal (the reader should hear an echo from
the program's planning imperatives):[26]

Limitations of innovative programs	Possible responses
1. The proposed model has not been developed, implemented, and evaluated. ("You're experimenting with our children!")	1. Most conventional programs have not been carefully developed, implemented and evaluated to the degree proposed for this accountability program. The focus of the proposed process should yield greater amounts of information on what both individuals and groups of students learn as a result of instructional strategies. In turn, this clarity of outcomes should permit: (a) closer diagnosis of individual learning problems (it should be possible to pinpoint a learner profile based on his performance toward the criterion-referenced objectives of the program); (b) more complete determination about what effects the instructional strategy used had upon the students as a group (suggesting ways the program might be modified in the future and identifying areas calling for review with current students); and (c) a way for staff to measure the relative effectiveness of their own efforts (enabling them to focus better their own professional efforts and, a side issue, to discover areas where they might be receptive to in-service workshop activity based on obvious needs). Specific knowledge of what is intended to happen, followed by an accounting of what did happen based on results, would not appear to be irresponsible experimentation.
2. Beyond adhering roughly to the general conditions of the concept, it is possible to get a wide variety of forms rather than one standard form to certify successful or unsuccessful. ("Why don't we just add 'accountability' to the title of our old programs and make the board happy?")	2. As long as the conditions of the concept are observed, flexibility of form is desirable. The fact that there are degrees of accountability should not be disturbing. Rigorousness of adhesion to the elements of the accountability concept should serve to indicate whether the program can be legitimately considered

Limitations of innovative programs	Possible responses

under that label. You be the judge. If nothing more, this design flexibility should prevent critics from stereotyping the program.

3. Usually, any application of the accountability concept to a local district has to undergo some tailoring to fit local conditions. ("If you use Jones, the principals won't speak to you. If you involve Smith, the teachers won't. So why don't you get some outsider so we can all get together and give him hell.")

3. Again, as long as it is possible to maintain the conditions of the concept with integrity, the local situation dictates the form (unless state or federal levels intervene with programs of their own). Whether you have "a little accountability" or a lot is left to your own discretion. As a rule of thumb, it might be wiser to accept a lesser degree of accountability than an all-or-none approach. For example, making only 50 percent of the objectives of a given program operationally accountable by results may prove to be more viable locally than attempting to account for a 100 percent operationally accountable program—a purity of form desirable for either research purposes or external performance contracts but maybe unnecessary for local service.

4. Implementing an accountability program usually requires several sets of interrelated, coordinated changes. ("Our staff believes in 'professional autonomy' where each member does what he thinks is right.").

4. Professional autonomy that translates into everyone "doing his own thing" makes the process of education haphazard and forever unable to become more effective than the sum of its individual parts (in this case, its parts are generally represented by the solitary classroom teacher—a teacher characteristically drawn from the lower standard scholastic achievement percentiles of college students). The accountability program suggested in our model clearly implies a necessity for people to coordinate their actions, which is requisite to any educational endeavor that hopes to have greater impact than the sum of its parts. Also, there can and should be specifically planned freedoms of operation within the external

Limitations of innovative programs	Possible responses

5. The innovation will not function successfully at the instructional level unless the staff has been appropriately trained and led in the handling of it. ("I'd like to see those bastards try to put that program in *my* class!")

    boundaries (objectives, budget, time, scheduling, etc.) of the program.

5. This limitation is critical. Unless the staff involved with the program views it as highly professional work (which it is) and is willing to try (with the appropriate amounts of time for training) or powerful external support comes from other sources (support capable of removing obstacles), there is little hope of successful operation. In part, this explains why we have stressed involvement of staff in the early planning of the program.

6. Like country doctors, it will probably be necessary to make do with the local leadership talent available. ("Who, me? I don't know anything about accountability!")

6. It is assumed that most local leadership talent can and ought to be developed. Any newly appointed administrator who has inherited his leadership team knows that this task may be formidable (particularly if local talents were either vying for his position or unenthusiastic about his appointment). Given a reasonably receptive group, however, it should be possible to develop local leadership talent to a point where it is capable of providing the necessary thrust. Exposure to the literature on the subject, perhaps attendance at national professional conferences (e.g., AASA's National Academy for School Executives, the "Accountability Conferences" of Educational Testing Service, etc.), and some well-planned discussion sessions should be helpful in gearing up the leadership. If the preliminary planning phase concludes with an unenthusiastic leadership group, some careful rethinking would be timely. Perhaps a performance contract with an external group might be worth seriously considering.

Limitations of innovative programs	Possible responses
7. Perhaps the most apparent limitation of innovative programs can be summarized in Donald Campbell's observation: "In the present political climate, reformers and administrators achieve their precarious permission to innovate by overpromising the certain efficacy of their new programs. This traps them so that they cannot afford to risk learning that the new programs were not effective."[27]	7. Our obvious response: be careful. Accountability programs, properly handled, yield visible results. You must be prepared to take that risk at the outset. The administrator who lightly purchases his ride on the accountability bandwagon with overpromises will be disappointed. Taken as a serious attempt to improve the process of educating children by focusing on their learning outcomes (or as a process to improve any operation), the conditions of the accountability process —especially those related to the level-of-confidence issue—are sobering. However, given affirmative answers to our imperatives, we think it is a risk worth taking.

The limitation of lack of research evidence in its general form is no stranger to educational practice. What evidence supports current educational practices? The critics' standard ploy, usually more rhetorical than sincere, is to point to a new proposal and loudly proclaim that it should be tested before it is used. They are right. It should be. To get below the surface of this issue, an appropriate response is to inquire further what evidence would be acceptable to warrant moving forward with the new practice. The point should be pursued. Get a determination of what might be regarded as a criteria for accepting or rejecting educational programs based on research evidence. The next step should be obvious: conduct a formal assessment of current programs. This can serve several purposes: (1) the standard, "tried and proven" practices under examination often turn out to be "tired and unproven"; (2) the rationale supporting both current and proposed practices should surface and be available for comparative analysis; and (3) formal needs assessment—the gathering of baseline data—is the first step toward developing program accountability.

Below the limitations raised by innovation characteristics and lack of research evidence lie more fundamental issues. Perhaps the key question might be to what degree can (and should) we really hold people and programs accountable? You are asked to accept a pragmatic answer: to a degree that is more than generally practiced, but far less than is theoretically possible. One reason for this answer is that the machinery for enacting accountability measures is still being developed and, while it has gotten beyond the threshold of primitive development, its usage has not reached a level of confidence akin to Caesar's wife. A second reason is found in human nature. A few people may regard themselves accountable to no one or for nothing, most will acknowledge a generalized accountability, and very few seek extensive accountability. To date, education has not called for the kind of accountable precision necessary for the launching of rockets in a space venture. This degree would be too cumbersome, unwieldy, and impractical for today. By the year 2001, who knows?

Part of our rationale supporting accountability programs runs on these assumptions:[28]

• The schools exist primarily to produce publicly endorsed changes in the learning behavior of their major client, the student;

• Learning behaviors, expressed as outcomes, can be achieved in multiple ways, some more effective than others;

• Because the resources (time, money, staff, etc.) available in any school district are customarily less than the demands made upon them, it is encumbent on the administrative staff to seek an optimum balance between the available resources and the most effective means of expending them in attaining publicly endorsed goals and objectives;

• Without the presence of some form of accountability process, it is difficult or impossible to gauge learner progress well—either individual or group—or instructional effectiveness for the purposes of decision making;

• Programs carrying the conditions of the accountability process lend themselves to better, more informed kinds of decision making toward seeking the optimum balance between resource expenditures and learning achievement;

• Given sufficient time and operation, programs identified by the accountability process as "ineffective" (i.e., failing to pass the level-of-confidence review of results) should be modified, eliminated, or replaced by more effective ones;

• The accountability process is a vehicle that holds promise for improving learning outcomes, decision making, and rational adjustments to change pressures.

The validity of any assumption is open to question; accordingly, these assumptions are offered as a variety of limitation.

It is, however, between these assumptions and their translation into practice that two or more serious questions arise: (1) is it possible to develop a set of effectiveness indicators that really indicate effectiveness? and (2) is the present state of the art of evaluating learning outcomes able to yield useful measurements for accountability purposes?

We have alluded earlier to the "criterion problem." The usual generalized practices used in seeking accountable employees hardly seem to meet minimum standards of reliability and relevancy.[29] At issue is whether the new proposals for accountability (e.g., management by objectives, PPBS, etc.) can actually offer (1) clear specifications for operating effectiveness, (2) objective measures that avoid being nonobjective or irrelevant, (3) subjective measures (where used) that are unbiased or unreliable, (4) criteria that are updated over time; and, in brief, (5) establishment of an effectiveness profile that measures what it is supposed to measure. Most adherents of the accountability movement appear to believe that it is possible to varying degrees.[30] It is a limitation. On the other hand, if you abandon honest attempts to measure effectiveness, on what grounds do you base your decisions?

Concerning the present state of the art of evaluating learner outcomes, there are some limitations—particularly in the use of standardized tests in meeting the demands for accountability. Where standardized tests are involved, Klein notes, for example, there is inclined to be: a poor fit between the objectives of the school and those of the standardized test; a problem inherent in the design and format of the test for a particular school population; poor instruction giving and administering of the tests; and a problem of using standardized tests that do not measure what they claim to measure.[31] Such limitations would caution against indiscriminate reliance on standardized tests for accountability purposes. On the other hand, adherents of formative evaluation appear to be moving in a direction that permits some useful measurements of instructional improvement.[32] In turn, this should be serviceable for accountability purposes.

A RAND study of five performance contracts (one approach toward accountability) listed several advantages and disadvantages accruing from performance contracts.[33] They are worth noting here. Performance contracting is only one approach toward accountability, but it is one that strongly embraces the major conditions of the concept, including the predetermined agreement on the level-of-confidence issue.

On the positive side, their study indicated that this form of accountability was capable of introducing radical changes in education, placed increased emphasis on accountability for student learning on the professional staff, and introduced new groups (external contractors) into education. Negatively, performance contracts were administratively complex, took a narrow focus "because of difficulties of defining objectives in subject areas other than those involving simple skills or, in some cases, difficulties in measuring the attainment of objectives,"[34] and tend to raise some old problems ("the most severe have been legal questions, issues of teacher status, difficulties in supplying the needed management skills, and especially, problems of test selection and administration").[35] As expressed by this study and in the recent controversy on the use of performance contracts,[36] the limitations appear formidable. At the same time, there remains cause for optimism. Accountable results were obtained. They were able to analyze and account for instructional processes, cognitive growth, resource requirements, evaluation procedures, program management, and returns to contractors. Like the Wright brothers' flight at Kitty Hawk, the accountability process works—not well yet, but it does function.

Are you game to try?

Notes for Chapter 2

1. Felix Lopez, "Accountability in Education," in *Emerging Patterns of Administrative Accountability*, ed. Lesley Browder, Jr. (Berkeley: McCutchan Publishing Corp., 1971), pp. 386-87.

2. Ibid., pp. 385-86; Joseph Mazur, "Operationalizing Accountability in Public School Systems," in *Emerging Patterns*, p. 513.

3. Ibid., p. 513.

4. Luvern L. Cunningham, *Governing Schools: New Approaches to Old Issues* (Columbus, Ohio: Charles E. Merrill Publishing Co., 1971), pp. 191-98.

5. Stated or implied, most who write about the application of accountability programs manage to indicate what they regard as essential or absolutely necessary. A casual review of *Emerging Patterns*, pp. 361-524, should give a sense of this imperative explicating.

See also *Conferences on Educational Accountability* (Princeton, N.J.: Educational Testing Service, 1971); E. Wayne Roberson, ed., *Educational Accountability Through Evaluation* (Englewood Cliffs, N.J.: Educational Technology Publications, 1971).

6. The reader should be further warned that Jacob Getzels, James Lipham, and Roald Campbell, *Educational Administration as a Social Process* (New

York: Harper & Row, 1968), raise serious questions about such forms of advice giving (see chapter 1). Their point is well taken. Hopefully our more academically oriented readers will review these imperatives as key variables in a conceptual framework that should become apparent as they read.

7. Charles Lindblom presents a classic rationale for administrators making decisions by successive limited comparisons (the "branch method") rather than by a rational-comprehensive approach (the "root method"). See Charles Lindblom, "The Science of Muddling Through," *Public Administration Review* 19 (1959): 79-88. We argue that accountability programs require more attention to the "root method" than practitioners normally use.

8. Getzels, *Educational Administration as a Social Process*, p. 378.

9. Amitai Etzioni, "Schools as a 'Guidable' System," in *Freedom, Bureaucracy, and Schooling*, ed. Vernon Haubrich (Washington, D.C.: Association of Supervision and Curriculum Development, 1971 yearbook), p. 45.

10. Marilyn Hapgood, "The Open Classroom: Protect It from Its Friends," *Saturday Review*, September 18, 1971, p. 66.

11. For a more extended explanation of this term and the norms surrounding it, see Lesley Browder, Jr., "A Suburban School Superintendent Plays Politics," in *The Politics of Education at the Local, State and Federal Levels*, ed. Michael Kirst (Berkeley: McCutchan Publishing Corp., 1970), pp. 191-93.

12. For further insights into the implications of good data, see Dorwin Cartwright, "Influence, Leadership, Control," in *Handbook of Organizations*, ed. James March (Chicago: Rand McNally, 1965), chapter 1; David Krech, Richard Crutchfield, and Egerton Ballachey, "The Changing of Attitudes," in *Individual in Society* (New York: McGraw-Hill, 1962), chapter 7; John Pfeiffer, *New Look at Education* (New York: Odyssey Press, 1966).

13. Desmond Cook, *Educational Project Management* (Columbus, Ohio: Charles E. Merrill Publishing Co., 1971), p. 203.

14. The literature on research project selection holds some works worth considering by administrators interested in what others do: N. R. Baker and W. H. Pound, "R and D Project Selection: Where We Stand," *IIEE Transactions on Engineering Management* (December 1964): 124-34; D. Z. Herz and P. C. Carlson, "Selection, Evaluation, and Control of Research and Development Projects," *Operations Research in Research and Development*, ed. B. Dean (New York: John Wiley & Sons, 1963).

15. Dale Mann, "Administrator/Community/School Relationships in New York State," *Newsday*, November 4, 1971, p. 13A.

16. For two interesting expressions of the zero-reject point of view, see Leon Lessinger, "A Zero-Reject Program in a Comprehensive School District: Some Concrete Steps to Eliminate School Dropouts," *The California School Administrator* 21, no. 4 (November 1966); Robert Weber, "The Early Warning System and the Zero Failure School: Professional Response to Accountability," *Journal of Secondary Education* 45, no. 8 (December 1970).

17. For a sophisticated expression of the zero-reject point of view, see Benjamin Bloom, "Learning for Mastery," *Evaluation Comment* 1, no. 2 (May 1968).

18. For some useful ideas on instruction, see Jerome Bruner, *The Process of Education* (Cambridge: Harvard University Press, 1961); D. P. Ausubel, *Educational Psychology: A Cognitive View* (New York: Holt, Rinehart & Winston, 1968); R. M. Gagne, *The Conditions of Learning* (New York: Holt,

Rinehart & Winston, 1965); Benjamin Bloom, J. Thomas Hastings, and George Madaus, *Handbook on Formative and Summative Evaluation of Student Learning* (New York: McGraw-Hill, 1971); John Carroll, "A Model of School Learning," *Teachers College Record* 64 (1963): 723-33.

19. For some insightful advice on the importance of this expectation, see Lee J. Cronbach, "Evaluation for Course Improvement," *Teachers College Record* 64 (1963): 8; Michael Scriven, "The Methodology of Evaluation," in *Perspectives of Curriculum Evaluation*, ed. R. Stake (Chicago: Rand McNally, 1967).

20. Douglas McGregor, "The Human Side of Enterprise," *Management Review* 46 (1957): 22-28, 88-92.

21. Frederick Herzberg, "One More Time: How Do You Motivate Employees?" *Harvard Business Review* (January-February 1968): 53-62.

22. For an excellent discussion on this topic, see Stephen Klein, "The Uses and Limitations of Standardized Tests in Meeting the Demands for Accountability," *Evaluation Comment* 2, no. 4 (January 1971); idem, "Evaluating Tests in Terms of the Information They Provide," *Evaluation Comment* 2, no. 2 (June 1970).

23. Although it was too late to return the exercise machine, it was found that a student could operate this machine and keep the records of student achievement on it, freeing the athletic director for other tasks. Following up later, the author learned that the student picked to operate the machine was from a retarded learner class. The high-priced athletic director, freed from this "professional" responsibility, is now teaching driver education. A cost-effectiveness analysis on the driver education program has not yet been run (what do you think they will find when it is done?). For obvious reasons, this district asked not to be identified.

24. Raymond Bernabei, American Association of School Administrators—National Academy for School Executives Conference on Accountability, Atlanta, Georgia, November 1971.

For a now classic approach to curriculum and instruction, see Ralph W. Tyler, *Basic Principles of Curriculum and Instruction* (Chicago: University of Chicago Press, 1950).

25. Undoubtedly there will be a few weeds in this garden. For example, think of some counterfeits you yourself have probably seen under the labels of team teaching and nongraded instruction. Some schoolmen, happy to see anything at all growing, seem willing to let be. Others are more fussy. It is our hope that both know what they have and what its effects are.

26. Glen Heathers has written much about problems of innovation in education; particularly useful is "Guidelines for Reorganizing the School and the Classroom," in *Rational Planning in Curriculum and Instruction* (Washington, D.C.: National Education Association, 1967), pp. 63-86.

27. Donald T. Campbell, "Considering the Case Against Experimental Evaluations of Social Innovations," *Administrative Science Quarterly* 15, no. 1 (March 1970): 111.

28. For a closely aligned set of assumptions, see The Research Corporation of the Association of School Business Officials, *Educational Resources Management System* (working draft, 1971), chapter 2.

29. Browder, *Emerging Patterns*, pp. 385-86. For an extended discussion of the "criterion problem" in research, see W. J. McKeachie's discussion in

Handbook for Research on Teaching, ed. N. L. Gage (Chicago: Rand McNally, 1963), pp. 1124-25.

30. See Browder, *Emerging Patterns*, pp. 361-525.

31. Klein, "Uses and Limitations of Standardized Tests."

32. For example, see Garth Sorenson, "Evaluation for the Improvement of Instructional Programs," *Evaluation Comment* 2, no. 4 (January 1971): 13-18.

33. Polly Carpenter and George Hall, *Case Studies in Educational Performance Contracting: Conclusions and Implications* (Santa Monica, Calif.: RAND Corporation, 1971).

34. Ibid.

35. Ibid.

36. The use of performance contracts to stimulate accountable forms of learning was given a considerable setback recently with the announcement (January 31, 1972) from the U.S. Office of Economic Opportunity that: "There is no evidence to support a massive move to utilize performance contracting for remedial education in the nation's schools. School districts should be skeptical of extravagant claims for the concept." The front page story in the *New York Times*, February 1, 1972, "Learning-Plan Test Is Called a Failure," projected a gloomy picture.

But there seems to be reasonable basis for doubt about OEO's contentions. The AASA Convention Report, prepared by the editors of *Education, USA* and covering the highlights of 1972 AASA convention, write (under the title "Performance Contracting—A Premature Burial?") that OEO may have reached its conclusions before performance contracting had an opportunity to work out its implementation problems. A number of factors (e.g., short lead times in operationalizing the contracts, "interface" problems with local schools, data on the improvement of student attitudes, motivation, attendance, lessening of discipline problems, etc.) seem to have been either lightly regarded or completely disregarded by OEO as significant. Charles Blaschke even countered the data offered by OEO. Some speculation was offered that the negative political pressure growing from teacher organizations toward OEO's educational venture in performance contracting (see, for example, UFT President Albert Shanker, "Performance Contracting in District 9: A Bronx Cheer for OEO," in the *New York Times*, January 2, 1972, p. E7) crumpled OEO's enthusiasm.

We draw two conclusions: (1) it is highly probable that the contractors hurt themselves with oversell of their product, and, (2) despite the counterclaims of the procontracting group, the shift of OEO funds from performance contracting experiments to something else is likely, in the absence of visible financial support from any other source, to kill off performance contracting. We still view it as promising and, with modification, viable. Among modifications that should be considered is the greater use of involvement techniques at the initial planning stages (i.e., involve parents, students, teachers, etc.), a reasonable time period for staff training, and closer analysis of the currently operating performance contracting to learn from their mistakes.

Jack Stenner and William Webster, in *Educational Program Audit Handbook* (Alabama State Department of Education, 1971), insist that accountability be separated as a concept from the means used to attain its ends. Using performance contracting as a case in point, they further note: "This delineation is important because it discourages the association of the concept itself with failures in specific applications" (p. iv).

Part II. Considerations in the Development of an Educationally Accountable Program

3. Needs Assessment

A Rational Basis for Educational Change

Over the past few decades the American school has been characterized, or plagued, by change. A bandwagon labeled "Educational Improvement and Innovation" has been joined by many, temporarily or permanently. It is not unusual to find school districts implementing large numbers of the latest fashionable educational projects without any clearly stated need or reason. When the jump on the bandwagon has resulted from irrational hasty decisions, change has emerged as primarily desirable for its own sake. When the attempt to change has had rational bases, clearly stated objectives, and clearly stated methods to achieve them, the original intent of improving the quality of education has had a better probability of success.

One might ask what constitutes rational bases, clear statement, and better probability of success. Within the concept of accountability in education, success has an economic analogy. Raymond Callahan's much cited work, *Education and the Cult of Efficiency,* surveying (with abundant examples) the uncritical application of business techniques in the early 1900s to educational administration, has probably done much over the past decade to discourage schoolmen from pursuing, in J. Alan Thomas's terms, *The Productive School.*[1] An educational program that yesterday was sought as "the finest product for the lowest cost" (with the emphasis on "the lowest cost" because there were few useful ways of determining "the finest product") is today seen as "the optimum level of educational outcomes balanced with an optimum level of inputs" (with the emphasis on searching for alternative ways to increase optimization). Returning to the analogy with business: an industrialist wishes to achieve his production objectives while optimizing the economic function that represents his annual profit. For example, he may wish to increase a given sales volume, minimize manufacturing costs, and maintain a fixed investment rate; but there is only one economic function that can be optimized. This function can be evaluated, according to circumstances, in terms of dollars, time, distance, number of employees, etc. The extent to which the economic function is optimized determines the success of the industrial program.

What is above called economic function might well be called "value function" in education. For example, where the industrialist is concerned about the amount and quality of production, the appropriateness of the product to the market, the relative costs and related items in determining the economic function, the schoolman may have roughly similar concerns: the amount and quality of student learning outcomes, the appropriateness (relevance?) of these outcomes to a changing world, the relative costs of obtaining these learning outcomes, plus parallel concerns in determining the educational value function. Like the industrialist, an educational administrator may want to increase the number of students, from most students to all, for example, who achieve some behaviorally defined objective (such as a specified increment of change in the student's reading behavior) while optimizing the value function in the program designed to result in the expected increase. The parameters—those common elements that are subject to change themselves (for example, the "cost" element changing with salary increases)—of the value function in education may be number and type of personnel, of curricular materials, cost of equipment, time, space, etc. Sometimes these parameters are very complex, both in economics and in education, so that the manager or the school administrator may wish to concentrate on "suboptimization" of a limited number of parameters at a time.

One may generalize from the above analogy that the determination and specification both of the product objectives and of the expected optimum method of achieving them is prerequisite to any rational change. *Rational* means that the change emerges out of need and consists of a set of well-specified operations that will reduce the need. If, furthermore, one is concerned with accountability connected with that change, two additional prerequisites must be met:

First, all factors that constitute either the product objectives or the expected optimum method of achieving them must be described by objective and quantifiable statements. Second, their functional relationships, that is, the means by which the method is expected to achieve the objectives, must be stated in at least a probabilistic manner.

At this point, the administrator who finds himself under the pressure of "accountability" must become familiar with some of the techniques available to the educational researchers in order to meet at least those two prerequisites. The behavioral specification and quantifiable statement of product objectives alone necessitate a number of steps which the administrator must perform prior to such specification. Change does not occur in a vacuum. Much like the industrialist who must take an inventory before he can talk about increasing production or sales volume, the educator must take an inventory of his system with its ongoing educational programs and products. Broadly, this educational inventory-taking is called need assessment.

A Systems Approach to Identifying Needs in Educational Systems

From an administrative viewpoint, need assessment is perhaps best described in systems terminology. No attempt will be made here to explain systems theory in any detail. A brief definition of terminology should suffice in considering the application of systems theory and system analysis to educational inventory-taking. Simply stated, a system is an "identifiable assemblage of elements (objects, persons, activities, information records, etc.) which are interrelated by process or structure and which are presumed to function as an organizational entity in generating an observable (or, sometimes merely inferable) product."[2] In education, the elements of a system are likely to be organized in a very complex way and often their interrelationships are difficult to discern. Sometimes the elements themselves may be subsystems within the larger structure (such as a classroom within a school). A system operates on a series of "inputs" to produce "outputs." Ideally, the elements of the system interact in an orderly fashion to produce the intended output efficiently. Few systems, however, achieve this ideal.

Systems Analysis in Determining Needs

One conducts system analysis to determine the structure and operation of the system. Its purposes are: (1) to discover ways of designing and operating systems which will minimize the probability of inefficient operation leading to a product of low quality, and (2) to develop any organization that will optimize the control and flow of information necessary to produce the desired product. Ryans, in his discussion of system study in education, makes four observations that may be useful to keep in mind in need assessment:[3]

First, the subsystems and elements of the educational system are *interdependent* and *interrelated.*

Second, interaction among the components or elements of a system is made possible by a *common information network.* Communication among the components is necessary to the functioning of a system as an organized entity which will produce the desired outputs.

Third, system functioning in education depends heavily on the control of the flow of information, both internally among the components (e.g., teacher to student, administrative unit to instructional units, etc.), and between the system and other external systems (e.g., administrative unit to community groups, policy-making board or state agency to administrator, professional organizations to local teacher groups, etc.).

Fourth, information processing is inherent in the functioning of systems. Information processing may mean any or all of the following: sensing, faltering, guessing, classifying, temporary sorting, synthesizing, and transforming available information; making decisions with respect to ways of transforming and conveying information; programming and arranging information content; and consequent forwarding of information.

These four observations facilitate dealing with the problem of need assessment. Inventory-taking amounts to describing: (1) the elements or components of the system, (2) their interrelationships and functions in the operation of the system, (3) how the operations lead to the desired output, and (4) where the structure and operations need to be redesigned to produce the desired quality product. In taking inventory, the administrator systematically utilizes the available methods of information processing that are inherent in the system.

The Process of Needs Assessment

It is not realistic to expect an administrator to conduct a complete system analysis to discover the elements and operations in the system that need repair or improvement; if one finds a leak in the plumbing system of a house, one does not have to take apart all the pipes. It is, however, necessary that the administrator view the school or the district as a complex dynamic system with many components that interact with and affect each other. Rarely can an educational problem be isolated as resulting from a single cause. For example, the fact that children read below the national norms of their age or grade level may be caused simultaneously by the children's past training at home or school, by their exposure to one teaching method instead of several alternatives, by their being taught in large groups instead of through tutorial methods, by the lack of time children spend actually reading, by inadequate curricular materials and equipment, by the lack of funds to hire reading specialists who can do the job, etc.[4] A systems approach to need assessment would suggest then, first specifying the problem in the product and, second, hypothesizing some possible "trouble-spots" in the system that may be producing the final, more visible, faulty product.

A third step in need assessment suggested by the systems approach is the establishment of priorities to deal with the hypothesized trouble spots. Since the interrelations are dynamic and complex, it is frequently impossible for the administrator to deal with all the elements at once. He must decide the order in which these are to be checked out and corrected. In the example used above of children reading below national norms, their home experience might be assigned the lowest priority whereas hiring a reading specialist might be assigned the highest priority since he could deal with several problems at once. Thus, the administrator's task becomes one of identifying some decision points where alternatives exist, arranging these alternatives in a hierarchy of priorities, and concentrating on the high priority needs to improve the quality of the product.

The three basic steps in the process of needs assessment discussed above are: (1) specifying or defining the problem observable in the product; (2) hypothesizing trouble spots in the elements and operation of the system leading to the product; (3) establishing priorities among these trouble spots so that the most important ones can be checked first.

The Far West Laboratory for Educational Research and Development has identified a similar set of three steps in its development of "integrated information systems."[5] The first step is concerned with the problems of information search, retrieval, and storage, the second with processing of information, and the third step involves the decisions in arranging the capabilities of the system to optimize the use of information. To be documented appropriately, the needs assessment process involves applying some research and data-gathering techniques to inventory-taking in the schools; the Far West Laboratory model of integrated information systems may be a good one for the administrator to keep in mind.

Scope of Needs Assessment as a Function of the System's Complexity

The three steps of identifying the problem, hypothesizing trouble spots, and establishing priorities among them exist in any needs assessment process regardless of the scope of the assessment task. The scope may be relatively simple (e.g., exposing culturally deprived children to the arts) or it may be very complex (e.g., bringing about more self-direction on the part of all children in the system in determining their own curricular objectives, courses of study, and areas of concentration). The inventory-taking connected with these problems may involve only a few components in the system, or the total system with all its components and operations. The scope of the assessment is determined by the complexity of the problem as exhibited in the product and by the number of components and operations showing trouble spots.

To search and retrieve information, the administrator must be familiar with the components of the system and their functional interdependence. Just as a pie may be sliced in a variety of ways, breaking a system into its component parts is somewhat arbitrary. Selecting the model to be used in the flow chart depends largely on the administrator's view both of the problem and the system, as well as on his philosophy. A few models are presented below to illustrate the arbitrariness and the complexity involved.

Suppose the problem is stated as students at a given grade level reading below the norms for that level. The system components and operations that may have a bearing on student achievement may be viewed as represented in figure 3.1.[6]

Once the model is drawn, as in figure 3.1, the administrator can systematically hypothesize which of the components in the system may be causing the problem. If he hypothesizes that all the components contribute to the existence of the problem, he next establishes priorities designating which ones are most important to tackle first. For example, he may decide to ignore all the source of curriculum information and concentrate on the network of curricular decision making. He may further ignore the processes on the left in that

Figure 3.1. Teaching/learning interrelationships

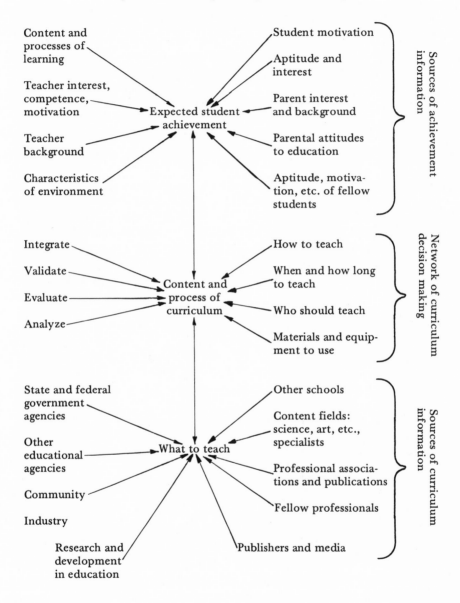

subsystem, and concentrate on "how to teach," "who should teach," "when and how long to teach."

A somewhat different model is suggested by Ebersole, who claims that only an insightful and enthusiastic individual within the system can design and bring about needed significant curricular changes since he is most familiar with all the elements in the system.[7] His model, if translated into a system model, would look like figure 3.2.

While both models refer to curriculum design and improvement, figure 3.2 represents a very different curricular philosophy from that of figure 3.1. Ebersole sees curriculum design as "a plan for presenting learning opportunities to students in the schooling system within

Figure 3.2. Ebersole's plan of learning opportunities

Foundations	Forces	Factors	Functions
Theory versus practice	Teachers	Involvement	Competence
Process versus content	Administrators	Confrontation	Compassion and caring
Cognition versus affect	Scholars in discipline	Shared decision making	Persistence
Clarity of reason for learning	Learning theorists	Right of expression	Joy
Amount of challenge in learning	Parents and citizens	Dramatic appeals	Risk taking
Role of choice in learning	School board	Bargaining demands	Perseverance
	Politicians	Power struggles	Imagination
	Professional associations	Politics	Logical reasoning
	Educational industries	Public relations	Integrating

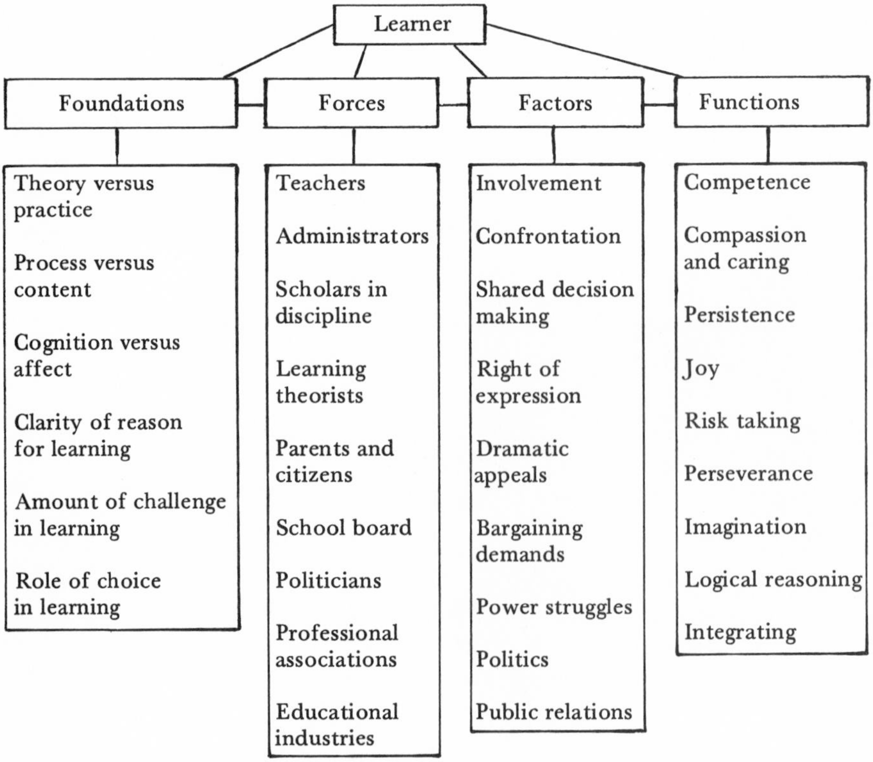

the institution of education. [He claims] some people look upon the design as a means to protect a domain, to further a sacred discipline, to maintain the status quo, to reinforce intellectual egos by esoteric exercises, or to attain a power base for trade-off in bargaining. These, however, are not adequate rationales."[8]

Clearly, the kind of component analysis used will depend to a large extent on the philosophy of the administrator or evaluator who is faced with the problem of need assessment. It will also depend on the complexity of the problem area on which one is focusing. Curriculum and student achievement, complex though they may be, are still more limited in scope than total educational planning for a total system whose outputs are much more complex than mere student achievement. To illustrate this complexity, a third sample model is suggested which represents the interaction and interdependence of at least three dimensions as they affect change on all of the student variables that educators might wish to produce.[9]

When the component analysis gets as complex as that presented in figure 3.3, the administrator can more readily perceive the need for assigning priorities to the trouble spots that must be checked out. Even though the total picture may be necessary to keep in mind and to refer back to at various stages of accountability, it is probably most practical for the busy school administrator to be concerned with subsystems of a more limited nature when attempting a full-scale need assessment.

Need for Documenting Identified Needs

The foregoing discussion using the systems model for information gathering and processing should have set the preliminary stage for the administrator who is faced with (1) identifying the problems in the system, (2) hypothesizing the trouble spots that exist in the elements and operations of the system, and (3) establishing the priorities among the hypothesized trouble spots to effectively determine the existing needs. So far, a *structure* for dealing with accountability information has been outlined. Nothing has been said about the actual assessment procedures. The final evaluation of operationally defined products is perhaps the ultimate task in accountability, while assessment of needs is among the first tasks. Yet the need for quantification exists at both ends and some of the techniques for evaluation are equally applicable at either stage.

Kaufman points out that "Needs Assessment procedures seem to be keyed to the concept that relevancy of education must be

Figure 3.3. Modified operations model for educational purposes

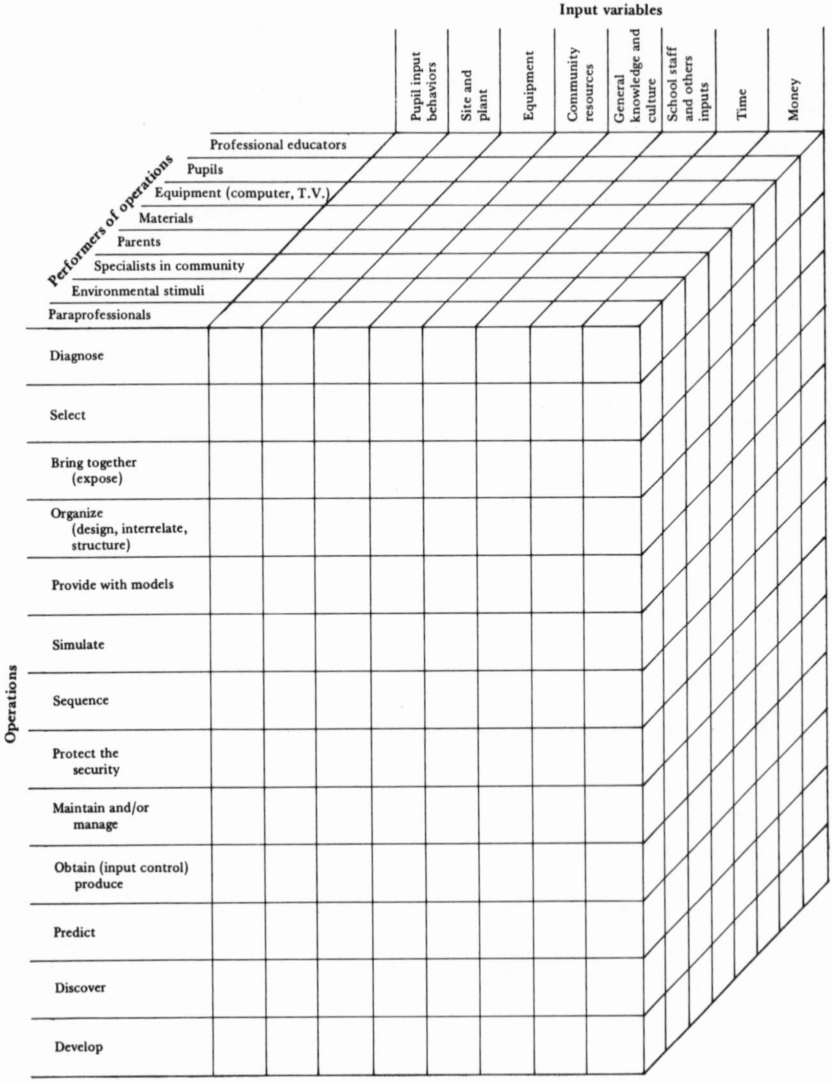

Input variables

Performers of operations:
Professional educators
Pupils
Equipment (computer, T.V.)
Materials
Parents
Specialists in community
Environmental stimuli
Paraprofessionals

Operations:

Diagnose

Select

Bring together
(expose)

Organize
(design, interrelate,
structure)

Provide with models

Simulate

Sequence

Protect the
security

Maintain and/or
manage

Obtain (input control)
produce

Predict

Discover

Develop

Input variables columns: Pupil input behaviors; Site and plant; Equipment; Community resources; General knowledge and culture; School staff and others inputs; Time; Money

Pupil outcomes: knowledge, tool skills, cognitive functioning, self direction and evaluation, attitudes and interests, social and emotional adjustment

empirically determined from the outset by a formal procedure, which precedes educational planning, design, and implementations. In most forms, Needs Assessment identifies and documents the discrepancies between 'what is' and 'what should be' and provides a valid starting point for education."[10] The process of identifying "what is" has been described. Documenting what is identified is done by using a variety of measurement techniques which will be described in some detail below. The identification of "what should be" will be dealt with in detail in chapter 6 in the context of specifying performance objectives.

Validating Existing Needs and Their Priorities

To some degree, the flow charting of the systems components is the first step toward documentation. Where the documentation may be limited to a mere description of the trouble spots, the flow charting may be used as a means of identifying and describing. It also provides a tangible descriptive analysis that may be presented to a variety of people, such as board members, outside consultants, and school staff, to obtain a degree of consensus among these members of the education community. Reaching or establishing consensus among different groups on the nature and priority of the trouble spots lends more validity to the existence of the specific need than one individual's descriptive claim. This concern with establishing consensus about the described need is one way to attempt objectivity and quantification.

At this point, the school administrator who is either not sufficiently familiar with statistical methodology or has only limited amounts of time to spare may prefer to consult with the educational researcher in order to apply quantification methods to the information he obtains in the process of establishing consensus. This chapter is not intended to turn the administrator into a statistician or researcher. However, it may be well to know that the statistician can, in fact, utilize quantifiable techniques and correlational analyses to document the consensus in which the administrator is interested. For example, priorities of needs established in the flow chart may be ranked by different individuals and rank-order correlations may be obtained to yield indices of consensus.

Documenting the Intensity of the Problems in the Product

Another area where quantified assessment is needed is in documenting the degree to which problems exist in the desired product.

Often these measures are found in the testing programs of the school system. However, it is no secret that not all the desired characteristics of the product are measurable by the tests commonly used in school districts. Furthermore, most testing programs in school districts have been criticized for yielding normative evaluation, which compares an individual's performance to the performance of a large group. Apparently more desirable is criterion-referenced evaluation, which indicates how much of a given trait (information, attitude, motivation, etc.) any given individual may demonstrate.[11] A number of curricula and teaching methods have been developed, such as IPI or pupil-contracts, that have built-in tests that fall in the criterion-referenced category. It must be recognized, however, that at present criterion-referenced tests are strictly limited to the area of achieving information and skills.

Whether normative or criterion referenced, schools have been practicing testing programs whose results may be used to document the degree to which some of the problems exist in the desired product. The administrator should be familiar with the use of these tests and their interpretation or have access to relevant supporting staff who are familiar with them. There are some advantages to using both the normative and criterion-referenced testing, depending on the situation and the aspect of the problem to be documented.

In areas where the available tests are inadequate or irrelevant, a number of alternatives for the administrator exist. The most obvious, and perhaps the simplest, is to invite an educational researcher to do the groundwork and deal with the problem of developing the quantitative techniques needed. These techniques may vary. They may involve (1) relevant test-development of the usual paper-and-pencil type, (2) application of observational or interview techniques, (3) the development or application of situational performance evaluation techniques not dependent on a paper-and-pencil testing approach.

Typically, educators have complained about a dearth of measures to determine student characteristics in the affective domain. Culture-free testing has also been typically less than adequate. Therefore, documentation of problems through testing in these areas has been difficult, at best. At this stage of development in educational evaluation, the administrator may well expect some developmental activity to precede the actual documentation of problems in the affective domain even after they have been identified and agreed upon. Otherwise, he must fall back on the use of such available records as rates of absenteeism, drop out rates, and incidences of vandalism and delinquency.

Another alternative is to depend heavily on self-reports of the students, on reports of parents and peers who are in constant contact with the individual, and on reports of his employees.

This type of documentation may be obtained either while the student is still in school or after he has graduated. It may be obtained once or several times over a period of years. If there is any periodic follow-up, or follow-up after graduation, longitudinal data-gathering techniques need to be applied. Since educational change occupies a major place in accountability, longitudinal methods of data gathering that are well suited to evaluate change will probably gain in importance as the concept of accountability continues to find its way into educational practice.[12]

Techniques for obtaining self-reports or reports of others are basically the same as survey techniques used in census-taking or in market research. These techniques utilize questionnaires and interviews as tools for data collection. If the tools have possible responses built into them, and thus are well "structured," their analysis is facilitated. Inclusion of many open-ended items may necessitate spending a great deal of time in content-analyzing the responses. Here again, if tools need to be developed, administered, and analyzed, it may suffice for the administrator to know what techniques are available so that the task may be delegated to the research technician or psychometrician.

Documentation Related to the Operation of the System

In all educational endeavor, it is assumed that the product is affected by what the "system" does to it. Even if one ignores the findings of the Coleman report[13] and other statistical studies of the determinants of pupil achievement,[14] one cannot help question what it is that the system in fact does[15] to bring about the desired product. The flow charting and task-analysis techniques enable the administrator systematically to hypothesize some trouble spots in the various components and operations of the system leading to the product. But these are merely hypotheses. Realistically, most administrators will not need any further documentation than their own hypotheses, at least not at the stage of needs assessment. However, it should be remembered that the concept of accountability will necessitate, at some point or another, the documentation and quantitative assessment of the system components and operations. The process and methods for such evaluation will be discussed in greater detail in chapter 10, under program evaluation, and in chapter 11, under program auditing. It is important for the administrator to be aware, however, that the availability of periodically obtained data in an ongoing program of evaluation and auditing would greatly facilitate his task of identifying the trouble spots in the components and operations of the system.

An Alternative: Getting a Preliminary Needs Assessment via a Positive/Negative Needs Analysis

We recognize that it may take some time for administrators to develop fully the system analysis needs assessment model described above. Its potential for giving a more accurate picture is considerable —especially when the performance objectives have become criterion referenced with an evaluation design purposely designed to measure them. We recommend it.

Assuming a different set of conditions, however, you may want to consider using a slightly different systems approach—one based on a primitive cost effectiveness model. We call it a "positive/negative analysis" and offer it as a possible procedure for reaching some preliminary conclusions about the state of educational needs. Assume, for example, that:

1. You need at this point only a rough index of need assessment;

2. Your district has many "conventional" programs in operation (that is, most of these programs have no sets of criterion-referenced objectives; a few have a rough kind of description of expectations located in curriculum guides; there has been little or no attempt to review programs in terms of their inputs and outputs; and, where an attempt has been made to get a rough index of the program's effectiveness and needs, it has generally depended on a standardized test or two and loosely organized reports of teacher attitudes toward the program);

3. Later, when you convert the positive/negative needs analysis steps in a criterion for cost/effectiveness:

a. In addition to making an assessment of needs for a given program, you desire to be able to compare one operating program with another (perhaps a similar program in a different building or class) or even with a proposed new one;

b. You would like to be able to determine the degree of effectiveness (more or less) of a given program as time passes;

c. You might like to assess the relative worth of the same

program as it is applied to different learner groups, different school settings or with different learning strategies, etc.

Establishing a Positive/Negative Needs Assessment Framework

Given these conditions, and noting that we recommend the first described systems analysis approach and do not suggest you place too much weight on these preliminary assessments, it is hoped that this approach might be helpful to you in the preliminary sifting among programs of their needs and priorities in building a sounder accountability program. A common problem with such approaches, because of the tendency to give superficially simple "answers" to highly complex problems, is to misuse them by placing too much faith in the results.[16] On the other hand, sometimes you want only a general approximation of the time and not an explanation on the making of clocks or celestial time measurement. In this preliminary phase, we have more confidence in our procedure than in a sun dial on a cloudy day—but not much more. Review the outline below and make your own determination whether it could be helpful to you or not. Figure 3.4 attempts to represent the process.

I. *Your objectives*
   A. For purposes of a rough preliminary needs assessment, to determine whether:
      1. An existing program has, as a matter of judgment (a postdetermined level of confidence), any identifiable "needs" (i.e., gaps between "what is" and "what should be" as a realistic optimum condition);
      2. If, as a matter of judgment (again as a postdetermined level of confidence), the identified needs (assuming some are found) are serious enough to warrant making the program more accountable.
   B. To establish some minimal basis for comparing this program with other programs, conditions, and times by converting the "positive/negative" needs analysis procedure into a cost effectiveness model.

II. *Steps toward realizing your objectives*
   A. Step 1: identify and describe the program
      1. What program is being considered?
      2. What group of students (age, grade level, socioeconomic backgrounds, range of learning abilities, etc.) does this program serve?
      3. What period of time is taken for your need assessment (from the calendar starting of the review period to the end point of the review; the number of days of program operation considered)?
      4. What are the generalized sets of expectations—assuming specific expectations to be lacking—for the program? (You may find curriculum guides, teacher lesson plans, textbooks, and learning materials used enough to give you some hints. You could draft a

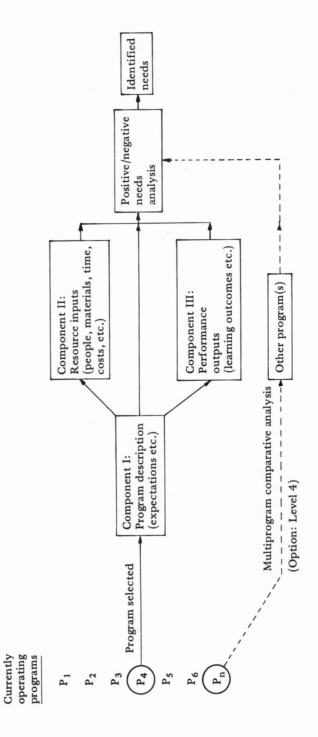

Figure 3.4. Positive/negative needs assessment model

Currently
operating
programs

P₁
P₂
P₃
P₄ Program selected
P₅
P₆
Pₙ

Component I:
Program description
(expectations etc.)

Component II:
Resource inputs
(people, materials, time, costs, etc.)

Component III:
Performance outputs
(learning outcomes etc.)

Positive/negative needs analysis

Identified needs

Other program(s)

Multiprogram comparative analysis
(Option: Level 4)

brief statement of program aims, if one does not exist, and circulate it among the staff for reaction, or request a brief statement from them. What is important to recognize is that later you will have to substitute your judgment—that is, make a level-of-confidence series of judgments—on the matching or mismatching of program aims, inputs, and outputs.)

5. What are the qualifications of the staff operating this program?
6. What teaching/learning strategy was used?

B. Step 2: determine program inputs
  1. Determine resources used
    a. Personnel
      (1) Teaching staff
      (2) Paraprofessional
      (3) Administration/coordination
      (4) Other (consultant etc.)
    b. Materials
    c. Equipment
    d. Facilities
    e. Other
    f. Staff-related utilization of time (estimated in hours) for:
      (1) Administration/coordination
      (2) Staff preparation
      (3) Staff/pupil contact
      (4) Formal pupil progress evaluation
      (5) Formal program effectiveness evaluation
      (6) Reporting pupil progress to parents
      (7) Reporting program effectiveness to board/public
      (8) Other
    g. Student-related utilization of time (rough approximations):
      (1) In-school time (group instruction, individualized instruction, independent study)
      (2) Out-of-school time
      (3) Other
  2. Convert input resources into input cost figures: through prorating staff salaries, etc., determine total cost and per student unit costs of program operation. These figures will also be useful later when comparing cost/effectiveness profiles of alternative programs. Where student time is concerned, the federal minimum hourly wage is a useful index.

C. Step 3: determine program outputs
  1. Determine performance outputs
    • Alternative Output Framework I: A taxonomy-based framework; evidence available should be categorized where it applies.
    a. Cognitive learning outcomes[17]
      (1) Knowledge
      (2) Comprehension
      (3) Application
      (4) Analysis
      (5) Synthesis
      (6) Evaluation

  b. Affective learning outcomes [18]
    (1) Receive
    (2) Respond
    (3) Value
    (4) Organization
    (5) Characterization
  c. Psychomotor learning outcomes [19]
    (1) Imitation
    (2) Manipulation
    (3) Precision
    (4) Articulation
    (5) Naturalization
• Alternative Output Framework II: a more conventional learning outcome framework used frequently in Title I applications; evidence can be categorized here, and, if desired, converted to fit the taxonomy-based framework. The comprehensiveness, specificity, and increasing usage of the taxonomy-based framework, especially as depicted in the works of Bloom and Krathwohl, make it an appealing way to classify outputs. You can see more clearly—after you have studied the taxonomies—where the collected data places the thrust of your program. At this preliminary stage, a mismatch between the aims of the program, for example, and the output analysis is likely to mean at least two things: either the data collected was inadequate to show forms of learning that did take place—a strong possibility—or the program failed in some way to achieve some of its aims. The establishment of criterion-referenced objectives should reduce such problems. Properly done, the output assessment should confirm or deny the matching of intended or expected learning outcomes with realized ones. In the meanwhile, the more conventional framework based on Title I might be more convenient. [20]

  a. Generalized learning outcomes
    (1) Application
    (2) Concept acquisition
    (3) Memorization of facts
    (4) Problem-solving
    (5) Reading comprehension
    (6) Skills (number, etc.)
    Common types of data collected for these outputs include: [21] objective tests (both standardized and locally made), product assessments of student work (reports, displays, models, etc.), rating scales, checklists, etc.
  b. Performance (common data collected: rating scales, checklists, product assessment, etc.)
  c. Classroom behavior (rating scales, checklists, attendance records, critical incident reports, anecdotal histories, etc.)
  d. Interest (questionnaire, checklist, interest inventory, factual vocabulary test based on words from interest fields, etc.)
  e. Attitude (rating scales, questionnaires, checklists, certain varieties of objective tests requiring attitude-responses, etc.)

     f. Aspiration level (rating scales, interviews, simple objective
       tests, word association tests, open-ended questions or sen-
       tences, etc.)
     g. Adjustment (rating scales, anecdotal reports, interviews, socio-
       grams, etc.)
   2. Determine unintended outcomes (any data that falls outside the
     regular classification system and appears to be a regulated but
     unintended outcome of the program).
   3. Determine the approximate degree to which the program rein-
     forces other programs (if the program, for example, is recognized
     as highly reinforcing or serving as a fundamental prerequisite to
     other programs, its relative priority in relation to other programs
     should rank accordingly higher. Expectations, priorities, commit-
     ment of resources, and the relative seriousness of identified needs
     are influenced accordingly).
  D. Step 4: summarize program description, inputs, and outputs into
    expressions for positive/negative analysis and identify needs

We know this last task is going to be difficult. In fact, given the
assumed state of data available at this preliminary stage, probably
most self-respecting cost/effectiveness analysts would throw their
hands up in dismay. They should. The chances are good that the data
available is insufficient for either cost/effectiveness or cost/benefit
purposes.[22] Cost/effectiveness analysis is useful in situations where
the outputs (learning outcomes) of the program are not likely to be
easily measured in dollars while the inputs customarily are or can be.
Cost/benefit analysis is very similar, only that it works toward
converting both inputs and outputs into monetary form. Both eco-
nomic-based forms of analysis seek to substitute the explicit for the
implicit, the quantitative for the qualitative, the precise for the
vague. Our positive/negative needs analysis attempts to do the same
thing only in a more subjective, intuitive manner.

The Criterion Problem: What Is Acceptable?

Up to this point, we are all—the cost/effectiveness, the cost/
benefit, and the positive/negative needs analysts—moving in generally
the same direction. It is here that we part company. If the kind of
data expected from an operating accountability program was available, the cost/effectiveness analyst would now apply his "criterion of
effectiveness," that is, the measure of the extent to which a program
objective (or weighted index) is achieved. As Carpenter and Haggert
point out: "It is necessary not only to weigh the relative importance
of measures and indicators of different aspects of effectiveness, but
to judge what levels of effectiveness are acceptable."[23] But, bluntly

expressed, how do you know when and where your program is acceptable or unacceptable? How do you make such a judgment? If, for example, the stated expectation is that the growth in reading achievement for each child should be one month-per-month of schooling, is a month-per-month growth rate unacceptable of .95? .85? .75? What if a program yielding the last result reaches other important objectives more "effectively" or reaches more students at a quarter of the cost? To make a judgment on the "acceptability" of such factors in a program, the cost-effectiveness analysis will continue to seek answers to these questions, applying cost-effectiveness curve analysis as the ultimate refinement of that system. We do not.

We do not because of the following assumptions: (1) the data available at the preliminary needs assessment stage (i.e., prior to developing an accountability program) is probably insufficient for such a task, and (2) even if the data were available, the task becomes cumbersome and time consuming for our purposes. It is expected that an analyst will have time to work out program structures, develop relevant alternatives (especially subtle ones), chart the interaction of key variables, etc. Most administrators, however, have other demands on their time. Accordingly, with the same variety of data before him as the cost-effectiveness analyst, the schoolman attempts to make a positive-negative needs analysis instead of applying the effectiveness criterion.

Making a Positive/Negative Needs Analysis

What is a positive/negative needs analysis? It is a way of assessing needs in an organized but subjective fashion. The critical ingredient in this process is the judgment of the practitioner making the assessment. As Cleland and King indicate:

Any formal analysis—or attempt at formal analysis—is usually valuable since it serves at least to make the decision maker think about the right things . . . Even if he does not know all that he should or have all the necessary information, a knowledge of just what he should have will usually provide him with a better basis for making a decision, such as to be wary and to choose conservatively or to err on the positive rather than the negative side of an issue. . . .[24]

Even a total lack of information is a significant discovery in assessing educational needs. Thus, in the sense of rendering a positive or negative level-of-confidence series of judgments on the three components of a given program (its goals and objectives as they are implied in the program's general aims and description; the resource inputs; and the performance outputs) and their interrelations, an assessment of need is determined.

In the ideal state, there should be a positive, matching relationship between the three program components. That is, the goals and objectives (Component I) of the program, stated as expectations or measures of achievement, should be equally matched with the amount of resource inputs (Component II) to fulfill the program. Similarly, the program's achievements or performance outcomes (Component III) should match the program's expectations. In turn, the program's outputs and inputs are theoretically equal and matching:

Component I: what program expects = Component II: what program requires
Component I: what program expects = Component III: what program achieves
Component II: what program requires = Component III: what program achieves

However, life seldom provides us with this ideal state. The relationships are not always equal or "acceptably equal" as a matter of judgment. Enter the mismatch. Where the mismatch occurs, a need is identified.

Determining matching and mismatching elements is not too difficult up to a point. It becomes more complicated, however, with missing or overly vague data. Yet most conventional educational programs operate in this condition. Accordingly, we suggest that two kinds of need analysis exist—a positive and a negative. We have indicated that a "need" is that gap between the current state of affairs and the state of affairs expected. Where there is *known* evidence that identifies "what is" and "what should be," a disclosed mismatch under this condition may be called a "positive need." If one or both of these conditions (what is/what should be) lack sufficient evidence to permit a match/mismatch of the elements, or otherwise offer *unknowns,* this condition may be referred to as a "negative need." Positive needs can be clearly identified, documented, and stated as "facts"—at least, for most practical purposes. Negative needs, however, require qualification, rationales, and should be offered as—at best—"informed opinions." To identify a negative need, the reviewer must substitute his own perceptions, standards, or interpretations of the missing data. Data on the state of affairs without a standard by which to interpret it, standards without any hard data available to indicate whether they are being met, or even the lack of any standard or extant data in a situation where the reviewer believes both should exist—these are characteristics of negative needs that require the reviewer to supply his own estimates.

Positive/negative need analysis is brought into use by subjecting each of the three program components and their interrelationships to a summary form of analysis. This form is admittedly impressionistic in part, but for our purposes, it should suffice. Whereas the research technician may wish to take each component apart, separate it into its elements and statistically assess each, such a task is clearly beyond our present intentions. If a conscientious job of collecting information on the three components has been done, it should be possible to render enough summary data to permit administrative decision making at this level.

At the same time, this positive/negative needs analysis approach—this blend of quantitative and qualitative analysis—might render data not normally apparent in purely quantitative analysis (although there appear to be ways of quantifying qualitative data).[25] As Charles Hitch expressed it:

How do you quantitatively distinguish between . . . (persons) who are highly motivated, and those who are demoralized? In fact, how do you quantitatively predict what it is that motivates or discourages a man? And which man? The fact that we simply cannot quantitize such things . . . does not mean that they have no effect on the outcome of . . . [an educational] endeavor—it simply means that our analytical techniques cannot answer every question.[26]

After collecting the data, it is processed in the following manner: (1) "what is" (the current state) is summarized, quantitatively and qualitatively, by the reviewer in roughly two paragraphs, one describing what is known, the other what is unknown; (2) the same exercise is followed in describing what ought to be; (3) the two descriptions (what is/what should be) are then compared, analyzed, and separated into "matching elements" and "mismatched needs." (See figure 3.5.)

The process of comparison and rendering judgments about what are "acceptable" (hence, matching) and "unacceptable" (mismatching) conditions is not easy. In effect, you are making a level-of-confidence series of decisions on program conditions. In the preliminary need assessment stage, they are conditions in your district based on available data and substituted estimates of missing data.

For the very thorough administrator, positive/negative comparative form of analysis is applied: (1) to each of the program components (Level 1: program component analysis); then (2) to the paired interrelationships between components (Level 2: interrelationship analysis of program components); then (3) to the joint interrelation-

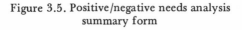

Figure 3.5. Positive/negative needs analysis
summary form

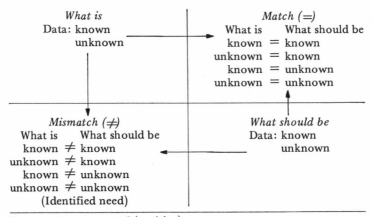

What is
Data: known
unknown

Match (=)
What is   What should be
known = known
unknown = known
known = unknown
unknown = unknown

Mismatch (≠)
What is   What should be
known ≠ known
unknown ≠ known
known ≠ unknown
unknown ≠ unknown
(Identified need)

What should be
Data: known
unknown

Known: data on record (positive)
Unknown: data unavailable, judgment substituted (negative)

ships of all three components (Level 3: program composite analysis);
and finally, after two or more programs have been analyzed through
Level 3, (4) to a comparison of two or more programs (Level 4:
multiprogram comparative analysis). Most administrators will probably be less conscientious and use only Levels 3 and 4. Figure 3.6
illustrates the total procedure.

While it may appear somewhat cumbersome at first sight—
especially if all four levels of analysis are attempted—we believe this
form of analysis to be helpful to the practitioner and likely to
identify the sort of needs schoolmen can do something about. The
procedure forces the administrator to think through educational
programs as components of an "educational system" whose stewardship, in part, is entrusted to his care. He must apply (in admittedly
primitive forms by research standards) the sorts of judgments that
later will be refined and expected of others. The usefulness of this
form of analysis will depend heavily on the professional insights of
the administrator, particularly in his role as an educator. Here we
have an expectation of our own: as long as an administrator considers himself an "educational administrator," he should be able,
within reasonable limits, to render explainable level-of-confidence
decisions concerning the operation of educational programs. If he

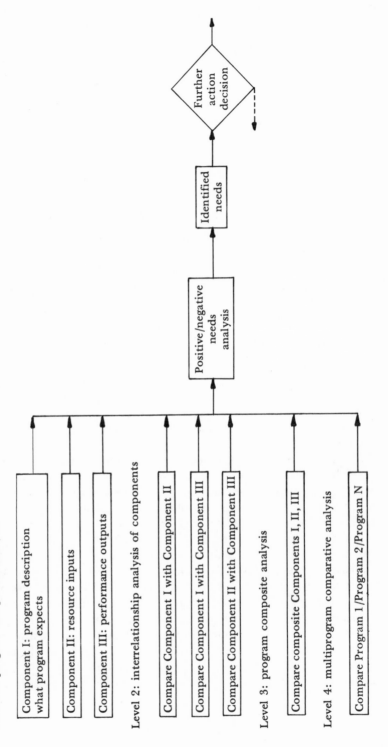

Figure 3.6. Program needs identification through positive/negative needs analysis

Level 1: program component analysis

Component I: program description what program expects

Component II: resource inputs

Component III: performance outputs

Level 2: interrelationship analysis of components

Compare Component I with Component II

Compare Component I with Component III

Compare Component II with Component III

Level 3: program composite analysis

Compare composite Components I, II, III

Level 4: multiprogram comparative analysis

Compare Program 1/Program 2/Program N

Positive/negative needs analysis

Identified needs

Further action decision

cannot, he should cease making any claims of "educational leadership" in the role he holds.

Some Results of Positive/Negative Need Assessment Procedures

Turning to another issue, what are some outcomes of such a positive/negative needs assessment procedure? What might we offer as a sample? Because positive/negative needs analysis as presented above has only been partially tested, our sample must be labeled "semihypothetical." It concerns a sixth-grade spelling program offered in two schools.

In the first instance, school *A* had a formal spelling program. The teachers claimed its objective was "to teach sixth-grade spelling." Two and a half hours a week was devoted to it by all students. While the focus was primarily on spelling, vocabulary work was part of it, as the students were to define the listed spelling words and use them correctly in a sentence. Sets of disposable spelling workbooks along with classroom dictionaries were the major materials used to support the program. The standardized achievement test showed their spelling performance to be a half-year above grade level norms in both spelling and related areas. The program did not require the teacher to prepare or otherwise spend time outside of class. Students with spelling problems were assisted by having them write the misspelled words five times each. The students maintained—by teacher observation—a passive attitude toward the program (neither enthusiastic nor rejecting). The teachers appeared—by the principal's observation—to be unexcited about the program, but not anxious to change it either. The program had been in operation nearly fifteen years. Input costs (calculating student time, materials, teacher's time, etc.) to maintain the school *A* spelling program were estimated to be $101 per student annually.

School *B*, drawing from a similar socioeconomic student population, had no formal spelling program, although it claimed to teach spelling. The aim was expressed as "teaching spelling as an outgrowth of self-expression." In practice, spelling was taught tangentially as part of the creative writing program, a program consuming about two hours a week class time (although requiring roughly four and a half hours weekly of teacher time outside of class). The teacher required that misspelled words be corrected with a dictionary and entered in a "corrections and additions" notebook. The teacher varied instruction also with the more able students by asking them to supply synonyms and antonyms for thoughts expressed in their writings. In the course of composition instruction, the thesaurus and dictionaries were used by all students (with the ablest students being asked to draw distinctions between nearly similar words). The student's notebooks were periodically checked for commonly misspelled words, recurring punctuation and grammar problems, and vocabulary work growing out of the compositions. The formal work for spelling (with some students spending more time on it resulting from a greater frequency of misspelled words and other students, having fewer misspellings and working more with the thesaurus, using less time) was approximated at a half hour a week. The same achievement test indicated that spelling achievement was also a half year above grade level for the class, but that vocabulary and word expression were nearly a full grade level ahead. The student's attitude toward the program—by teacher observation—was neutral. The teachers were enthusiastic about the program they had developed two years before. Input costs for maintaining the spelling program were $84 per student.

In the matching/mismatching process following the summary reviews, the superintendent determined that school B had an "acceptable" program. School A, although the superintendent determined that he would be willing to accept the program until a better one could be devised (there were other programs requiring more immediate attention), was "mismatched" with the superintendent's judgment. It became identified in his mind as a "need" in the district and the focus of a later change effort. Among the mismatching elements that concerned the superintendent were:

(1) The objectives were too vague and not adequately defined (the same was true for school B, but the superintendent took the attitude of a "why argue acceptable success" and let it pass. He preferred an objective stating a learning outcome that each student should gain at least a year-by-year achievement level advancement with a special teaching procedure to be used for those students who gain less than .85 achievement year-by-year);

(2) The methods of instruction and efforts to individualize instruction appeared too mechanical and unsuited (the superintendent originally had a difficult time establishing a judgment measure for this program, until he compared it with school B. Being a pragmatic man, school B's procedures then became the superintendent's basis of judgment);

(3) Because of hoped-for changes in the manner of instruction and efforts to individualize it, the use of the spelling workbook appeared dubious (in the superintendent's mind, the manner in

which the workbook was being used suggested a sort of make-work approach; eliminating the workbooks and the use of a few thesauruses seemed more appropriate);

(4) Again, because the results achieved by school B appeared more significant in the mind of the superintendent, while school A's spelling achievements were roughly "acceptable," the reinforcement potential of school A's program did not appear too strong (the superintendent hoped to see greater "transfer of learning" potential through active usage than appeared);

(5) The manner in which class time was utilized at first did not bother the superintendent, but later bothered him enough to make a mismatch judgment after comparing the two schools (the comparison indicated to him a significant difference in teacher inputs into the program. He believed that program reinforcement, individualization of instruction, and similar forms of teaching require more careful attention and greater outside class time effort by the teachers. While he hoped that the students would achieve well as a group, he hoped more for individual achievement. The lock-step approach toward spelling—used in other school A programs—or as much class time demanded uniformly for students toward achieving the goals of the spelling program—did not seem acceptable).

There were some things about the school A program that did not apparently disturb the superintendent, although they may disturb others. These include student and teacher attitudes toward it and the cost of maintaining it (it was 17 percent more than school B's program).

What did the superintendent do? He began working with the building principal of school A through management by objectives, which entailed plans to attempt to change the program by focusing first on staff attitudes toward it. But first he had to decide what to do with the needs he identified.

Deciding What to Do with Assessed Needs

What do *you* do with the identified needs? After having made a few positive/negative need assessments, you should find yourself in a position to make some decisions—decisions that ought to be sharper and more informed than those you would have made before you began your assessment. The key decision (for purposes here) is to determine whether the number of identified needs warrant taking one of four courses of future action: (1) to leave the program(s) alone; (2) to modify or otherwise change the existing program(s); (3)

to eliminate it (them); or (4) to eliminate it (them) and replace it (them) with some other alternative program(s). If you choose either to modify or search for an alternative program, you also have the option of making the program(s) more accountable. (Figure 3.7 illustrates these decision options.)

Figure 3.7. Some decision options resulting from needs assessment

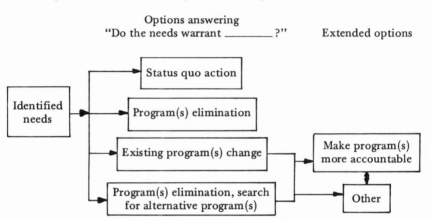

Certainly this level of analysis and decision making does not correspond with the sophisticated cost/effectiveness analysis of an analyst. Henry Levin, for example, using regression equations on quantified inputs and outputs, was able to estimate the approximate cost for increasing student verbal scores by an average of one point as an output measure by using either teachers who had high verbal scores of their own or teachers with length-of-service experience as isolated inputs.[27] Levin found that it required only $26 for both black and white students to raise their scores with the high "verbal" teachers. On the other hand, where the major input consideration was teacher experience, the costs were $128 for black and $253 for white students. The superintendent is offered an interesting decision making alternative with this kind of analysis. Given the choice of hiring either teachers with high verbal scores or those with length of experience, Levin concludes that the best solution might be "the recruitment and retention of verbally able teachers while paying somewhat less attention to experience."[28]

While the positive/negative need analysis procedure is not likely to yield the kind of data offered in the Levin study, it should offer enough information—at least until the systems procedures presented at the opening of this chapter can be developed—to assist an administrator in charting a course of action. If you decide to explore further the possibility of making the program more accountable, it is suggested that you next consider strategies offered in chapter 4.

Notes for Chapter 3

1. Raymond Callahan, *Education and the Cult of Efficiency* (Chicago: University of Chicago Press, 1962); J. Allan Thomas, *The Productive School* (New York: John Wiley & Sons, 1971).
For a present-day interpretation of Callahan's theme, see H. Thomas James, *The New Cult of Efficiency and Education* (1968 Horace Mann Lecture: University of Pittsburgh Press, 1969).
For a detailed description of how the economic function is determined and optimized, see Arnold Kaufman, *Methods and Models of Operations Research* (Englewood Cliffs, N.J.: Prentice-Hall, 1963).

2. David G. Ryan, "System Analysis in Educational Planning," *Tech Memo* 7, no. 6 (1964): 5.

3. Ibid., pp. 3-9.

4. For additional examples of educational programs considered in systems terminology, see "Some Aspects of Education Viewed in a System Framework," ibid., pp. 11-17.

5. B. H. Banathy, "Information Systems for Curriculum Planning," *Educational Technology* (November 1970).

6. Ibid., pp. 26-27.

7. Benjamin P. Ebersole, "Opening the System from the Inside," *Educational Leadership* 28, no. 5 (February 1971): 469-71.

8. Ibid., p. 469.

9. Esin Kaya et al., *Developing a Theory of Educational Practice for the Elementary School*, final project report to the Ford Foundation, Fund for the Advancement of Education (June 1967), p. 91a.

10. Roger A. Kaufman, "Accountability, A System Approach and the Quantitative Improvement of Education—An Attempted Integration," *Educational Technology* (January 1971): 21-26.

11. For a detailed treatment of criterion-referenced measurement, see R. L. Ebel, "Content Standard Test Scores," *Educational Psychology Measurement* (spring 1962): 15-25; Robert Glaser, "Psychological Bases for Instructional Design," *AV Communication Review* (winter 1966); idem, "Instructional Technology and Measurement of Learning Outcomes: Some Questions," *American Psychologist* (August 1963); Jason Millman, "Reporting Student Progress: A Case for Criterion-Referenced Marking Systems," *Phi Delta Kappan* (December 1970): 226-30; James Popham, ed., *Criterion-Referenced Measurement: An Introduction* (Englewood Cliffs, N.J.: Educational Technology Publications, 1971).

12. For a detailed treatment of the use and importance of studies, see articles by Walter Emmerich, Samuel Messick, Scarvia Anderson, and John

McDavid in *Untangling the Tangled Web of Education,* a special symposium sponsored by the National Council on Measurement in Education (Princeton, N.J.: Educational Testing Service, 1969).

13. James Coleman et al., *Equality of Educational Opportunity* (Washington, D.C.: U.S. Office of Education, 1966).

14. Herbert J. Kiesling, *The Relationship of School Inputs to Public School Performance in New York State,* Report P-4211 (Santa Monica, Calif.: RAND Corporation, October 1969).

15. Henry M. Levin, "A New Model of School Effectiveness," *Do Teachers Make a Difference?* (Washington, D.C.: U.S. Office of Education, 1970), pp. 56-57.

16. For interesting discussions on cost effectiveness, its use and limitations, see Margaret Carpenter and Sue Haggart, *Cost-Effectiveness Analysis for Educational Planning,* Report P-4327 (Santa Monica, Calif.: RAND Corporation, March 1970); Donald Levine, *Structuring Program Analysis for Educational Research,* Report P-4565 (Santa Monica, Calif.: RAND Corporation, March 1971).

17. For a close definition of these terms, see Benjamin Bloom et al., eds., *Taxonomy of Educational Objectives, Handbook I: Cognitive Domain* (New York: David McKay Co., 1956).

18. This set of outcomes is defined in David Krathwohl et al., eds., *Taxonomy of Educational Objectives, Handbook II: Affective Domain* (New York: David McKay Co., 1956).

19. R. H. Dave, "Psychomotor Variables," *Developing and Writing Behavioral Objectives* (Tucson, Ariz.: Educational Innovators Press, 1970); idem, "The Identification and Measurement of Environmental Process Variables That Are Related to Educational Achievement" (Ph.D. diss., University of Chicago, 1963).

20. For definitions of terms and general coding, see *Instructions for Title I 1967 Application Forms,* Report no. 37003 (Washington, D.C.: U.S. Office of Education, 1967), p. 13.

For suggestions on organization and kinds of data collection, see New England Educational Assessment Project, *A Guide to Assessment and Evaluation Procedures* (Providence, R.I.: NEEAP, 1966).

21. There is a proliferation of literature on tests, testing, and varieties of obtaining usable data. One of the most recent and interesting was developed and is published by UCLA School of Education, *Elementary School Test Evaluations* (July 1970). It is a compendium of tests, keyed to educational objectives and evaluated by experts for meaningfulness, examinee appropriateness, administrative usability, quality of standardization, etc. Interesting sources of data collecting on affective learning outcomes is found in R. Fox, M. B. Luski, and R. Schmuck, *Diagnosing Classroom Learning Environments* (Chicago: Science Research Associates, 1966).

See also Arthur Storey, *The Measurement of Classroom Learning* (Chicago: Science Research Associates, 1970); Robert Ebel, *Measuring Educational Achievement* (Englewood Cliffs, N.J.: Prentice-Hall, 1965); Benjamin Bloom, J. Thomas Hastings, and George Madaus, *Handbook on Formative and Summative Evaluation of Student Learning* (New York: McGraw-Hill, 1971).

22. See J. Allen Thomas, *The Productive School,* p. 82.

See also Daniel Rogers and Hirsch Ruchlin, *Economics and Education*

(New York: Free Press, 1971), pp. 134-40, 161-66; Robert Spiegelman et al., *A Benefit/Cost Model to Evaluate Educational Programs* (Menlo Park, Calif.: Stanford Research Institute, 1968).

23. Carpenter and Haggart, *Cost-Effectiveness Analysis for Educational Planning*.

See also Harry Hatry, "Criteria for Evaluation in Planning State and Local Programs," in *Program Budgeting and Benefit-Cost Analysis*, ed. H. Hinrichs and G. M. Taylor (Pacific Palisades, Calif.: Goodyear Publishing Co., 1969), pp. 94-119.

24. David Cleland and William King, *Systems Analysis and Project Management* (New York: McGraw-Hill, 1968), p. 37.

25. For example, see Mark Holmes, "Prediction of Educational Outcomes from Institutional Variables in a Population of Junior High Schools" (Ph.D. diss., University of Chicago, 1969).

26. Charles J. Hitch, Assistant Secretary of Defense, address before the U.S. Army Operations Research Symposium, Duke University, Durham, N.C., March 26, 1962. Quoted in Cleland and King, *Systems Analysis and Project Management*, p. 80.

27. Henry M. Levin, "Cost-Effectiveness Analysis and Educational Policy —Profusion, Confusion, Promise," Pamphlet no. 41 (Palo Alto, Calif.: Stanford University Center for Research and Development in Teaching, 1968).

28. Ibid., p. 12.

4. Change Strategies

That school districts tend to resist change is a commonly accepted truism. They are not alone. Even a suggested change in an organization based on research finds resistance. President Richard Nixon states:

Even when good and relevant research is achieved, its utilization is not automatic. Dissemination is not utilization, and much more than brief summaries, announcement of results, and general research conferences are probably required to translate good research products into good program results. A whole new system of research delivery and application needs to be developed. Above all, research—to be utilizable and utilized—must be problem oriented. It must help identify the problems, the hang-ups, the needs, and the gaps in program operation. What works, what doesn't work—and why? The linkage of research, and especially followup and evaluation research, must be with change, with redesign of programs and adjustments in methods of operation.[1]

It appears not enough to request change based solely on research evidence or on needs assessment. Significant change rendering intended consequences seldom succeeds by accident. To increase the likelihood of success, a *strategy* for change—that is, a plan for aligning the critical elements in the change situation into the most advantageous position prior to the actual undertaking—should be developed for implementing the change. This chapter presents some approaches toward developing such a strategy. It starts with a review of some commonly used change strategies.

A Look at Some Change Strategies

In 1901, John Dewey gave the following description of the educational change process:

Consider the way by which a new study is introduced into the curriculum. Someone feels that the school system of his . . . town is falling behind the times. There are rumors of great progress in education being made elsewhere. Something new and important has been introduced; education is being revolutionized by it; the superintendent and board become somewhat uneasy; the matter is taken up by individuals and clubs; pressure is brought to bear on the school system; letters are written to the newspapers, . . . editorials appear; finally the school board ordains that on and after a certain date the particular new brand . . . shall be taught in the public schools. The victory is won, and everybody—unless it be some already overburdened and distracted teachers—congratulates everybody else that such advanced steps are taken.[2]

Dewey's description (alas, still too true for many changes in our schools!) is not the kind of change strategy we have in mind. True, such procedures do produce changes. They also tend to produce hard-to-handle problems that undermine the effectiveness of the change. The goal of a change strategy, then, is not merely to create a change, but to create a change that does what it is intended to do. Reaching such a goal normally requires that the change be a *planned* one.

In seeking guidelines for the successful implementation of a planned change, many strategies are possible. In fact, one has already been offered in the form of the six "imperatives" in chapter 2. These "imperatives" attempted to point out elements in the local situation believed to be critical in planning a change to develop new programs that are educationally accountable. Each imperative suggested a condition that must be brought into some kind of alignment before the program is believed ready for successful operation. For example, it was held that, in order to function successfully, the program must (1) have knowledgeable designers, (2) lead to improved education, (3) recognize and accommodate diverse forms of participation, (4) train personnel before and during implementation, (5) fulfill the conditions of the accountability concept, and (6) be judged politically attainable. In turn, a change procedure, a strategy offered as a model, was presented. Theoretically, such models depicting a change strategy put into operation are intended to be helpful in either the successful orchestration of an educationally accountable program or any other kind of planned change.

But models of planned change are not restricted to education or accountability programs alone. Some of the most successful models employing a planned change strategy have been those aimed at changing farm practices.

Typically, the strategy begins with increasing a sense of *awareness*—that is, the agricultural change agent brings to the attention of the farmer (through mass media, meetings, word of mouth) new practices that either solve a recognized problem or carry strong potential for improving the practice. Next, the strategy allows for the nurturing of *interest* by supplying the farmer with information and advice about the new practice (through booklets, demonstrations, give-and-take discussions). When awareness and interest have had time to work, there appears to be a point at which the individual *evaluates* for himself whether to try the new practice or forget about it. If the evaluation is affirmative, usually a small *trial* of the practice is attempted—a point where the agricultural change agent generally receives his strongest appeals for help. If the trial practice works well, the chances of its *adoption* into standard procedures are high.[3]

The major premise in this change strategy, however, is the notion that the decision to change or not to change is ultimately controlled by the party being changed. The agricultural change agent cannot easily resort to other means (e.g., organizational authority structures) to bring about this behavioral change. Instead, he relies heavily on the persuasive merits of the new practice. At the same time, he knows what changes he wants to see made and why.

Industrial psychologists also offer change strategies. For example, Robert Blake and Jane Mouton contend that, to change an organization, it is necessary (1) to be prepared to change the entire organization, (2) for those who head the organization to lead—not merely authorize, delegate, or approve—the change, (3) for those involved in the change to do it themselves, (4) to apply systematic ways of thinking and analysis to achieve a model of excellence that distinguishes between *what is* and *what should be,* (5) to make clear and get people committed to changing *all* of those conditions that are not what they should be, (6) for those leading and managing the organization to study it in specific operational terms, and (7) from the operational study of the organization, to proceed in a sequential, orderly way.[4]

Similar change themes run through the literature of education. For J. Lloyd Trump, a suitable change strategy would:

1. Analyze cooperatively the reasons for present practices.

2. Discover what people want that is different from what they are doing.

3. Make tentative decisions, general and specific, regarding the priority of recommended changes.

4. Plan the innovation carefully in terms of teacher preparation, student preparation, procedures to be followed, and the anticipated effects of the changes.

5. Set the times and techniques for evaluation.[5]

Without attempting an exhaustive analysis of all varieties of change strategies,[6] what might be concluded from the above samples and the literature? It appears that most change strategies imply recognition of first knowing clearly what is to be changed, recognizing next that this knowledge must be communicated, shared, and understood by those others to be influenced by the proposed change. Perhaps the major thrust of the change strategy, however, is directed at the attitudes of those persons involved in the change. If the attitudes of these individuals can be favorably disposed toward the change, there is assumed to be a greater likelihood of success. If you can favorably change an individual's attitude, the possibility of also favorably altering his working behavior seems greatly increased. Again, the degree of success for the strategy used is determined by the extent to which the desired new conditions are reached without negative factors, anticipated or unanticipated, nullifying the outcomes.

Developing a Change Strategy

A useful concept for guiding the construction of a change strategy is provided by Kurt Lewin, a pioneer in change theory.[7] Lewin hypothesized that all social environments (e.g., homes, offices, schools, factories, clubs, etc.) contain forces for change and counterforces that resist change. The task of a maker of change is to identify those forces in the particular social environment as quickly as possible. Because some forces will facilitate a contemplated change while others will oppose it, the would-be change agent must either strengthen the facilitating forces or reduce the potential opposition. Experience indicates that conflict arises if the change agent's efforts are concentrated solely on strengthening the facilitator forces without attempting to reduce the resisting ones. A good change strategy therefore embraces both efforts.

Some guidelines based on Lewin's concept that may be included in a change strategy are:
1. Assessing the forces for and against change.
2. Understanding the values and goals of the system.
3. Reviewing the organizational structure.
4. Understanding opposition to change.
5. Understanding the roles of people within the school system:
   a. The teacher's role.
   b. The school administrator's role.
   c. The role of the school board collectively.

d. Influence of individual school board members.

Each of these guidelines is described here in greater detail. Figure 4.1 provides an outline of some forces in the school's social environment used to construct a change strategy.

Guidelines

1. Assessing the forces for and against change. One of the first things that must be done in applying Lewin's concept to the schools as a social environment is to assess the forces already present in the community that are facilitators of the change as well as those that might oppose it. Of course, most school administrators and school board members will have a relatively good idea of the "pulse" of the community, but we cannot always be sure. These forces may not readily be seen since they may be in a state of equilibrium, i.e., acting to neutralize each other. It may not be until the suggested change has been openly stated that these forces become apparent.

Figure 4.1. An outline of some forces in the school's social environment used to construct a change strategy

The dynamics of change concept

Social environment

Forces for change ⟷ Forces resistant to change

Strengthen these   Reduce these

produces

a change strategy

• Identify facilitators	• Identify opposition
• Involve people in planning	• Change should not increase people's work load
• Develop "ownership"	
• Is change compatible with the values of the district?	• Is there agreement on the purposes and aims of the school district?
• Are the districts goals established? accepted? understood?	• Does organizational structure help or hinder change?
	• Does change cause a loss of power? status?
• Capitalize on the desire for a new experience	• Too much previous change?
	• Visit other similar projects
• Understand the opposition and respect it	• Do not become discouraged!

A recent example may be seen in attempts to integrate schools in northern communities. No problem was apparent until it was suggested that the schools be integrated by busing children from a neighboring town or section of the community. In many cases there were drastic and dramatic results, including burning of buses, assaults on students, damage to homes and schools, and an exodus of people to a "safe" community. While there are many reasons for such reactions, it can be said that present in the community were forces that favored integration and forces that opposed it. Prior to the suggested change they were not visible. Once change *was* suggested, however, these forces surfaced. They had been in a state of equilibrium, but conflict arose since the demand was strengthened without reducing the resistance. Similar examples could be cited in cases of attempts to introduce sex education into the curriculum. Do not assume that there are no opposing forces just because there has not been a problem or because they have not been openly expressed. They may be present but under the surface like an iceberg, ready to tear a hole in the hull of the best-laid plans of the school board and superintendent.

Goodwin Watson has suggested that "the more an innovation is owned by those affected by it, the greater the probability it will be accepted."[8] In other words, unless people who are to be affected by a change feel that they took part in developing it, they may oppose it. This is one reason for assessing the needs of a school district to determine what changes, if any, should occur. The assessment process should identify people likely to be affected by the change and who are, hence, to be involved in the planning of it. Many educators are now aware that the consumers of education must be involved in the planning of it. This includes not only students, but parents, teachers, and employers. Dr. Wilson Riles, state superintendent of schools in California, expressed it well when he said:

Accountability is a term that has been bandied around by many people, but to me it means gaining consensus of goals, involving the students, the teachers and the parents, saying "these are our objectives; this is what we mean"; secondly, determining what resources are necessary to do the job and telling the people what it will cost; and thirdly, to provide flexibility necessary to match resources with needs and the people qualified to do the job.[9]

Change pushed from above or from outside the district will probably have less chance of succeeding than change that has been developed by people within the district. Sometimes change must occur as a result of some outside force (when, for instance, the state reduces the amount of state aid to a district) but the basic point is that people must feel they "own" the change if it is to be implemented with a minimum of disruption.

Some will feel that the example of state aid being reduced would not be a change but a catastrophe. While that may be true, it is also true that sometimes such a change may have unexpected desirable outcomes, perhaps uniting the forces in the district against the "bad guys" at the state level, and making other changes within the system easier to accomplish. For example, with reduced funds it may be easier to reduce overhead costs, or to release some teachers, or to cut out some unnecessary programs that have been difficult to discard. The whipping boy can be the state, yet change is accomplished.

Change must be responsive to needs that have been felt by the district and it must be diagnosed and designed with the involvement of those who will be affected by it. The same people should be involved in implementing change if possible. Any strategy for change that does not take these factors into account will not be as successful as it could have been.

Another dynamic of the change process that should be understood by planners is that, where possible, people should see change as reducing their work rather than adding to it; it should lighten their load, not make it heavier. No one is likely to resent change if he can be shown that as a result his work will be easier. But if we add responsibilities to a person who already feels he is overworked, it will be more difficult to gain his acceptance. He may in fact oppose the change and encourage others to do likewise, to a point where the innovation may be impossible to achieve.

Suppose, for instance, that the district is planning to implement a program of accountability that includes cost accounting. If the teachers see this change as adding to their work because they will be required to fill out extra forms, they may resist it. However, it need not be assumed that the teachers have to do this. Many districts now use paraprofessionals for many of the clerical chores formerly performed by teachers. Rather than replacing the teachers, these aides *re*-place the teacher into the role best performed by the teacher, that of working individually with children. We endorse such plans if properly conceived and when they are not used to reduce the number of teachers who come in contact with students.

2. *Understanding values and goals of the system.* The proposed change must be reasonably compatible with the values of the system in order for the change to take place. To the degree that a change challenges the values held by the people in the system, it is corres-

pondingly more difficult to achieve. Changes whose content and purposes agree with the traditional values and goals of the system are more likely to be accepted than those disagreeing with those values. One of the jobs of the change agent is to attempt to harmonize the goals and values of the system with the intent of the change. This task is easier to describe theoretically than to accomplish in practice. One of the functions served by the ubiquitous committee meetings is to bring proposed change into a reasonably acceptable alignment with the goals and values of the school system. But it is difficult. Values change, people change, institutions change.

A dilemma in education, stemming from this acceleration of change, is a lack of agreement on the purposes and aims of education. For example, two trends in education seem on a collision course. The first trend aims at alleviating the pressure of increasing costs, to reduce the financial strain on the schools and the pocketbook.

The second trend aims at unburdening the learner from the restrictions of pace and time; we attempt to individualize instruction for each pupil and let him work independently from other students and at his own rate of speed.

Both trends have wide acceptance in our schools. Most people are likely to agree that they are indeed good aims. But they tend to lead in opposite directions. The first trend is usually translated to mean larger classes and fewer teachers; the second, to require more teachers and smaller groups. In short, one set of values and aims tends to conflict with the other. Pressure to achieve both is great. Obviously both cannot be accomplished at the same time in the same way; if the participants do not recognize that they are arguing from different points of view, they may not understand the reason for the conflict that inevitably arises. It is the task of the change agent to deal with both pressures by clearly establishing the interrelationships of cost and instruction, showing what effect pressing one aim has on the other.

At the same time, proposed changes should agree with the goals of the institution in order for them to be accomplished more easily. If the goals of the change are not (1) clearly stated and (2) in agreement with existing goals, the change process will be correspondingly more difficult. It will be necessary for the change agent to alter the goals of the proposed change or attempt to change the existing goal. Not infrequently a compromise is devised whereby the existing goal is more broadly (or narrowly) interpreted and the proposed goal is suitably changed to present an acceptable alignment.

3. Reviewing the organizational structure. Another point considered in developing change strategies is how the change influences the organizational structure. Organizations characteristically have two structures. One is *formal* and inclined to appear on organizational charts, letter headings, and in all the nuances that mark the individual's official position in the organization. The other structure, an *informal* one, appears in the social chemistry of human interaction: who speaks to whom (or does not), who people search out for advice and help, who is avoided, what unwritten procedures are used to circumvent written "official" procedures that press too hard, etc. These structures, both formal or informal, do not change easily. The particular existing structure is there for a reason—or at least originally it was there for a reason, or it developed for a reason. While the original reason may no longer exist, the organizational structure remains.

Some individuals are likely to feel personally threatened if the proposed change causes some change in the present structure. They know how to deal with both the current formal and informal structures, they know whom to see to get something accomplished, and they know on whom they can count and who cannot be trusted. The change may mean that they will no longer have this confidence.

The change can also mean that they may personally be affected and lose status or power because of it; sometimes this may in fact be the purpose of the change. Or they may believe this "negative" motive to be the purpose when actually there is another reason. In any case, one must be aware that resistance may develop because of the perception that the change will affect the organizational structure and therefore people's relationships within it.

On the other hand, sometimes people are bored with the same old patterns and the opportunity to do something new and exciting may be sufficiently strong to assist (with a little encouragement) in gaining acceptance of the proposed change. Sometimes the desire for a new experience may be strong enough to overcome other objections of the "we've always done it this way" variety. Often we can capitalize on this desire and help these individuals to become supporters of the project.

For example, one building principal experiencing a high rate of program innovation was asked why his school seemed to have so many more successful changes than three other similar schools in the district (similar in terms of faculty, students, and neighborhood characteristics). All four schools were charged with making the same changes as directed by the board of education. His school, however, stood out in terms of its success in making these directed changes as well as initiating others of its own.

The principal confided that he first observed very closely the informal organizational structure in his building. Between lunches in the faculty lounge and the regular ongoing operation of the school, he developed a knowledge of the faculty "pecking order," the informal dominance structure among the teachers. In this case, the principal studied the order ranging from those staff members whose good will and support were most necessary to those whose support etc. was least effective in convincing the entire faculty in the building to accept a change. From his observations, the principal identified four teachers in his building whose support he regarded as requisite for innovating change in that building.

His approach was to woo each of these teachers separately, casually sounding out opinion, asking for advice, and—incidentally— planting ideas and building support. Almost invariably each teacher suggested bringing it before the entire faculty for discussion. When the principal did (or had contrived to have one of these teachers make the proposal), the staff's acceptance of the change was positive and morale remained high.[10]

In short, as in employing any good change strategy, the principal aligned (albeit through a form of manipulation he calls "human relations engineering") the critical elements in the situation—these four teachers in the building's informal dominance hierarchy—into the most advantageous position prior to the actual undertaking. The other building principals handled these change matters as "directives from the board," and made no attempt at aligning the critical elements in their organizational structures before presenting the task to the staff. Unenthusiastic foot-dragging generally followed, with the staffs usually resigning themselves gloomily to "live with" the change.

When change causes a shift in the formal organizational structure, attention also should be given to preparing people to accept their new roles. New job descriptions may be needed. At minimum, the person needs to know what is expected of him in his new position. If additional materials are needed, they should be available before the change takes place so that the lack cannot be used as an excuse for not performing in the new role. When appropriate, everyone in the organization should be aware of the new organizational pattern so that they too can know to whom they now go with their problems and questions.

Frequently, a change in one part of the organizational structure will have both expected and unexpected consequences for the other. These consequences may or may not be desirable but if at all possible they should be anticipated. Like the childrens' game "Pick Up Sticks," greater success goes to those who are aware of the consequences of moving particular elements in the structure; moving elements without forethought is likely to jiggle other elements better left undisturbed for the present. But sometimes it cannot be avoided. In one instance, a school district shifted from a four-year to a three-year high school. Most things went well—the shifting of teachers, new administrative organization, reallocation of textbooks and supplies, and so on. However, a morale problem soon developed, and it took some time for someone to realize that the informal arrangements for depositing paychecks in the bank on Friday at noon had been disrupted. The new middle school, which now housed the ninth grade teachers, was too far from the bank for teachers to get there during the twenty-five minute lunch period, and the bank was closed by the time school was dismissed. As a result teachers were late in covering some checks they had written. The district decided to deposit checks directly into the bank to overcome the problem. Shortly afterwards, much of the mysteriously arisen faculty criticism of the change—more remarkable for its suddenness, magnification, and heat than its substance—rapidly died away. Faculty morale improved. This was an unexpected development which, had it not been discovered, could have had detrimental effects on the change. The adverse reaction had nothing to do with the actual change, but affected an informal arrangement that was very important to the teachers.

Because things do not always work as expected the first time, planned changes usually attempt to be flexible enough to permit modifications once inaugurated. Ideally, a monitoring system of some sort, built into the change to identify trouble spots as early as possible, is a useful device. Expect some problems from changes affecting the organization's structure and be ready for them.

4. *Understanding opposition to change.* We should never assume that the opposition is stupid or ignorant; instead, we should respect it and attempt to understand it. Much worthwhile instruction can occur with a close listening to the opposition's arguments. The popular term today for listening to such information is "feedback." As part of a change strategy, it is suggested that some mechanism (frequently a committee meeting) be established that permits feedback from sources where opposition is anticipated. Resistance that

surfaces is usually easier to deal with and reduce than is unarticulated opposition.

Because searching out the opposition and asking their advice about improving upon a contemplated change (or one already in operation) is likely to produce as much heat as reason in the feedback sessions, there is a tendency for administrators to avoid such unpleasantness—like resisting going to the dentist when you know he has some drilling to do. However, planned, periodic feedback check-up on the opposition's thoughts and feelings is recommended.

Sometimes the problems uncovered in feedback sessions are *less* painful than they appear on the surface. For instance, to get more time for instruction at the upper grade levels so that a French program could be started in a school without lengthening the school day, we discussed with the teachers the possibility of doing away with the afternoon recess for the students. The teachers already had a break since they would not have to be in the room while instruction was taking place. The children had a twenty-minute recess each afternoon, during which time they went outside to play on the school grounds. We could not understand the resistance of the teachers to dropping this out of the program until we suddenly realized that when we used the term "recess" we were referring to the whole time period. The teachers were insisting on the recess so the children could get a drink and go to the lavatory, a process requiring five minutes instead of twenty. The program had almost been shelved because of the opposition until we discovered through the feedback that we had not been talking about the same thing.

Those opposed to change usually have some reason for legitimate concern. Sometimes this can be answered relatively easily, sometimes not. But the reason is perfectly sound to them and should not be minimized or ridiculed. They may very well be right. Wisdom does not rest with only a few.

A recent Gallup poll found an almost even division, over a two-year period, among too many innovations, not enough, just about right, and don't know.[11] However, this was a survey of adults. Students felt at a rate of about three to one that not enough innovations were being tried. The so-called generation gap might lead us to expect this but we must remember that the students are the real consumers of what is being taught in the schools. By and large adults only hear about what is going on. Be sure to include some feedback sessions from both parents and students.

Probably one of the most frequently used ways to gain support for a proposed change is to have people visit another district where a similar program is being tried. Of course this is not always possible, but often a nearby district has been doing the same thing or nearly the same thing. It is important, on a number of counts, that the district be as close to yours as possible so people cannot use the excuse that the two programs are not similar. An industrial district will have little in common with a rich suburban district—at least that is what most people are likely to think. Similarly, a rural district will learn little from an urban district. Excuses will be given that they have newer buildings, or more money, or smaller classes, or something that is not "like us." However, a visit can be very helpful if people come back and say that such-and-such a district is using that new program and they like it. This may help overcome some opposition. A successfully operating change in a similar district is a powerfully persuasive factor in allaying doubts and skepticism.

Much can also be learned by looking at past history in your own district. How have the people reacted in the past to suggestions for change? Who was opposed to the change? Has another, nonschool, issue recently been the source of controversy? The answers to these and similar questions in your community may save you much time and trouble in locating likely sources of resistance.

Foreseeing and preventing opposition may be as importnat as the plans for the change you are attempting to accomplish. Once the opposition has mobilized it may be too late to do anything about it. Arguments should be anticipated and plans should formulate what to do so you do not create the conditions that may lead to opposition.

5. *Understanding the role of people within the school system.* Any change strategy must consider how the change will affect directly the people within the system. This includes teachers, school administrators at various levels, school boards, and individual school board members. Not only will these people be affected by the change, but they may also help in the change process in various ways. In the following sections the roles of each of these groups are touched on briefly. (The roles of parents, students, and community groups are discussed in chapter 5.)

a. The teacher's role: What kinds of change can a teacher really bring about? According to Henry Brickell, "classroom teachers can make only three types of instructional changes in the absence of administrative initiative."[12] The changes to which he refers are, first, altering practices within the classroom. An example might be changing from a multiple choice test to an essay test, or using group discussions rather than teacher presentations. The second type of change is relocating existing curriculum content, which usually occurs between two or more teachers—for example, putting a unit on butterflies into the third grade science program in place of a unit on rocks which is moved into the fourth grade. The third type of change is in the introduction of single courses at the high school level. These are often introduced as a result of a teacher's individual experience, such as a graduate course, summer institute, or travel abroad. Brickell notes that both the first and third types of change have little effect on the work of other teachers.

It might be also noted that in these days of collective bargaining (or "professional negotiations" if you prefer that term) there is seldom any emphasis on change in the curriculum contained in the written agreements signed between the teachers' association and the school board. Usually these contracts stipulate working hours, salary, fringe benefits, and often they state under what circumstances teachers may be required to stay after school to work on curriculum matters. Some contracts even state that changes in course content or curriculum may not be made without the advice and consent of the teachers, but very few place the initiative for change on the teaching staff.

Not only should a suggested change reduce the person's burden rather than add to it, but the change should provide at least as much reward to the people after the change as they had before. The reward can, of course, be in the form of money, meaning that salaries should not be reduced as a result of the change. However, since most school districts are on salary schedules this usually will not occur, i.e., the teacher is likely to receive more salary next year than was received this year, based on length of service. Both major teacher groups, the National Education Association and the American Federation of Teachers, have long been on record as opposing pure merit salary schedules, and few school systems have them. It is possible in most districts to have additional compensation for staff members for extra work or increased responsibilities. Either or both may be a result of the planned change and may serve as an incentive for support of the change. In preparing your change strategy, however, it is useful to consider the question, What incentives do our people have for making this change?

In answering this question, there are other rewards that are very important to teachers that may also be considered when planning. Since teachers' salaries are determined according to a schedule, and they usually do not have offices and secretaries—common indicators of status in the business world—the innovators might seek other things important to teachers. Among these are teaching loads, size of classes, adequate supervision of cafeterias, parking spaces, teachers' lounges, and a chance to participate in decisions. It is probably the last that is most important and the best motivator of people. But, if the change will increase class size, or change the teaching load from four classes to five, or require supervision of the playground, or buses, or cafeteria, or require a teacher to make three preparations daily instead of two, we can almost be sure to encounter resistance.

b. The school administrator's role: Without the cooperation of the teaching staff it will be almost impossible to initiate successfully any change involving them. However, it is equally improbable that effective change will occur without the support of the administration. As Donald Tope concludes from research on the change process in the public schools, "the administrator *does* make a difference."[13] In some cases it will be the building principal or some other pivotal administrator. Very few innovations can succeed without the commitment of those at the top or in key positions. Not only does the "buck" stop there, the "buck" also often comes from there. Many changes require money in some form—not always additional funds, but perhaps a reordering of existing funds. It should be apparent that change can take place more easily if additional funds are not required, and that there will be less resistance if no tax increase is needed. This may be especially important in these days of "taxpayer revolt."

Richard Carlson's study on the adoption of educational innovations indicates that administrators are chiefly responsible for innovations.[14] To effect change, it appears necessary to convince administrators of its value. We do not mean to imply that our earlier statement about changes effected by teachers is any less true. Most of these changes were in classroom practices, while here we are thinking of new types of instructional programs that involve many teachers and mean a large change in existing programs. An example would be the introduction of modern mathematics into the curriculum, an innovation of several years ago. Without administrative support it would have been extremely difficult for systemwide changes to occur.

While the teacher has no way to reward his peers, or to stimulate them to do something, the administrator has some power and authority in this realm by virtue of his position in the formal organizational structure and authority, even if he is a poor leader. A poor leader who is an administrator is still able to initiate change more readily than a teacher who is an outstanding leader. Seldom is a group as effective as a single individual in being the change agent, especially when that individual occupies a key position of authority.[15] Clearly the administrator is the most important single person in a school district when it comes to facilitating the change process. Without his support, change is almost impossible; with it, change may be facilitated. Be certain the administrative team is supportive and also feels a degree of "ownership" of the change too.

    c. The collective role of the school board: Among groups of people who can assist the change process and are influential in the dynamics of change are school boards. Boards of education usually do not originate demands for new instructional or educational changes, but their influence is decisive—either "for" or "against"—when it is exerted.[16]

Boards of education tend to act in the matter of educational change rather like the public they represent. That is, they may respond positively or negatively to a suggested change, or they may suggest a general change for the administration to study and report back. This role may result from the board's spending most of its time on items other than those related to the curriculum. Boards of education open bids for supplies, approve financial statements, listen to reports from committees, and are generally (sometimes too heavily) involved in the ongoing administrative details of the school system.

If a board does suggest an educational change for the district, it is usually along the lines of asking the administration to look into a particular program or activity. Very few boards think in comprehensive terms about the school's educational programs. Instead they operate in piecemeal fashion. True, they seldom involve themselves intimately in the methods and techniques of teaching, but in this regard members of the board reflect their perceptions of their roles as representatives of the people or taxpayers. If they show higher concern with the cost of a new program and its effect on the tax rate than with the educationally offered justifications for it, that may be a political fact of life in that community. To retain his position, a board member must pragmatically balance what is acceptable to the community with what his common sense and the professional staff tell him. Work on developing the "big picture" for the board so that the members can respond intelligently to inquiries about where and why this particular change is to be made; if the board opposes the change, halt efforts until their support can be secured.

One of the commonest elements of board resistance to change

programs is the cost factor. It may be interesting to note that while one hears about "taxpayer revolt," there is more commonly a lack of interest among tax *voters*. These are two quite different things. The sad fact is that most voters do not vote on school issues.[17] Only a little over a third of the eligible voters in most communities turn out to vote in school elections. Whatever the decision, clearly a minority of the voters have made it. If, for example, out of one hundred eligible voters thirty-six vote in the election, normally it would take only nineteen voters to pass or defeat the issue. Perhaps it can be assumed that those who do not vote would have voted with the majority, but one can never be sure. In most districts the school tax is over half of a community's tax bill, and it is often the one tax voters can vote on directly, yet less than half the voters turn out for the election. It would appear to make sense to take into consideration such behavioral patterns by local voters in mapping out a change strategy. Remember that the school board is in a much better position to accept the change if they do not have to explain an increased tax burden to their constituencies. At the same time, too many new programs have died through financial starvation. Search for a trade-off. If you can put something new into the educational program, can you take something else out? Some work with cost/effectiveness analysis, and a bit of political testing and speculating is useful at this juncture. Removal of an ongoing program, especially to make room for a new one, is delicate.

d. Influence of individual school board members: There is one area in which it has been our experience that school board members do exercise considerable influence, and that is as individuals. Theoretically, the school board member is only a member when the board is sitting as a full board. Outside of the board room he is supposed to have no more power than any other private citizen. To believe this is to be unaware of the dynamics of change or influence. Legally a board member has the same power as every other board member, but just as individual people have a greater capacity for leadership, so do individual board members. Some are listened to by other board members, and some are not. They too have a "pecking order."

Individual board members also exert influence on change in areas in which they have a particular competency. For example, a member who is an architect is nearly certain to be highly influential with other members of the board when the construction of a new school is considered. Similarly, a member who is an insuranceman is likely to become more involved and more influential in the decision-making process when the district is considering bids for fire insurance. Likewise, the physician may be called upon to help draft a medical policy statement for the board. This is understandable, and as long as there is not a conflict of interest, we do not object to utilizing the talents and capabilities of the individual board members. The situation can become "interesting" when one of the board members is a teacher (by law, usually not from that district.) To whom will the board look for advice on instructional matters? to the teacher who is the board member, or to the superintendent? We would hope that the *total* board would regard the superintendent as the instructional leader and that the teacher-board member would be viewed as a board member.

We stated earlier that the board's influence is decisive when it is exerted in matters of change. This should not be overlooked in a change strategy. The board must approve the change or else the change will not occur. The board has too many legal options to resist change for one to ignore their importance, among them refusal to vote funds, not approving the hiring of additional staff, charging insubordination to direct legal orders of the board, and blocking other projects. Any one of these is enough to squelch the change, and a combination will make change impossible. Where the chief school administrator is concerned in developing a change strategy, he must know the pulse of the individual board member as well as the collective board's. Boards are heavily influenced by the opinions of their own members.

The ideal situation would seem to be one where the superintendent and the board agree on the need for the change. Whether it was the superintendent's idea, the board's idea, or someone else's idea is not as important as whether or not the board and superintendent are in accord on it. The board will set the necessary policy for the change, if it is required, and the superintendent can then administer the policy. It sounds simple. It is not. Experience indicates, however, this pattern is of the utmost importance and must be planned for in any change strategy.

Changes Vary Widely

In this chapter we have presented some ideas that may be helpful in developing a change strategy. It should be emphasized that changes will vary widely in terms of who and what they affect. For example, a curriculum change may affect only a single room in the case where a teacher changes some practice; or the change may be K-12 in nature as when an entire curriculum is changed; or the change may affect only the teachers in one building, as when a nongraded approach or an open classroom is tried.

Changes involve people. An example might be shifting children from one building to another to equalize school enrollments or to inaugurate a new middle school, or "busing" children to overcome racial imbalance. Teachers may be relocated, or positions may be added or reduced to accommodate changing enrollment patterns.

Other changes may affect more than one district. This would be the case during a consolidation or reorganization of school districts. The pairing of school districts to achieve a racial balance will possibly affect several districts. These changes may also have an impact on curriculum or people, which may make the change more complicated. For example, if two districts are joined together for some reason, the reading programs may vary between the schools which may necessitate some adjustments.

The proposed change might involve institutions besides the schools. For example, a change in the vocational education curriculum may have consequences for the businesses and industries in the community. Likewise, a new industry in the city may require some changes in the school's vocational program. The new after-school sports program may have an effect on the recreation program offered in the community, or the Little League soccer teams may be a "farm system" for the high school soccer team. A decision by the city to abandon the recreation program could mean a losing season in future years for the high school coach.

Change may develop from within the system, or it may come from outside when the state or federal education department develops new requirements for the local schools. In addition to requirements to overcome de facto segregation, we can think of new state testing programs, facility requirements, and mandated curriculum changes such as the inclusion of driver education at the high school level.

Judges in state and federal courts may be agents of change. Some people maintain that judges are the most effective change agents since they can accomplish in a single ruling what might have been debated for decades. The recent rulings in regard to the property tax as the source of school revenue are examples of the power that a judge has to effect change in the local schools.

Our list could go on and on, but the point has been made: change may take a variety of forms, stem from a variety of causes, have a variety of effects, and serve a variety of purposes. This chapter has presented some guidelines for a change strategy. It does not purport to be all inclusive. All of the elements presented may not be necessary in every change, and some of the elements offered did not explore in depth, or perhaps at all, everything which could and should be done. They were only suggestive. For example, we did not discuss means of publicizing the proposed change, the uses of citizens' advisory groups, the roles of parents and students, public meetings and hearings, and other information seeking and gathering devices. These are valuable components in some change strategies, but may not be necessary in all such programs.

From their study of the last seventy-five years of educational changes, Donald Orlosky and Othanel Smith have drawn some interesting conclusions.[18] Among these, it stands out that successful changes in instruction where teaching behavior is expected to alter are considerably more difficult than changes in curriculum or administration:

A change that requires the teacher to abandon an existing practice and to displace it with a new practice risks defeat. If teachers must be retrained in order for a change to be made, as in team teaching, the chances for success are reduced unless strong incentives to be retained are provided.[19]

If, as these researchers suggest, "in no case in the past did a successful change in instruction come from outside of education,"[20] it would appear prudent in preparing a change strategy for developing an educationally accountable program to establish merely the framework of a policy of educational outcomes expected and let the professional staff take it from that point. To be sure, involve every appropriate person in the planning of the accountability framework and provide a supportive climate (i.e., encouragement, a sense of direction, time, money, and technical assistance) for the staff as it determines how it will cope with the task of accounting for educational results. In this sense it might be wise to think in terms of roles similar to the Malay fishermen in working with the staff once the accountability framework has been established:

The relation between the expert (fisherman) and his crew is one of free association, either party being at liberty to break the bond at any time. He is the leader and commander of the crew . . . but they are not simply wage-earners and they are not bound to obey him. While he leads them, and sometimes drives them in matters of technique and organization, he shows what, to the outsider, is often a surprising readiness to consult them on matters of policy. Their mutual relations are governed not by any set formula of rights and duties, but by a number of practical assumptions about what is reasonable in the circumstances of their work.[21]

In the end, our notion of a good change strategy is one that gets the results intended from its application. Because the process of change is complex and the state of the art imperfect, we essentially assume that it is necessary to be pragmatic in the construction of a change strategy for the local situation. We fully understand that "a focus on change also requires a focus on courage."[22]

Notes for Chapter 4

1. Quoted in G. J. Goldin, K. N. Margolin, and B. A. Stotsky, *The Utilization of Rehabilitation Research*, New England Rehabilitation Research Institute Monograph no. 6 (Boston: Northeastern University, 1969), pp. 1-2.

2. John Dewey, *NEA Proceedings, 1901* (Washington, D. C.: National Education Association, 1901), pp. 334-35.

3. See Subcommittee for the Study of Diffusion of Farm Practices, *How Farm People Accept New Ideas*, Regional Publication no. 1 (Ames, Iowa: North Central Rural Sociology Committee, 1962); Herbert Lionberger, *Legitimation of Decisions to Adopt Farm Practices and Purchase Farm Supplies in Two Missouri Farm Communities: Ozark and Prairie*, Research Bulletin no. 826 (Columbia, Mo.: University of Missouri, 1963).

4. Robert Blake and Jane Mouton, *Building a Dynamic Corporation Through Grid Organization Development* (Reading, Mass.: Addison-Wesley Publishing Co., 1969), pp. 10-15.

See also E. Ginzberg and E. W. Reilley, *Effecting Change in Large Organizations* (New York: Columbia University Press, 1957), pp. 130-39. Ginzberg and Reilley note a change process that can be roughly broken into ten distinguishable parts: (1) initial recognition of difficulties, (2) determination to take corrective action, (3) finding appropriate methods of analyzing the situation, (4) developing the plan, (5) decision to accept the plan, (6) announcement of the plan to the organization, (7) detailing new functions and responsibilities, (8) alignment of various operating systems and incentives to reinforce the plan, (9) active instruction of key personnel in new methods to facilitate a change in their behavior, monitoring the plan, and (10) adjusting it in light of experience.

5. J. Lloyd Trump, "Influencing Change at the Secondary Level," in *Perspectives on Educational Change*, ed. Richard I. Miller (New York: Appleton-Century-Crofts, 1967), p. 66.

6. A considerable literature on the topic of change strategies is presented in Louis Maguire, Sanford Temkin, and C. Peter Cummings, *An Annotated Bibliography on Administering for Change* (Philadelphia, Pa.: Research for Better Schools, Inc., 1971).

7. Kurt Lewin, "Quasi-Stationary Social Equilibria and the Problem of Permanent Change," in *The Planning of Change*, ed. Warren Bennis, Kenneth Benne, and Robert Chin (New York: Holt, Rinehart and Winston, 1961), pp. 235ff.

8. Presentation by Goodwin Watson, "Strategies for Change Conference," Philadelphia, October 28, 1971.

9. Quoted in Paul C. Fawley, "Professors of Educational Administration Look at Preparation Programs for Community Education Leadership," *Community Education* 1, no. 4 (November 1971): 24.

10. It should be noted that none of these changes seriously altered the "pecking order." Where some change tended to modify relations, the principal was quick to bring other things into the situation to keep the informal structure in balance—things usually not directly related to the change but that retained the integrity of the pecking order (e.g., chairing an important committee when a change meant performing a necessary but low status task).

11. George Gallup, "The Third Annual Survey of the Public's Attitude Toward the Public Schools," *Phi Delta Kappan* (September 1971): 37.

12. Henry Brickell, *Organizing New York State for Educational Change* (Albany, New York: State Department of Education, 1961), p. 24.

13. Donald Tope, "Summary," in *Change Processes in the Public Schools,* ed. Richard Carlson et. al (Eugene, Ore.: University of Oregon, 1965), p. 89.

14. Richard Carlson, *Adoption of Educational Innovations* (Eugene, Ore: University of Oregon, 1965).

15. For further insight, see Edwin Ghiselli and Thomas Lodahl, "Patterns of Managerial Traits and Group Effectiveness," *Journal of Abnormal Psychology* 57 (1958): 61-66.

16. Brickell, *Organizing New York State for Educational Change*, p. 21

17. William Savard and Richard Caret, *Influence of Voter Turnout on School Board and Tax Elections* (Washington, D. C.: Government Printing Office, 1961).

18. Donald Orlosky and Othanel Smith, "Educational Change: Its Origins and Characteristics," *Phi Delta Kappan* (March 1972): 412-14.

19. Ibid., p. 414.

20. Ibid.

21. Raymond Firth, *Malay Fisherman* (London: Trench, Trubner, 1946), p. 104.

22. J. Lloyd Trump and Dorsey Baynham, *Guide to Better Schools* (Chicago: Rand McNally, 1961), p. 130.

5. Community-Staff Involvement

Who Decides What: Curriculum Policy Making

Should the schools be responsible for the child's intellectual development only, or should they be responsible for his social, moral, religious, vocational, physical, emotional, and recreational needs also? If the schools are to be responsible for everything, are all these things of equal importance, and if not, what is the order of priority—what comes first?[1] This set of questions, offered in chapter 1, is implicitly raised in curriculum policy making—that is, the determination of "a body of principles to guide action"[2] (policy) toward what the learner is expected to learn from his school experience (the curriculum). Whether an educational program is large or small in scope and size, it requires definition in terms of its goals and objectives. This definition of purpose is the process of curriculum policy making. The generalized goals and objectives of the school, usually expressed as a "philosophy," have until recently characterized the local school district's answers to these questions. The issue of "who decides what" in curriculum policy making, although always a part of education's historical scene, has not received as much attention as it appears to be getting today and it promises to grow more volatile tomorrow. To enhance understanding of the proposed basis of community-staff involvement, we ask two questions: (1) why is "who decides what" in curriculum policy making receiving more attention today, and (2) what are the implications of this at the local district level?

Legally and within prescribed limits, the power for local

128

curriculum decision making is vested (along with other powers) in the local board of education by the state government. Most persons, however, are aware of certain other realities. A knowledge of who the law designates to make decisions seems less important than a personal knowledge of those who actually make and interpret the decisions; where real decision-making power can be located, influence can be brought to bear. The manner in which influence is wielded—whether by confrontation and conflict or by efforts to build consensus and forms of accommodation—is part of "who decides what." The increased focus on who it is that makes decisions concerning what children should learn is easier to describe in general terms than to document specifically, and the question of why people bother at all seems related in part to the values they hold. Ultimately, one is pressed to discuss the place of values in our society as the source of motivation for community involvement in curriculum policy making.

If we think of values as "standards of desirability"[3] that tell us what is acceptable and unacceptable as a behavior or condition (or, what is good or bad, pleasant or unpleasant, beautiful or ugly, appropriate or inappropriate), we are led to an observation: in the public sector, where there is substantial agreement on what the dominant values of a society should be (those values held or shared commonly by most people over a period of time, reflected in the actions of their leaders, and experienced through their own actions to have a higher intensity than other values), there is more willingness to delegate the responsibility for translating these values into practices and programs. We delegate custodianship and maintenance of our social values to elected or appointed officials responsible for these practices and programs—public servants believed to share our value orientation. The willingness to delegate such responsibility might be called "public trust" or the attainment of a positive level of confidence vested in its stewards by the public.

If Robin Williams is correct, examples of the major value orientations in American society include: "achievement" and "success," "activity" and "work," "moral orientation," humanitarian mores, efficiency and practicality, "progress," material comfort, equality, freedom, external conformity, science and secular rationality, nationalism-patriotism, democracy, individual personality, racism, and related group-superiority themes.[4]

For our purposes, it is not necessary to trace the course of each of these values from the founding of the colonies to their current position in American society. It should be enough to suggest that if one compared the messages of the media in the 1920s and 1930s with those of the 1940s and 1950s, one could note national shifts in the emphasis and interpretation of all these dominant value themes. Today, however, the contrast is even more marked for two reasons: (1) the acceleration of change (as Toffler notes, "value turnover is now faster than ever before in history"[5]) and (2) we are encountering a period of deteriorating consensus. In sum:

Most previous societies have operated with a broad central core of commonly shared values. This core is now contracting, and there is little reason to anticipate the formation of a new broad consensus within the decades ahead. The pressures are outward toward diversity, not inward toward unity.[6]

In part, because modern media (particularly television) has such a powerful ability to focus national attention, because what is "newsworthy" or attention getting frequently runs counter to or diverges from the commonly held view, and because so many subcultural interest groups have successfully dramatized—almost daily—their positions—positions confronting selected values among the hegemony of values nationally subscribed to—before a national audience, there has been an eroding away of the commonly shared values. As different individuals find closer bonds with previously unknown (or dimly perceived) subcultural interest groups, they find themselves realigning their constellation of values and becoming more critical in general of "desirability standards," frequently experiencing conflict with associates and friends who have not made the same shifts or have shifted even further. "Uptight" aptly expresses the feelings experienced by many persons caught up in the juggling of standards of desirability.

If, added to this state of affairs, events occur where the actions of public servants do not appear consistent with their words—as the term "credibility gap" (coined in President Lyndon Johnson's administration) suggests—there is further strain. Whatever the label, the results are the same: public trust in its servants deteriorates and suspicion arises that the "right" set of values is not being used to base programs on, or that the programs do not succeed in doing what they are expected to do. In short, a negative level of confidence emerges.

Thus, particularly in communities where there is a marked diminution of commonly shared values, one finds today a high proportion of humorless, "uptight" persons who are: (1) caught up in the national turmoil of value shifts; (2) highly conscious that the locally applied standards of desirability can be shifted or otherwise manipulated; (3) distrustful of those who hold values divergent from their own; and (4) suspicious of the efforts of those public servants who must translate values into practices and programs. In its most visible form, the observation of one harassed superintendent is worth repeating: "There's a lack of good will. That's the problem. They come on as members of a political party to fight and they fight."[7] In communities where groups of citizens believe that "we must destroy the (school) system before it destroys our children,"[8] there is bound to be a lively interest in and attention paid to matters of curriculum policy making. Cunningham portrays this negative level of confidence of various groups:

We are now witnessing vigorous attempts to strike out against school organization by individuals and groups—parents, nonparents, black, white, American Indian, and Spanish American—who seek to achieve a wide range of purposes. Some want action on a private or individual grievance; others want improved political access to the points of decision; others demand large-scale shifts in specific policy; still others want complete community control over "their" schools including operational responsibility.[9]

But a community concerned with the enforcement and/or shaping of different value codes in the schools is only one part of the issue of the local level. Two other groups—groups also lacking the board of education's legal powers to make curriculum policy decisions—show concern about what standards of desirability are reflected in the formally designated expectations of learners: the professional teaching staff and the students. Without attempting to explore the subgroup differences among the teaching staff (elementary-secondary, male-female, subject matter—child orientation, teacher-quasi administrator, etc.) or the students (conformists-nonconformists, black-white, vocational—college-bound, student council-SDS, etc.), one can note conflicting points of interest radiating from these groups in regard to other groups in the process of curriculum policy making.

For teachers, concern and claim to involvement in curriculum policy making has a long history that quickened in the 1960s. Under a sometimes exaggerated notion of "professionalism" and perhaps expressed best in Myron Lieberman's writings, the teachers' position on curriculum policy making might be stated:

A profession is an occupation which possesses some kind of expertness. It is in the public interest to accord the professional worker the autonomy to make the decisions which require this expertness. This is why it is undesirable to have non-professional control over the curriculum in any school system.[10]

As seen by Lieberman and reflected in the drives of militant teacher organizations, "the problem is not which public . . . should establish the educational program, but how to make certain it is in the hands of the teachers, where it belongs."[11]

Teachers have shown increased willingness to put their claims to the test. Aiming primarily at the distribution and allocation of economic resources, teachers opened the past decade with three strikes in 1960-61 and ended it with 180 strikes in 1969-70—500 strikes for the ten-year period, a work stoppage involving over a half million teachers and more than five million man-days of instruction.[12] Certainly the majority of these strikes did not focus per se on curriculum policy making, but the extended influence of these strikes and countless threatened near-strikes, by teacher organizations in quest of equal decision-making powers with the board of education through formal contracts, has made the issue of teacher involvement in curriculum policy making highly visible.

In many communities, it might be argued that the power struggle is reaching new proportions. Some observers believe the struggle is for control of the local public school.[13] In an oversimplified sense, the group having the power of control seeks to yield as little as strategically possible of its position. The "have-nots," finding that aggressive attack wins concessions, encouraged by opportune legislation, and their efforts legitimized by court decisions, increasingly press their own standards of desirability.

Locally, the major participants in the "have" group are the local board of education, presenting the prevailing will of the community, and the board's uneasy ally, the school administration (uneasy because school boards frequently appear willing to sacrifice the administrator as expedience demands).

Among the "have-not" groups seeking access to decision-making power are subcultural community interest groups, teachers, and a new, previously "overlooked," group[14]: the students. C. Wright Mills noted: "Power has to do with whatever decision men make about the arrangements under which they live . . . . Insofar as such decisions are made, the problem of who is involved in making them is the basic problem of power."[15] The desire to be included in the decision-making process is a prominent motif in the use of confrontation and protest by students.[16] Among the findings of a Louis Harris Poll conducted nationally in spring 1969—probably the high-water mark of recent student unrest—was the disclosure that more than half (58 percent) of high school students were impatient with the limited degree of participation afforded to them in the running of educational affairs. Harris reported: "The key to what is going on among high school students today is that a majority clearly want to participate more in deciding their future."[17] Further, a report from the same period by the National Association of Secondary School Principals (NASSP) says that three out of five principals noted some form of active protest in their schools.[18] It appears that students in many localities, learning from their adult models, have had success in their drive for inclusion in curriculum policy making—if Educational Research Service's publication, *Framework for Student Involvement,* is any kind of barometer.[19] Student unrest may have lessened recently, but there are strong indications that efforts have been made in many communities to include students in curriculum policy making.

What can be concluded about the local issue of who-decides-what regarding curriculum policy making? Several conclusions might be tentatively offered:

1. It is an exceedingly complex issue—far more complex than presented above and, in Neal Gross's words, "very slippery"—involving a community-by-community analysis to determine the actual interplay of forces on the board of education. On the matter of how boards use their formal position in the authority structure to discharge their legal responsibilities, Gross concludes:

Some school boards know that they have the formal authority and use it and do not get especially pressured; they make the basic policies and see that these are carried out. Other school boards are rubber stamps for the superintendent. Still others are representatives of special interest groups. And many school boards operate on their own but, in hot issues, yield to local pressures.[20]

2. The formulation of curriculum policy has strong roots in educational theory and practice. As Taba described it: "Scientific curriculum development needs to draw upon analyses of society and culture, studies of the learner and the learning process, and analyses of the nature of knowledge in order to determine the purposes of the school and the nature of its curriculum."[21]

3. While educational theory and practice do have contributions to make, it is both dangerous and naive for educators to believe that they have a monopoly in curriculum matters and to assume:

Engineers cannot solve the problem. Politicians cannot make significant changes, nor can physicians, economists, or industrialists. Only schoolmen can find ways to help young people learn and live in creative and satisfying ways.[22]

4. Curriculum policy making today has developed equally strong roots embedded in political processes (not just influenced by political events). As Kirst and Walker view it:

Throughout curriculum policy-making political conflict is generated by the existence of competing values concerning the proper basis for deciding what to teach. The local school system and the other public agencies responsible for these decisions must allocate these competing values in some way, even though this means that some factions or interests win and others lose on any given curriculum issue.[23]

5. Therefore, local procedures to involve the community, staff, students, etc., in the process of curriculum policy making should be frankly recognized for what they are: an exercise in politics as well as education.

What are the implications? If involving others beyond administrators and board in the curriculum policy-making process appears fraught with so many potential difficulties and conflicts, why bother to make the effort? For example, some persons contend that, indeed, the board is elected (or appointed) to implement the wishes of the community as well as of the state, while the administration is expected to represent expertise in the field (as is the staff). Many among these two parties—administrators and board members—are likely to share the conviction that the responsibility for determining curriculum policy making is exclusively theirs as a part of their legitimate roles. They see in the process for extending involvement as much potential for increasing conflict as there is for resolving it. The thought of having to share decision-making powers, of being placed in an "exposed position" publicly, of permitting a sort of "role emasculation" as others claim parts of heretofore exclusive roles— these thoughts are likely to produce the reaction, "Who needs it"? As one superintendent remarked to the suggestion that he go out into his divided community, "to heal the wounds" and "meaningfully involve people" in the planning of the school's curriculum: "Fellows willing to put their head in a lion's mouth work in circuses."

Against this inclination (i.e., to avoid potential conflict and a struggle for power where the board and the administrator appear to have more to lose than to gain), however, stand sound arguments. One of the oldest is the basic American concept of democracy—a standard of desirability stating that decision-making power is derived from the advice and consent of the governed. In today's society, the local expression of this value is usually made through soliciting people to involve themselves voluntarily in decision making—that is, to give them a direct voice rather than a representative voice that may or may not truly represent the individual's position. The current emphasis on civil rights adds another dimension: majority decisions should be tempered with respect to minority rights. In short, today's climate of opinion produces in many places a standard of desirability holding that it is necessary for all persons—young and old, teacher and taxpayer, parent and nonparent, majority and minority, powerful and powerless—to have an "input" into determining public school policy at the local level.

But the fact that this value is widespread may not be as powerful an argument as naked political force. It can be impossible for administrators and school boards to function without serious gestures toward authentic community/staff involvement ("authentic" meaning that the parties involved truly believe their participation is capable of influencing policy making). Strikes, boycotts, riots, serious budget defeats—all are expressions from external parties capable of bringing the process of education to a standstill. It is a common experience for boards and administrators to find themselves the target of conflicting demands from different groups, each group pressing to levy its demands without regard to other groups and their interests. In such situations, it becomes tempting to cease having to defend what appears to be an "unpopular" position, and serving as the target for pressures. The alternative is to invite all these groups to become involved and allow them the opportunity to resolve their conflicts or, failing that, allow them to perceive better some of the heat as well as the merits of other points of view. It can also be reassuring when a board member or administrator is able to say that "this curriculum" or "that program" is the will of the people in this community and know that, in fact, it is.

Whether extended involvement of other parties in curriculum or other forms of policy making is solicited or unsolicited, the chances are that with the passage of time and acceleration of change, the choice will become academic. If our contention is correct that the issue of who decides what in local curriculum policy making is today (and will be) receiving more attention because of decreasing commonly shared values and the increase of special interest groups, and that, for practical purposes, the implications of this increased local attention are (1) heightened political activity (rather than exclusively pedagogical considerations) and (2) increased involvement of others —then a further question emerges: what is the role of the administrator—as the steward of the board—in curriculum policy making?

The Administrator and Curriculum Policy Making

There are many points of view on the role of the local administrator in the process of involving others in curriculum policy making. Like most public executives, he gets much free advice—particularly

from those who do not face his problems. There are those who seem
to exhort the administrator to take a strong leadership position, not
infrequently meaning a strong position *against* some opposing pressure group. For example, Lieberman sees curriculum as remaining in
the teachers' hands "where it belongs," yet he assigns to administrators the role of *telling* the public what should be taught in school,
stating that administrators should be criticized for "catering to
public opinion."[24]

Then there are those who tend to view administrators as part of
a "professional priesthood" who should be humbled for not paying
enough attention to public opinion. Dean Bowles writes:

There is no further need to separate and entrust educational policy to a
consensus of the professional priesthood in lieu of the political process. The
demands of today require that educational policy be the product of a political
policy brought about by an accommodation of conflicting public interests as
opposed to the narrower goals of the professionals.[25]

With these conflicting viewpoints, what might be considered a
fair appraisal of the administrator's role? Probably the observations
of Art Gallaher and George Spindler come closer to meeting the
perceptions of most practicing administrators.

Gallaher sees the administrator as "the man in the middle,"
taking a balancing role among several different audiences with different claims—school boards, parents, parent groups, special interest
community groups, teachers, students, and even other administrators, while avoiding advocacy. "Since the role of advocate is pur-
posive and one that involves commitment that, even under the best
of change circumstances, sometimes involves conflict, the school
administrator might reduce his balancing role effectiveness if he
assumes advocacy."[26]

Spindler concurs with this "man in the middle" balancing role
for the administrator:

His job is in large part that of maintaining a working equilibrium of at best
antagonistically cooperative forces. This is one of the reasons why school
administrators are rarely outspoken protagonists of a consistent and vigorously
profiled point of view. Given the nature of our culture and social system, and
the close connection between the public and the schools, he cannot alienate
significant segments of that public and stay in business.[27]

Charles Lindblom speaks of the "reconstructive leader," who
perceives and exploits opportunities to alter the preferences of others
that constrain him:

He neither resigns himself to the constraint of preferences as he finds them, nor,
on the other hand, does he necessarily attempt the impossible task of winning all

other participants over to his views or preferences. He takes the middle course of shifting others' preferences so that the policies he desires fall within (whereas they formerly fell outside) the constraints imposed by the preferences of other participants in policy making. And he then uses what power or influence he has to get the policy he wants.[28]

The complexity of handling this pragmatic reconstructive balancing role is great. It suggests that the administrator influences the course of events primarily through more subtle manipulative acts that bend with the weight of conditions rather than a leadership style that marches forth—banner in hand—into the fray. The mute presumption is that a man of integrity knows when to take a stand and when not. In a negative sense, it implies that at times he must manage to keep certain of his convictions under control, risking the condemnation of those who would apply Abraham Lincoln's admonition: "To sin by silence when they should speak out, makes cowards of men." Whether or not that is true, we hope the man in the middle has a professional conscience.

A further qualification might be added: much of what the administrator does or does not do—the role he plays—is strongly influenced by the behavior of his superiors (the board of education and/or higher level administrators in the case of subordinate administrators) and the kind of community power structure existing where he works. From their research on the effects of community power structures on boards of education and school administrators in fifty-one different communities, Donald McCarty and Charles Ramsey have suggested a rough four-part categorization of effects:

(1) In communities where there are strongly held common views expressed forcefully by the board, the superintendent tends to act as a dominated "functionary," carrying out board policy decisions;

(2) Divided communities with split-and-changing board majorities, however, produce a guarded "political strategist" administrator who acts in such a way that he is able to work effectively with any current or future majority by never taking strong stands likely to offend any board member, always restricting himself to advisement (usually of moderate courses of action), and avoiding becoming openly supportive of any given faction;

(3) In communities reflecting a split value structure ("pluralistic") but having board members who consciously act less as faction members and more as individual peers facing sets of common problems, the more statesmanlike qualities of the superintendent are apparent in a "professional adviser's" role—a role where he "can

express to the board alternatives to any policy and can delineate the consequences of any action openly and objectively";

(4) Finally, there are even some communities where the inertia of both community and board is so great that the superintendent becomes, indeed, the decision maker to a rubber stamp board.[29] Where conditions permit, the role of the balancing administrator as "professional adviser" seems most appealing to us.

Whatever community power structure or board exists, some further thoughts on the role of the administrator in regard to curriculum policy making might be advanced. For example, we have consistently viewed him as playing a dual role as both leader and follower-participant. The role of man in the middle has subtle complexities in performance. Krech, Crutchfield, and Ballachey define "leaders" as members of a group, community, or society who (by degree in comparison with other members of the group) "outstandingly" influence the other members of the group (who also exert influence) and also play a central role in helping to define group goals and "in determining the ideology of the group."[30] This influencing behavior, i.e., this ability to get others acting, thinking, or feeling in the direction one intends, has two dimensions: "consideration" and "initiating and directing." Where consideration is concerned, the leader works to motivate members of a group to accept the goals of the group and the efforts toward their accomplishment, while he attempts to maintain harmony and member satisfaction. In "initiating and directing," the leader attempts to help specify ways and means for achieving the goals of the group and coordinating its activities. Translating this concept into curriculum policy making for educational accountability programs, it seems possible to view the administrator's role in this manner:

1. Recognizing that the board holds the ultimate power of decision, the local administrator will probably want first to obtain the advice and consent of his board before moving too far along. If the accountability program is to be of modest proportions, this action may not be necessary. However, it would almost certainly be deemed necessary if numbers of people from different groups were to be involved. Students of formal organizations are likely to refer to this procedure as paying attention to the "chain of command." Less patient persons may view it as so much red tape and counsel the administrator to get on with the task, letting the resulting political pressures come to rest on the board and the school and spur them along. Still others may consider it a simple act of courtesy. Perhaps closer to the mark, it may also be regarded as part of the procedure

for maintaining trust that sustains a positive level of confidence by the reviewer in his steward. At any rate, in the process of developing an educational accountability program, the administrator will want to know the board's position on a number of issues:

• Is the board of education interested in making district programs (all programs or only certain ones) more accountable?

• Is it aware of the amount of time, effort, and expenditure necessary to do this task?

• Is it fully aware of the particular educational (as well as other) needs of the district (needs determined by the administrator through the preliminary needs assessment procedure)?

• Is it willing to pursue a particular change strategy being tentatively suggested?

• Is it interested in or agreeable to having others involved in an advisory planning committee that is charged with the task of determining the educational goals and objectives for the district (or, less broadly, for a specific program) and submitting their findings and/or program plan to the board for approval? (If "yes," does the board desire to lead this committee, be represented on it, or otherwise maintain some liaison with it?)

• Does the board understand that if such a committee is formed (even with detailed charges) it may assume a momentum of its own (particularly if no board members are represented on it and the leadership influence of the administrator is less than other influences) and may present a set of recommendations to the board that appear more like "demands" than "requests for consideration"?

• Is the board and the proposed advisory planning committee likely to recognize that the recommendations of the committee are neither to be rubber stamped nor ignored by the board but very seriously considered?

• In brief, is there sufficient commitment by the board to the entire project to justify making the attempt?

2. In determining answers to the above questions, it is assumed that the administrator (in addition to having reviewed the imperatives offered in chapter 2) has a sense of timing—knowing when to present his request, the manner of presentation, the reasons for the request, and all things dependent on the schoolman's political awareness. When the matter is broached with the board (or, in the case of a subordinate administrator, with his superior), the administrator's leadership is put to the test. Presumably the request will be granted, perhaps in modified form. If not, the administrator should recognize that in this instance his role is that of a follower participant, in which

case he can: accept the board's wishes and not pursue the matter further; present it again at a more advantageous time or in another form; play politics and determine another way to bring influence to bear on the board; or disregard the board's wishes by either pretending to misread their real wishes (if a recorded vote was not taken) or merely moving ahead ("damn the torpedoes") in spite of the board. Most administrators would probably find the first two options acceptable, some even the third, but only a few the last. Each successive option runs the risk of diminishing the board's level of confidence in its administrator, with the third and particularly the fourth courting disaster.

3. Assuming the administrator's influence was strong enough to obtain a positive response from the board (i.e., the administrator proves to be a leader in this instance), he may be expected to perform the following leadership tasks:

(a) Develop for board approval a specified charge that empowers him (or another designated administrator) to proceed with the formation of a planning advisory committee;

(b) Identify and solicit a group of "relevant" participants desiring involvement in curriculum policy making and/or program planning;

(c) Help this group (committee) structure itself and develop a data-based focus (via needs assessment information) on the issue or problems;

(d) Provide guidelines for enabling the committee to determine the community-at-large's concerns, goals, and objectives for the given program;

(e) Allow the teaching staff and students to be involved, with the expectation that the teaching staff will play a prominent role in translating program goals and objectives into measurable learning outcomes;

(f) Move the committee toward a workable consensus or program goals and objectives and/or preliminary program design;

(g) Require the committee to complete its planning activities within a reasonable length of time (probably with formal progress reports periodically made to the board if the latter group is not represented on the committee as an entire board);

(h) See that the committee's final report and/or program proposal receives an appropriate hearing by the board and is given serious consideration.

While these tasks appear to fall largely in the "initiating and directing" leadership dimension, it is likely that the harder dimension will be that of getting the proposals considered. If the range of opinion on goals and objectives for any given school program is as broad as we suspect it to be, the administrator is going to have a difficult time building a supportable consensus for any program. But if efforts to resolve conflict are not made, it is doubtful that a workable program will result, or that there will be much useful support if it does.

What happens to the pragmatic, balancing leadership role of the administrator when the conflict becomes overly intense and the situation out of hand? Perhaps it is at this point the moment of truth arrives. The counsel of Stephen Bailey may be useful:

The wise administrator when confronted with crisis-type conflict that has gone beyond rational negotiations takes to heart the five-point strategy of Harry S. Truman: first, estimate your own resources; second, estimate your enemy's resources; third, form a judgment as to what is to be done; fourth; implement your judgment with a plan; fifth, persuade your leaders of the value of that plan and mass your forces for the attack. . . . "Forces" may mean sensible students and faculty, a skillful downtown lawyer, cooperative media, a fast-talking chaplain, neighborhood parents or older siblings.[31]

And, as observed in an account of a superintendent who followed this strategy in another issue:

The folklore of the practitioner is heavily oriented toward insulating schools and school men from the taintings of "politics" in the popular sense. These powerful norms of practice mean, among school men, that unless you are willing to risk your position in an all-or-nothing gamble (a gamble that should only be made in a morally correct cause), you should not play politics. A corollary piece of advice states: If you do play politics, don't get caught.[32]

Finally, in depicting the administrator's role in curriculum policy making, we wish to remind the reader that:

· The ultimate source of power in the local community, the board of education, is first solicited and sounded out by the administrator to determine its interest in and willingness to share or delegate some of its power to a planning advisory committee for purposes of developing an educational accountability program.

· The administrator, once the board has indicated to him the latitude of operation permitted, searches out "the relevant community" for the planning task:

The relevant community for formulation and choice of the preference dimension in planning must ultimately be that community which has the *right* to make the political decision. Sometimes a sub-unit or neighborhood may be permitted considerable leeway, within wide boundaries, in recognition of the fact that its residents are affected by the decisions and that the results have few implications for others.[33]

• The relevant community is determined by reviewing the scope of the change proposed. If the tentatively proposed accountability program affects only a given building unit, the parties immediately involved become "the relevant community." If it affects the entire district, the entire district has the right to participate.

• The purpose of the search for a relevant community is to involve it. "Involvement" means to assure formally through solicited participation of the members of the relevant community that the program being instituted is the one desired by it in terms of the program's goals and objectives (and, sometimes, its general design). Involvement implies: searching out the relevant community; communicating to it the nature of the task or problem; soliciting its help; listening to its advice; crystallizing the issues or questions; and—most difficult—forming a consensus. Forming a consensus may mean that:

Control over govermental decisions is shared so that the preferences of no one citizen are weighted more heavily than the preferences of any other one citizen . . . . Governmental decisions should be controlled by the greatest number expressing their preferences in the "last say."[34]

• Involving many parties in building consensus recognizes that: "As an institution resistant to violation of societal norms, the school political system is designed to delay response to new societal demands until need and the demand are unequivocally clear."[35] Accordingly, because of the accelerating rates of change and the resulting shifts in our standards of desirability, more formal, frequent, and extended probing of the public's will is necessary.

• The administrator uses his position and exerts influence to preempt conflict by solving problems before they become burning issues, to develop support for certain changes before they are enacted, and, where possible, to resolve conflict and build consensus. His actions and the programs of the school are expected to reflect the public trust—a trust built and maintained by determining, sometimes following, and sometimes shaping a public's will. Before taking any action, he has an objective in mind and has weighed the possible consequences and alternatives.

• Through community-staff involvement, the burden to initiate change or preserve the status quo is shared. Summerfield concludes:

If interested publics want change, they must be willing and able to properly organize to pursue their goals. They must endure frustrations and be willing to counter competition such as strong support for continuing the status quo.[36]

• In the ideal situation, an educational accountability program for a relevant community expresses the will of that community. This valuing of increased involvement and participation is not isolated. According to a 1969 nationwide survey of thousands of 1950s college graduates and upperclassmen of 1969, the statement, "A new style of politics, involving broader and more active participation at all levels, is emerging," was regarded as generally true by 69 percent of the alumni and 62 percent of the upperclassmen. Even more impressive, 83 percent of the alumni and 80 percent of the upperclassmen perceived this trend to be "generally desirable."[37]

Other Influences on Local Curriculum Policy Making

The business of curriculum policy making is not done in a vacuum, untouched by the rest of the world. A framework of external pressures shapes the process, presents external standards of desirability, and otherwise imposes forms of limitations on local decision-making latitudes.

Without attempting to tease out and assess closely the contribution of each external influence, one should be aware that a host of influences impinge upon and otherwise contribute toward shaping local curriculum policy making. Outside the local district, these influences can be traced to the national and state levels. At the national level, there is the U.S. Office of Education (influenced in turn by Congress, the president, and the Supreme Court). There are also nationally oriented educational (professional, lay, and scholarly) groups, national testing agencies, foundations, prominent persons using the media, nationally organized special interest groups and (perhaps most influential) commercial companies that produce textbooks and instructional materials.

At the state level, the state education department (under the state board of education) looms large as a source of pressure. Because of the prominence of education as a state function, the state's legislative process (e.g., passing more educational legislation, appropriating proportionally larger funds, etc.) is more influential than the less educationally active federal one. State and regional accrediting agencies, a multitude of state and regional educational groups, colleges and universities, and other special interest lobby groups are also in evidence.

Figure 5.1 attempts to provide a rough generalized view of the impact of these groups on daily instruction. The focus on daily instruction rather than on curriculum policy making is deliberate. It is a rather rude reminder as to what parties play major roles in *what actually happens* as opposed to *what should happen* in the school

Figure 5.1. Generalized distribution of influence on daily instruction of the curriculum

Level of influences	Major influences (constant influence)	Moderate influences (periodic influence)	Minor influences (occasional or episodic influence)
National	Textbook and instructional materials producers	HEW-USOE; national professional and scholarly associations; national testing agencies	Federal legislative groups (Congress, president, Supreme Court); foundations; national interest groups (NAACP, CBE, etc.); individual authors, journalists, scholars, etc.)
State	State education departments	State legislative groups (legislative, governor, courts); state and regional education associations; state accrediting associations	Other state lobby groups (taxpayers etc.); state universities and colleges
Local district	Board of education; superintendent; central office staff	Vocal community interest groups; teacher associations/union; local press; building principals	General community; local, state, or national chapters of civil or political groups; local community government
Building unit	Principal; department heads; teachers	Central office staff (or, in small district, superintendent); parent groups; students	Superintendent; board of education; teachers associations; neighborhood groups
Classroom	Teachers; students	Principal; department heads; individual parents	Central office staff

(particularly at the most critical point in the process, the classroom). At the same time, it illustrates the relative position of groups that influence policy making at the district level.

It may be academically interesting to distinguish ways in which these groups affect curriculum policy making (Kirst and Walker offer three: "by establishing minimum standards, by generating curricular alternatives, and by demanding curriculum change"[38]), but here we will merely note that the acceleration of change—if we are correct in our assumption—tends in figure 5.1 to shift both the minor and moderate influentials closer toward the major influentials at the point of curriculum policy making.

Adapting the figures of the Council of Chief School Officers' 1971 "Position Statement," figure 5.2 reflects more or less their generalized view and expectation of educational participation in the matter of policy determination (they also include indications of participation in the areas of decision making, implementation, and evaluation).[39]

Over time, one might expect to see a redistribution of power in educational policy making. Teacher organizations can be expected to pick up power through formal contract negotiation and threats of strike, "job action," etc. Civil rights and other citizens groups will also gain influence, eventually clashing with teachers, boards, and administrators over the issue of pupil control (especially in curriculum matters), while students will acquire some specific rights of their own. These conflicts should escalate political activity to higher levels. According to Iannacone:

Greater political party involvement in educational policy making through legislation will be seen from the U.S. Congress and state legislatures. The traditional educational lobbies will continue to lose influence. The initiative for legislation will, instead, most probably be found lodged in the executive branch of government.[40]

There are already signs that a shift is occurring. Without making an exhaustive attempt to illustrate the point, some examples might be offered both at the national and state level to illustrate the influence on curriculum policy making, both toward increased educational accountability and more extended forms of involvement.

Influences from Washington

Larger issues in Washington, D. C. (civil rights, federal funding, etc.), tend to dominate the visible portion of the national educa-

Figure 5.2. Educational participation in policy determination

Past-present levels

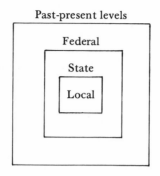

Emerging pattern of levels

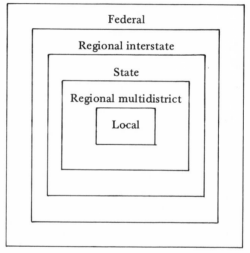

tional scene, but it is the interpretation and funneling of these issues through federal administrative offices that transmits pressures downward to the local districts. A simple example of this influence may be seen in the issue of community involvement in Title I projects. The Bell Memo of October 30, 1970 (mentioned in chapter 1) states clearly that "parental involvement at the local level is important in increasing the effectiveness of programs under Title I."[41] The memo then details (over four single-spaced pages) the specific nature and form of this involvement. Among the conditions for receiving Title I funds are that: (1) a parent council be set up that includes "a majority of parents of children to be served" and "broadly representative of the group to be served"; (2) the local educational agency shall develop and maintain "an affirmative information program for parents" and "provide open access to information" on the program; (3) the parent council shall be involved in the planning, development, and operation of the program; and (4) the parent council has access to other sources (presumably federal and state) to "present its views" and "voice complaints."

This is given further impact both by federal legislation and the activities of personnel in the U.S. Office of Education. A sample of both appears in a speech by Richard Fairley, director of compensatory education—a man who sees accountability as "performance objectives, comparability, and parental involvement":

> We need accountability. . . . We need goals which can be understood easily and appraised accurately by everyone . . . . With this in mind, Congress inserted a provision in the 1970 amendments to Title I, ESEA, requiring performance criteria . . . . Public Law 91-230 actually included mandates for accountability at all levels of school supervision.[42]

Thus, through legislation—its translation into administrative rules and regulations and its propagation by various governmental agencies—influences from Washington flow into the state and local curriculum policy-making process. If the thrust of the local program involves federal funding, the influence from Washington is more than casual where curriculum policy making is concerned.

National Assessment

Another national movement likely to have increasing influence on the state and local curriculum policy-making scene is the National Assessment of Educational Progress (NAEP). It began formally in 1966 under the Education Commission of the States, amid fears of the major professional organizations (not unlike their fears of "merit rating") that the assessment process would lead to state-by-state, district-by-district comparisons, with corresponding competitive pressures on schools to achieve desirable profiles. It was perceived as shaping a "national curriculum" (a negatively viewed American value that may be shifting) with state and local districts developing their curriculums around the NAEP test items, always aware that it is potentially dangerous to have the commonly inflated self-images of state or local communities changed in any direction but up. (If your program should cost more to operate than a nearly identical neighboring state's or community's, imagine the embarrassment if one's neighbor scores higher.[43]) To date these fears have not been realized, largely because NAEP, stung by critics, has moved very cautiously, maintained a low political profile, and done only assessment samplings on attitudes, skills, and knowledge in writing, science, and citizenship at four age levels (nine, thirteen, seventeen, twenty-six—thirty-five). The samplings were taken in 1969 and will not be released until late 1972. Former director Frank Womer maintains:

National assessment can serve and has served as one of the many stimuli in the movement toward educational accountability. It can serve and has served as a model of criterion-referenced assessment. . . . It is beginning to release results that have considerable immediate utility for curriculum evaluation.[44]

A National Professional Group

The Council of Chief State School Officers wields more influence than its small numerical size would indicate by virtue of the power of its membership. The influence of this organization is directed at shaping the standards of desirability for public education. Among its positions are: (1) "public education" should and must be held accountable for its results"; (2) state education departments should lead in the evaluation of all programs involving "student time and public funds"; (3) the process of program assessment should be encouraged and supported at the local, state, and national levels; (4) lay and parental involvement is to be encouraged (although not as prescriptively as the federal government urges), and (5) students should be involved in the "planning, developing, and evaluating of educational programs that directly affect them."[45]

A State-Level Professional Group

These positions—usually taken piecemeal—appear almost simultaneously and are echoed at other levels. On student participation, for example, consider the resolution of the New York State Council of School District Administrators:

Whereas, high school students, because of their learning experiences, are in a unique position to make positive contributions to the improvement of the educational process and

Whereas, the experiences of a number of school districts have indicated that when high school students are given the opportunity to participate in ways to improve the educational process and in determining guidelines for student conduct, the effects have been better learning, better student-teacher, student-administration, and student-board relationships, greater mutual respect, and greater student interest in school, and

Whereas experience has shown that direct student contacts lead to constructive educational improvements and a better relationship, be it

RESOLVED, that the New York State Council of School District Administrators go on record as strongly supportive of participation by high school students in ways to improve the educational process . . . [and that the Council] believes it would prove beneficial to the educational process and to administrator-board-teacher-student relationships for high school boards and administrators to seek out and to encourage regular contacts with high school student representatives.[46]

Whether or not the assumptions behind such resolutions and position statements are actually verified, the net effect of taking these positions by professional and other groups is to forge new standards of desirability for the operation and conduct of the public schools. Enacting these standards into practice at the state level promises to exert powerful influences on local curriculum policy and those participating in its making.

Influences from State Legislatures and Departments of Education

Currently movements toward educational accountability via establishment of measurable goals and objectives at the state level are apparent in several states—for example, California, Colorado, Florida, Georgia, Michigan, Nevada, New Jersey, Texas, Utah, Virginia, Wisconsin. The resolution on page 150 is a dramatic illustration of California's efforts to increase community-staff involvement in the curriculum policy-making process.

The first state to move forward formally was Pennsylvania. The 1963 General Assembly of Pennsylvania passed Act 299, containing a mandate for commonwealth educational performance standards.[47] Subsequently, Educational Testing Services of Princeton, New Jersey, was hired to help develop a plan for implementing the legislation.

Educational Testing Service returned its recommendation, "Ten Goals of Quality Education for Pennsylvania."[48] No attempt was made to involve people extensively in drafting these goals (an advisory committee of thirty public and teaching representatives was used), which were adopted by the State Board of Education in 1965, but work to develop the plan was delayed until 1968 when a Title III ESEA grant was obtained. The development of measuring tools, field testing, and sampling procedures in six counties and two cities yielded, in June 1971, a series of twenty-three booklets describing the manner of assessing the performance objectives that add meaning to Pennsylvania's "Ten Goals of Quality Education": (1) self-understanding; (2) understanding others; (3) basic skills; (4) interest in school and learning; (5) good citizenship; (6) good health habits; (7) creativity; (8) vocational development; (9) understanding human

---

Joint Committee on Educational Goals and Evaluation,
California Legislature—Resolution ACR 127 (November 1971)

WHEREAS, The Legislature declared its intent through the passage of the George Miller, Jr., Education Act of 1968 to provide for the development, conduct, and enforcement of educational programs in the elementary and secondary schools; and

WHEREAS, The intent was further declared to set broad minimum standards and guidelines for educational programs, and to encourage local districts to develop programs that will best fit the needs and interests of the pupils; and

WHEREAS, The Joint Committee on Educational Goals and Evaluation is directed to fulfill this intent by encouraging public involvement in determining the philosophy, goals, program objectives, and priorities of educational programs in local communities and for the state system of instruction; now, therefore, be it

RESOLVED BY THE ASSEMBLY OF THE STATE OF CALIFORNIA, the Senate thereof concurring, That it is the intent and purpose of the Legislature that teachers, students, administrators, parents and other community members be given the opportunity to meet together for the purpose of developing educational goals relevant to the instructional program of the schools in their district. The Legislature encourages school districts to recognize the need to meet with students, parents and other community members in order that all people served by the schools can have a voice in determining the philosophy, goals, program objectives, and priorities for their schools; and be it further

RESOLVED, That the governing board of any school district is encouraged to grant certificated employees and students of the district time away from the regularly constituted schoolday in order to meet with school administrators, parents, and other community members for the purpose of developing educational programs relevant to the needs of the community served by the schools of the district; and be it further

RESOLVED, That the governing board of any school district is encouraged to keep and maintain current records, which should be open to inspection of the public, showing the number of certificated employees and student hours involved in such meetings and the specific objectives and results of the meetings; and be it further

RESOLVED, That the Chief Clerk of the Assembly transmit a copy of this resolution to the Superintendent of Public Instruction.

accomplishments; and (10) preparation for a world of change.[49] It is an ambitious undertaking and probably will not yield clear data until 1973—a full decade after the passage of the authorizing legislation.

To illustrate the scope of Pennsylvania's efforts, figure 5.3 attempts to provide a random sample breakdown of "creativity," one of the ten goals; it depicts how such goals are elaborated and specified in terms of both effective and ineffective student behaviors in their attainment. Figure 5.5 extends the "creativity" sample to suggestions, offered as "teacher strategies," believed to help foster creativity in some learners. Figure 5.4 gives a glimpse of how "creativity" might be established as a local goal priority through "needs assessment," expressed as a review made by parents, students, teachers, and administrators (or any combination of these parties), who would identify what, in their opinion, are the most important things either the school or the individual student should be accomplishing. In turn, an individual assessment of progress toward certain identified objectives can be maintained by a self-assessing learner with a reviewing teacher to verify attainment. Various standardized tests are employed where appropriate as external benchmarks of progress.

Involvement and the Local Curriculum Policy-Making Process

What are the likely results of such influences on local curriculum policy making as it involves various groups in identifying measurable goals and objectives for developing educational accountability programs?

In *The Social Contract* Rousseau observed that since no man has a natural authority over his fellow, and force creates no right, we must conclude that conventions form the basis of all legitimate authority among men. The task is usually to develop a suitable convention for a "joint-fortune situation," in which the separate parties (individuals, groups, organizations, etc.) are all affected by the actions of others (some parties, as in the case of national and state influences, are outside the situation) and, because they cannot ignore each other, must either compete or cooperate to forward their separate ends. If competitiveness is the dominant characteristic of the situation, conflict can be expected as each party maneuvers for maximum advantage. If cooperation dominates, consultation seeking mutual advantage through the exchange of views and information will emerge as the parties attempt to maximize their joint gains while sublimating individual differences or losses. Normally, joint-fortune situations produce both competitive and cooperative elements.

Figure 5.3. Sample breakdown of a section of one of

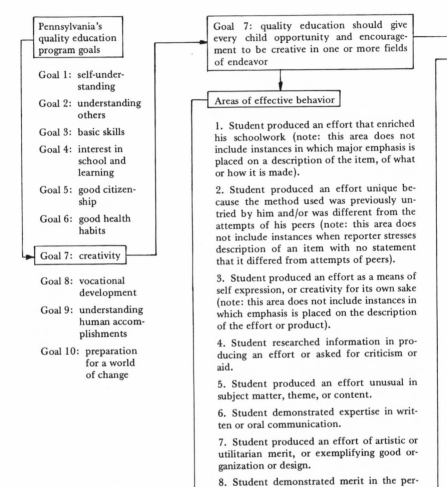

Pennsylvania's quality education program goals

Goal 1: self-understanding

Goal 2: understanding others

Goal 3: basic skills

Goal 4: interest in school and learning

Goal 5: good citizenship

Goal 6: good health habits

Goal 7: creativity

Goal 8: vocational development

Goal 9: understanding human accomplishments

Goal 10: preparation for a world of change

Goal 7: quality education should give every child opportunity and encouragement to be creative in one or more fields of endeavor

Areas of effective behavior

1. Student produced an effort that enriched his schoolwork (note: this area does not include instances in which major emphasis is placed on a description of the item, of what or how it is made).

2. Student produced an effort unique because the method used was previously untried by him and/or was different from the attempts of his peers (note: this area does not include instances when reporter stresses description of an item with no statement that it differed from attempts of peers).

3. Student produced an effort as a means of self expression, or creativity for its own sake (note: this area does not include instances in which emphasis is placed on the description of the effort or product).

4. Student researched information in producing an effort or asked for criticism or aid.

5. Student produced an effort unusual in subject matter, theme, or content.

6. Student demonstrated expertise in written or oral communication.

7. Student produced an effort of artistic or utilitarian merit, or exemplifying good organization or design.

8. Student demonstrated merit in the performing arts or in a physical activity.

9. Student demonstrated merit in problem-solving ability.

10. Student demonstrated adeptness in social interaction situations.

Pennsylvania's "quality education" goals: goal specification

Areas of ineffective behavior

Category of effective behavior in problem solving

9.1. Student originated a game.

9.2. Student, confronted with a lack of equipment or other resources, thought of and utilized adequate substitute equipment, or restructured the situation to fit available equipment.

9.3. Student suggested or utilized an operational procedure suited to a task or better suited than any previous one, or that adequately structured a previously unattempted task.

    a. Student rethought a procedure, came up with a new, more workable idea.

    b. Student assembled an object without directions.

9.4. Student originated a different (though not necessarily more effective) way of doing a job, solving a problem, etc.; student originated a different way to do a mathematical operation.

9.5. Student experimented with or tested an idea.

    a. Student experimented in that he tried to determine if a given process would work with different materials or in a different setting.

    b. Student designed an experiment that would test a scientific principle.

    c. Student originated a way to test social awareness of his fellow students.

    d. Student worked mathematical puzzles.

9.6. Student demonstrated ingenuity by originating an activity that benefited others or himself.

3. Student demonstrated he did not value creativity or self-expression.

6. Student demonstrated lack of expertise in written or oral communication.

7. Student produced an effort lacking artistic or utilitarian merit (including poor method of presentation).

8. Student demonstrated lack of merit in the performing arts or in a physical activity.

9. Student demonstrated lack of merit in problem-solving ability.

Category of ineffective behavior in problem solving

9.2. Student, confronted with a lack of equipment, stopped working.

9.3. Student did nothing or used a relatively poor operational procedure rather than developing or adopting a better procedure.

9.4. Student was unable to originate a different (not necessarily more effective) way to do something.

9.6. Student failed to discover similarities or relationships in given ideas or failed to make comparisons; participating in a sport, student demonstrated lack of foresight by inappropriate actions or by not doing what was indicated.

Figure 5.4. Sample breakdown of a section of one of

	1	2	3	4	5
Goal 7: quality education should give every child opportunity and encouragement to be creative in one or more fields of endeavor	Least important	Marginal importance	Average importance	Important	Most important

General needs assessment: creativity (derived by parents, teachers, and students)

Areas 1, 2, 3: produces things that are unique
Draws something, makes a model or chart, etc., to go with a class report or project; makes or tries something he has not tried before; goes beyond a class demonstration or lesson; prepares food, sews something or writes a creative poem, story, or essay.
        1   2   3   4   5

Area 4: researches information
Researches material to write a report that is not assigned; to prepare for a job, or to give a report a different or unusual treatment
        1   2   3   4   5

Area 5: uses unusual treatment of schoolwork
Draws an original picture or makes an original project or invention; presents ideas in a new way; draws sketch or pictures that express a poem or story.
        1   2   3   4   5

Area 6: uses unusual written or oral communication
Can reason through use of words; writes unusual phrases, headings; gives a report in an unusual way; can report easily and convincingly.
        1   2   3   4   5

Area 7: produces unusual artistic design or organization
Makes original art design; designs a costume for a particular use; makes an effective arrangement of materials; shows unusual talents.
        1   2   3   4   5

Area 8: shows unusual talent in performing arts or physical activity
Prepares, presents, or directs a show, skit, etc.; writes a song or music, composes a ballet; develops a dance; does an athletic stunt learned on his own.
        1   2   3   4   5

Area 9: shows problem-solving ability
Puts an object together without directions; does mathematical puzzles; makes up a game; suggests a better way to do something; designs an experiment for science.
        1   2   3   4   5

Pennsylvania's "quality education" goals: needs assessment

Area 9: shows problem-solving ability: individual needs assessment instrument (student checks self, compares with teacher)	1 Never	2 Seldom	3 Usually	4 Often	5 Always
9.1. Makes up a game.	1	2	3	4	5
9.2. Substitutes equipment and materials that are lacking to accomplish a task.	1	2	3	4	5
9.3. Suggests or uses a way of doing a task better than the way it was done before.	1	2	3	4	5
9.4. Makes up a different way of doing a job or solving a problem.	1	2	3	4	5
9.5. Experiments with or tests an idea.	1	2	3	4	5
9.6. Shows originality through an idea for an activity that benefits others or himself.	1	2	3	4	5

Standardized test instruments for Goal 7 (creativity): measure and/or identify such factors as logical thinking, divergent thinking, ideational fluency, expressional fluency, optimistic imagination, style preferences, generalizing, analyzing, synthesizing, and evaluating.

P. R. Christensen, "Consequences" (Sherill Supply Co., 1962).

Industrial Relations Center, "AC Test of Creative Ability," Form B (University of Chicago, 1960).

"Ship Destination Test," Form A (Sheridan Psychological Services, 1956).

Christensen and Guilford, "Christensen-Guilford Fluency Test."

"Torrence Tests for Creative Thinking" (Princeton, N.J.: Personnel Press, 1966).

W. H. Winker, "Creative Ability Inventory" (Detroit, Mich.: Winker Publications, 1961).

Elinor Hatch, "A Test of Creative Writing Aptitude and Ability" (Eugene, Ore.: University of Oregon, 1942).

M. T. Macy, "Test of Critical Thinking" (Eugene, Ore.: University of Oregon, 1951).

David Miles, "Creativity Problem Test" (Carbondale, Ill.: Southern Illinois University, 1968).

Pamela Pearson, "Novelty Experiencing Scale" (Chicago: University of Illinois Medical Center, 1960).

Figure 5.5. Sample breakdown of a section of one of Pennsylvania's
"quality education" goals: teacher strategies

Goal 7: quality education should give every child opportunity and encouragement to be creative in one or more fields of endeavor.

↓

General teacher strategies

1. Teacher encouraged originality, verbally or through an assignment or discussion.

2. Teacher developed or attempted to develop the students' creative interests.

3. Teacher was flexible in relating to students.

4. Teacher gave students instructions in creative matters or encouraged them to do something.

5. Teacher allowed or encouraged a student with talent or creative interest to make use of his creative skills.

6. Teacher aided a bored, disinterested, or unenthusiastic student by using or encouraging the use of creative efforts or self-responsibility.

7. Teacher worked at increasing a student's self-image.

7. Teacher worked at increasing a student's self-image.

7.1. Teacher provided encouragement or showed interest in endeavors of a student who lacked confidence in a skill or creative ability.

7.2. Teacher provided guidance, directions, pointers, hints, etc., for a student who lacked confidence in a skill or creative ability, or talked with him about his interests, hobbies, etc., in order to help him get started.

7.3. Teacher gave a student who was shy or lacked confidence the opportunity to gain confidence through a creative medium.

7.3. Teacher gave verbal assurances or assistance to a student who stated a lack of confidence, or arranged for a favorable comparison of his ideas to those of other students, or challenged him to perform.

7.5. Teacher informed another teacher or student's parents of the student's talent, skill, progress, etc.

If local curriculum policy making is a joint-fortune situation, what conventions might be used to produce an agreement on an educational program's goals and objectives as well as its design? How are we going to achieve a policy decision?

In the search for "civilized" conventions that permit decisions to be made with minimal conflict, the most popular is consensus seeking, i.e., the search for a shared collective will or opinion. Consensus implies that the opinions of persons are examined not only in terms of the number of persons holding them but also in terms of the intensity with which they are held. Frequently in a small group situation (typically a committee) members are informally polled immediately, not as a voting matter but to bring into the open various points of view and to measure their intensity. As a part of the group dynamics process, they either move away from that point or attempt (through extended discussion, more "analysis" and "facts," plus other subtle means) to bring about some reconciliation of views by persuading dissenting parties to abandon their position or by producing an alternative position likely to carry mutual support. Harold Leavitt refers to this approach to decision making as a "lots of talk" approach where an issue is "kicked around, talked about, written about in a great many quarters over an extended period of time" and finally it is apparent that a decision has emerged although "nobody can ever put his finger on the individual or body who made the decision, or the precise alternatives that were considered."[50]

This form of consensus seeking in joint-venture situations frequently finds expression in what Lindblom and Braybrooke describe as "disjointed incrementalism." Under this process, change from existing conditions is made only incrementally or marginally (like the annual budget increase in most schools).[51] The policy makers focus their attention primarily on the better-known areas of existing situations with the intention of changing gradually rather than by a sharp break with past understandings, policies, or practices. Accordingly, the number of possible alternatives—especially radical ones—are sharply reduced, and the goals and objectives of the policy limited (both in number and complexity) to the more familiar (as expressed in the comments of persons inquiring "where they are doing" this or that before being willing to consider seriously a more extreme policy). The risk with incrementalism is that under ordinary circumstances it may neither keep pace with the tempo of change nor permit the degree of change necessary to meet new conditions, or fully explore anything but conventional approaches.

Whether disjointed incrementalism in consensus seeking is

carried out through negotiation meetings (final decisions are reached only by unanimous consent), committee meetings (final decisions are reached by majority consent), or command meetings (a specific body, e.g., the board of education, is empowered to make the final decision after receiving the advice and recommendations of others), the aim is the same: to reduce outright conflict through milder forms of competition within some agreed-upon system of constraints.

But something more than merely the making of decisions is desired. We are looking for an *informed* decision—not merely a decision resulting from the simple compromise of committee references. As John Stuart Mill warned, there is

danger of a low grade intelligence in the representative body, and in the popular opinion which controls it; and danger of class legislation on the part of the numerical majority, these being all composed of the same class.[52]

Further, we hope that it will be an *educationally* informed decision.

Recognizing that we are dealing with a rather murky process, what conventions can we employ to increase the informed nature of our policy-making process while also decreasing conflict? There is a good deal of sophisticated information and speculation on this question from the fields of political science and social psychology; exploration of it, however, would move this discussion away from our more immediate concerns. Accordingly, when the time comes to put the Advisory Planning Committee into action, what are some simple, sometimes overlooked, forethoughts that might be considered?[53] At the most elemental level (frequently bungled through oversight), there is a range of consideration from simple thoughtfulness to more complex foresight:

1. Meeting essentials for the advisory committee:

• Convenience to participants (have you considered the problem of distance? access? parking? space requirements? storage facilities? using multimedia presentations? providing baby-sitters and/or transportation? etc.).

• Settings for meetings (has consideration been given to the political appropriateness of the meeting site? comfortable seating and work space? working methods? noise and aesthetics? smoking and refreshments? etc.).

• Time schedules (what thought has been given to time of day? frequency of meetings? calendars of events with activity deadlines? advance notice reminders of upcoming meetings? As a rule of thumb, the participants should work out their schedule after the first organizational and task overview meeting. Probably the meetings should not exceed two and one-half hours with more than forty-five minutes for large group presentations).

2. Ways of structuring the advisory planning committee—do you plan (and know how) to use:

• Large group meetings of twelve or more participants (with perhaps these functions contemplated: committee organization and task charge review; reporting information; summarizing results; sounding for consensus; etc.).

• Small group meetings of three to twelve participants (for exchanging ideas and concerns, sharing information, assessing needs, searching for supportable consensus, etc.).

• Subcommittee(s) of three to twenty-five participants (for planning, doing research and investigations, carrying out assignments and charges of the central advisory committee, etc.).

• Three-member "triads" (for training in techniques for listening, observing, and reporting).

3. Working toward effective communication procedures—have you thought about: establishing ground rules, allowing leadership to emerge from the group, getting a mix of ideas and views, providing feedback mechanisms and access to necessary information, etc.?

4. The use of techniques to increase consensus making—do you plan on using (and how):

• Research solicitations of the larger community, staff, and student populations (through opinion questionnaires, surveys, interviews, etc.).[54]

• Public hearings and school-community forums.

• Delphi forecasting and methods of ranking.

• Charrette process.

• Filing minority reports.

• Feasibility studies.

A considerable number of techniques have grown around ways of increasing the rational quality, range, and scope of decision making. A working paper from the California Elementary School Administrators Association lists forty-five "planning techniques" (see figure 5.6).[55] Among the most interesting to us, however, is the Delphi Technique.

The Delphi Technique was originally and still is used as an intuitive technique for organizing the speculations of experts on the future. In part developed to estimate the chronology of scientific and technological breakthroughs, it was used as a device to keep individual judgments from being warped in the interplay of group dynamics when heatedly expressed positions (once openly stated)

Figure 5.6. Planning techniques—listed competencies suggested for
program planning (working paper, California Elementary School
Administrators Association, 1969)

Phase 1. Initating a planning program

1. Performance objective setting
2. Task force selection/role definition
3. Consensus decision making
4. Graphic modeling
5. Internal resource definition/audit
6. Information need specification
7. Estimating and costing
8. System/function/task analysis
9. Formative evaluation design
10. Event network design
11. In-service training requirement identification

Phase 2. Operating a planning program

12. Negotiating
13. Priority setting
14. Needs assessment (curricular/instructional
15. Performance objective modification
16. Task force management
17. Feasibility analysis
18. Resource allocation
19. Forecasting
20. Information need analysis
21. Fault free analysis
22. Critical path analysis
23. Brainstorming/heuristics/imagineering
24. Optimal tryout environment selection
25. Backup/contingency planning
26. Management by exception
27. Resource reallocation/slippage
28. PPB system design
29. Communication network design
30. In-service training program management
31. Master planning
32. Data base design

Phase 3. Advanced operations

33. Performance objectives integration
34. Extrapolation/prediction/advanced forecasting
35. PPBAR system reallocations
36. Simulation and gaming/system exercising
37. Sociotechnical system analysis/development
38. Quality control management
39. Management information system design
40. Summative analysis
41. Opposition reduction management
42. Permanent Hawthorne effect design
43. Ensharette management
44. Self-renewing system design
45. Planner exchange scheduling

become difficult to abandon and high status persons are more likely to have their statements unduly inflated. Thus, along with scenario writing, future history analysis, and cross-impact matrices, Delphi is a future-oriented method of pooling opinions, hunches, and subjective judgments by orderly design.

In one of its intial uses, a panel of experts was asked to estimate individually and anonymously what year a machine with a thinking IQ potential above 150 would be developed. The intial written responses ran from 1975 to 2100. A second questionnaire was then given containing a summary of the first questionnaire responses expressed as the median estimate and the accompanying interquartile range (that is, the middle 50 percent of the answers, with the highest or the lowest 25 percent of the estimates dropped). Each panel member was then requested to reconsider his first answer, revising it if he desired. If the second response was outside the interquartile range of consensus, the individual was asked to write on the questionnaire his reasons for moving outside the judgment of the majority. This procedure was followed through two more rounds, each round coming closer to a workable group consensus. Notes Helmer: "Placing the onus of justifying relatively extreme responses on the respondents had the effect of causing those without strong convictions to move their estimates closer to the median, while those who felt they had a good argument for a 'deviationist' opinion tended to retain their original estimate and defend it."[56]

As interesting as future forecasting might be, Delphi has other uses too. It can be used as a tool for analysis of assumptions, values, goals, and priorities. For example, Cyphert and Gant used the technique to establish goals for the School of Education at the University of Virginia. A large group of persons was involved, ranging from the school's faculty members and selected students to other university people, key persons (educators, politicians, and civic leaders) in the state, and others. Suggestions and, later, opinions were solicited on identified tasks for the School of Education from the targeted group of 421 persons. Through these solicitation mailings, they were asked to offer suggestions on the prime targets on which the school should focus its efforts over the coming decade. Then items were identified and the shaping of opinion into a viable consensus began. Cyphert's and Gant's use of the Delphi Technique, however, differed in several ways from the original aim and procedure of the method. They used over 400 persons (the normal method seldom exceeded fifty participants); their participants were a mixture of professionals and laymen (the original method relied exclusively on "expert" professional opinion); and—most dramatically for our purposes—their focus was on *what should happen* as goals for the school rather than on *what will happen* as future events likely to befall the school of education. To establish consensus, they also preferred to use the mode of distribution rather than the ever-narrowing interquartile range.

How happy were they with the results?

The data generated by this study are quite usable for assisting in formulating the future targets of the School . . . . They also have face validity; yet, they differ significantly from the emphases postulated prior to the study. Under similar circumstances, the experiment would be repeated. In addition to the satisfaction of planning one's future with the assistance of data . . . the survey made influential persons in the Commonwealth aware of the School's existence and awakened them to a realization of its future accomplishments.[57]

A planning technique that tends to operate on the opposite premise is the Charrette, a French term derived from a little cart, or *charrette,* used to carry student architectural exhibits to the academy for display while the students made frantic, last-minute finishes on the project. The term came to connote among architects intensive "cramming" to solve problems. Where the Delphi Technique attempts to minimize heated conflict by rationalizing the process through analysis, the Charrette meets conflict head-on by design in an intensive confrontation setting. Used in ghetto districts of Baltimore, New Jersey, and San Francisco to involve the neighborhood community in educational facility planning, groups of architects, administrators, students, teachers, politicians, public officials, and various residents of the neighborhood met for extended, concentrated periods of time to develop consensus solutions to planning problems. Inevitably, conflict of interests emerge.

The basic rationale of the Charrette is that conflict can be created *and* constructively channeled. This constructive shaping is supposed to occur by reducing the social distance between the Establishment (authority) and the other participants. By creating a situation in which the key decision makers of the Establishment, neighborhood representatives, and others meet face to face in the belief that the organization (i.e., the proposed school or other potentially community-supported organization) cannot isolate itself and must find support for its operation in the neighborhood, much faith is placed in the open forum manner of resolving conflict. When a spirit of cooperation emerges from the Charrette (a spirit somewhat similar to successful around-the-clock negotiating sessions when key issues are resolved), decisions can be made rapidly and the basis of involvement judged fruitful—as happened in Baltimore and New Jersey.

If, however, conflict continues as groups continue to operate as factions rather than problem solvers, sets of demands usually arise. In turn, these demands tend to escalate until they run into a set of counter demands that have some clout and must be negotiated. Success for a faction is not likely to bring satisfaction but is likely to bring more demands. Until trade-offs can be made—gaining something in return for giving something—the situation may not stabilize. The pressure for *some decision* is expected to help. We are not enamored with the Charrette concept as a means of curriculum policy making, but offer it for its stark contrast with the Delphi Technique in community-staff involvement. Figure 5.7 portrays a typical Charrette schedule.[58]

A more familiar approach in gaining a perspective on the will of the community and forming a consensus among its members is the technique of polling. In Oakland County, Michigan, it is possible for schools to get information through the use of an "inforet" system— an "information return" polling procedure that gathers, computer analyzes, and reports information in a month's time. By using consultant expertise, volunteers (housewives, senior citizens, etc.), random sampling techniques on the target populations (e.g., the general community, subgroups within the community, teachers, and students), and a computer to sort out information, Waterford has been able to keep the costs of the inforet program fairly low—about $250 per polling. The volunteers (twenty to thirty of them) are trained in telephone as well as face-to-face group and individual interview techniques. When possible they use the telephone (questionnaire mailings are seldom used because of limited response). On the normal single-issue poll, little more than fifteen hours of work are required "by a single interviewer to produce 95 percent reliability."[59]

What information have the decision makers received? Over half the students believed that school rules were being inequitably enforced to the disadvantage of their own racial group (black or white); more than half the parents believed that the time being spent on various subjects is about right; and, given "the sky is the limit," 248 of 251 teachers favored better instructional materials, facilities, and more training first (the other three thought of their salaries first).

As a feedback system for members of a planning committee searching for agreement, techniques like inforet, properly done, appear to be useful tools in drawing together an impression of the community's standards of desirability as well as identifying areas of difficulty and priorities. And as the forty-five items listed in figure 5.6 suggest, there is no lack of approaches to the tasks.

But there are two more points to be touched upon in the

Figure 5.7. Educational facilities Charrette schedule

Time	Friday	Saturday	Sunday	Monday	Tuesday	Wednesday	Thursday	Friday	Saturday	Sunday
8:00 a.m.		General session	General session							
9:00					Small work groups: proposal development	Small work groups: proposal development	Small work groups: proposal development		General session	Section meetings
10:00		Section and small group meetings:	Section and small group meetings:						Section and group reaction to panel comments	
11:00									First round of decision-making and commitment by institutional representatives	Second round reactions to panels' comments
12:00 noon				General session				General session		Final decision making
1:00 p.m.		"generating ideas"	"generating ideas"							
2:00								Reaction by ethnic panels		
3:00										Prepare for open house
4:00				Small work groups: proposal development				Reaction by community panels		
5:00									General session	Open house for community
6:00	Registration and social hour							Reaction by decision-making bodies		
7:00	Dinner and orientation				General session	General session	Set up display of proposals			Charrette closes
8:00										
9:00					Community caucuses	Community caucuses				
10:00										
11:00										

joint-venture involvement process: (1) the definition of tasks and roles played in the process; and (2) the end result of the advisory planning committee's efforts, a board-approved accountability policy.

Noting that role and task assignments may be handled in a multiple of ways and combinations (see figures 2.3 and 2.4, for example), figure 5.8 presents a generalized manner of assigning responsibilities.[60] It is intended to be suggestive rather than prescriptive, and was constructed with the idea that it can be altered as the situation dictates. The creation of an advisory planning committee at the building unit level, for example, would place the unit principal in the role position of the superintendent, moving the role of the superintendent closer to the board's role.

As presented in figure 5.8, no attempt is made to spell out the membership of each group of participants in detail (in some cases there is no need). However, one might expect to find the superintendent (or assistant superintendent for instruction), a couple of board members, some representative principals, teachers, students and community groups serving on the advisory planning committee. These representatives might be selected by inviting each group (principals, the teachers association, the student council, the civic associations in the community, and perhaps some local officials likely to review the school budget) to select a given number of representatives for committee service. Where known segments of the community are not likely to be represented in any civic or other kind of organization, direct contact with their informal leaders is used to solicit names and, ultimately, representative persons.

As the advisory planning committee takes form, one of the most delicate balancing acts of leadership by the administrator is the task of helping the committee pace itself toward reaching the educationally informed level of decision making desired. He has an obligation to see that the committee is organized and functioning well enough to maintain a forward thrust of its own while making certain that, as so often happens, the committee neither wallows in apathy or overcomplexity nor moves too rapidly to make simplistic decisions.

Because it is probable that the advisory planning committee will have between twenty-five and fifty persons on it (sometimes these committees have several hundred members), it may be necessary to structure this deliberative body into reporting subcommittees to accomplish many of the tasks. The use of a "professional support staff" is suggested for handling the technical aspects of the planning

Figure 5.8. Responsibility matrix for community-staff involvement
in curriculum policy making and program design

Roles played by participants

Steps in the process	Board of education	Superintendent	Advisory planning committee	Professional support staff	Professional staff	Community	Students
Initiates community-staff involvement through advisory planning com.	m	t_{1-2}			i	i	i
Stipulates responsibility of the advisory planning committee	m	t_{1-2}					
Establishes a working advisory planning committee	r, p_2	t_1	m, p_1		c, p_2	c, p_2	c, p_2
Creates a professional support staff team		t_2	m		i	i	i
Identifies educational needs and change strategies	i	i	m	i	i	i	i
Identifies goals for task by approximate consensus	p_2	p_2	m, p_1	t_1	i, p_2	i, p_2	i, p_2
Develops general objectives			m	t_1			
Relates selected goals and objectives to specific needs for program design		c, t_2	m	t_1			
Charges professional support staff to design alternative program plans	p_2	c	m, p_2	t_{1-2}	p_2	p_2	p_2
Translates goals and objectives into performance objectives			m	t_{1-2}			
Designs alternative program plans for consideration			p_2	m, p_1			
Projects resource allocations to performance objectives (PPBS format)			p_2	m, p_1			
Selects optimum plan design	p_2	c	m, p_1	t_{1-2}	p_2	p_2	p_2
Organizes selected plan for implementation and operation			m	t_{1-2}			
Designs a plan of evaluation for selected program design			m	t_{1-2}			
Considers educational program auditor for independent evaluation			m	t_{1-2}			
Reports planning recommendations to the board	r, p_2	c, t_2	m, p_1	t_1	p_2	p_2	p_2
Board decides action on planning recommendations	m, p_1	c, t_{1-2}	c, p_2		c, p_2	c, p_2	c, p_2
If favorably disposed, board passes a policy resolution	m, p_1	t_{1-2}	p_2		p_2	p_2	p_2

t_1: Initiates action on tasks through recommendation
t_2: Studies and interacts with recommendation (or decision) received, may wish to modify and get reconsideration
m: Major decision maker
r: Technical responsibility, should be kept informed of progress
c: To be consulted (via meetings, pollings, questionnaires, forums, etc.) for indications of approval and support
i: Information source
p_1: Responsible for posting a progress report of events to this point
p_2: To receive progress report

process. This team is likely to be small (five to seven members) and to use consultant help,[61] a central office administrator, a principal, and a few teachers. Optionally, some might like to add a couple of students and parents to it.

Naturally, all these roles may be done somewhat differently. Before we discuss the board's policy, two further examples might illustrate this point. An almost parallel set of guidelines influencing roles for involvement is suggested in "Principles of School-Community Planning and Action" by the Joint Committee on Educational Goals and Evaluation of the California State Legislature (see box below). This illustration represents the Joint Committee's idealized view of what should occur (it also serves as another example of state influence on local operation).

The second example is currently in motion at the local level. An interesting but different sort of community-staff involvement in curriculum policy making is utilized by George Caldwell, superintendent of the San Bernardino (California) Unified School District. In what he describes as an "educational management system," Caldwell approaches involvement simultaneously at all levels. He has students, teachers, and administrators all developing objectives (i.e., 95 percent of the elementary teachers, 50 percent of the high school teachers, and 100 percent of the administrative staff voluntarily participate). A teacher, for example, will develop his work plan, state objectives according to an accepted format, construct some monitoring plan, and schedule a performance interview with the principal (along the lines of the management-by-objective technique[62]). In turn, the student works out his own learning objectives with his teacher and takes them home to his parents—to get the parents involved and committed to the child's education.

While the central district office and the individual schools, teachers, and students concern themselves with objectives, Caldwell has the board and the community working on the overall direction of the district: the goals. The board, after several sessions of debate, develops a set of interim goals and circulates them, getting people to react and getting a focus on the task. Meeting with businessmen, PTA groups, different groups in the community, teachers and others, the board receives direct feedback from its constituents and clients.

Some of the more interesting feedback has to do with the community's acceptance of criterion objectives (e.g., 60 percent, 75 percent, 90 percent etc., of the students will achieve these tasks). Caldwell contends that many groups, particularly minority groups, will probably resent an objective stating anything less than 100

Principles of school-community planning and action*

    1. The board of education and superintendent of schools should jointly propose and initiate the goal-setting process as a response to felt needs within the community.

    2. Every community member should be invited to participate in the goal-setting process.

    3. The search for goals and objectives relevant for education in the 1970s should be the start of an on-going effort to involve the community in school policy development.

    4. The goal-setting process should be kept open to all points of view without domination or intimidation by any special interest group.

    5. The purpose of bringing people together is not to dwell on past deficiencies, or lay blame, but to evolve a philosophy, identify needs. determine goals and program objectives, and establish priorities.

    6. Participants should not expect to have everything their way; they should come seeking a better understanding of the community, its people and problems.

    7. A spirit of cooperation and trust should be established among individuals and groups involved in the process.

    8. Roles of leadership in school-community planning should be earned on the basis of consensus rather than on authority.

    9. Individuals and groups who are instrumental to the goal-setting process should provide for the open flow of information.

    10. The individual school should be the base of operation for bringing people together.

    11. In the process of determining goals and objectives, opinion must be balanced with fact.

    12. The interaction process must begin with concerns which have high priority for the people involved.

    13. The school board should commit the resources necessary to see the goal-setting process through to a satisfying conclusion: board members should be encouraged to participate in the interaction process, not as board members, but as private citizens.

    14. Teachers and administrators should honor their responsibility to the community by taking an active part in the goal-setting process.

    15. A variety of meetings should be held as part of the goal-setting process: mixed groups assist consensus building.

    16. Inasmuch as the learning process is recognized as being dynamic and individualistic, any objectives of education that are established should not be so specific or restrictive as to pre-program the learning process for any student.

    17. To ensure that the goals and objectives of public education continue to be relevant, a recycling process should be designed.

    18. The goal-setting and planning process should result in observable action.

*Joint Committee on Educational Goals and Evaluation, *Education For the People* 1, section 3 (Sacramento, Calif.: California State Legislature, 1971).

percent of the students reaching a specified level of attainment—even though it is acknowledged that not all students are likely to reach that objective. Thus, making the districtwide objectives more "saleable," Caldwell comments:

Then, on a school-by-school basis, we are going to be talking about certain numbers of students achieving at certain levels and we are going to try and communicate this on the basis that there will be continued improvement in those areas that have priority.[63]

Under the umbrella of community-school board goals and districtwide objectives (with each level reconciling within its own framework the efforts of the level immediately below), a strong effort is now being made to "decentralize" individual schools by having each form its own parent advisory group, along the lines of a limited mini-board—an intensified level of community-staff involvement.

Adopting an Educationally Accountable Program Policy

In the case we have proposed, there is—finally—the matter of adopting a school board policy: an educationally accountable policy that reflects the consensus of the community and staff. Appendix A is a sample of this sort of policy. Its anatomy is fairly simple; it opens with a stated recognized need, offers a policy (with a rationale, goals, and objectives), indicates the procedures used in implementing the policy (in this case, presumed attached as a plan design from the advisory planning committee), states how the account shall be rendered, and (as an option) suggests some predetermined conditions to be accorded by results.[64]

In the last analysis, it is the board's obligation, as an agent of the state, to decide on local curriculum policy making. Our effort has been aimed at providing this board with direction and purpose as the goals, objectives, and priorities of many persons are reconciled and find expression in a policy for an educationally accountable program. If it is a good policy, it should help the board keep the public informed in a manageable way, as well as give promise to resolving an educational need.

To John Stuart Mill's observation that responsibility is null when nobody knows who is responsible, we might add that accountability is void when the expectations are undefined. Hopefully, this chapter has shed some light on the manner of bringing answerable definition to work roles through the involvement of people in the curriculum policy making process.

Notes for Chapter 5

1. These questions were suggested by Paul Woodring in *A Fourth of a Nation* (New York: McGraw-Hill, 1957). These same questions continue to be raised anew. The journal of the Association for Supervision and Curriculum Development, *Educational Leadership* (May 1972), contains a special feature, "Community Involvement in Curriculum." For different perspectives, see William Alexander, "Community Involvement in Curriculum: Editorial," p. 655; Norman Hamilton, "The Decision-Making Structure of a School System," p. 668; Rhody McCoy, "Ingredients of Leadership," p. 672; Mario Fantini, "Community Participation: Many Faces, Many Directions," p. 674; Preston Wilcox, "Changing Conceptions of Community," p. 681.

2. D. Lerner and H. D. Lasswell, eds., *The Policy Sciences: Recent Developments in Scope and Method* (Stanford, Calif.: Stanford University Press, 1951), p. 12.

3. Robin M. Williams, *American Society* (New York: Alfred A. Knopf, 1960), p. 24.

4. Ibid., pp. 415-70.

5. Alvin Toffler, *Future Shock* (New York: Random House, 1970), p. 304.

6. Ibid. For an interesting study on the degree of conformity to the American core culture (a study that could be profitably updated and show interesting shifts), see J. Reusch, Annemarie Jacobsen, and M. B. Loeb, "Acculturation and Illness," *Psychology Monograph* 62, no. 5 (1948): 1-40.

7. Christopher Weber, "Three R's—Rows, Rifts, Resignations," *Newsday*, February 1, 1971.

8. Ellen Lurie, *How to Change the Schools* (New York: Vintage Books, 1970), p. 9.

9. Luvern L. Cunningham, "Trends and Issues in Participation," in *Emerging Patterns of Administrative Accountability*, ed. Lesley H. Browder, Jr. (Berkeley: McCutchan Publishing Corp., 1971), p. 100.

10. Myron Lieberman, *The Future of Public Education* (Chicago: University of Chicago Press, 1960), p. 72.

11. Ibid., p. 75. For a detailed analysis of militant teacher organization "ends" and "means," see Lesley Browder, Jr., "Teacher Unionism in America" (Ed.D diss., School of Education, Cornell University, 1965).

12. National Education Association, "Research Memo 1970-19" (August 1970).

13. This contention appears to underlie the writings of Charles Billings and Barbara Sizemore. See Charles Billings, "Community Control of the School and the Quest for Power," *Phi Delta Kappan* (January 1972): 277-78; Barbara Sizemore, "Is There a Case for Separate Schools," *Phi Delta Kappan* (January 1972): 281-84; Philip Piele, "Conflict Management in Education," *R & D Perspectives* (fall 1971).

14. Lesley Browder, Jr., "The Overlooked Student: A New Power" (unpublished). For a much-modified version, see idem, "The New American Success Story Is Called Student Confrontation," *American School Board Journal* (June 1970): 23-25.

15. C. Wright Mills, *Power, Politics, and People,* ed. I. L. Horowitz (New York: Oxford University Press, 1963), p. 23.

16. Irving Hendrick and Reginald Jones, ed., *Student Dissent in the Schools* (New York: Houghton-Mifflin, 1972).

17. Louis Harris, "What People Think About Their High Schools," *Life,* May 16, 1969, p. 24.

18. J. Lloyd Trump and Jane Hunt, "Report on a National Survey of Secondary School Principals as the Nature and Extent of Student Activism," mimeographed (spring 1969).

19. Educational Research Service, *Framework for Student Involvement,* Circular no. 6 (Washington, D.C.: ERS, 1970).

20. Neal Gross, "Who Controls the Schools?" in *Education and Public Policy,* ed. Seymour Harris (Berkeley: McCutchan Publishing Corp., 1965), p. 25.

21. Hilda Taba, *Curriculum Development: Theory and Practice* (New York: Harcourt, Brace & World, 1962), p. 10.

22. Jack Frymier and Horace Hawn, *Curriculum Improvement for Better Schools* (Worthington, Ohio: Charles A. Jones Publishing Co., 1970), p. 251.

23. Michael Kirst and Decker Walker, "An Analysis of Curriculum Policy Making," *Review of Educational Research* 41, no. 5 (December 1971): 480-81.

24. Lieberman, *Future of Public Education,* p. 60.

25. Dean Bowles, "The Power Structure in State Education Politics," *Phi Delta Kappan* (February 1968): 240.

For a strongly stated antiprofessional leadership position, see James Koerner, *Who Controls American Education* (Boston: Beacon Press, 1968).

26. Art Gallaher, "Directed Change in Formal Organizations: The School System," *Change Processes in the Public Schools* (Eugene, Oregon: University of Oregon, 1965), p. 50.

27. George Spindler, ed., *Education and Culture: Anthropological Approaches* (New York: Holt, Rinehart & Winston, 1963), p. 238.

28. Charles Lindblom, *The Policy Making Process* (Englewood Cliffs, N.J.: Prentice-Hall, 1968), p. 105.

29. Donald McCarty and Charles Ramsey, *The School Managers: Power and Conflict in American Public Education* (Westport, Conn.: Greenwood Publishing Corp., 1971).

See also Donald McCarty, "Community Influence Systems and Local Educational Policy Making," *The School Administrator* (February 1971): 7-10.

30. David Krech, Richard Crutchfield, and Egerton Ballachey, *Individual in Society* (New York: McGraw-Hill, 1962), p. 453.

31. Stephen K. Bailey, quoted in *The School Administrator* (February 1972): 13.

32. Lesley Browder, Jr., "A Suburban School Superintendent Plays Politics," in *The Politics of Education at the Local, State and Federal Levels,* ed. Michael Kirst (Berkeley: McCutchan Publishing Corp., 1970), p. 193.

33. Alfred Kahn, *Theory and Practice of Social Planning* (New York: Russell Sage Foundation, 1969), pp. 123-24.

34. Robert Dahl and Charles Lindblom, *Politics, Economics and Welfare* (New York: Harper & Bros., 1953), p. 41.

35. Harry Summerfield, *The Neighborhood-Based Politics of Education* (Columbus, Ohio: Charles E. Merrill Publishing Co., 1971), p. 101.

36. Ibid., p. 103.

37. C. Robert Pine and Mary Milne, "College Graduates: Highlights from a Nationwide Survey," *Evaluation Comment* 3, no. 2 (November 1971): 3.

38. Kirst and Walker, "Analysis of Curriculum Policy Making," p. 488.

39. Council of Chief State School Officers, *State and Federal Relationships in Education: A Position Statement* (Washington, D. C.: CCSSO, 1971), p. 27.

40. Laurence Iannacone, "The Forces Shaping Education" (unpublished paper, NASE reading materials, 1971), p. 8. For a published version of Iannacone's insights, see idem, *Politics in Education* (New York: Center for Applied Research in Education, 1969).

41. Terrell H. Bell, acting commissioner, USOE, "Memorandum to Chief State School Officers: Advisory Statement on Development of Policy on Parental Involvement in Title I, ESEA Projects" (Washington, D. C.: U.S. Office of Education, October 30, 1970).

42. Richard L. Fairley, director, Division of Compensatory Education, USOE, "Accountability—Title I, ESEA," Ohio Title I Conference (Columbus, Ohio: September 29, 1971).

43. There are signs that such embarrassments already occur. Powerful influences also come from the state; in New York State, for example, standardized test results are released. Writes Gayle Tunnell: "Each year, with the publication of standardized test scores in third and sixth grade reading and mathematics for Long Island school districts, shock waves of surprise hit many communities. Parents are surprised that the scores in some districts are so low or compare unfavorably with those in neighboring districts." *Newsday*, June 21, 1971, p. 13A

It is parenthetically interesting to note that out of five of the most affluent communities that scored most poorly, there has been (or is currently underway) a replacement of the superintendent in four of them. Perhaps it is merely coincidental.

44. Frank Womer and Marjorie Mastie, "How Will National Assessment Change American Education?" *Phi Delta Kappan* (October 1971). An interesting article on the topic is Eleanor Norris, "What We Are Learning From the National Assessment," *American Education* (July 1971): 19-23. For extended information, write to NAEP Information Services, Suite 300, Lincoln Tower Building, 1860 Lincoln Street, Denver, Colorado 80203.

45. Council of Chief State School Officers, *State and Federal Relationships in Education*.

46. "Resolutions Adopted October, 1971," New York State Council of School District Administrators, Albany, New York.

47. Act 299: School District Reorganization Act of 1963, Commonwealth of Pennsylvania:

"Section 290.1: *Education Performance Standards*—to implement the purpose of this subdivision, the State Board of Education, as soon as possible and, in any event, no later than July 1, 1965, shall develop or cause to be developed an evaluation procedure designed to measure objectively the adequacy and efficiency of the educational programs offered by the public schools of the Commonwealth. The evaluation procedure to be developed shall include tests measuring the achievement and performance of students and courses comprising the curricula. The evaluation procedure shall be so construed and developed as to provide each school district with relevant comparative data to enable directors and administrators to more readily appraise the educational performance and to effectuate without delay the strengthening of the district's educational program. Tests developed under the authority of this section to be administered to pupils shall be used for the purpose of providing a uniform evaluation of each school district and the other set forth in this subdivision. The State Board of Education shall devise performance standards upon the completion of the evaluation procedure required by this section."

48. Educational Testing Service, *A Plan for Evaluating the Quality of Educational Programs in Pennsylvania* (Princeton, New Jersey: ETA, June 1965).

49. *Quality Education Program Study*, an ESEA Title III Project, coordinated and directed by the Bucks County Superintendents Office in cooperation with the Pennsylvania Department of Education (June 1971).

50. Harold J. Leavitt, *Managerial Psychology* 2d ed. (Chicago: University of Chicago Press, 1964), p. 347.

51. C. Lindblom and D. Braybrooke, *A Strategy of Decision* (New York: Free Press, 1963).

52. John Stuart Mill, *Considerations on Representative Government* (Chicago: Henry Regney Co.—Gateway edition, 1962), p. 139.

53. The listing of items by the authors is intended to be merely suggestive. For more thorough pursuit of these items, see Herbert Thelen, *Dynamics of Groups at Work* (Chicago: University of Chicago Press, 1954); Matthew Miles, *Learning to Work in Groups* (New York: Teachers College Press, 1959); William Savage, *Interpersonal and Group Relations in Educational Administration* (Glenview, Ill.: Scott, Foresman & Co., 1968).

The authors are indebted to Dr. Keith Echeverii, consultant to the Joint Committee on Educational Goals and Evaluation of the California Legislature.

54. Standard reference works on social relations research would be helpful on this aspect. See, for example, Claire Selltiz et al., *Research Methods in Social Relations* (New York: Holt, Rinehart & Winston, 1959); Delbert Miller, *Handbook of Research Design and Social Measurement* 2d ed. (New York: David McKay Co., 1970).

55. "Tentative Draft: Planning Techiques," California Elementary School Administrators Association (fall 1969).

56. Olaf Helmer, *Analysis of the Future: The Delphi Method* (Santa Monica, Calif.: RAND Corp., 1967), p. 7.

57. Frederick Cyphert and Walter Gant, "The Delphi Technique: A Tool for Collective Opinions in Teacher Education," in *Emerging Patterns of Administrative Accountability*, p. 194.

For an extended analysis of the Delphi Technique, see W. Timothy Weaver, "The Delphi Forecasting Method," in *Emerging Patterns of Administrative Accountability*, pp. 171-83.

For applications of the technique, see Olaf Helmer, "The Use of the Delphi Technique in Problems of Educational Innovations," Report P-3499 (Santa Monica, Calif.: RAND Corp., December 1966); D. P. Anderson, "Clarifying and Setting Objectives on an Intermediate School District's Objectives Utilizing the Delphi Technique," paper presented at the American Education Research Association (Minneapolis, Minn., March 4, 1970).

58. Robert D. Williams, "Patterns of Influence Attempts in Decision-

Making Groups in the Educational Facilities Charrette" (Ed.D. diss. School of Education, Stanford University, 1970).

See also Walter Mylecraine, "The Charrette Process," in *Education for the People: A Resource Book for School-Community Decision-Making,* ed. Joint Committee on Educational Goals and Evaluation (Sacramento, Calif.: California Legislature, 1971), §D-8.

59. Nancy Stark, "How Schools Can Listen to the Community," *American Education* (July 1971): 10.

60. Figure 5.8 has similarities with the four matrix tables presented in the second chapter of the Research Corporation of the Association of School Business Officials' draft, *Educational Resources Management System* (pursuant to USOE Project no. 8-0290, 1971). Their four-table arrangement, however, includes separately planning, programming, budgeting and evaluating. These four components form the basis of their "educational resources management system," an accountability system akin to plan-program-budgeting systems (PPBS).

61. For some good insights into the use of consultants, see Richard Walton, *Interpersonal Peacemaking: Confrontations and Third Party Consultation* (Reading, Mass.: Addison-Wesley Publishing Co., 1969).

62. For a closer look at management-by-objectives technique, see George Odiorne, *Management by Objectives* (New York: Pitman Publishing Corp., 1965); Peter Drucker, *The Practice of Management* (New York: Harper & Bros., 1954); A.P.A. Raia, "A Second Look at Management Goals and Controls," *The California Management Review* (1966).

63. George Caldwell, "The Educational Management System," *Viewpoints on Accountability* (Tucson, Ariz.: Educational Innovators Press, 1971), p. 7.

64. The area of developing board of education accountability policies has received commercial attention recently by the Croft Educational Services (100 Garfield Avenue, New London, Connecticut 06320). Leon Lessinger, Dale Parnell, and Roger Kaufman have a series of model policies entitled "Accountability: Policies and Procedures." A fee of $195 is charged for this service.

6. Performance Objectives

Recognition of the need for schools to define their educational objectives operationally dates from the early 1930s and 40s, when Ralph Tyler and others wrote about their rationale for curriculum development and evaluation.[1] Since then many educational experts have written on the subject. Some point out the need for specification of objectives; some apply such specification to educational testing; some emphasize the importance of observable performance and behavior rather than test performance; some accumulate a data bank of behaviorally stated objectives; and some caution on the overuse of such specification leading to educational trivia.[2] Yet, in the context of "accountability," the school administrator is finally faced with the responsibility of actually having to do something about specifying performance objectives.

Richard Suchman wrote in 1966, "Thus far, education has not come up with a precise language of its own to permit the systematic description and analysis of educational events."[3] He placed the blame on "educationese," an argot of educators full of sound and devoid of clarity and precision. It is the old problem of blaming "semantics" for long arguments and disagreements that can be resolved when the terms are clearly defined. Bertrand Russell discussed the need for defining one's terms, and scientists such as Bridgman have brought into the behavioral sciences the need to define terms operationally. Education as a discipline has also been affected by these movements; this, however, has been manifested more in research than in the practice of the discipline.

For example, in a study made to determine research findings

applicable to educational practice, three different uses were discovered for the term "regrouping."[4] One use referred to subgrouping children daily into different small study groups according to what they had accomplished on the preceding day. A second meaning referred to grouping children twice a year on the basis of their achievement scores and teacher's judgments. A third referred to placing children in a different group in each subject matter area, on the basis of the child's achievement in and talent for each subject.

Since these differences exist in the use of educational terminology, and since educational goals are presumed to vary from one community and region to another, the task of determining or selecting behaviorally stated objectives that are relevant to the school's established needs must be performed locally. The objectives should reflect the general guidelines and minimum requirements issued by federal and state governments, but the actual specification that goes beyond the minimum requirements needs to be handled in the district.

In addition to the reasons discussed in chapter 5, there are at least two more reasons for involving the local district in the task of specification. First, Rogers has pointed out that, to adopt change, an institution must feel from within the need for that change.[5] If the need assessment has been adequately carried out, it will provide the guidelines for specifying the objectives that are relevant to local needs. Second, the selection of educational objectives would be purposeful only if the expressed objectives were put into practice in the classroom; it is therefore advisable to involve all groups that directly influence instruction in specifying and selecting educational objectives and priorities.

Educators in local school districts frequently resist the specification of performance objectives. Some legitimate concerns about the problems of specification have been expressed by Myron Atkin and James Raths.[6] These center around the danger that specification may possibly lead to and perpetuate only objectives that are easy to specify. Doubtless, there is some evidence that some objectives specified so far and included in the data bank established at UCLA, are relatively trivial. Almost all of Mager's behaviors deal with a cognitive level, which according to Bloom's taxonomy would be identified as the lowest level.[7] However, there is some evidence that more desirable and idealistic objectives are also being dealt with. For example, Taba, Gagné, Kaya, have succeeded in specifying a number of behaviors that would in fact fall in the higher-cognitive processes and affective social development of the child.[8] The Behavioral Outcomes Project of the Norwalk (Connecticut) public schools used some of these behavioral objectives to improve classroom teaching.[9] Other school systems have made similar attempts through a variety of innovative projects, in-service training, and curriculum development activities.

Popham wrote an excellent summary of arguments against the use of performance objectives as well as in favor of the desirability of specification.[10] Since proponents of both sides would benefit from the opposite viewpoint, Popham's points are briefly summarized, with some modification:

Argument against specification	Argument for specification
1. Trivial objectives are easiest to operationalize and will lead to underemphasizing important ones.	1. Explicit objectives make it easier for educators to attend to and differentiate the important objectives from the unimportant.
2. Prespecification of goals prevents teachers from pursuing learning opportunities that occur spontaneously.	2. Prespecification does not interfere with spontaneously arising opportunity if relevant. Instead, it eliminates sidetracking into irrelevant classroom events.
3. Specification does not involve some important outcomes, e.g., changes in parental attitudes, professional staff, community values.	3. Primary responsibility is to educate the youth; if other outcomes are met, they should also be specified and justified in terms of their relevance to educating the youth.
4. Measurement of behavior implies an objective, mechanistic approach which is dehumanizing.	4. It is possible to assess many qualitative and complicated human behaviors with reliability and validity.
5. It is undemocratic to prescribe how the learner should behave after instruction.	5. Whether the objectives are specified or not, the same degree of "democracy" exists in educating the youth. Schools do not purport to allow students to deviate "democratically" from socially desirable goals.
6. It is unrealistic to expect teachers to specify their objectives, because they simply don't.	6. Teachers should be trained to specify their objectives rather than perpetuate an ineffective status quo.
7. In areas like arts and humanities it is difficult to specify performance objectives.	7. Teachers in arts and humanities constantly make judgments about the quality of students' products. They only refuse to specify the criteria for their judgments.

Argument against specification	Argument for specification
8. Measurability implies accountability. Teachers may then be judged on their ability to produce results in the learners instead of their competence in instructing.	8. Teachers should be judged on whether they produce results in the learners. What other criterion is there for "competence in instructing"?
9. General statements of objectives appear worthwhile to outsiders. Most educational goals, when stated precisely, would be revealed as innocuous.	9. Schools must abandon the ploy of "obfuscation by generality" and face squarely what it is they are achieving.
10. It is more difficult and time consuming to generate precise objectives than to talk about them in customary undefined terms.	10. Resources should be allocated to allow teachers to spend the necessary time either in generating the specific objective or in selecting from among those already specified.
11. Since specification cannot be exhaustive, the prespecification of some objectives may make the evaluator inattentive to unanticipated results.	11. Prespecification of objectives indicates what may be the primary but not exclusive focus in evaluating instruction. If dramatic unanticipated outcomes occur, their determination would only be facilitated since much of the "noise" in the system would already be clarified.

Although most of these arguments refer to the specification of student performance objectives, several points imply as well a concern with criteria for teacher performance. Two recent developments necessitate that the administrator concern himself with specifying performance objectives both for students and teachers. First is the development of a new trend in states like Washington, Texas, Florida, and New York towards certifying teachers on the basis of performance criteria. This trend, at least on the surface, appears to be supported by professional teacher associations in these states who are discontented with the type of preparation they have received in the past, and wish to have more voice in determining the criteria for certification. Second, the accountability movement pressures the administrator to look for professionals, besides himself, who are also accountable for the achievement of educational objectives. Without a clear specification of teacher performances and criteria for evaluation, both teachers and administrators are faced with the possibility that the interpretation of "competence" may be limited solely to the learner's achievement level.

Assuming that the administrator is in fact concerned with the specification of performances both for students and for teachers, some discussion of specified performances in these two categories may be useful to the administrator faced with the task.

Some Generic Student Objectives

A category system with a list (by no means exhaustive) of sample student performances is offered which may be used by the educator as a starting point. The category system and the behaviors apply across subject-matter areas and are therefore considered generic and contentless. Anyone interested in applying them to specific subject-matter areas would need to specify further the context in which these behaviors are expected to occur. Later in the chapter, we will discuss in greater detail means of further specifying these generic objectives.

Knowledge of Factual Information (Category 1)

This category corresponds to the lowest cognitive level in Bloom's taxonomy. It consists of behaviors indicating that a child recalls or recognizes facts, principles, events, definitions. Some sample behaviors are:

1. Child identifies facts, theories, and principles in a given discipline.

2. Child recognizes an object, fact, or event.

3. Child recites given principles, facts, or accounts of events and phenomena.

4. Child defines terminology.

5. Child recalls the details of an account, event, or material read.

6. Child identifies technical terms specific to the area of study.

7. Child defines abstract terms.

8. Child recites the steps in a sequence he has studied.

9. Child repeats instructions.

10. Child repeats information he was given previously.

11. Child recites a passage from memory.

12. Child reports an event as it took place.

13. Child repeats the rules of the game.

14. Child behaves in accordance with previously established rules.

15. Child finds his way back to a place where he has been before.

Tool-skills (Category 2)

This category has customarily referred to reading, writing, and arithmetic computation skills. A skill is defined as a learned set of behaviors that are carried out almost automatically with no requirement of further thought or instruction. To the extent that the three Rs represent this kind of automatic behavior, it is appropriate to classify them as tool skills. It is more likely, however, that some behaviors under the three Rs may be skills, while others may involve information recall, recognition, and perhaps even some higher cognitive processes. Other behaviors falling into the tool-skill category concern the utilization of tools, equipment, materials, etc. Some of these skills are developed in the context of the three Rs, others are developed in special classes like "shop." Sample behaviors are:

1. Child follows written directions.
2. Child reads a passage.
3. Child uses equipment such as cameras, projectors, typewriter, calculator, microscope, accurately and within accepted time limits.
4. Child takes dictation.
5. Child spells correctly.
6. Child uses card catalog in library to locate materials.
7. Child budgets his time.
8. Child alphabetizes.
9. Child locates places on maps.
10. Child follows instructions to build models or equipment.
11. Child displays physical skills necessary in games or in taking care of his personal needs.
12. Child gives oral directions that can be followed.
13. Child performs the four fundamental arithmetic computations.
14. Child reads scale drawings.
15. Child draws.
16. Child sings.

Higher Cognitive Manipulation of Information (Category 3)

This category refers to the way the child copes with his environment through applying the knowledge and skills he has acquired.

Behaviors represent reasoning, judgment, problem solving, novel crea-
tions, and a number of cognitive processes discussed in the psychological literature, including classification, association, comparison,
divergent and convergent production, analysis, synthesis, inductive
and deductive reasoning, translation and transformation, and evaluation.[11] Some sample behaviors in this category are:

1. Child formulates hypotheses.
2. Child modifies hypotheses in light of new evidence.
3. Child guesses.
4. Child differentiates between two objects, phenomena,
events, and gives his criteria for the differentiation.
5. Child plans a course of action.
6. Child indicates logical fallacies in an argument.
7. Child gives approximations.
8. Child predicts future events after he analyzes current trends.
9. Child labels objects, events, and phenomena according to
common characteristics.
10. Child matches objects, people, and events according to some
rules.
11. Child develops rules.
12. Child criticizes events, phenomena, and arguments.
13. Child translates passages into his own words.
14. Child gives alternative solutions to a problem.
15. Child uses analogies and metaphors.
16. Child selects facts, theories, and principles that are relevant
to the solution of a specific problem.
17. Child identifies unspoken assumptions.
18. Child organizes seemingly unrelated objects, words, or data
into one whole composition.
19. Child generalizes accurately from given data.
20. Child arranges objects, events, or data in a sequential or
hierarchical order.

Affective Development

This general area has perhaps been the most difficult to specify
and the most controversial. The focus of the controversy is whether
or not the school should be responsible for the affective development
of the child. The contention is that there are a number of behaviors
that fall into the affective domain which the school, in fact, attempts
to develop. Some of these are globally stated as interest in learning;
values consistent with the societal, legal, cultural, moral, and ethical

heritage of the individual; attitudes that enable healthy, cooperative, harmonious living in a complex society characterized by interdependence. Obviously, some of these affective goals are dealt with in the schools, at least in the context of some subject-matter areas. It is perhaps because of subject matter providing the context that Krathwohl's taxonomy[12] of the affective domain (dealing with receiving, responding, valuing, organization and characterization by a value system) seems rather limited in scope and highly confounded by the cognitive aspects of the child's development. Perhaps an educator's interpretation of affective behaviors is different from the psychologists' interpretation. In any event, we follow here a broader approach to the affective domain. Two subcategories are offered and a sampling of behaviors are listed in each.

Affective-interactive development (category 4). This category includes behaviors that represent acquired affective social abilities. Leadership, cooperation, productive and positive interaction with others, positive values, attitudes, interest in one's social, cultural, and political environment are concepts that belong to this category. For example:

1. Child participates in extracurricular activities.
2. Child adheres to group-made rules and laws.
3. Child assists others when needed.
4. Child shares with others either personal property, experiences, or ideas.
5. Child participates in tasks that directly involve him with other children.
6. Child performs before a group.
7. Child makes and sustains conversation.
8. Child practices social amenities and courtesies when exchanging ideas.
9. Child draws reticent members of a group into conversation.
10. Child performs his share of specific chores in the classroom.
11. Child points out the "good" aspects of something rather than what is wrong with it.
12. Child keeps still when the situation calls for silence.
13. Child refers to others those problems they can handle better than he can.
14. Child invites others to share experiences, thoughts, or objects with him.
15. Child conducts a meeting and moderates discussion.
16. Child compliments others on things they have done well.
17. Child defends himself and others.

18. Child laughs a great deal with others.

19. Child explores possibilities of new interests by attending activities new to him.

20. Child comments on the relationships between himself and others with sensitivity.

Affective-personal development (category 5). This category includes such objectives as self-assessment, self-analysis, self-direction, achievement motivation, happiness, enjoyment of one's environment and of one's activities, having good mental and physical health habits. Illustrative behaviors include:

1. Child designs a course of study for himself.

2. Child acts quickly in an emergency to alleviate or escape the problem.

3. Child gives an account of what his objectives are and how far he has advanced in attaining them.

4. Child voluntarily learns a poem or song.

5. Child expresses his feelings through whatever medium he can.

6. Child chooses activities independently and carries them out.

7. Child expresses curiosity and seeks answers.

8. Child accepts blame when a self-initiated activity fails.

9. Child expresses satisfaction at completing a difficult task.

10. Child specifies a few things which he believes he does well.

11. Child's claims about himself are realistic and unexaggerated.

12. Child tries new things and new activities when presented with the opportunity.

13. Child finds a humorous side to events that might otherwise upset him.

14. Child demonstrates eagerness to participate in enjoyable activity.

15. Child more often smiles and laughs than he cries or frowns.

16. Child collects things that he thinks are beautiful.

17. Child prefers building things to destroying them.

18. Child keeps himself busy in activities by himself.

19. Child requests to go or be taken to activities that are pleasing to him.

20. Child voluntarily engages in physical activity that is good for him.

In summary, the five categories of pupil objectives with sample generic behaviors in each are offered to illustrate that some rather important goals can be translated into behavioral terminology. These may be useful to the administrator in his attempt to coordinate or carry out further specification in the local school district.[13]

Some Generic Teacher Performances

The Division of Teacher Education and Certification of the the New York State Education Department raised two main questions in its guideline, "A New Style of Certification."[14] First, what are the stated objectives and priorities of the schools involved? Second, what competencies should a teacher have to serve in those schools? If one agrees that the objectives and priorities must be established locally by a school system, it would follow that the desired teacher performances leading to them must also be determined locally in view of the assessed needs of the school.

A great deal of research has been conducted concerning teacher characteristics and "effective" or "good" teaching behaviors.[15] Conceptual models for teacher education have been theorized and sometimes experimented with.[16] Yet most state departments of education find themselves unable to specify the criteria by which teachers should be certified. Teacher-training institutions are criticized for not meeting the ambiguously stated needs of school districts and for not providing leadership in bringing more system to what is potentially a chaotic situation. The test developers find themselves blamed for providing limited definitions of effective teaching, thus setting narrower goals for new teachers than those goals supposed by teacher groups to reflect their proper image—a problem of professional ego.

Teachers have typically been expected to be all things to all people, an expectation that stems from an undefined role. They are called upon to diagnose student needs; to act as pseudopsychologists in coping with students' social, motivational, and emotional needs; to develop or modify curricula for individual needs where interdisciplinary teams of curriculum specialists have failed to do so; to manage, direct, and supervise groups of children; to counsel children and be sensitive to their vocational interests; to be experts in at least one, and often more, subject-matter areas; and, after all that, to be dedicated professionals who continue to better themselves and love children in a community that sometimes has little love or respect for teachers. Add to all these tasks the current views held by many teacher associations that teachers should take part in policy and administrative decision making, and the job of teaching mounts to a herculean effort. Few teachers can effectively perform under these conditions.

With so many tasks required of teachers, it is difficult but necessary to analyze the behaviors desired of teachers for each task.

Thus, once again a generic list of teacher performance categories and some sample behaviors are offered as a starting point for the administrator faced with specification of performance. The categories are based on a functional analysis of the tasks required of a teacher and should be accepted as arbitrary and heuristic.

Diagnosing and Evaluating Children

At a time when individualizing instruction has received very favorable reaction from both educators and the public, it has become essential to assess the child's level before prescribing instructional activities. Some of this assessment is done on a schoolwide basis, utilizing standard tests. Some is done individually by psychologists or counselors, and some by the teacher. Regardless of who performs assessment, various functions are given below:

1. Administers tests.

2. Keeps records on individual performance.

3. Conducts observations.

4. Gives personal evaluations of individual pupils based on some evidence.

5. Prepares growth charts on some important student outcomes.

6. Prepares student profiles on several cognitive and affective objectives.

7. Reviews individual profiles and makes recommendations for instructional placement.

8. Establishes a system whereby the child's daily or weekly performance may be recorded by the child, and reviewed by any instructional staff.

9. Utilizes some systematic performance evaluation techniques.

10. Finds out information about the child from his parents and peers.

These functions may be further specified to indicate more clearly what the teacher may do in assessing the child. The teacher:

1. Checks and determines the time child spends in a given activity.

2. Finds child's rate of learning by checking the time spent in the activity against the amount learned.

3. Compares the amount of time child spends in each of a variety of activities to determine "interest."

4. Identifies causes of errors when child makes mistakes.

5. Asks the child to identify possible causes of errors.

6. Compares child's self-assessment with the child's work.

7. Asks others' opinions of the child.

8. Presents children with tasks and records differences in styles of attacking the problem, and rates and means of solving it.

9. Estimates child's individual characteristics such as attention span, interest, special drives, activity level, and periodically records these for each child.

10. Identifies inconsistencies in child's behavior, if they exist.

11. Asks the child about his own objectives, likes, and dislikes.

12. Checks own assessment of the child against available data from other sources.

13. Makes up situational and paper-and-pencil tests.

14. Uses appropriate techniques for analyzing the information obtained.

15. Has a record-keeping system where all systematic information is recorded for each child at regular intervals both by those assessing the child and the child himself.

Preparation for Instruction

The teacher spends some time preparing to teach. Selection of appropriate curricular topics, materials, and activities, translation of state and local guides into specific objectives, arranging for utilization of appropriate community and school resources available to supplement instruction, are all functions that fall in this category. Here are some sample behaviors:

1. Specifies expected student outcomes in behavioral terms.

2. Specifies alternative teaching strategies to achieve a given objective.

3. Identifies curricular materials relevant to the topic, which children may utilize.

4. Identifies alternative activities for children that are designed to achieve the objectives.

5. Sequences activities in order of either difficulty or logical continuity; defines prerequisites for learning tasks.

6. Designs a course of study for each child on the basis of the diagnostic information.

7. Involves the child in the planning of his course of study.

8. Sets up and/or utilizes reference files to locate curricular materials that are relevant to specific objectives.

9. Produces learning materials to meet specific requirements of

pupils, e.g., printed instructions, displays, stories, transparencies, games, etc.

10. Checks out the relevance of his selections, plans, and preparations with other professionals in and out of school.

Communicating with Students for Instructional Purposes

Generally, one tends to think of the teacher as the sole instructional agent. This false assumption has led to many criticisms of the instructional process. It is more realistic to think of the teacher as one of the many instructional agents available to the child. Other agents may be the parents, the peers in and out of class, instructional materials such as programmed materials, books, movies, etc., and even the not-so-instructional television set! Thus, the teacher's function may be reflected better in preparation *for* rather than *in* actual instruction. However, the teacher serves in an instructional communication function, which may be reflected in transmitting information, clarifying and explaining concepts and principles, or in utilizing the child's own thinking and resources to achieve the specified educational outcome. Some sample teacher behaviors are:

1. Elicits frequent responses from each child about his knowledge and experiences relevant to the objectives.

2. Either gives factual information or refers the child to where he can obtain it.

3. Elicits from children hypotheses to explain phenomena.

4. Gives accurate and relevant explanations when necessary.

5. Asks the child to correct his errors; if the child cannot, assists him by providing relevant cues.

6. Uses positive reinforcement for desired responses from children, e.g., informing them that their responses are good, correct, creative, etc.

7. Informs students of objectives, plans, and criteria.

8. Invites student participation in solving problems.

9. Raises relevant questions and frequently asks for alternative solutions rather than *one* correct answer.

10. Checks with the child to determine that explanations are clear for feedback purposes.

11. Tutors individual children.

12. Utilizes audiovisual techniques of communicating.

13. Asks children to put information into their own words.

14. Elicits discussion about children's own experiences relating to a curricular objective to provide a context for applying information.

15. Frequently uses techniques such as dramatizing, role-playing, and simulating games in which children participate to generate information as well as discover and acquire information.

Communicating with Students for Counseling Purposes

Often the teacher's counseling role is at least as important as his instructional role. In the affective domain it may even be difficult to separate the two. However, there are some counseling behaviors that do differ from instructional behaviors to the extent that they involve less directive, less prescriptive approaches than does instructional communication. Some sample teacher behaviors are:

1. Engages the student in talking about himself, his life pattern, his personal and social relations in the school, to bring about some awareness of self.

2. Reinforces student's positive comments about himself and about others.

3. Reinforces student's voluntary participation in a variety of activities.

4. Exposes student to new and various activities he may find of interest.

5. Presents students with available alternatives in scheduling, in courses of study, in extracurricular participation so that the student can make choices.

6. Guides student to seek remedial help or to do additional projects when needed.

7. Confers with parents and advises them about their participation in the student's school-related activities.

8. Places individual student with peers who are likely to have positive interaction with him.

9. Establishes free time for students to see him on a voluntary basis.

10. Participates in extracurricular student activities.

11. Discusses his evaluation of the student with the student.

12. Consults other school staff about his knowledge of the student.

13. Shares with the student his own experiences relevant to student's problem.

14. Asks student to talk about his positive educational and personal experiences connected with his objectives.

15. Discusses with student some possible career objectives which the student may have as long-term goals.

Classroom Management

This category includes not only the "housekeeping" activities of a teacher but also such functions as grouping and subgrouping children, organizing trips, using and maintaining equipment, furniture, and facilities, and creating a cheerful and comfortable class atmosphere conducive to learning. Examples of teacher behaviors are:

1. Establishes and varies seating arrangement according to the needs of different children and different activities.

2. Arranges for children to work alone, in teams, or subgroups as the need arises.

3. Decorates the room with the help of the students.

4. Allows children to set up research groups and divide activities among themselves.

5. Brings together classes for large group activities.

6. Functions without being disturbed by noise that can occur in a class busy with a variety of activities.

7. Invites students to participate in selecting and organizing field trips.

8. Deviates from established routines without getting upset if the students request it for a good reason.

9. Utilizes parental and paraprofessional assistance in class.

10. Involves students in establishing class rules so that these become their own rules.

11. Structures classroom environment so that learning via pupil interaction can occur without involving the teacher.

12. Ignores rather than punishes students who do not conform to his expectations.

13. Reinforces by public approval children who behave in desired ways.

14. Invites or assigns children to be responsible for housekeeping routines (watering plants, collecting money, etc.).

15. Involves children in discussing the solution of class management problems so that they are participants rather than recipients.

In sum, the teacher behavior categories discussed above all relate to achieving student objectives. There are other teacher functions relating to the professional growth of the teacher, his service to his school and community, his interpersonal relations with other staff members, and his participation in the activities of professional organizations. Here, however, the intent is to provide the administrator with some examples of performance objectives mainly involving the student. However, these other functions should not be minimized.

Helpful Hints on How to Specify Performance Objectives

No one will dispute the value of "motherhood." Few will attempt to define what it is. A number of people have written on how to specify behavioral objectives.[17] Mager points out three criteria for a behavioral objective.[18] One might add to these three, bringing the list up to five; the objective, when specified, should:

1. Describe what the learner will be doing to demonstrate he has attained the objective.

2. Describe the setting and conditions under which the learner will demonstrate his achievement.

3. State the expected standard of performance.

4. Be recognizable as relevant to the educational goal it represents.

5. Be of a level of specificity that is useful in the instructional or decision-making process.

These criteria are useful once the specification is accomplished, but they do not describe a procedure for the specification. Individuals will vary in their method of specifying objectives; for those who may not have a method, one is offered here.

Usually one starts with the general educational goal, which is stated as a concept—for example, self-direction or good citizenship.

Next, one might ask: "How do I know when an individual has achieved this desired goal?" or "What does the individual do that makes me think he has achieved the desired goal?" or "What would I do if I were . . . ?"

These questions often generate a series of actions and behaviors, some at a general level, some very specific. It is best not to be concerned with the quality of the statement at this stage. It is more important to produce as many behaviors as possible. This process of producing behavioral statements may be facilitated by using analogies and brain-storming techniques.

Once the varieties of behavior are listed, the criteria listed earlier may be applied to match and select "good" behavioral objectives. At this stage of the process it is very helpful to ask other qualified persons to judge the statements against the criteria. Agreement about the quality and usefulness of the statement usually assures a degree of objectivity and validity.

Perhaps the most difficult step in this process is deciding what level of specificity to accept. This decision must be made according to the context in which the objective is applicable. If, for example, the context is writing behaviors for programmed instruction in a given topic, the statements must be extremely specific ("the child adds two and two and obtains four"). If the context is writing terminal behaviors for the graduating elementary school pupil, the statement must be both more generic (such as the ones given earlier in the chapter) and less specific. Two general rules to remember are (1) never lose sight of the context and the purpose for which the behavioral objectives are specified, and, (2) when in doubt, check with other qualified people.

Specifying Criteria to Determine When an Objective Is Achieved

Specifying performance objectives of a desired level is perhaps the most difficult step in a performance-based approach to accountability. However, a logical sequence to it involves delineating the criteria to determine when an objective is achieved. For example, the objective may be: "The child adds two digit numbers correctly." The question then becomes: How often does he have to add correctly for us to accept that this objective has been achieved? One may find some stated criteria, such as adding correctly 90 percent of the time, or 80 percent of the time, etc. Establishing the criteria for the achievement of the objective is a step toward criterion-referenced evaluation.

Criterion-referenced evaluation attempts to describe how well a given individual has achieved the specified objectives, without any attempt to compare him with others.[19] It is an *absolute* rather than *relative* type of evaluation; either the individual achieves the specified criterion or he doesn't. One is not concerned here with normative curves based on group performance, or the position of the individual in relation to his group. The interest lies in determining the position of the individual in relation to the criterion he must achieve. Because of its apparent rejection of group-related norms, it has a strong appeal to persons interested in forms of "individualized instruction" wherein the learner proceeds at his own pace through arbitrarily arranged sets of criteria.

There is one main problem: the educator is often unable to find any rationale to serve as a guideline in selecting a particular criterion. For example, why should one select as the criterion a 90 percent accuracy level in adding numbers, as opposed to 80 percent or 100 percent accuracy?

To date, there appears to be no good discussion of the possible solutions to this problem. A few approaches are suggested here to facilitate the decision making in selecting and/or specifying such criteria.

First, the criterion level should eliminate or reduce the probability that the desired performance occurred by chance, rather than as a result of true achievement. If the desired performance is highly specific, such as adding two-digit numbers accurately, a representative sample of addition problems should yield accurate results approximately 95 percent of the time. This figure, however, is partially dependent on the number of times the task is to be performed to begin with. Suppose a child can add three sets of two-digit numbers in a row accurately, makes a mistake on the fourth one, but adds the fifth set accurately again. He has achieved a criterion level of 80 percent and not 95 percent. Yet, since he would have to take a 100-item two-digit addition test to demonstrate a 95 percent proficiency level, it would be to some both inefficient and undesirable to specify 95 percent as the criterion for determining his true achievement level. In short, it becomes a matter of judgment and value preferences.

The nature of the task to be performed should provide another guideline. For some tasks there can be no margin of error in performance. Crossing the street without getting hit by a car is an example. Other tasks, such as exploring alternative solutions to a physics problem, require a wide margin of error since the child must feel free to experiment, err, and find alternatives through eliminating his mistakes.

In sum, the educator must remember that there is no one criterion that is equally applicable to all performance objectives. The crucial factors to keep in mind in selecting criterion levels are: (a) the maximum reduction of the probability of a chance occurrence; (b) the number of times the task can be performed within limits of practicality and efficiency; (c) the level of specificity with which the task is stated; and (d) the nature of the task.

Handling Your Own Performance Objectives

We subscribe to the notion of developing one's own sets of performance objectives, but it is also possible to follow another path mentioned earlier—namely, to borrow from a bank of performance objectives. On the theory that it is not always necessary to reinvent the wheel, many staffs have preferred to order their set of objectives for instruction from a collection point of such items, the Instructional Objective Exchange (IOX) at UCLA.[20] It is possible to designate the instructional areas involved in your program plans and request IOX to send a package of "banked" instructional objectives for these areas.

It then becomes a matter of reviewing these objectives, culling out appropriate ones for the task plans, and/or modifying them to fit the local situation. Like getting new clothes, some people prefer their own tailors; some do it themselves; others order from Sears. Take your pick.

Notes for Chapter 6

1. Eugene Smith, Ralph Tyler, et al., *Appraising and Recording Student Progress* (New York: Harper and Bros., 1942), chapters 3 and 10. See also Wilford Aikin, *The Story of the Eight-Year Study* (New York: Harper and Bros., 1942).

2. See Myron J. Atkin, "Behavioral Objectives in Curriculum Design: A Cautionary Note," *Science Teacher* 35, no. 5 (May 1968); Robert F. Mager, *Preparing Instructional Objectives* (San Francisco: Fearon Publishers, 1962); James W. Popham, "The Performance Test: A New Approach to the Assessment of Teaching Proficiency," *The Journal of Teacher Education* 19, no. 2 (1968): 216-22; idem, "Probing the Validity of Arguments Against Behavioral Goals," paper presented at AERA (Chicago, February 1968); James Raths, "Specificity as a Threat to Curriculum Reform," paper presented at AERA (Chicago, February 1968).

3. Richard Suchman, "A Model for the Language of Education," *The Instructor* (fall 1966): 33.

4. Esin Kaya et al., *Developing a Theory of Educational Practice for the Elementary School,* report to the Ford Foundation Fund for Advancement of Education (Norwalk, Conn.: Norwalk Board of Education, 1967).

5. Everett Rogers, *Diffusion of Innovations* (New York: Free Press of Glen Cove, 1962); Robert Glaser, "Instructional Objectives and Programmed Instruction: A Case Study," in *Defining Educational Objectives,* ed. C. M. Lindvall (Pittsburgh, Pa.: University of Pittsburgh Press, 1964), p. 51.

6. Myron Atkin, "Behavioral Objectives in Curriculum Design"; James Raths, "Specificity as a Threat to Curriculum Reform."

7. Robert F. Mager, *Preparing Instructional Objectives;* Benjamin Bloom et al., eds., *A Taxonomy of Educational Objectives: Cognitive and Affective Domains,* 2 vols. (New York: Congmans Green & Co., 1956, 1964).

8. Hilda Taba, *Curriculum Development: Theory and Practice* (New York: Harcourt, Brace & World, 1962); idem, "Learning by Discovery: Psychological and Educational Rationale," *Elementary School Journal* 63 (1962): 308-15; Hilda Taba and F. Elsey, "Teaching Strategies and Thought Processes," *Teachers College Record* 65 (1964): 524-29; R. M. Gagne, "The Analysis of Instructional Objectives for the Design of Instruction," in *Teaching Machines and Programmed Learning II: Data and Directions,* ed. R. Glaser (Washington, D.C.: National Education Association, 1965), pp. 21-65; idem, "Educational Objectives and Human Performance," in *Learning and the Educational Process,* ed.

J. E. Krumboltz (Chicago: Rand McNally, 1965), pp. 1-24; Esin Kaya, "A Curricular Sequence Based on Psychological Processes Rather Than Subject Content," *Exceptional Children* 27 (1961): 425-28; idem, "Improving the Cognitive Functioning of Pupils through Teacher-Training in Process-Objectives: A Field Experiment," paper delivered at AERA (Los Angeles, February 1969).

9. See all the articles by members of the Norwalk public schools faculty reporting on their project in *Grade Teacher* (April 1967).

10. James Popham, "Probing the Validity of Arguments Against Behavioral Goals," paper presented at AERA (Chicago, February 1968). For two recent views, see Philip Smith, "On the Logic of Behavioral Objectives," and James Popham, "Objectives '72," both in *Phi Delta Kappan* (March 1972).

11. For a detailed definition of these processes, see Esin Kaya, "Improving the Cognitive Functioning of Pupils."

12. David R. Krathwohl, Benjamin Bloom, and Bertram Masia, *Taxonomy of Educational Objectives, Handbook II: Affective Domain* (New York: David McKay Co., 1964).

13. For some guidance, see Philip G. Kapfer, *Behavioral Objectives in the Cognitive and Affective Domains* (Englewood Cliffs, N.J.: Educational Technology, 1968); Robert Armstrong et al., *The Development and Evaluation of Behavioral Objectives* (Worthington, Ohio: Charles A. Jones Publishing Co., 1970); Robert Mager, *Developing Attitude Toward Learning* (Palo Alto, Calif.: Fearon Publishers, 1968).

14. University of the State of New York, Division of Teacher Education and Certification, "A New Style of Certification" (Albany: The State Education Department, 1970), p. 8.

15. J. Amidon and N. A. Flanders, "The Role of the Teacher in the Classroom: A Manual for Understanding and Improving Teacher's Classroom Behavior" (Minneapolis, Minn.: Paul S. Amidon & Associates, 1963); Arnold Bellack et al., "The Language of the Classroom: Meanings Communicated in High School Teaching, Part II," Cooperative Research Project no. 2023, U.S. Office of Education and U.S. Department of Health, Education and Welfare (New York: Columbia University, Teachers College Press, 1965); O. L. Davis, Jr., "Laboratory Components in Teacher Education," *Peabody Journal of Education* 47 (January 1970): 202-7; Donald Medley, "The Language of Teacher Behavior: Communicating the Results of Structured Observations to Teachers," *Journal of Teacher Education* 22, no. 2 (1971): 157-65; H. V. Perkins, "A Procedure for Assessing Classroom Behavior of Students and Teachers," *American Educational Research Journal* 1 (November 1964): 249-60; David Ryans, *Characteristics of Teachers: Their Description, Comparison, and Appraisal* (Washington, D.C.: American Council on Education, 1960); J. Whithall, "The Development of a Technique for the Measurement of Social Emotional Climate in Classrooms," *Journal of Experimental Education* 17 (March 1949): 347-61.

16. Tri-University Project in Elementary Education, *A Behavioral Approach to the Teaching of Social Studies* (Seattle, Wash.: University of Washington, May 1968); *Annual Progress Report of Teacher Education* (Bellingham, Wash.: Western Washington State College, 1971); Stephen K. Bailey, "Teachers' Centers: A British First," *Phi Delta Kappan* (November 1971): 146-49; A. A. Clegg and A. S. Ochoa, "What Does Today's Teacher Need to Know and to Do?" *Educational Leadership* (March 1970): 568-72; Marie Gaasholt, "Precision Techniques in the Management of Teacher and Child Behaviors," *Exceptional Chil-*

dren 37 (1970): 129-35; N. L. Gage, ed., *Handbook of Research on Teaching* (Chicago: Rand McNally, 1967).

17. Sam Leles and Raymond Bernabei, *Writing and Using Behavioral Objectives: A Learning Packet for Teachers, Students and Administrators* (Montgomery, Ala.: W. B. Drake & Son, Printers, 1969); C. M. Lindvall, *Defining Educational Objectives;* Robert Mager, *Preparing Instructional Objectives.*

18. Ibid., p. 53.

19. For a good discussion of criterion-referenced evaluation contrasted with norm-referenced evaluation, see Robert Glaser, "Instructional Technology and the Measurement of Learning Outcomes," *American Psychologist* 18, no. 8 (August 1963): 519-21; James W. Popham, *Criterion Referenced Measurement* (Englewood Cliffs, N.J.: Educational Technology, 1971).

20. For information write:
Instructional Objectives Exchange
University of California at Los Angeles
Los Angeles, California 90024

7. Planning-Programming-Budgeting-Evaluating

Any modern work on accountability would hardly be complete without a look at planning, programming, budgeting, and evaluating systems (PPBES). Sometimes this is referred to as PPBS without the evaluating component, but we prefer to emphasize the fourfold nature of the process. The Association of School Business Officials (ASBO), an association of people who have a major responsibility in the area of school administration, refers to the process as an "educational resources management system."[1] Others merely call the procedure "program budgeting."[2] No matter what name is used, our emphasis is on using the process as a means of being more "accountable." We should make clear at the outset that we do not recommend PPBES as the *only* possible procedure to be used. Obviously each district must decide for itself what is most appropriate for its needs. We do maintain, however, that present fiscal procedures in most school districts do not provide a resource for the administrators and others to make intelligent decisions on the money matters. We feel that PPBES can be a useful tool to assist administrators in making better decisions.

What Is PPBES?

There are a number of different definitions of PPBES by a variety of authors. Harry Hartley has devoted a book to the subject, and defines it:

Program budgeting relates the output-oriented programs, or activities, of an organization to specific resources that are then stated in terms of budget dollars.

Both programs and resources are projected for at least several years into the future. Emphasis is upon outputs, cost effectiveness methods, rational planning techniques, long-range objectives and analytical tools for decision making. Probably the most important single task that must be accomplished in moving to this kind of planning and budgeting is the development of a program structure.[3]

Another author indicates that PPBES is in "many ways more a decision-making process than an operations research tool. PPBS utilizes the mathematical analysis of operations research in the decision process, but PPBS is not a tool that can be applied to a specific problem situation. In this sense, it is more of a planning tool than a specific problem solution oriented tool."[4]

Charles Schultze, the former director of the U.S. Bureau of the Budget, describes PPBES as "a means of *helping* responsible officials make decisions. It is *not* a mechanical substitute for the good judgment, political wisdom and leadership of those officials."[5]

Another perspective:

Program budgeting has no standard definition. The general idea is that budgetary decisions should be made by focusing on output categories like governmental objectives, and products or programs instead of inputs like personnel, equipment, and maintenance. As in cost-benefit analysis, to which it owes a great deal, program budgeting lays stress on estimating the total financial cost of accomplishing objectives.[6]

Planning, programming, budgeting and evaluation systems, then, are a process by which long- and short-range planning for fiscal management occurs in such a way that the objectives of the organization can more effectively be met. Perhaps the key word is *process,* since we do not view the four components as separate but rather as a continuous flow of ideas and information, leading to responsible and accountable decisions.[7]

What PPBES Is Not

PPBES cannot ordinarily be applied in isolation to a specific situation. It will not, for instance, *tell* you whether or not to add a new bus run or build a gym or hire more teachers or fire some teachers or buy more instructional materials. PPBES can *help* you make these decisions, and will assist you in situation like those above as part of a total process, but not individually.

PPBES is not a synonym for computer programming, in spite of the use of *programming* in its title. A computer is not necessary in PPBES, although it may be helpful if a school district already has one. Unless they can be quantified, many of the procedures used in

PPBES do not readily lend themselves to computer programming. Instead they rely on careful planning and discussion so that alternatives may be considered.

PPBES is also not a substitute for a good administrator any more than an adding machine is a substitute for a good administrator. PPBES, however, will assist a good administrator, school board, and community to understand what and how well their educational dollars have been or appear likely to be spent.

Finally, PPBES is not a device to hold down expenditures for education. It can assist you to spend money more effectively but it is not going to cost less, any more than merit pay for teachers will save money.

Why Use PPBES?

PPBES, or program budgeting, first appeared in operation during the Kennedy administration, in the Department of Defense under Secretary Robert S. McNamara in 1961. Although the Hoover Commission of 1950 recommended "program budgets," it was President Lyndon Johnson in 1965 who instructed twenty-one nondefense departments to institute similar techniques, thereby spreading the practice broadly. RAND Corporation was also instrumental in the early research on PPBES (RAND stands for "research and development"). It was not, however, until 1968 that articles discussing the possibility of using PPBES began to appear in professional education journals, although the process was operational in many other fields several years earlier. (Why is it that education is generally one of the last fields to adopt new practices?)

But more of an argument is needed for PPBES than the fact that it is used by government or business. A school system is not a government or a business—or is it? For one thing, aren't most school board members *elected* officials? In some states, school board members run for election as members of political parties, yes, as Democrats or Republicans, selected at party caucuses or through primary elections. Elsewhere school board members are elected on a nonpartisan basis or they may be appointed by a mayor or other elected official. Also, school board members everywhere are *state* officials, not local officials. The U.S. Constitution does not mention education as a federal function but leaves it to the states, which (in all cases except Hawaii) delegate responsibility for operating the schools to smaller local subgroups, sometimes a county, often a city or village school board. There are about 17,000 school districts in the country, each of which has board members, elects officers, levies taxes or spends money, and operates like other *governmental* offices. School boards can set policy that affects the actions of others, take punitive action, often condemn property, construct buildings, and do many things that governmental agencies also do.

Whether we like it or not, school districts are also big business. Especially in the suburbs and rural areas, the schools frequently spend more money and hire more people than any other governmental agency or private business, and often the schools are the largest agency in terms of dollars spent, people employed, and property owned. Doesn't it make sense to apply good business practices, *when appropriate,* to our schools? The common abhorrence to business methods among schoolmen, stemming from excessive application in the early 1900s, needs reexamination.[8] The fear that the business dictum, "the finest product at the lowest cost," still emphasizes "the lowest cost," remains as strong today as ever. When cost is the only criteria offered for reaching a decision, the traditional schools appear more likely to yield solely "the lowest cost" without any firm notion of what this means for the educational program it supports.

There are other reasons why PPBES may be useful. It is apparent to most of us that there is resistance on the part of many taxpayers to rising school costs with no noticeable improvement in the educational program. That is what accountability focuses upon, and what PPBES may help alleviate. School districts have limited resources in terms of money. The property tax can only go so high, and there have recently been court decisions in a number of states indicating that the property tax may be a poor way of financing schools. But even if another source of funds is found, or if the state assumes a greater share of the costs, only so much can be spent for education. Other services compete for the tax dollar, including the police, fire departments, hospitals, highways, garbage collection, street lighting, libraries, playgrounds, and welfare. However, the demands for school services continue to increase. Schools are asked, or told, to teach driver education, sex education, several languages, black studies, advanced placement courses, vocational training, speech therapy, remedial reading, and so on. These demands or desires are probably greater than the funds available to support them, under present conditions and procedures. But the schools have resources besides money: people, facilities, equipment, and time. By considering how these additional resources are to be used—and PPBES will help you do just that—it is possible to consider alternatives and set priorities on how the dollars are to be spent.

Another factor for school boards to consider is how well the district uses its present funds. We suspect that much of taxpayer resistance results from lack of knowledge about how the money is now being spent. Most school budgets are fairly difficult to read and understand, and many people feel there is "plenty of fat" in the budget or that extra amounts are put into the budget by the school administration so the board can cut the budget and "look good." In other words, if the public does not think the money is being spent wisely, or does not know how it is spent, it may be reluctant to approve an increase. One district discovered that, with the PPBES approach, the school budget was approved by "the greatest margin in the recent history of school budget elections."[9] This is not to say that you can be assured of passing a school budget just by using PPBES. But the total process can go a long way toward gaining support and understanding of the budget, thereby reducing the negative vote.

Perhaps this is a good place to remind ourselves why schools exist in the first place. Schools exist to educate children. They do not exist to operate buildings, or to provide something to administer, or to provide jobs for teachers or maintenance workers, or to run transportation, or to operate cafeterias. However, if we look at most school budget documents we see under expenditures: administration, instructional salaries, maintenance, food service, transportation, and fixed charges. Is it any wonder that people resist paying higher taxes when the budget indicates nothing about educating children! Under PPBES, however, the educational program is more clearly defined, showing how much money is spent to teach reading, French, music, and physical education; the present budget system has no way to show this relationship.[10]

Another reason to consider PPBES is found in the tendency of most school budgets not to look at the long-range implications of programs that are being started, or salary schedules that have been adopted, or equipment that is being purchased. Under a PPBES plan, each of these would be explored before making the decision. Building a new school facility, for instance, means that in future years there will be additional staff, equipment replacement, utilities costs, maintenance and preventive maintenance, and increased insurance (one of the "fixed charges" that somehow is not really fixed). Future expenditures should be part of the original decision whether to build the facility or not.

There may be a variety of ways to achieve a certain goal. By using PPBES, these alternatives can be explored to determine which is the best one, and what it will cost, before embarking on a new program. For example, let us say that the district has decided to have a driver education program. Among the possible ways to accomplish this are: to have a private company teach the course, use specially equipped automobiles owned by the district, lease automobiles from outside, ask local dealers to furnish automobiles, use "driver-trainers" instead of automobiles, practice on the city street, build a driving range, use the parking lot after school as a driving range, give each student a certain amount of money and let the student purchase driver training, use motion pictures and filmstrips, use videotapes, hire part-time teachers, use regular teachers, use regular teachers and pay them extra to teach driver training, offer the program during the school year, offer it only in the summer, use only automatic transmission vehicles, use both standard and automatic, use only standard-sized cars, use only compact cars, have the students furnish their own cars, etc. The point is that each of these alternatives must be examined with regard to (1) cost and (2) how well it will accomplish the stated goal. Well-conceived program budgets are specific about their goals and use some performance objectives, which indicate what skills are expected on completion of the course, or what outcomes may be expected, such as a reduction in the number of accidents in the community. A PPBES procedure would force the district to examine what it is doing, rather than burying a new series of items in the budget under several headings, since there are elements of administration, teachers' salaries, instructional materials, maintenance on the vehicles, insurance, and other costs scattered throughout the budget document. Using the PPBES approach, the driver education program could be clearly detailed, as far as costs are concerned, in the budget document, with a supporting statement for public presentation that shows what alternatives were considered and why they were not selected.

In sum, if there is a common thread that runs through the advantages of using PPBES, it is that the *PPBES procedure* pulls together long-separated strands in education: the educational program, its costs, and its expectations. Accordingly, the process should aid schoolmen in (1) formulating educational programs based on goals and objectives, (2) creating models that present alternatives and comparison data for decision making, (3) aiding in establishing more clearly what the district's educational and financial priorities are over a period of time, and (4) permitting schoolmen the chance to be more educationally accountable to the board and public for the results achieved in relation to the resources expended. As a process, PPBES forces a district to ask five questions of any educational program with a financial commitment undertaken:

1. Where is this program going?

2. How does it intend to get there?

3. How will the district know if and when this program has succeeded?

4. What are the alternatives to this program?

5. What are the financial and educational implications over a period of time for the proposed program and its alternatives?

The search for answers to these questions discourages, as Harold Noah points out, "the usual shibboleths of 'education for life,' or 'educating each child to the extent of his capacities,' or 'integrating the child into the community,' for all of these are, as they stand, nonoperational goals, mere sloganizing."[11] Faced with the necessity of making hard decisions among competing demands on the scarce resources (time, talent, and money), PPBES offers a powerful tool for both the steward and reviewer in the accountability process.

The Major Components of PPBES

There are four major components of PPBES: *planning, programming, budgeting,* and *evaluating.* We cannot emphasize too strongly that these are *not* separate components, but are interrelated and interdependent. Granted, any one of the components is useful, but we insist that the total process or system should be utilized to realize fullest possible potential. The key relationship among the processes is that of decision making, which is the central activity that occurs in PPBES. It is made possible because the district has planned, programmed, budgeted, and evaluated itself, thus highlighting some important analytical components in decision making: objectives, alternatives, costs, and effectiveness.

Figure 7.1 shows the relationship of the four processes. Note especially that the arrows indicate a back-and-forth flow of information and ideas; the process is not necessarily sequential. Although we present the process sequentially, school practice may not always work that mechanically. It may not first plan, then program, then budget, and then evaluate, but rather plan, program, evaluate, plan,

Figure 7.1. The major components of PPBES

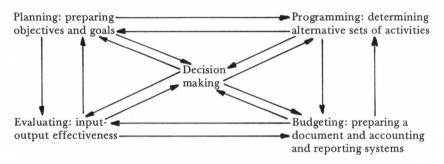

program, budget, plan, evaluate, program, budget, plan, evaluate, and so on. This happens because the school system is constantly changing—or should be—to meet the needs of students. What was appropriate in a science class the day before man walked on the moon was not appropriate the day after that magnificent event. (As we write this chapter we are struck by the fact that "one giant step for mankind" took place three years ago; have science courses and textbooks really been updated?) We must constantly plan, program, budget, and evaluate our school system, not just in November or at "budget time." We *do* need to establish a budget, and to be fiscally responsible, but by expressing the budget in terms of programs—e.g., science—rather than people, we have the opportunity to reevaluate our science program more realistically, perhaps even reallocating science funds to take advantage of new concepts. We would not be tied down by line items in the budget, with little room to maneuver, nor would it necessarily be a case of shifting funds from one line to another, e.g., from cafeteria to instructional equipment, but rather of looking at the science budget and deciding how best to spend these funds. Funds might be shifted, for example, from music to science, but it would be from one program to another with everyone aware of what was happening. An examination of our goals and objectives, the planning component, is required before we can change the priority one program has over another. In this way, each of the components of PPBES interrelates with the other components to assist in the process of decision making.

Planning

Planning may be defined as "the process of preparing a set of decisions for action in the future, directed at achieving goals by optimal means."[12] In practice, planning—as we use the term—means reducing program intentions to the form of a model that can be systematically analyzed. E. S. Quade notes:

In areas . . . where there is no accepted theoretical foundation, advice obtained from experts working individually or as a committee must depend largely on judgment and intuition. *So must the advice from systems analysis.* But the virtue of such analysis is that it permits the judgment and intuition of the experts in relevant fields to be combined systematically and efficiently. The essence of the method is to construct and operate within a "model," a simplified abstraction of the real situation appropriate to the question.[13]

This planning model attempts to make as *rational* and *visible* as possible "decisions in and about education . . . [that] continue to come from the political process, influenced by value judgments, and from the pressures coming from the various interested parties as well as from the process of systematic analysis."[14] A model's form may range from mathematical equations to simple verbal descriptions extrapolated from experience, intuition, and best guesses.

Many of the ingredients for planning ought to be already on hand if our model for developing educationally accountable programs has been followed. A sense of direction presumably exists now through the identification of needs (chapter 3) and the involvement of appropriate persons in establishing the goals and objectives of programs that meet those identified needs (chapter 5). Further, the objectives of the program have also presumably been refined to a point where their performance lends itself to evaluating or generally asssessing the degree of relative success achieved (chapter 6). In short, if we now have a relatively clear notion of where we want our program to go (the ends), it behooves us to consider alternative ways of getting there (the means), what the costs of these different alternatives are, and, finally, how desirable each alternative is in the weighting of its costs against its effectiveness (the criterion). Figure 7.2 indicates briefly the steps that have led us to the point of selecting an alternative from our planning to develop further into a program, the "programming" element of PPBS.

Concerning the construction of *your* planning model, two procedures (among many possibilities[15]) might be considered: the framework used in chapter 3 for gathering data for the positive/negative

Figure 7.2. Precedence of *planning* in a planning-programming-budgeting-evaluation system for educationally accountable programs

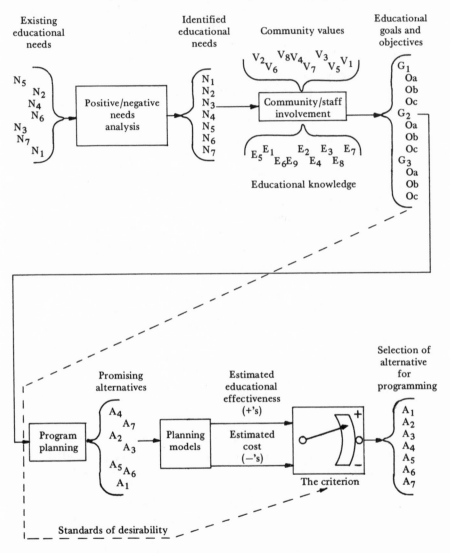

needs asssessment (see pages 89-93), or the procedure offered below. If the positive/negative needs assessment framework is used, it is assumed that its user possesses sufficient imagination not to be troubled by the conversion of currently operating educational programs (the focus of the needs assessment) into hypothetically operating programs (referred to in figure 7.2 as "promising alternatives"), in order to project the cost and degree of effectiveness expected if that alternative was used.

The second suggestion for building a planning model might be: (1) to begin with the goals and objectives offered as expressions of the school district's policy, (2) search for alternatives that appear to promise some success in meeting those goals and objectives, and then (3) project them through a series of categories over a time period. A series of answers should arise as different alternatives are projected. It then becomes the task of the reviewing body (e.g., the building principal, superintendent, board of education, advisory committee, etc.) to select the alternative most suited for further development or programming.

Suppose, for example, that the board of education adopted formally some goals and objectives committing the district to offering a driver education program: "That every child may learn to drive, this district shall offer to students (of at least sixteen years of age who elect it) a driver education program with the expectation that, upon completion of the eight-week course, the student will know and understand proper driving procedures as demonstrated by passing the state's driving test and obtaining a driver's license."

With a policy stated in that manner, there should be little doubt in the administrator's mind about what is expected. But what is the *most reasonable* way to accomplish it? Enter alternative plans and a model to test them.

The question, however, was not a random one. If it asked for the *best* way rather than the *most reasonable* one, controlled tests and a research design would be required, and we would have a problem too cumbersome for immediate administrative decision making. On the other hand, if we asked only for *"a* way" to accomplish our goal, any way that appears to offer some promise of success could be used (a common practice where immediate time pressures seemingly force one to solve problems on the spot, taking usually a short-term view expressed in the notion "if it solves the problem, use it"). Our quest, however, is to find what appears to be the most plausible way of reaching our goal, given local conditions, etc. If we consider that such a program, once selected and in operation, has the potential to influence many hundreds or thousands of lives, requires valuable time and space in the school program (if that is where the program is placed), and costs in the thousands of dollars (particularly as the years pass), it seems worth a little time to consider the "most reasonable" way for the program to grow. While we assume that implemented programs can be changed, it may be akin to transplanting oak trees, i.e., very difficult. Choosing to do a little work now rather than a lot of work later, our task then is to take the objectives of the board's policy and develop a planning model:

What is essential is a model that enables expert intuition and judgment to be applied efficiently. The method provides its answer by processes that are accessible to critical examination, capable of duplication by others, and, more or less, readily modified as new information becomes available. And, in contrast to other aids to decision-making, which share the same limitations, it extracts everything possible from scientific methods, and therefore its virtues are the virtues of those methods.[16]

Returning to our task, what alternatives for accomplishing it might be considered? A little research into what other school districts do or where similar goals are attempted would be helpful at this point. Even more useful is taking time to do some hard thinking about the task and various ways of handling it (there is no substitute for hard thinking!). On the goal of driver education, we listed about twenty items that might be considered in putting together packages of plan alternatives (e.g., contracting an outside driver training school on a fee basis, hiring part-time staff, using "trainer" models, etc.). These alternatives, grouped appropriately together (a function requiring a degree of intuition and judgment), might be fit into four or five packages of alternative plans (e.g., alternative plan 1 might consist of simply contracting an independent agency, alternative 2 of using part-time teachers with driver trainer films and other simulated materials, alternative 3 of using regular faculty on an extracurricular basis with leased dealer cars, and so on).

Significant for our purposes here, however, is the format used in establishing the planning model. A three-dimensional model may be used to portray, in the parlance of the U.S. Bureau of the Budget, a "multiyear program and financial plan" (PFP). Essentially, the PFP includes reviewing each of the packaged plan alternatives by breaking them into "program elements" and projecting these elements into the future, usually three to five years depending on the nature of the objectives being planned (e.g., planning building facilities normally means many more years of projection, etc.). If the particular

alternative has already been in operation, the review typically includes its past and present performance before projecting into the
future. Regarding the items projected, the "program elements," the
Bureau of the Budget describes them in this manner:

> C. *Program elements.* A program element covers agency activities related
> directly to the production of a discrete agency output, or group of related
> outputs. Agency activities which contribute directly to the output should be
> included in the program element, even though they may be conducted within
> different organizations, or financed from different appropriations. Thus, pro-
> gram elements are the basic units of the program structure.
>
> Program elements have these characteristics: (1) they should produce
> clearly definable outputs, which are quantified wherever possible; (2) wherever
> feasible, the output of a program element should be an agency end-product—not
> an intermediate product that supports another element; and (3) the inputs of a
> program element should vary with changes in the level of output, but not
> necessarily proportionally.[17]

Figure 7.3 offers a three-dimensional view of projecting the
program elements in an educational PFP, while figure 7.4 suggests an
outline for projecting and analyzing data and alternative plans.

The procedure used on the federal level includes following up
the PFP with a "program memorandum" (PM). The PM supports the
conclusions and offers recommendations from the data of the PFP. It
is the steward's way of influencing his reviewers as they decide
among the alternative plans. The program memorandum presents a
succinct evaluation and justification of the PFP, and should:

> (1) Spell out the specific programs recommended by the agency head for
> the multi-year time period being considered, show how these programs meet the
> needs of the (school district) in this area, show the total costs of recommended
> programs, and show the specific ways in which they differ from current pro-
> grams and those of the past several years.
>
> (2) Describe program objectives and expected concrete accomplishments
> and costs for several years into the future.
>
> (3) Describe program objectives insofar as possible in quantitative physical
> terms.
>
> (4) Compare the effectiveness and the cost of alternative objectives, of
> alternative *types* of programs designed to meet the same or comparable objec-
> tives, and of different levels within any given program category. This comparison
> should identify past experience, the alternatives which are believed worthy of
> consideration, earlier differing recommendations, earlier cost and performance
> estimates, and the reasons for change in these estimates.
>
> (5) Make explicit the assumptions and criteria which support recom-
> mended programs.
>
> (6) Identify and analyze the main uncertainties in the assumptions and in
> estimated program effectiveness or costs, and show the sensitivity of recommen-
> dations to these uncertainties.[18]

Figure 7.3. A three-dimensional procedure for developing educational multiyear program and financial plans

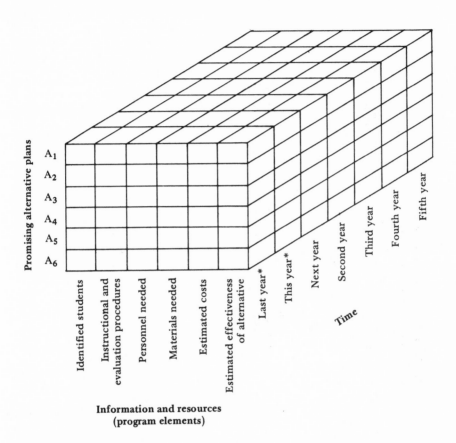

Promising alternative plans

A_1
A_2
A_3
A_4
A_5
A_6

Identified students

Instructional and evaluation procedures

Personnel needed

Materials needed

Estimated costs

Estimated effectiveness of alternative

Last year*

This year*

Next year

Second year

Third year

Fourth year

Fifth year

Time

Information and resources (program elements)

*If appropriate.

Figure 7.4. Outline of a multiyear program and financial plan (PFP) used to analyze alternative plans

Statement of objective(s): _____

Plan Alternative 1: _____

(Statement of desired outcomes that the alternative plans seek to attain)

Time	Students identified (characteristics and number)	Instructional and evaluation procedures to be used	Personnel needed	Estimated costs	Estimated effectiveness of alternatives
Last year (if appropriate)		(Brief description)			
This year (if appropriate)					
Next year					
Second year					
Third year					
Fourth year					
Fifth year					

Plan Alternative 2: _____

(Brief description)

These expectations, accepted by federal agencies as normal operating procedure for presenting recommendations to political decision makers, far exceed normal school practice. While the effort necessary to generate such memoranda is more formidable than schoolmen usually attempt, some virtues attend making the effort. Among these are that the steward should have a positive notion of what appears to be the "most reasonable" alternative plan for a given situation. He should also have a grasp of the situation that permits him to withstand tight review of his recommendations. His command of the situation, with its cards-on-the-table approach, should help the steward to build a higher level of confidence in the reviewer's mind toward the steward's performance. As you will recall, the heart of the accountability process is for the steward to explain *as rationally as possible* the results of efforts to achieve specific task objectives of his stewardship. If planning for programs is one of the steward's specific tasks, the procedure outlined above ought to help.

There is an additional note to be offered. At this point a perennial source of difficulty commonly arises between stewards and their reviewers. Whether the steward is an administrator, teacher, advisory committee, etc., who reports to the reviewing party (e.g., the board of education, advisory committee, other administrator, etc.), the expectation exists that the reviewing party will seriously consider the report. Often the reviewers do not, or give only perfunctory attention. Frustration grows even stronger when reviewers seemingly disregard such efforts altogether and embark without explanation on a different course of action. Whether or not this behavior is intentional, the result is usually predictable: a strong desire on the steward's part—teacher, administrator or lay professional committee —to shout "Damn you!" at the reviewers. Building trust works both ways, for reviewers as well as stewards. When reviewers show apparent indifference to the planning efforts of stewards, it is hard for a steward to escape an attitude of "why bother." Under these circumstances, both rational planning and the accountability process suffer.

Programming

A second component of PPBES is programming, the further development of the selected program's plans. The programming document is very specific, spelling out in greater detail what will be done to achieve the goals and objectives stated in the chosen planning component. In a sense, planning establishes the strategic outline of the program, while programming represents its tactical rudiments.

The program plan might be developed by the school district staff, perhaps with outside consultants and resources. The participation of students might also be considered. Obviously, the size and makeup of the planning group is a function of the size of the district: larger districts need some form of representation while smaller districts may be able to involve more people directly. Programming at the building unit level would be less cumbersome.

The program plan is made up of a number of parts. It makes sense to have a standard pattern for programming so that programs can be more easily compared and to make sure nothing is overlooked. Each district will want to decide for itself how much specificity is contained in the program plan. However, programming is not a lesson plan, nor a substitute for individual creativity on the part of teachers. The purpose of programming is to ensure through logical means the attainment of the objectives stated within the planning framework selected. From the details of the programming come the last translations into budget figures and the means of evaluating program progress and outcomes. Among some items commonly considered in educational programming are:

The planning framework. The planning framework (i.e., the alternative plan selected) indicates what the program is (e.g., reading, French, physical education, art, etc.). It serves as a charge to the programmers. It provides the direction and denotes the general boundaries within which the programmers are expected to "flesh out" or otherwise develop the plan further.

Performance objectives. Because the planning framework seldom provides more than a few major objectives, it is usually necessary for the programmers to provide a closer, more detailed listing of performance objectives necessary to realize the program's goals as well as to evaluate its progress and outcomes. Chapter 6 has reviewed the process of creating performance objectives in some detail.

Identified or targeted students. An indication should be given of what group of students the program will serve: young children, college-bound students, blind students, etc. Any number of questions might be raised in the identification of the students targeted from this program. How many students will be served? Are they found in all schools? Do these students have special needs? Perhaps this is an adult education program, or for students who elect the program or for students who have special talents. Again, the planning framework may *generally* indicate which students are to be considered; the programmer must be specific.

Content. Programming provides detailed statements of what

happens during the program. These statements may come in the form of a course syllabus, a course outline as is found in college catalogs, or a highly sequenced set of learning skills and knowledge as is found in the "individualized program instruction materials." It is not a lesson plan. It is, however, the identification of that body of knowledge and skills that we desire to impart to the learner.

Coordination. Is this to be an isolated program, or is it related to other programs? For instance, the reading program in the primary grades may be related to the social studies program, or a student may have to complete the first high school mathematics course before taking the physics course. It is also possible that some sort of team teaching, or shared teaching, or open classroom, or nongraded program may be a part of the statement. Perhaps the terms "integrating" and "fitting" apply equally well here to describe coordination, for the programmer attempts to both integrate and fit the program into the larger ongoing school system of programs as well as to seek internal coordination among the plan's details.

Responsibility. Who is responsible for the program? Perhaps a single teacher or a curriculum coordinator has the responsibility, or maybe a building principal. This will vary from district to district, but should be clearly indicated in the programming. Delineating who is responsible to whom for what results is an important part of this process. It is at this point that it is also possible to consider the negotiation of this responsibility either as an internal or external performance contract (see chapter 9).

Resources. What is needed for this program? Special equipment may be necessary, or special facilities, or special teachers. Does the program require a large room, a stable, newspapers, videotapes? Obviously this information will be needed when the budget is developed. More important, it permits the allocation of costs where they appropriately belong, to the program that incurs them.

Time. Is the program offered every semester, every day, every period, several times during the same period, twice a week, after school, only in the summer? This is needed for budgetary purposes as well as for space allocation. A common pitfall in programming is the lack of attention given to the implications of time usage.

Evaluation and program monitoring. How is the program to be evaluated? How is its progress to be checked? We said earlier that performance objectives would be developed for each program. But how will we be kept posted on progress toward their attainment? How will they be measured? Are standardized tests to be used? observation of students? outside testing such as passing the driver's

exam? statistical data on how many students enter college? This list
will vary from program to program. Different programs may have to
be monitored and evaluated in different ways. It is the task of the
programmer, however, to specify the form and manner. (Chapter 8
describes, in part, program monitoring, while chapter 10 deals with
evaluation more closely, and chapter 11 touches upon the use of the
educational program auditor.)

In essence, programming structures the educational plan by
converting the abstract elements in the plan—that is, who-what-
whom-when-where-how—into educational elements. For example, (1)
who: students (grade level, age, sex, mental ability, etc.); (2) what:
curriculum (driver education, mathematics, science, reading, etc.);
(3) whom: personnel (teachers, parents, paraprofessionals, specialists,
etc.); (4) when: time (hours, periods, days, years, etc.); (5) where:
location (classroom, city streets, home, museums, etc.); and (6) how:
pedagogy (lecture, simulation, discussion, lab, etc.).[19] As the program takes shape, alternative options of another variety will suggest
themselves. Various trade-off possibilities among the different ways
of handling the programming will unfold, compelling the programmers to reach decisions at this tactical planning level akin to those
faced by the planning strategies. Programmers too must be able to
justify to their reviewers the paths they took in spelling out the
planning framework. This need is especially true if the programmer
challenges any constraints in the planning framework.

Budgeting

Budgeting is the component of PPBES in which the programs
and available resources are examined, and a budget document is
prepared that expresses the educational plan of the district in terms
of expenditures. It is "the process of authorizing the use of resources
to accomplish the objectives and programs developed in the planning
and programming process."[20] Budgeting is thus an integral component of PPBES, since the planning and programming usually have
little impact unless translated into a budget. The actual process of
budgeting should be familiar to most practitioners. The emphasis in
PPBES budgets, however, is placed on isolating the expenditures to
be incurred in a particular program rather than common expenditure
requests into a category of expenditures shared by all other programs
without delineation. While state fiscal requirements usually call for
these traditional line-item budgetary procedures for auditing purposes, in PPBES the effort is made to estimate what problems of

time, personnel, materials, etc., are actually utilized by the particular program. It is such estimates and prorations, however, that frequently raise important overlooked questions about the educational priorities of the district, uncovered by the visibility of program allocation in the PPBES document.

In the following paragraphs we will present some of the ideas that might be helpful, in a general way, in considering the budgeting component.

Defining Available Resources

One of the first steps in the budgeting process is to define the available resources. We indicated earlier that the resources of the district in financial terms will probably be less than the demands and requests of the staff. But, to determine the gap (if any), we must find out what the resources are.

There are other resources besides money, among them people, facilities, equipment, and time. We suggest an inventory of these available resources. They were briefly sketched in the planning framework and projected for several years into the future. Do not forget to include the number of students anticipated, replacement costs, rising salaries of personnel and similar items.

Most of these figures are easy to determine from information that is readily available. The number of students can be determined from population projections. There are many ways of projecting the number of students, and it is not too difficult to do. Close coordination with community officials is necessary, especially if zoning changes are contemplated. It is equally important to consider the possible effects of the closing of a private or parochial school. The latter may be a touchy subject politically, but is necessary lest the district be caught unprepared for a sudden influx of students.

The resources of personnel should be broken down to indicate the number of administrators, teachers, paraprofessionals, staff, and others. It is probably best to deal in full-time equivalent staff, combining two half-time positions into one full-time person.

Materials and equipment can be listed together or separately, depending on preference. Usually equipment consists of items that have a useful life of longer than a year and are not consumed in use; desks, chairs, tables, typewriters, textbooks, and wastebaskets are usually considered to be equipment. Materials include paper, pencils, crayons, workbooks, and other supplies. We suggest a separate listing unless there are good reasons for combining the items.

The facilities inventory includes the number of rooms available for instruction, offices, playground, gyms, cafeterias, and special use rooms. There may be state laws on the number of students who can occupy certain sized rooms, generally in terms of the square feet of floor space for each student. Some of the emerging trends in open-spaced rooms and team teaching make space comparisons more difficult, but they must be done to determine whether the number of students will be adequately taken care of in the available facilities.

A listing of the available financial resources should include money from local, regional, state, and federal sources, including any private funds available from endowments, gifts, tuition, and other receipts such as admissions and rentals. Again, any changes contemplated on the local level should be indicated. A change in assessment practices (for instance from 30 percent to 50 percent of market value) may significantly alter funding patterns.

In some ways, defining available resources is similar to the situation of a newly appointed superintendent moving into the school district. On the one hand, he faces the problems of planning and programming his family's living needs and the realities of where it is politically "proper" for him to live. On the other, there is the question of estimating his available resources (e.g., what kind of down payment can he make? How big a mortgage will his salary carry? Will his wife need to work? Should he cash in his retirement benefits from the state he is moving from?). Hopefully the real estate agent will locate a house that fits the appropriate planning and programming needs and that can be bought and carried without undue hardship by the available resources. But, in house hunting as in educational program development, it is not necessary to wait until a specific point before doing some preliminary work on determining what resources are available once the project has been identified. However, when an offer is to be made on the located house or the educational programmers believe they have developed *the* program to be recommended, the time has come to match the handiwork of the programmers against the reality of potentially available resources.

Matching Program Requirements and Resources

The next step is to compare the available resources with the required resources indicated by the programming. It is the wedding of available resources with the requirements indicated in the programming, or spelling out financially the program's inputs. We suggest following the same format offered in figure 7.4, only with the addition of greater detail plus a listing of available resources. Figure 7.5 makes this attempt. A summary sheet should be prepared, compiled from each of the program sheets. It is then a simple matter of comparing what is requested with what is available. Figure 7.6 presents a possible format for performing this task.

Again, our task here is to reconcile the program requirements with the resources available. If a mismatch occurs, a problem is identified and a decision must be reached on how to adjust the matter. Again, the guideline to be used in resolving the problem is the search for the "most reasonable" solution. Remember that solutions need to be projected over a time period to determine possible distortions that might arise later in the program.

Preparing the Budget Document

Next, the budget document is prepared to present to the school board and other groups. The budget may use the program format. For variety, a slightly different budget sheet is shown in figure 7.7. Each program is described at the top of the budget document in terms of what happens, not who does it, followed by the breakdown of how the money is to be spent.

In preparing the budget document, some system of account numbers should be used. Any one that works for you is appropriate, but the system should be consistent from one program to another so accurate comparisons can be made. It will also make the job of using data processing equipment much easier. If legal stipulations require that the budget document assume a specific format, the means of making such account transfers has been developed through a procedure called "crosswalk," a cross-referencing of budgets on different classification dimensions.[21]

The final step in the process is approval of the budget by the appropriate group. In most cases this is the board of education, but occasionally the town governing board has some veto power. Often the budget is approved by the school board but the money must be raised by a tax levy approved by the voters. Both groups should be aware that they are setting educational policy when they approve or disapprove the budget or certain items in the budget. However, if the system of priorities has worked correctly, any cuts in the budget should be made according to the established priorities, not on an across-the-board basis.

Figure 7.5. Possible format for projecting resource availability

	Last year (units)*	This year (units)	Projected			
			Next year (units)	Second year (units)	. . . . .	Fifth year (units)
Students						
Preschool	——	——	——	——		——
Primary	——	——	——	——		——
Elementary	——	——	——	——		——
Junior high	——	——	——	——		——
Senior high	——	——	——	——		——
Adult education	——	——	——	——		——
Instructional and evaluation procedures						
Time estimates	——	——	——	——		——
Personnel						
Administrators	——	——	——	——		——
Teachers	——	——	——	——		——
Specialists	——	——	——	——		——
Paraprofessionals	——	——	——	——		——
Other	——	——	——	——		——
Materials						
Instruction	——	——	——	——		——
Evaluation	——	——	——	——		——
Equipment	——	——	——	——		——
Facilities	——	——	——	——		——
Other	——	——	——	——		——
Revenues						
Local	$ ——	$ ——	$ ——	$ ——		$ ——
State	——	——	——	——		——
Federal	——	——	——	——		——
Other	——	——	——	——		——

*Unit: cost per student hour of a given service.

Figure 7.6. Possible format for matching program requirements with resources available

Identification no. _____   Program objectives: _____   Program description: _____

	Last year (units)		This year (units)		Next year (units)		Second year (units)		. . . .	Fifth year (units)	
	Program requires	Resource available	Program requires	Resource available	Program requires	Resource available	Program requires	Resource available		Program requires	Resource available
Students identified (number)											
Instructional evaluation procedures (time estimates)											
Personnel											
Administrators											
Teachers											
Specialists											
Paraprofessionals											
Other											
Materials											
Instruction											
Evaluation											
Equipment											
Facilities											
Other											

Figure 7.7. Pearl River School District program budget, 1971-72

Program title: Mathematics, K-12   Program code: 37

	Elementary	Middle school	High school	District-wide	Total
Certificated staff					
Regular salaries	$145,133	$114,766	$144,515	$1,850	$406,264
Substitutes and					
overtime	4,444	3,918	4,605	—	12,967
Employee benefits	36,068	28,619	35,958	446	101,091
Total	$185,645	$147,303	$185,078	$2,296	$520,322
Noncertificated					
Regular salaries	$420	$1,008	$3,226	—	$4,654
Substitutes and					
overtime	—	—	—	—	—
Employee benefits	117	282	1,674	—	2,073
Total	$537	$1,290	$4,900	—	$6,727
Other expenses					
Equipment	$ 100	$ 240	$ 160	—	$ 500
Supplies	8,600	3,900	2,500	—	15,000
Textbooks	2,182	602	3,145	—	5,929
Purchased services	1,628	855	4,965	—	7,448
Total	$12,510	$5,597	$10,770	—	$28,877
Grand total	$198,692	$154,190	$200,748	$2,296	$555,926
Number of students served	1,512	849	930	3,291	3,291
Budget per student served (whole dollars)	131	182	216	1	169

Evaluating

The last component of PPBES is evaluating, which is the process of finding out how well the program's objectives have been met. We indicated earlier that during the programming component, evaluation plans were formulated both for monitoring the progress of the program and assessing the effectiveness of its outcomes. Sometimes the evaluation component is utilized even before the program is made operational, gathering base-line data for comparative purposes later.

The information gained from the evaluation process also helps in the decision-making process shown in figure 7.1. Again, the four components are not isolated but are interrelated, and interact with each other. The results of the evaluation will be used to determine the effectiveness of the program, and to assist in ongoing and future planning. In other words, if the program is effective, as determined from the evaluation, it would probably be continued. If the program is not as effective as anticipated, some decisions will have to be made concerning the program's future.

One should expect to find included in a description of the evaluation component statements indicating (1) the methods of evaluation, (2) when and how they are to be employed, (3) the procedures used to collect data, (4) what amounts of objective and subjective data are to be collected, (5) whether a sampling technique is to be used, (6) an estimate of "reasonable expectations" to be attained at stages in the program's development as well as at its conclusion, and perhaps (7) a final cost/effectiveness ratio for the program. Thus, evaluating seeks to stimulate self-evaluation, to encompass the objectives of the program, to enable more successful learning and teaching, to record necessary data, and to provide a means for continuous feedback for educational policy makers.[22]

Because chapter 10 is devoted to the topic of evaluation, we will not press the reader's attention beyond pointing again to the parallel between the accountability process and the four interrelated components of PPBES. The evaluating component corresponds also with the rendering of the steward's account to the reviewers, touched on in chapter 11.

Implementing PPBES

Harry Hartley concludes: "Personal visits to schools in thirty states in the past three years have convinced me that *there is no single 'best way' to 'do' PPBS.*"[23] He then proceeds to offer three steps he believes worth considering for implementation purposes.[24]

The first step is to develop, under the superintendent's coordination, a district *program structure* that identifies and lists all programs—instructional and supportive—in descending order of detail with goals, objectives, and evaluative criteria.

Next is the selection by the curriculum coordinator or principal of particular curriculum, areas for *program analysis* by the staff, developing a model that includes all the ingredients of an instructional program (e.g., program goals, instructional objectives, learner skills, evaluative criteria, alternatives, estimated effectiveness, costs, etc.) and results in a twenty-page memorandum for each program.

The final step is the preparation of a *program budget* (under the guidance of the business administrator) that identifies each program as a "cost center" and spells out its budget in cost accounting procedures.

This approach makes sense to us. So too do the procedures we have offered it. Yet we recognize the possibility that much skepticism remains. According to the Western New York Study Council, skepticism toward the PPBES tool is usually based on two factors: (1) uncertainty in understanding precisely what is required at each step in the PPBES process; and (2) a feeling that the qualitative aspect of educational objectives limits the usefulness of the tool.[25] However, the same study shows that other groups with hard-to-quantify objectives and uncertain beginnings have tended to have positive experiences with their use of the PPBES tool once started— for example, the United States Information Agency, the Agency for International Development, the U.S. Department of State, and the Peace Corps. Surely if such groups can profitably use such a tool, we in education can also.

Notes for Chapter 7

1. Charles W. Foster, ed., *Educational Resources Management Systems* (Chicago: Association of School Business Officials, 1972).

2. Harry Hartley, one of the national leaders in the PPBS movement, objects to the equating of *program budgeting* with PPBS. He notes, "The two are not the same, although a myth repeated often enough can become accepted truth. A program budget is simply one component of a much more comprehensive PPB System." (Harry Hartley, "PPBS: Status and Implications," *Educational Leadership* 29 no. 8 (May 1972): 658.)

We do not make this distinction largely because the general literature of the field has not been consistent in making Hartley's distinction.

3. Harry Hartley, *Educational Planning-Programming-Budgeting: A Systems Approach* (Englewood Cliffs, N.J.: Prentice-Hall, 1968), p. 76.

4. Ralph Van Dusseldorp, Duane Richardson, and Walter Foley, *Educational Decision-Making Through Operations Research* (Boston: Allyn and Bacon, 1971), pp. 134-35.

5. Charles Schultze, "Why Benefit-Cost Analysis?" in *Program Budgeting and Benefit-Cost Analysis*, ed. Harley Hinrichs and Graeme Taylor (Pacific Palisades, Calif.: Goodyear Publishing Co., 1969), p. 1.

6. Aaron Wildavsky, "The Political Economy of Efficiency: Cost-Benefit Analysis, Systems Analysis, and Program Budgeting," in *Planning Programming Budgeting: A Systems Approach to Management*, ed. Fremont Lyden and Ernest Miller (Chicago: Markham Publishing Co., 1968), p. 371.

7. A three-volume work designed to help educators understand and train other educators in the essentials of the approach is available from the Center for

Vocational and Technical Education, The Ohio State University, Columbus, Ohio, and from the ERIC (Educational Resources Information Center) system in microfiche. These volumes include Joseph McGivney and William Nelson, *PPBS for Educators: A Training Outline* (Columbus, Ohio: Ohio State University, 1969); idem, *PPBS for Educators: A Case Problem* (Columbus, Ohio: Ohio State University, 1969); idem, *PPBS for Educators: An Annotated Bibliography* (Columbus, Ohio: Ohio State University, 1969).

8. Raymond Callahan, *Education and the Cult of Efficiency* (Chicago: University of Chicago Press, 1962).

9. Robert Alioto and J. A. Jungherr, "Using PPBS to Overcome Taxpayers' Resistance," in *Emerging Patterns of Administrative Accountability*, ed. Lesley H. Browder, Jr. (Berkeley, Calif.: McCutchan Publishing Corp., 1971), p. 257.

10. One school district's attempt to develop PPBES is portrayed in Todd Anton, "Planning, Programming, Budgeting System for Hillsborough City School District," *Emerging Patterns*, pp. 260-74.

11. Harold Noah, "Education Needs Rational Decisionmaking," *Emerging Patterns*, p. 207.

12. Yehezkel Dror, "The Planning Process: A Facet Design," in *Planning Programming Budgeting: A Systems Approach to Management*, p. 99.

13. E. S. Quade, "Systems Analysis Techniques for Planning-Programming-Budgeting," report P-3322 (Santa Monica, Calif.: RAND Corp., March 1966), p. 5.

14. Robert J. Garvue, *Modern Public School Finance* (New York: Macmillan Co., 1969), p. 104.

15. Among standard works on planning, see B. E. Goetz, *Management Planning and Control* (New York: McGraw-Hill, 1949); H. D. Koontz and C. J. O'Donnell, *Principles of Management*, 3d ed. (New York: McGraw-Hill, 1964); W. H. Newman, *Administrative Action—The Techniques of Organization and Management* (Englewood Cliffs, N.J.: Prentice-Hall, 1951).

A series of document résumés concerned with the applications of various planning techniques in education is contained in Educational Resources Information Center, *Educational Planning* (Washington, D. C.: American Association of School Administrators, 1971).

16. Quade, "Systems Analysis Techniques for Planning-Programming-Budgeting," p. 40.

17. U.S., Bureau of the Budget, Bulletin 68-9 (April 12, 1968), section 4c.

18. U.S., Bureau of the Budget, Bulletin 66-3 (October 12, 1965), p. 8.

19. Joseph McGiveney and Robert Hedges, *An Introduction to PPBS* (Columbus, Ohio: Charles E. Merrill Publishing Co., 1972), p. 50.

20. Ibid., p. 83.

21. Foster, *Educational Resources Management Systems*, chapter 6.

22. Van Dusseldorp, Richardson, and Foley, *Educational Decision-Making Through Operations Research*, p. 143.

23. Hartley, "PPBS: Status and Implications," p. 659.

24. Ibid., pp. 659-60.

25. Western New York School Study Council, *Development of an Operational Model for the Application of Planning-Programming-Budgeting Systems in Local School Districts: Program Budgeting Note 2—Program Budgeting in the Federal Government* (Buffalo: Western New York School Study Council, February 1969).

8. Staff Development and Program Implementation

Before the staff is developed and the program put into effect, a number of things should have happened. For example, we presume that a survey of the district's needs was made to establish some notion of what educational problems have priority in receiving the district's (or building's) allocation of scarce resources (i.e., time, money, and effort). A change strategy was adopted, either implicitly or explicitly, concerned with anticipating generally what needs to be done at various points along the way to ensure the successful development of the program. A pivotal consideration was involving people—particularly those expected to be directly influenced by the new program—in the process of planning the program, working out its goals and objectives, determining how it is to be evaluated and with what kinds of evidence, and other details that lead to the authorization to move forward with the program.

We are now at the point of preparing the staff to undertake the new program. Because the program's development is not specified beyond being educationally accountable, we focus more on general procedures that may be used (1) to develop the staff and (2) to implement the program.

Developing the Staff

Some Expectations

What results are expected from the development preparations of the staff? To implement an educationally accountable program, the following outcomes seem reasonable expectations:

1. The staff members clearly understand the purpose, goals, and objectives of the new program and their role in it—that is, they can answer in logical detail any related questions asked by an outside observer.

2. The staff members know and can identify the measurable changes expected to occur in the targeted group of learners, and will be able later to make this knowledge clear to the learners.

3. An attitude or point of view is held by the staff members as part of their professional role that if the expected changes do not occur in individual learners, other possibilities and alternatives will be explored until appropriate ways to produce the desired changes are found—that is, at least three or four alternative learning plans are available for individual students who do not seem to be learning under the new program, and additional efforts will be made if these plans do not work, but under no circumstances will the child be rejected as a potential learner.

4. The staff demonstrates (by performance test) a knowledge of the theory or model of instruction used to support the program and has been instructed (through demonstrations, workshops, and practice sessions) how to apply it.

5. The proposed program is given a few practice sessions, first on the staff and then on a small group of students.

6. The staff is able to operate procedures for monitoring program progress and to make appropriate shifts in the on-going program as problems appear.

7. The staff knows and can answer questions on how the program is to be assessed and the results reported.
Further refinement of these general expectations is, of course, dependent on the nature of the designated program.

In brief, these seven general outcomes desired for developing a staff require providing it with particular knowledge, skills, and an attitude—all combined for the purpose of developing this staff into an effective working group in implementing an educationally accountable program.

A Strategy Employed

In most of our efforts up to now, we have subscribed to a general change theory (chapter 4) holding that to make a successful organizational change one reduces resistance forces while increasing facilitator forces in the organizational environment. This task requires that one can identify and manipulate appropriately these forces.

An outgrowth of this approach was the notion that, in order to change people's behavior (i.e., move them from resistance to support, or at least acquiescence), one focuses first on changing the attitudes of the parties most directly influenced by the change (these parties are perceived as major forces for resistance or support in the change process). If people had a positive attitude toward the change (or at least a neutral one), they would be amenable to it; in fact, if we were successful, the parties most involved might even be willing to behave so as to accommodate the change. This hope was held particularly for staff members.

Accordingly, opportunities for staff involvement abounded in the early stages of program planning and development. Many people with different perspectives—parents, teachers, students, administrators, etc.—were involved, for a variety of reasons. One reason was to develop a sense of "ownership" in the emerging program. Another was to build a system of checks and balances among the individual interest groups by making them accountable to each other from the outset. The major reason was the belief that, through involvement, attitudes (particularly the attitudes of individuals paid to provide professional service for the new program, the staff) would become amenable to the change. Involvement of the professional staff was therefore the "order of the day" in selecting goals, specifying objectives, and framing plans, programs, budgets, and evaluation systems.

Involvement of the professional staff was frequently accompanied by the help of citizens, students, and significant "others," because such aid: (1) conformed to notions of the "democratic process" and was therefore politic; (2) kept pressure on the staff to look and act "professional" in the company of "concerned" others; (3) allowed the staff an opportunity to keep the expectations of the others closer to the reality of what was possible; and, (4) for purposes of administrating change, permitted use of today's most accepted form of "authentic" participation/manipulation: the interplay of group dynamics.

At this point the time may have come to shift from attempts at modifying *attitudes* to more direct efforts at modifying *behavior* (to the extent necessary for implementing the new program). Even if efforts to produce a favorable attitude among the staff have failed (and there are likely to be failures), the policy of educational accountability (chapter 5 and appendix A) places a responsibility on the administration and staff that cannot be taken lightly. Thus, our strategy alters slightly; instead of our major concern being that of changing attitudes, we now seek to change behavior (where necessary). We certainly have not given up the hope of gaining staff support and reducing resistance, but it now becomes paramount to train operationally the staff members who are to use the selected program. This training process is *staff development.*

How are we to train or develop our staff to handle an educationally accountable program?[1] First, we *analyze the tasks* arising from the new program. For example, what behaviors will be required to play a successful role in the new program's operation? The seven expectations offered above serve as general guidelines for further specifying the behaviors that will be needed. For training purposes, it might also be helpful if one could describe current teaching role behavior and then indicate in detail what the desired new role behavior is and the consequences that flow from it—that is, let the staff see the difference for themselves. A review of the positive/ negative needs analysis in chapter 3 might provide the framework for establishing an understanding of "what is" in the current role, while the objectives of the new program determine the "what should be" role behavior model. The gap between these positions identifies the focus for staff training efforts.

Many persons—educators included—become defensive if the description of what they do (or do not do) presses too hard on their self-images; you should be aware of what they do but take care how you convey this information to them. For example, if an individual or group uses a professional skill improperly or ineffectively, pointing out that fact is not likely to be appreciated. They will spend a disproportionate amount of energy trying to redeem their lessened professional self-esteem by attacking the training efforts and "proving" them ineffective, rather than learning from them. It is, therefore, worth placing more emphasis on firming up the skills, knowledge, and attitudes that bear on the desired results.

The approach to the staff might be expressed in this manner: "As you know, these are the results we are getting from our present program. [Cite results.] We think we can improve upon these results. The new program is aimed at making these improvements. [Cite objectives.] To make the improvements, we believe our staff should be able to do the following things. [List the behaviors desired.] This staff development program is supposed to help us review and sharpen our skills in those areas as well as to work out problems and details in the new program."

If staff involvement has been genuine and the program design well done, this approach should make sense to the staff and come as no surprise. It is now the task of the staff developer (principal?

curriculum coordinator? master teacher?) to present a carefully prepared training program related to attaining or developing the identified requisite skills, knowledges, and role attitudes that form the
desired operational behavior of the staff members. At the same time,
the new accountability program itself will require some pretesting.
Thus, the staff development strategy includes: (1) an instructional
role model of what is desired and the ways of producing that state;
(2) opportunities to try out the new instructional role behaviors (or
old behaviors revitalized) in as nonthreatening circumstances as possible (unfortunately, any situation requiring an analysis of ability is
likely to be perceived as threatening); and (3) feedback mechanisms
(many of the "self-discovery" variety) to staff members on the
results of how they handled applications of the desired behaviors.
Write Kepner and Tregoe:

> The . . . [teacher] needs awareness of new concepts, practice in applying them,
> and feedback on the results of his performance. The kind of feedback is critical,
> for it will determine the kind of learning that takes place. It is not enough to
> know that the end results were poor. The feedback must also enable the learner
> to see *how* the ideas, specific procedures, and actions he used contributed to the
> final outcome. One learns by taking an idea, trying it out, and seeing how and
> why it works, or fails to work.[2]

Some Procedures

Through the analysis of tasks, the trainer or staff developer is
able to develop a pattern of organization that arranges the training
tasks into teachable components. For our purposes, task analysis
presumes that the trainer: (1) can identify the area of behavioral
change required; (2) knows the nature and size of the staff group he
is to develop; (3) is aware of the current practices of this group; (4)
possesses a model of the new desired role behaviors; (5) has a clear
idea of what the staff development effort is expected to accomplish;
and (6) has some objective indicators available to determine whether
the training effort worked.[3]

Once the trainer comes to some satisfactory conclusions on
these six points, he is ready to arrange the program into teachable
components. An overview of such an arrangement might include:

• Phase 1: devoted to acquiring or renewing a background of
information and knowledge about the program and their roles in it
(answers, Who does what and why?);

• Phase 2: isolates critical role skills and techniques needed in
the program's operation (answers, How? When? Where?);

• Phase 3: tries out both the program and the requisite staff role behaviors on a trial basis (answers, Can we operate it and make it work?);

• Phase 4: analyzes the results of the trial run of the program and the operational role behaviors of the staff (answers, Where are the problems of our operation?);

• Phase 5: focuses on how the program's progress is to be monitored once implemented, and reviews the tools of evaluation to accompany accounting for the program's results (answers, How is the progress of the program to be controlled, and how will we know if the program is "on target" and gets the results expected?);

• Phase 6: is a trouble-shooting process, resulting from working out the training or planning flaws uncovered in the monitoring process during the program's operation (answers, What do we do about problems arising in the program's operation?);

• Phase 7: concerns itself with the conclusion of the program's operation, summing up assessments of the program's effectiveness, insights into what was learned during its operation, implications for what the data reveals, recommendations for its future, and a final report for the reviewer (answers, What account is to be rendered to the reviewers?).

The staff developer can pour into these different phases the training techniques he requires: readings, simulations, lectures, role playing, in-baskets, case studies, films, video tapes, demonstrations, instructional diagnosis, computerized analysis, interaction analysis, chalk-talk, and other items in the repertoire of teaching role behaviors.[4] Feyereisen, Fiorino, and Nowak's list for "continuing teacher education" (in-service work) is even longer:

[Instructional] teachers' meetings; service bulletins and curriculum guides; conferences (individual and group); institutes; seminars; workshops; work-study groups, clinics; classroom visitation; intervisitation; demonstrations; professional organizations; informal get-togethers; the use of consultants; microteaching; and simulation techniques.[5]

Whatever blend of devices and procedures is used we leave to the discretion of the staff developer.[6] In speaking about "clinical supervision" (focusing on what and how teachers teach *as* they teach), Mosher and Purpel remind us generally that:

Teaching, as an intellectual and social act, is subject to intellectual analysis. . . . [We] believe that the analysis of teaching can be rigorous and systematic, that it should be ongoing, that it requires specific analytical skills and that the professional teacher should be a careful critic of his own practice.[7]

Performance-Based Teacher Education as a Training Device

There are many training devices available to the staff developer in bringing about the role behaviors believed necessary to implement the new program. The devices and procedures listed above are assumed to be familiar enough to our readers not to require further elaboration. However, a relatively new (in terms of emphasis) training device has made its appearance on the educational scene. Because of its nature, it has been linked with the accountability "movement." We refer to *performance-based teacher education* (PBTE), in which the teacher is trained to produce and demonstrate by results his ability to make prespecified changes in the learner's behavior.

Some authorities hold that PBTE is potentially superior to the traditional "credit-course-apprenticeship degree" oriented form of teacher preparation in developing teacher knowledge, skills, and attitudes necessary to promote learning in students.[8] In its current state of development, PBTE has involved mainly teacher education institutions, state departments of education concerned with teacher certification, and teacher organizations seeking to gain control over the entrance requirements to the profession. The implications for PBTE on teacher preparation and the educational political scene seem considerable (especially for colleges and universities), but we limit ourselves here to describing PBTE as a heuristic device to aid in training staffs for specific new programs—not the broad framework for preparing preservice teachers for the profession.

Essential elements of performance-based teaching, according to the American Association of Colleges for Teacher Education,[9] include:

1. Spelling out behaviorally (i.e., capable of being measured) the competencies (knowledge, skills, behaviors) that are to be demonstrated by the teacher based on an analysis of the teaching task and stated publicly as something the teacher "ought" to be able to do as part of his professional role;

2. Making public the distinctions used as criteria for evaluating the effectiveness of role competencies the teacher is to demonstrate under stated conditions;

3. Assessing objectively the teacher's role competency, primarily in terms of his ability to demonstrate it in a teaching situation in which children learn what is expected and the teacher exhibits evidence of planning for, analyzing, interpreting, and assessing the learning situation;

4. Moving the teacher through the training program on the basis of his ability to demonstrate levels of role mastery rather than according to a predetermined course schedule for all to begin and finish at the same time;

5. Developing the prespecified teaching role competencies through an especially designed instructional training program geared for them.

A frequent characteristic of PBTE is a give-and-take discussion (involvement?) about the nature of the prespecified conditions. Similarities between PBTE and the emerging patterns of accountability discussed in chapter 1 should be apparent (i.e., specified objectives, rationality, results oriented, predetermined levels of confidence, negotiable accountability, etc.).

In using the concept of PBTE as a heuristic training device, the staff developer constructs from his task analysis of the new program explicit sets of instructional objectives to be attained in the role, coupled with items for measuring their achievement. If the purpose of the training is to develop a particular set of role skills (rather than, for example, amounts of subject content) in the teachers, the trainer will use an unfamiliar content format so that the student-learners are less likely to have had previous contact with the specific content (if, for example, you wish to test the teacher's performance teaching map-reading skills, it is better to use hypothetical maps rather than real ones with which some students may already be familiar). For the training sessions, a staff member is selected to teach, given the specific set of objectives, a sample assessment item that indicates how the learning might be evaluated later, and some appropriate background material. The teacher is allowed some time to review the materials and prepare a lesson before teaching a group of students selected especially for that purpose. After being taught for a set period of time (the lesson may be videotaped for other analysis later), the students are tested on their achievement of the learning objectives and their attitude toward the instruction (cognitive and affective measures). The teacher had not previously seen these tests and presumably could not teach the test items. The resulting measures provide an index of the teacher's effectiveness in the teaching role.

The same task, repeated with other staff members under circumstances as nearly identical as possible (i.e., using different groups of students with similar learner characteristics, etc.), makes it possible to make individual comparisons of teaching skills. It also provides a basis for sharper role analysis and means of improvement. If each teacher is provided the same task and gets markedly different results for the same objectives with similar learners, presumably the teaching skills used contrast. Popham remarks:

The trick, clearly, is to control other relevant conditions so that all teachers have the same opportunity to display whatever instructional skill they possess. This means randomly assigning learners to teachers and, if necessary, statistically adjusting for remaining inequities in disparate learners' entry behavior.[10]

It is possible now to obtain packaged sets of teaching performance tests.[11] Meanwhile, research efforts (like John O'Neil's at UCLA to identify good reading teachers[12]) continue.

Evaluating Readiness to Implement the New Program

When can we implement the new program? In the best of all possible worlds we could simply say, When we are ready. But reality is not usually so kind. The calendar mercilessly records the passage of time; the kids continue to grow up—with or without us; the close interdependence of other schedules places us in the position of having to establish arbitrary time lines. At a given date (usually the start of the school year), the new program is to be implemented, whether Miss Jones has demonstrated the requisite role behaviors to cope with it or not. The reality that needed educational programs cannot afford the luxury of waiting too long to be implemented is cause for further reflection.

From a technical standpoint, the expected and ideal situation is to have all staff members reach their training objectives through phase 5 of the staff development effort before the program is implemented. Presumably, the program was back planned, that is, after the training phases were planned chronologically forward and a target date was posted for beginning instruction, the training program was planned backward from this date, phase by phase, in terms of the estimated minimum and maximum times required to complete each training phase. Back planning should have yielded a realistic starting date for the training to begin. If the planning estimates were correct and the right amount of maximum and minimum times were scheduled around the "most likely" expected times to complete each training phase through phase 5 (more attention is given to scheduling below), one has every right to expect that the staff will be ready on the targeted starting date. They *should* be ready.

But what if these plans go wrong? What if certain staff members are not (for a number of possible reasons) able to demonstrate successfully the requisite behaviors for operating the program—even utilizing the maximum contingency of training time? Such a situation raises some hard issues for persons accountable for the program, issues somewhat different to education in their implications. Do we use the approach of "ready or not, here we come," or do we wait until all the staff members are "ready on the mark"? It is a matter of judgment on the steward's part.

To overgeneralize: In the customary teaching situation, a teacher is hired and put into the classroom on the basis of having the "proper" credentials, which usually include taking some required courses, practice teaching, attaining a bachelor's degree from an institution recognized by the state, and finding two or three persons qualified and willing to say a few kind words regarding the individual's character. The state duly certifies such individuals as "teachers," permitting school districts to hire them on the assumption that they possess the requisite (but unspecified) skills for the job; most of them do. On the job, the criteria for successful practice tends to boil down to being able to control a classroom, receiving few complaints from parents, producing the semblance of student "learning" (i.e., not too many students are failed or given As, most are automatically advanced to the next class or grade level, and, where standardized achievement tests are used, the class average reflects a loosely acceptable norm), and a tolerant relationship with peers, administrators, and parents. Seldom is heard a discouraging word about the teacher's actual performance ability (assumed to be "professional" and hence beyond reproach). One merely asks if the teacher is certified; not if he is able to perform. As Fantini describes it:

Not having been prepared to teach for cultural pluralism or to deal with the wide range of different learning styles that converge in the classroom, teachers attempt to survive. They learn to teach on the job, developing their own teaching style in the process. Many find it natural simply to impose their learning style on a group of youngsters and to blame the youngsters who do not respond for failure.[13]

In our efforts to develop an educationally accountable program we reject the reasoning that simply because a person is certified, he is able to teach. We hold rather that, if the individual can demonstrate meeting our training expectations, he is ready to teach in an educationally accountable program.

In the event the staff member cannot demonstrate some of the requisite role behaviors, what happens then? Among the options, these three alternatives (or a mixture of them) seem probable:

• Begin the program hoping for the best, but continue to work on improving the deficit areas in the staff's background;

• Start the program but be careful to maximize the use of those teachers who possess demonstrated skills and to minimize (eliminate?) deficit role areas as much as possible, of staff members unable to demonstrate those particular abilities—a premise that underlies the notion of "differentiated staffing";[14]

• Briefly postpone the starting date of the program until the teachers have been able to attain the requisite skills (advisable if a sizable number have not reached a particular threshold but appear to be likely to reach it shortly).

Naturally, the selection of any of these or other alternatives depends heavily on the actual field situation (e.g., the number and degree of deficit skills etc.) and the steward's judgment. Still, our question remains only partially answered. What if the staff or an individual staff member can not or will not demonstrate the requisite performance abilities to attain the program's objectives?

In the case of the individual member, the steward of the program (the person or group charged with that responsibility) should have authority to drop the particular member, modify his role as necessary, or replace him. This action may not appear noteworthy to outside observers, but it is significant in public education. It grants administrative authority to the steward at a time when negotiated teacher contracts have generally reduced or sought to eliminate such administrative authority. Under the authority offered to this steward goes the right to determine who is fit or unfit according to prespecified criteria jointly established. The point of view applied to students, that one never rejects them as potential learners, is *not* carried into the professional staff. For the individual staff member who is unable to learn the new role requirements after reasonable training efforts, we merely suggest that you do not give this individual a task to perform that he can not. If possible, have someone else perform the task. If that is impossible, seek to excuse this staff member from participation in the program.

In the case of the staff itself, much depends on the circumstances surrounding the inability to perform the desired role behaviors. If the staff has made an honest effort to learn its new roles and cannot achieve the objectives, the role should be carefully reexamined—with concurrence from the steward's reviewers—or the objectives of the program should be restated. No matter how hard a group of ordinary people train, for example, few are ever able to jump as high as six feet.

If on the other hand the staff simply refuses to take the program seriously or to invest its energy in training, the steward should talk it over with the staff and then take the matter to the reviewers. The steward might recommend aborting the program or replacing the staff with more willing members (depending on the size of the program), or another course of action. With all our involvement efforts to date we do not believe such action would be necessary unless some new issues—perhaps not even related to the program—emerged and required immediate resolution.

Our aim, however, is to begin implementing the new program with a staff trained and ready to handle it. When the staff is ready (i.e., can satisfactorily perform in their new roles at least through phase 5), and barring mishaps, we are ready to move forward with the program.

Implementing the Program

Implementation usually implies getting the program into operation and providing it with direction and control. In education, however, more attention tends to be given to getting the program into operation than to the tasks of discerning its direction and providing effective controls. This may result from the common practice of implementing new educational programs by handing the task to the teaching staff with minimum administrative involvement and the unspoken directive: "Here it is; do it!"

Under this condition, the teaching staff, operating under the sometimes strange norms of the profession, is inclined to show signs of believing that as "professionals" it is expected that:

1. They are able to handle the new program on their own (a norm fostered by the self-contained classroom where the solitary teacher does everything himself and comes to believe that autonomy is a natural condition);

2. Too many questions about how to operate the program (unless the questions are used as an educationally acceptable political means of resisting the program's implementation through nit-picking) are a sign of the "green" teacher (the mature, experienced, autonomous teacher, says the norm, does not need advice on how to teach, and few teachers ask for any after their first or second year of teaching);

3. If it is necessary to work with other professionals, it should only be done in a peer relationship context, democratically and by consensus decision making, with every precaution made not to

breach the professional autonomy of another (the integrity of professional autonomy, suggests the norm, would be compromised under any other arrangement).

Programs so implemented not surprisingly tend to obtain widely varying results. Like a football team without a quarterback to call the plays, a good deal of hit-or-miss action (instruction) results amid known and unknown fumbling even though the players know the goals to be reached, the objectives necessary to obtain them, and can perform their requisite role behaviors. Without direction and control their talents, however great, lack the orchestration necessary for success.

In education, the teaching staff's need for direction and control is greater than many teachers (their behavior styled by the professional norm for individual autonomy) might care to admit. Our experience with staffs left completely to their own devices in educational programs calling for coordination among the staff members has been disappointing. True, some staffs have done a good job, but the greater tendency is for the staffs to divide tasks in such a way that the opportunity for future feedback and interaction is sharply reduced. Many team teaching efforts, for example, quickly resolve into to "you take my math, and I'll take your English" or "you teach them Monday, and I'll teach them Wednesday," rather than suffer through the difficulties of jointly planning, teaching, and evaluating the teaching/learning outcomes. Thus the major intent of the program—its team approach to educational performance and problem solving—is lost.

In recent years the norms supporting individual autonomy in teaching have made it difficult (especially with the advent of militant professionalism) to provide these deemphasized ingredients—direction and control—in the implementation process. Therefore, beyond first developing the staff to cope with new role expectations, our task is to accomplish three objectives in the implementation process: (1) to provide continuing direction to the program; (2) to preserve a degree of professional autonomy in the process; and (3) to ensure that the program moves in the directions intended via a monitoring system of control. Accordingly, we offer three approaches to accomplishing these tasks: (1) project management; (2) management by objectives (MBO); and (3) program evaluation and review technique (PERT). All three can be interrelated and, like PPBES and our accountability model, are system based. At the same time, they are worth a close look individually.

Project Management

The notion of project management is closely tied with program evaluation and review technique (PERT), a management device growing out of project management and used to monitor and control the development of a program or project. Project management emerged in 1954 out of a need to bring together many different people, materials, procedures, and ways of thinking for a specific project: to produce an operational ballistic missile in the shortest possible time.[15] The first missile was ready by 1959, a significant achievement of organization and purpose, and with it, a new form of management was recognized—project management. Since then it has grown and developed further, and shows signs of entering education.[16]

What is project management? John Baumgartner says that it "consists of the actions involved in producing project deliverable items on time, within the contemplated cost [and] with the required reliability and performance," while the role of the project manager is "one of planning, controlling, and motivating the project team."[17] Desmond Cook echoes this definition: "The project manager's principal role is the production of a product by integrating professional persons into a team . . . which operates within some lines of organizational responsibility and authority, [and] also operates within time, cost, and performance parameters."[18] As we use the term, project management is the assignment of a particular individual (or small group)—the project manager(s)—to the ongoing tasks of planning, directing, and controlling a project or program. This project or program is finite (i.e., is aimed at accomplishing specific objectives in a given time period within budgetary ranges); complex (i.e., involves many persons—perhaps teachers, specialists, paraprofessionals, parents and students—and requires coordination of time, money, and effort); related solely to the project (i.e., is concerned *only* with the tasks of the project and their accomplishment), and usually terminates after the experimental defects have been located and corrected. The project—if it is to be continued—then fits into the regular structure of the organization after the initial implementation.

Blurring many fine distinctions on when a project *is* a project or the dozen or so alternative ways of structuring it,[19] we visualize project management as a way to give needed special attention to a new program's implementation. This is typically lacking where the ordinary requirements attending the regular school program's operation prevent more than cursory attention, follow-up, and trouble

shooting. Whether the project manager is called team leader, committee chairman, master teacher, task force coordinator, etc., his job is
to see that the objectives of the program are met during the period of
its initial implementation. Within the confines of the program plan,
he is granted defined authority to do this task; in effect, he is the
program's steward.

When the board of education has passed its policy on accountability in a specific area and asks the superintendent to implement it
in a program, the superintendent then appoints the project man-
ager(s)—most likely, a key professional staff member or small group
of members involved in the workings of the advisory planning committee which initiated the program specified by the board. While the
basic planning outline of programs may have been accomplished
through the advisory planning committee (chapter 5) and is perhaps
cast in a PPBES format (chapter 7), much remains to be done.
Schedules need to be established or further refined, a training program instituted (staff development), and the remaining procedures
accomplished, of (1) identifying the targeted students (if this task
has not been performed by the advisory planning committee), (2)
working out the instructional elements of the program, (3) refining
and implementing the evaluation design, (4) establishing a monitoring system (PERT), (5) developing a progress report format, and (6)
making the arrangements necessary to operate a new program and tie
up loose ends. Many parties may be involved in each of these tasks,
but the project manager controls pace and direction of the program.
While in that role he is accountable for the results obtained.

At the same time, he shares control (via management by objectives) of the work of others in relation to the specific program. The
project manager determines the budgetary guidelines, issues instructions, selects and releases (but does not hire or fire or regularly
supervise) personnel related to the project, and reports on both the
progress of the project team and the individual role performance of
its members in relation to the program and its accomplishments.

In short, the project manager lives within the framework of the
program plan (time, costs, and specified objectives) as authorized by
the superintendent and/or board of education (or, where appropriate, the building principal). If he does not believe that the authorized framework is sufficient in terms of resources, authority, or
whatever, he normally should have the option of refusing the assignment or causing the areas of concern to be revised; in effect, he
negotiates his own accountability. This idea of negotiating the
project manager's accountability (as defined earlier in this chapter)

also coincides with Alkin's notion of accountability: "Accountability is a negotiated relationship in which the participants agree in advance to accept specified rewards and costs on the basis of evaluation findings as to the attainment of specified ends."[20] In assuming the role of steward of the program, the project manager thus becomes accountable to his reviewers under the conditions specified in the contract.

Who are the project manager's reviewers? It is appealing to borrow from and adapt Alkin's view of three levels of accountability to answer this question.[21]

First, the school board is accountable to the public (and to the state) for *goal accountability*—the district's ability to achieve the goals and objectives stated in its policies.

Second, there is a form of *program accountability* for operating a specified program whose overall procedures meet the objectives established for it. This responsibility is undertaken by the school district's regular administration or is delegated to a project manager or even to an external group (e.g., performance contractors). Under this management responsibility, the program is further developed, refined, and carried out. The purpose of program accountability is to ensure that the appropriate procedures (i.e., those designated) are used for reaching the total performance objectives specified in the goal accountability guidelines. Because teachers and other members of the instructional team only operate in portions of the program, they can only be held accountable for their activities within their particular sector of the program.

In the ultimate sense, if the superintendent of schools is granted authority to implement the board's policies, he is responsible to the school board for the program's outcomes. However, the superintendent may elect or be directed to delegate some of his authority in the form of a negotiated contract (or, less legally binding, a memorandum of agreement) with a project manager or, with concurrence of the school board, a performance contracting firm. The superintendent remains generally responsible to the school board for the results obtained, but clearly the individuals or groups charged with the action portion of program management carry an immediate degree of accountability for the program. When a legally binding contract is used, the reviewers are the board of education, since normally only boards can enter into formal contracts on behalf of the school district. If the superintendent or other administrator (e.g., the building principal) retains control (i.e., if he remains the major reviewer), either through a project manager or the regular staff members, it is understood that this reviewer/administrator later becomes a steward/administrator in reporting results to the school board. If predetermined levels of confidence (i.e., the rewards and/or punishments stipulated for the results to be achieved) are included in the agreement between stewards and reviewers, this normally is in the form of a legally-based contract between the board, usually with the superintendent as its key reviewer agent, and the project manager or—more likely in formal contracts—the performance contractors (discussed in more detail in chapter 9).

The third and grass-roots level of accountability, *outcome accountability,* occurs in the relationship between the individual instructional team members (i.e., teachers, specialists, paraprofessionals, etc.) and the project manager. The vehicle we have chosen for implementation is management by objectives (MBO). In assigning responsibility, we have followed Barro's general principle: "Each participant in the educational process should be held responsible only for those educational outcomes that he can affect by his actions or decisions and only to the extent that he can affect them."[22]

Management by Objectives

As a system, management by objectives (MBO) has its roots in the works of Douglas McGregor, Abraham Maslow, Peter Drucker, and others.[23] George Odiorne's efforts have done much to summarize and popularize its concepts. According to Odiorne:

The system of management by objectives can be described as a process whereby the superior and the subordinate officers in an organization jointly identify its common goals, define each individual's major areas of responsibility in terms of the results expected of him, and use these measures as guides for operating the unit and assessing the contribution of each of its members.[24]

The MBO process recognizes that managers carry responsibility to achieve organizational objectives and that staff personnel too have responsibilities for meeting their share of these objectives. MBO tries to combine these responsibilities into one system of operation, enabling both groups to work toward their joint objectives—missions first and methods second—as a team: "The key premise of Management by Objectives is that the objectives established between the staffman and the manager will achieve better results than random or hit-and-miss methods could produce."[25]

In the typical application of MBO, the manager and the staffman discuss face-to-face five questions about their work (questions usually asked in connection with the individual's job description or in terms of the role he plays in a particular project):

1. What is it that needs to be accomplished? (Where are we going?)

2. Why do we want to accomplish it? (For what purpose?)

3. How will it be done? (What steps need to be taken?)

4. How will we measure the accomplishment? (By what criteria?)

5. Who will do what? (Who is responsible?)

The results of these informal discussions provide the staffman a frame of reference with which to think about his work. From this frame of reference, he attempts to formulate in writing some specific objectives related to fulfilling the recognized responsibilities of his role. He next works out the details associated with carrying out these objectives. This planning sets the scene for another discussion between the staffman and the manager.

Now the staffman presents his written ideas on how he proposes to fulfill the objectives of his work (usually the manager has reviewed this written plan before their discussion). Included in the staffman's presentation will be:

1. *Performance objectives* (what needs to be done): the performance objectives are expected to support and complement the general objectives of the work unit, and should be as specific and measurable as possible;

2. *Resources* (what is needed): what resources are needed in terms of time, money, equipment, materials, facilities, additional personnel assistance, etc. (particular attention is customarily given to time in scheduling intermediate and final project review target dates);

3. *Actions* (what to do): actions are usually a series of steps in a plan that leads to achieving the performance objectives;

4. *Results* (what is expected): what can be expected in terms of an increase in quality and/or quantity (e.g., of student learning outcomes), time and money, etc.

The reader should recognize a format that closely parallels the one offered for establishing plan-program-budget-evaluation systems (PPBES as discussed in chapter 7).

From this review procedure at least three things should be determined: the staffman's job responsibilities, the standards of performance, and the objectives he is to attain. In reviewing the staffman's plan, the manager and the staffman first seek to clarify the *job responsibilities* of each person as they relate to the project or work. The major focus is, of course, on firming up their mutual knowledge of the project and the staffman's part in it. A common procedure for establishing a desired mutual point of view on job responsibilities is to have both the staffman and manager draw up a list of what each sees as the task objectives of the staffman. They then compare and discuss their lists, seeking mutual agreement.

Once the staffman's job responsibilities are clarified, a discussion ensues about the *standards of performance* expected on the job. These standards should establish guidelines for estimating whether the task is being achieved or not. They are statements of the conditions that exist when the work has been performed satisfactorily and they establish some criteria for later reference.

With job responsibilities and performance standards agreed upon, *objectives* may be set to improve the staffman's performance. Remembering that MBO has most frequently been used as a device for improving individual performance (as well as a means of giving organizational direction and control to individual work situations and for getting forms of feedback in return), the objectives for the individual can be established "near" (but under) the standard of performance (usually applicable to new staffmen), "on" the standard, or "over" it. The staffman then attempts to meet the objectives set in the joint conference on the job.

With the passage of time and the arrival of a predetermined target date (usually from one to six months following approval of the staffman's plan of action), a follow-up conference is held to gauge the progress made toward attaining the objectives. In most places of business, this conference has the title *performance appraisal.* Our concern, however, is less focused on appraisal and more directed toward *progress reporting.* Normally, the periodic progress report contains:

1. Areas of achievement (results obtained);
2. Areas of difficulty (problems encountered);
3. Recommendations for coping with the difficulties (action to be taken);
4. When (date and time schedule);
5. Additional resources needed or other circumstances reported (general information).

If, from the joint review of the progress report, it becomes necessary to reshuffle the staffman's priorities and/or performance objectives, the necessary action may be taken. At the same time, the manager is in a position to assess the significance of the progress being made as it relates to and affects the operation of the entire project and the work of others. It is a means for him to exert the influence necessary to give the project direction and control.

How would a system of management by objectives work in implementing an educationally accountable program?

Turning our attention to combining MBO procedures with the implementation process, we might offer several observations. For a start, before the project manager and, for example, the teacher sit down to their first discussion, many things have already happened to shape this moment. It is not a "from scratch" discussion or one otherwise unbounded to the topic at hand, that is, the operation of a new program. Specifically, the goals and objectives of the program have been publicly stated; a plan-program-budget-evaluation system may have been adopted; and, most importantly, the personnel selected for implementing the program—personnel likely to have participated extensively in the planning of the program—have received training in its background and operation. Thus, at this point the two parties should have a pretty fair idea of what is expected. It remains their task, however, to block out the assignment of the individual teacher (or perhaps a team of teachers).

Using the adopted program plan as their frame of reference, the project manager and the teacher discuss the program objectives as given conditions in their work situation. These conditions must be accepted, especially if the objectives have been stated as board policy. The objectives express the ends desired and the program plan offers some means to that end, but the project manager and teacher concentrate on defining these terms more closely—especially the means. In effect, the project manager offers the teacher some objectives and a knowledge of the resources likely to be available; in return, the teacher works out a sequence of instruction that he believes will accomplish the objectives within the parameters of the available resources. The training program has already offered the teacher some suggestions, materials, and ways for reaching the desired objectives, but, respecting the professional need for autonomy, these remain suggestions to the teacher, not prescriptions on *how* to teach (although the program objectives dictate plainly *what* to teach and, under prespecified conditions, what is *expected to result* from the instruction). In other words, only the ends are specified and a rough approximation offered of resources available; the pedagogical means are left to the teacher.

Accordingly, the teacher (like the staffman and using the same format) prepares a plan of action centered around accomplishing the objectives. A second conference is then held with the project manager to work out and discuss joint problems, reporting schedules, and to obtain plan approval.

We draw a finer distinction, however, between the plan approval procedure used in the business world, with its regularized superior-subordinate relationships, and education. Business customarily expects the superior to feel free to say yes or no to *all* aspects of a subordinate's plan, but we do not operate under this assumption. Rather, we attempt to set terminal boundaries of authority between the necessary management functions of the project manager and the professional discretion of the teacher. The project manager draws from the program plan to establish the external boundaries of resources and expectations; the teacher is free within these constraints. Approval of the teacher's plan formally recognizes the boundaries of terminal authority. The relationship is not entirely a peer relationship, for the project manager retains the authority to move these boundaries if necessary (most probably to coordinate the joint efforts of other teachers) and to hold the teacher answerable for the results achieved, at least to the extent of releasing the teacher from the program (but not the school district) for failing to meet reasonable expectations. Thus, the teacher's plan is reviewed with care, (1) to understand what the teacher intends and (2) to coordinate a schedule with other participants in the program. Portions of it that abut the project manager's management function must meet with his approval. A similar progress-reporting schedule and procedure is followed for charting results achieved.

Outcome accountability. In determining how the instructor is to be held accountable for the learning outcomes of his students, a number of plans have been suggested.[26] Teacher accountability per se is a major concern to many parties. However, we are more concerned with developing educationally accountable programs and less interested in focusing on teacher accountability, but for the sake of intelligent educational program development, we recognize the necessity of charting progress or its lack and identifying problem areas for trouble shooting. We are also serious about applying the zero reject philosophy to learners who are experiencing difficulty. To be able to do these things requires some assessment or measurement feedback that, ideally, can be considered reliable and above reproach. True, the criteria for evaluation and for forming a judgment on the quality of work done is present in the standards of performance part of the action plans (under performance objectives and results expected), but the use of information on achieved learning outcomes for purposes of rewarding or punishing the instructors is beyond our scope.

Our first concern is that tests be developed and used as diagnostic tools to chart the program's development and the student's learning mastery level. If teacher accountability for outcomes is desired (with attendant rewards and punishments included in the program), it should be handled as a separately negotiated, predetermined level-of-confidence contract condition.

In any event, when student learning outcomes are assessed—whether used to evaluate teacher performance or merely to learn if the program and the students are on target—Barro's second principle is useful to us: "The range over which a teacher, a school principal, or an administrator may be expected to affect outcomes is to be determined empirically from analysis of results obtained by all personnel working in comparable circumstances."[27] This principle implies that: (1) teacher and other forms of accountability, as well as the benchmarks of program progress, are going to be relative and based on comparisons of pre and postinstruction results for individuals and groups; (2) the larger the number of persons and groups involved, the more reliable the comparative information will become; and (3) we will need to appeal to statistical models—particularly regression analysis—to infer contributions made. Klein and Alkin have suggested a process to accomplish this task.[28] Adapting their process for our purpose, we would:

1. Administer a pretest to all students identified for the program to assess their performance on the program's relevant learning objectives; the test might be a standardized test that closely matches the program's objectives, or a specially constructed one;[29]

2. Repeat the testing at the end of a given time period when most of the instruction has been completed; this posttesting, using different items on the test, should cover the instructional objectives of the program;

3. Compare the pre and posttest scores for each student; the difference between these scores should represent the relative learning gain for the individual student;

4. For purposes of comparing teacher performances as well as establishing some norms for student learning expectations, plot the pre and posttest scores on a graph, identifying each student and his teacher (or teacher team). By using regression analysis, fit a line among the plot points that represents the average relationship among the pre and posttest scores. Review the results.

From the information available one should be able to compare teacher performances, arriving at some conclusions about the individual teacher's relative on-the-job effectiveness and degree of accountability for outcomes. Klein and Alkin note that this procedure "takes into account the students' skill and knowledge before instruction begins, it is flexible enough (via a technique called multiple regression) to take into account several input factors (such as minority group membership and different instructional programs), and it examines more than just the class's average performance."[30]

With this information and other data, the project manager and the teacher can analyze different teaching approaches more effectively, utilizing strengths and identifying weaknesses in the program as well as in the teacher's role performance. To the extent that the teacher recognizes a need for improvement from the data received and seeks help or advice, the project manager should be ready to help—through his own efforts or through a consultant. Hopefully, by now a relationship has grown between the teacher and the project manager that allows each to discuss openly and candidly his professional problems with the program. While we do not expect human relations miracles, it is hoped that each can become a greater assistance to the other as they establish follow-up procedures and schedules with new performance standards to determine progress. This is a sign of professional growth.

On the darker side, if a particular teacher or other participant in the program has really proven "undesirable" on the job (either through inability to achieve significant student learning gains or by refusal to cooperate with others in the program), the project manager should be free to exercise management discretion and drop that individual from participation (note: we have not granted the project manager the right to fire or hire, merely to select or reject in relation to the program). We recognize that circumstances may sometimes make this authority impossible to use. If the project manager has recommended that an individual be dropped and the district is unable to accommodate his recommendation, it seems just that, when the project manager's account of program results is weighed, the teaching results of the undesired staff member be striken (if possible) off the steward's account, from the date of the manager's recommendation onward. Popham found in his research that:

Experienced teachers are not particularly skilled at bringing about prespecified behavior changes in learners. When it comes to a task such as that presented by the performance test in which they must promote learner attainment of specific instructional objectives, perhaps most experienced teachers are no better qualified than a person who has never taught.[31]

Our training program fortunately screened out the unskilled before implementation began, but mistakes and unforeseen circumstances do occur. If the project manager believes it necessary to drop a staff member during the implementation of a new program, we encourage his right to this management discretion. It should be part of the agreement when he undertook responsibility for the project.

At the same time, it should be clear whether or not staff members have a similar option for themselves—whether they render service at their own pleasure for the duration of the project, anytime during its operation, or otherwise. Whether service is voluntary or assigned, it probably ought to be at least for the duration of the implementation period.

Program Evaluation and Review Technique

The last of our three suggestions for program implementation is "program evaluation and review technique" (PERT). Our implementation efforts were designed to accomplish three things in the process of putting your educationally accountable program into operation: (1) to provide direction and control for the program (we recommended the use of a project manager whose appointment to that position is geared to the life of the project);[32] (2) to preserve a degree of professional autonomy in the process while also increasing professional outcome accountability (we suggested a management-by-objectives approach); and (3) to ensure that the program moves in the directions intended via a monitoring system of control. For accomplishing this last task, PERT seems uniquely suitable.

Because PERT procedures (like putting together your kid's swing set) are inclined to be extremely detailed (but, at a basic level, easily learned), we will present little more than a generalized description of PERT's basic features. One either seems to learn a lot about PERT or a little; there is no easily recognized halfway point once one begins to discuss the jargon of "perting." Therefore we offer you a little and urge you, if our hint catches your fancy, to learn a lot about it, particularly if *you* must provide coordination and control to any activities of complexity occurring at the same time (e.g., the manager of a three-ring circus would find PERT useful—does this fit your situation?).

What is PERT? Many would answer that PERT is what project managers do, so closely related are the two concepts of project management and "program evaluation and review technique." We have separated them, however. The first relates to an individual, the second to a procedure he may or may not use. As a procedure, PERT has been defined as "an integrated management planning and control technique."[33] We could even more appropriately label our suggestion *network-based management systems* (except that PERT has come to dominate the scene of procedures of this type), and include both PERT and critical path method (CPM), and a variety of other alphabet-designated network systems (e.g., MAPS, SCANS, TOPS, PEP, TRACE, LESS, PAR, etc.).[34]

Conceptually, PERT operates on the principle that there is one path or way through the many concurrent activities of a complex program. This particular path is the longest path, and the project is dependent in terms of its priorities on completing it. The longest path is the most time consuming and hence the most critical; a delay along it represents a delay in the completion time of the entire project—like going on a trip and discovering that someone forgot to put enough gas in the tank, everyone sits in hostile silence while someone scouts for gas and completes an overlooked task responsibility.

To determine this path it is necessary to construct a project or program plan that shows graphically the sequence and interrelation of all activities needed to accomplish the program objectives. Estimates of the activity time needed for accomplishing various events along the graphically laid-out plan can be gotten through discussion with the people who are to take responsibility for completing particular activities (this discussion is provided for in our MBO approach where the project manager seeks estimates of time needs from the staff). These time estimates are then refined by statistical methods (at the level of simple manual calculations), allowing for plotting the critical path and identifying activities most in need of management attention. With a full network of all necessary activities and a critical path charted through the maze, the project manager can keep track of activities, knowing where to anticipate serious problems, what slack resources of time and manpower are available for emergencies in other program areas, and how the entire project is likely to be influenced by given sets of decisions during its operation.

In operation, the network system acts like a monitor, alerting the manager when things are in danger of getting out of control and pinpointing the source. At the same time, it permits many of the activities to continue without direct supervision of the project manager (beyond expected progress feedback reports), allowing for a healthy degree of staff autonomy within the constraints of their activity responsibilities. This activity autonomy enables the project manager to devote his attention to trouble shooting in the problem areas, a practical example of management by exception.

Historically, PERT (and its faithful companion CPM) grew up in the late 1950s. While the concept of project management blossomed around the ICBM, PERT blossomed with the Fleet Ballistic Missile program (Polaris) as a natural extension of project management. It was successful because it seemed to meet research and development needs. These included recognition of:

1. The importance of a timely, orderly sequential flow of activities, intangible and intellectual, as well as tangible or hardware activities leading to the achievement of objectives (do not educational programs have a similar need?);

2. The wide range of uncertainty involved in many aspects of the Polaris program (is there not normally a wide range of uncertainty attending the implementation of any new educational programs?);

3. The significance of time as the "scarcest resource," emphasized by the success of Sputnik I (is time not the scarcest resource in learning, emphasized by the fact that kids grow up anyway, taught or untaught, graduated or dropped out?);

4. The interdependence of time, resources, and technical performance (does not successful education as offered in the public schools depend on the skillful use of time, resources, and professional technical performance?);

5. The unsystematic traditional procedures for setting schedules (toward what ends and how are schedules made in your school?).

Thus, through the uses of visual records, arrow diagrams, statistical procedures, and all the other aspects of network construction and operation, PERT proved successful. It replaced the useful (but less flexible) Gannt Bar Chart methodology commonly associated with the planning of construction projects.

Without going into the details of network construction (which would require elaboration of work breakdown structures, flow plans, time estimates, scheduling, costing, etc.), we conclude our brief presentation by citing some advantages commonly attributed to network approaches. The use of networks commonly:

• Facilitates task definition;

• Clarifies the technical responsibilities of project personnel;

• Enables all persons to see the interrelations of all the tasks performed for the project (gives them the "big picture");

• Forces design decisions earlier than normally procrastinated decisions are customarily made (avoiding "what do I do now, coach?" later);

• Ensures that the project will be performed in a well-defined order (an order that can be rationally accounted for later);
• Provides a clear picture of the project scope (what it is intended to do and not to do);
• Aids in preventing omission of tasks needed for project completion;
• Reduces problems normally associated with lack of communication.

In short, the use of networks, PERT particularly, seems made to order for stewards seeking to accomplish specified tasks as well as explaining attainment levels in a manner that maintains or builds the reviewers' confidence in his stewards. If your interest is caught, a number of good reference books are available.[35]

The Continuing Task of Staff Development

Under whatever procedures the program is put into operation, we still need to emphasize that developing the staff to handle the program does not stop at the preimplementation stage. The use of a project manager, MBO, and PERT should add unity, direction, and control to the new program's operation, but problems are bound to be uncovered by the staff as they work through their new roles. Many of these problems are likely to be peculiar to individual situations, others may be more generic in kind and common to several staff members. It is probably impossible for a project manager to anticipate all the problems that will arise from the field for incorporation into the preimplementation training program. It makes sense for him now to attempt to group or package defined, repeating field problems for purposes of further analysis and staff development to cope with them. At the same time, a staff member experiencing real difficulties in the field is more likely to be an attentive learner than one who is uncertain whether the particular problem concerns him or not.

If a recurring problem is pesky but not overly complicated, the staff members as a group may be able to talk it through and act to solve their own problem. If the problem appears to require more expertise than is immediately available on the staff, common sense suggests seeking advice from an outside source—either a professional consultant or another authoritative source. This sort of action is what is proposed under phase 4 of our procedures for developing the staff.

Our final concern for staff development and program implementation is recorded in phase 7, the conclusion of the program's operation. While evaluation per se is discussed in chapter 10, there is much growth to be gained for all staff members from involvement in pulling together final information about the program's operation. Among the things bound to be of interest and worth knowing to most staff members from the review and analysis of data will be signs of their individual impact on the program (to the extent that it is possible to infer). How were they perceived by their students? Did parents notice any differences? Did the students show any learning gains? etc.

At the same time, the project manager will be seeking feedback on his own performance. Did the program meet objectives? How was it perceived by students, staff, and parents? What suggestions do these groups have for improvement? etc. If an independent educational program auditor (discussed in chapter 11) has been hired to provide a program audit, certainly the project manager and the staff will be anxious to find out what the educational auditor reports.

Aside from preparing to render the account of the program's outcomes to the reviewers, most good stewards will be thinking ahead. A major question for the staff in this regard is, If we operate this program again (or one like it), what should we change?

Hopefully, the results obtained from *this* program will encourage all parties—stewards and reviewers—to continue. Play it again Sam!

Notes for Chapter 8

1. An extended explanation of staff training applicable to accountability programs is provided in Robert G. Smith, Jr., *The Engineering of Educational and Training Systems* (Lexington, Mass.: Heath Lexington Books, 1971); Educational Innovators Press, *Sourcebook for Implementing Accountability* (Tucson, Ariz.: Educational Innovators Press, 1971).

2. Charles Kepner and Benjamin Tregoe, *The Rational Manager* (New York: McGraw-Hill, 1965), p. 231.

3. George Odiorne, *Training by Objectives* (New York: Macmillan, 1970), pp. 150-52.

4. David Young, "Instructional Methods," in *The Teacher's Handbook*, ed. Dwight Allen and Eli Seifman (Glenview, Ill.: Scott, Foresman and Co., 1971), pp. 220-28.

5. Kathryn Feyereisen, John Fiorino, and Arlene Nowak, *Supervision and Curriculum Renewal: A Systems Approach* (New York: Appleton-Century-Crofts, 1970), p. 243.

6. A carefully worked-out program for staff development generally is presented in Ben Harris and Wailand Bessent, *In-Service Education: A Guide to Better Practice* (Englewood Cliffs, N.J.: Prentice-Hall, 1969).

A series of ways to organize training efforts for instituting forms of "continuous progress" education appears in Maurie Hillson and Joseph Bongo, *Continuous-Progress Education: A Practical Approach* (Palo Alto, Calif.: Science Research Associates, 1971), pp. 135-52.

7. Ralph Mosher and David Purpel, *Supervision: The Reluctant Profession* (Boston: Houghton Mifflin, 1972), p. 79.

8. Stanley Elam, *Performance-Based Teacher Education: What Is the State of the Art?* (Washington, D. C.: American Association of Colleges for Teacher Education, 1971), p. 1.

9. Ibid., pp. 6-7.

10. W. James Popham, "Found: A Practical Procedure to Appraise Teacher Achievement in the Classroom," *Nation's Schools* 89, no. 5 (May 1972): 60.

11. For more information on teaching performance services available to school districts, write Instructional Appraisal Services, 105 Christopher Circle, Ithaca, New York 14850.

12. "Researcher Devises Test to Spot Good Reading Teachers," *Report on Education Research* (March 15, 1972): 10.

See also W. James Popham, "Performance Tests of Teaching Proficiency: Rationale, Development, and Validation," *American Educational Research Journal* 8, no. 1 (January 1971): 105-17.

13. Mario Fantini, "Needed: Radical Reform of Schools to Make Accountability Work," *Nation's Schools* 89, no. 5 (May 1972): 57-58.

14. Fenwick English and Donald Sharpes, *Strategies for Differentiated Staffing* (Berkeley: McCutchan Publishing Corp., 1972).

15. John S. Baumgartner, *Project Management* (Homewood, Ill.: Richard D. Irwin, Inc., 1963), pp. 4-5.

16. Desmond Cook, *Educational Project Management* (Columbus, Ohio: Charles E. Merrill Publishing Co., 1971).

17. Baumgartner, *Project Management*, p. 8.

18. Cook, *Educational Project Management*, p. 4.

19. In addition to the already cited works of Baumgartner and Cook, the reader may be interested in reviewing *Project Manager's Handbook* (New York: Booz, Allen, and Hamilton, Inc., 1967); David Clelland, "Project Management," in *Systems, Organizations, Analysis, Management: A Book of Readings*, ed. David Clelland and William King (New York: McGraw-Hill, 1969), pp. 281-90; idem, "Why Project Management?" *Business Horizons* 8 (1964): 81-88; idem and William King, *Systems Analysis and Project Management* (New York: McGraw-Hill, 1968); Paul Gaddis, "The Project Manager," *Harvard Business Review* 37, no. 3 (June 1959): 89-97; Joseph Hansen, "The Case of the Precarious Program," *Harvard Business Review* 46, no. 1 (January-February 1968): 14 ff; E. S. Keats, "How to Become a Good Project Manager," *Aerospace Management* (August 1963): 20-23; Paul Lawrence and Jay Lorsch, "New Management Job: The Integrator," *Harvard Business Review* 45, no. 6 (November-December 1967): 142-50; C. J. Middleton, "How to Set Up a Project Organization," *Harvard Business Review* 45, no. 2 (March-April 1967): 73-82; Ross Mooney, "Problems in Initiating a Project," *Theory into Practice* 5 (June 1966): 139-43; D. C. Robertson, *Project Planning and Control* (Cleveland, Ohio: Chemical Rubber Co., 1967); John M. Steward, "Making Project Management Work," *Business Horizons* 8, no. 3 (fall 1965): 54-68.

20. Marvin C. Alkin, "Accountability Defined," *Evaluation Comment* 3, no. 5 (May 1972): 2.

21. Ibid., pp. 2-4.

22. Stephen M. Barro, "An Approach to Developing Accountability Measures for the Public Schools," *Emerging Patterns of Administrative Accountability*, ed. Lesley Browder, Jr. (Berkeley: McCutchan Publishing Corp., 1971), p. 368.

23. Douglas McGregor, *The Human Side of Enterprise* (New York: McGraw-Hill, 1960); Abraham Maslow, *Motivation and Personality* (New York: Harper & Row, 1954); Peter Drucker, *The Practice of Management* (New York: Harper & Row, 1954); Rensis Likert, *New Patterns of Management* (New York: McGraw-Hill, 1961); C. L. Hughes, *Goal Setting* (New York: American Management Association, 1965); M. S. Kellogg, *What To Do About Performance Appraisal* (New York: American Management Association, 1965).

24. George S. Odiorne, *Management by Objectives—A System of Managerial Leadership* (New York: Pitman, 1965), pp. 55-56.

See also idem, *Management Decisions by Objectives* (Englewood Cliffs, N.J.: Prentice Hall, 1969).

25. Goodyear Management Training Department, *Management by Objectives II*, brochure (Akron, Ohio: Goodyear Tire and Rubber Co., 1968), p. 2.

For a comment on the use of MBO in a school district, see William Ingraham and John Keefe, "Values of Management by Objectives," *School Management* 16, no. 6 (June 1972): 28-29.

26. See "Section B: Some Applications of Accountability," in *Emerging Patterns*, pp. 361-523.

See also Frank Sciara and Richard Jantz, eds., *Accountability in American Education* (Boston: Allyn and Bacon, 1972), chapters 3 and 4.

27. Barro, "An Approach to Developing Accountability Measures," p. 368.

28. Stephen Klein and Marvin Alkin, "Evaluating Teachers for Outcome Accountability," *Evaluation Comment* 3, no. 3 (May 1972): 5-11.

29. Five varieties of tests are suggested in David Shoemaker, "Evaluating the Effectiveness of Competing Instructional Programs," *Educational Researcher* 1, no. 5 (May 1972): 5-8, 12.

30. Klein and Alkin, "Evaluating Teachers for Outcome Accountability," p. 10.

31. Popham, "Performance Tests of Teaching Proficiency: Rationale, Development, and Validation," p. 115.

32. It might be added that as a form of management project management can be expected to increase as bureaucratic forms of organizational structure attempt to adapt and respond to accelerated change pressures. The comments of Warren Bennis appear to carry foresight in this regard. See Warren Bennis, "The Coming Death of Bureaucracy," *Emerging Patterns*, pp. 541-551.

33. Russell Archibald and Richard Villoria, *Network-Based Management Systems* (New York: John Wiley and Sons, 1967), p. 14.

34. Ibid., pp. 12 - 14.

35. Among the references on networks and PERT (in addition to the works of Baumgartner, Cook, Archibald, and Villoria) are Bruce Baker and Rene Eris, *An Introduction to PERT-CPM* (Homewood, Ill.: Richard D. Irwin, Inc.,

1964); Desmond Cook, *Program Evaluation and Review Technique: Applications in Education* (Washington, D. C.: U. S. Government Printing Office, 1966); D. H. Dillman and D. L. Cook, "Simulation in the Training of R and D Project Managers," *Educational Technology* 9, no. 5 (May 1969): 39 - 43; H. W. Handy and K. M. Hussan, *Network Analysis for Educational Management* (Englewood Cliffs, N.J.: Prentice-Hall, Inc., 1969); L. S. Hill, "Some Possible Pitfalls in the Design and Use of PERT Networking," *Academy of Management Journal* 8, no. 2 (June 1965): 139-45; J. J. Moder and C. R. Philips, *Project Management with PERT and CPM* (New York: Reinhold Publishing Corp., 1964); C. R. Philips and C. R. Beer, *Computer Programs for PERT and CPM*, Technical Paper no. 13 (Silver Springs, Md.: Operations Research, Inc., 1963); P. Schoderbeek, "A Study of the Applications of PERT," *Academy of Management Journal* (September 1965): 190 - 210; G. S. Stillan et al., *PERT: A New Management Planning and Control Technique* (New York: American Management Association, 1962); H. S. Woodgate, *Planning by Network* (London: Business Publications Ltd., 1964).

9. Performance Contracting

"Pupils Improve in School Run by Private Company" was the headline for a *New York Times* article that greeted readers with their morning coffee recently.[1] The article described the apparent success of a performance contract in Gary, Indiana, where one of the city's schools was being run for a four-year period by the Behavioral Research Laboratories under a $2.6 million contract. The children in the school achieved well on tests and at "10 percent less than the $924 spent on each student in other Gary schools." Five months later, the Office of Economic Opportunity announced performance contracting to be a failure.[2] Is it? As mentioned earlier (note 36 to chapter 2), it *is* controversial and, we think, still worth a close look.

Performance contracting is considered by some to be a possible method of achieving accountability in education. In this chapter we will discuss performance contracting, its advantages and disadvantages. Various types of contracts will be examined. Finally, some steps toward developing a performance contract will be discussed.

There are many types of performance contracts, but those most commonly discussed are agreements between a school district and another agency to provide instructional services. In this form of contracting the school district pays a fee for these services, sometimes on a fixed basis and sometimes on some sort of incentive (e.g., if the contractor "overperforms" and demonstrates an appreciably larger learning gain than requested, he may be paid a bonus). The other agency can be a group of teachers (this is called "internal" performance contracting), a private commercial firm, a university, a professional society, or an "external" ad hoc group. The agreement is usually in the form of a contract that specifies the desired outcomes, defines what pupils will be taught, and establishes other parameters within which instruction is to take place. In return for the accomplishments of the students—or lack thereof—the fee is determined (a form of level-of-confidence predetermination). Sometimes the accomplishment is evaluated on the basis of standardized tests that may be given to the students by an outside evaluating agency.

We discussed in chapter 1 some of the reasons for the current interest in educational accountability. Performance contracts have been viewed by some as the major means of accomplishing this, but we hold to the position that a performance contract is only one of the many means a school district might examine and consider in its quest for better educational results. Opinions on performance contracting vary. The *New York Times* reported two viewpoints; Albert Shanker, president of the United Federation of Teachers in New York City, responded to the article on Gary's experiment in the same paper, downgrading the reported results and referring to the program as "Gary's dubious venture."[3]

On the other hand, a Gallup poll raised the question of performance contracts in education in a public survey of American education. The survey showed that 49 percent of those polled favored the idea of performance contracts while 28 percent were opposed. A sizable group—23 percent—was still undecided. This report maintains that people see the performance contract as a way to make sure that the public gets its money's worth, and it concludes: "Unless cogent arguments can be advanced, *unless experience proves that this is not an effective way of reaching educational goals at present cost levels, this movement is likely to gain momentum.*"[4] (Emphasis added.) This point is currently under question. In the 1969-70 school year, two school districts entered into performance contracts with educational firms; in 1970-71 the number was over a hundred.[5] It is highly probable, however, that opposition from the powerful United Federation of Teachers and other groups has—despite counterclaims—diminished this growth rate for external contracting.[6]

The National Education Association polled its members about performance contracting to determine whether they favored school systems contracting with private businesses that guarantee improvement in reading and other school subjects. Nearly one-half the respondents indicated some degree of opposition, but these were divided almost evenly between those who *tended* to oppose and those who *strongly* opposed such a practice. Thirty percent tended to favor it, but fewer than one in ten were strongly in favor.[7]

When these same teachers were asked whether local teacher associations should themselves contract with school systems for performance contracts (rather than some outsider group), 24 percent said yes, 38.4 percent said no, and 37.6 percent had no opinion.[8] There was no difference in responses on either question that could be attributed to grade level taught, sex, size of the school system, geographic region, or type of community. In sum, "public school teachers . . . do not believe that the type of competition for money customary in the business world should be applied to education."[9]

The National Education Association opposes performance contracts unless they meet a set of conditions that includes the involvement of teachers, a variety of testing devices, a "turn-key" provision (i.e., a process whereby the contractor turns over—like turning a key—the operation of a proven program to the local school system), maximum use of school personnel, supervision of students by professionals, genuinely innovative programs, no conflict with negotiated agreements, and no copyright provisions.[10]

The American Federation of Teachers has taken a stronger position, stating that "all AFT locals be urged to educate their members, boards of education, as well as parent and community groups, to the educationally negative aspects of performance contracting and that the AFT sponsor a major nationwide campaign to oppose performance contracting."[11]

It is interesting but not entirely unexpected that both major national teachers' organizations oppose performance contracting. It is really the teachers who are criticized by the suggestion of a need for a performance contract; the clear implication is that teachers are not doing their job. Most teacher salary schedules are based on how many degrees teachers have and now long they have been teaching. Very few districts have "merit" salary schedules, and none of these, as far as we can determine, base merit on student performance as does a performance contract. Performance contracts threaten teachers because they may imply that paraprofessionals or teaching machines can do the same job (and more cheaply) that the teacher does. Teachers' salaries typically account for 75 percent or more of a school district's annual operating budget, and have risen so dramatically in the past few years that local school costs have increased to the point of bringing on a taxpayer revolt. Faced on the one hand with the embarrassing implication that teachers are not doing their job (and hence schools must appeal to outside groups—performance contractors—for help), and on the other with vigorous teacher demands for increases in salaries and benefits, it is small wonder that teacher organization leaders, accountable only to their memberships, attack performance contracting overtly or "qualify it to death."

The teachers are correct on at least one count. To date most performance contracts have used less money for teachers' salaries and more for paraprofessionals and instructional equipment and materials. One study shows that the percentage spent on performance contracts for teachers' salaries varied from nothing to 66 percent, while the control programs in the same districts were spending from 64 to 81 percent of the money for salaries. Conversely, the money for instructional materials in the performance contract programs ranged from 8 to 27 percent while the control programs were spending from 1 to 4.8 percent. Only one control group used paraprofessionals at all, while the performance groups used from 9.5 to 66 percent of the money for paraprofessionals.[12] It is clearly evident from these results that most performance contracts have used funds for purposes other than teachers' salaries. Is it any wonder that teacher leaders oppose performance contracts?

However, the National Association of State Boards of Education has stated that, "if they hold promise, the Association suggests consideration of future development of similar performance contracts with teachers, relating levels of student achievement to teacher compensation."[13] The American Association of School Administrators has passed resolutions at annual conventions favoring the concept of performance contracts as a means for effecting positive change.[14]

To generalize, it might be fair to say that a conflict is brewing. The public and boards of education say they want school costs reduced and see performance contracting as a means of achieving this goal and at the same time getting the kids demonstrably educated. Teachers' organizations are opposed to performance contracting, and administrators sit in the middle, taking a "neutral" position.

The Growth of Performance Contracting

Just how prevalent is performance contracting, anyway? Performance contracts are presently under way in such diverse communities as Boston; Cherry Creek, Denver, and Englewood (Colorado); Taft and Dallas (Texas); Flint, Monroe, and Grand Rapids (Michigan); Gary and Hammond (Indiana); Fresno, Oakland, and Gilroy (California); Greenville (South Carolina); Philadelphia; Texarkana (Texas-Arkansas); Norfolk (Virginia); Jacksonville, Duval County (Florida); Savannah (Georgia); Providence; Anchorage (Alaska);

Wichita; Chicago; Hartford (Connecticut); Las Vegas; McComb (Mississippi); McNairy County (Tennessee); New Orleans; Bronx; Portland and Rockland (Maine); and Seattle.[15] Thus, contracts are in effect from coast to coast, in big and small towns, and in urban and rural settings. Suffice it to say that there is considerable interest in performance contracting by a number of people.

In a few cases, the internal performance contracts are being done by groups of local teachers with their school boards (e.g., Mesa, Arizona, and Stockton, California), but most are external contracts with private companies. These include Behavioral Research Labs, Learning Research Associates, Macmillan Educational Services, Educational Development Laboratories, Harcourt Brace Jovanovich, Westinghouse Learning Corporation, Quality Education Development, Dorsett Educational Systems, Alpha Learning Systems, Learning Foundations, Inc., Plan Education Centers, Singer/Graphflex, Thiokol Chemical Corporation, and Education Solutions, Inc. The contracts vary in size from several thousand to several million dollars. Most, however, are in the range of 200 to 350 thousand dollars.[16] Practically all of these contracts have been financed with *federal* money, either from Title I of the Elementary and Secondary Education Act or from the Office of Economic Opportunity. Most of the programs deal in one way or another with reading.[17]

It may be interesting to note that very few of the companies listed above were in existence ten years ago. Most were formed to become involved in the educational market as a result of the recent influx of federal dollars to public schools. Before 1965, there was little involvement of the private sector in education except in the textbook and school supply fields, and the total amount spent was relatively small compared with other school expenditures. Then, in 1965, the Elementary and Secondary Education Act was passed, which provided funds to local school districts to develop experimental programs. This was really the first time that massive federal funds were made available to local public school systems in noncategorical grants. Previously most federal money was for vocational education, school construction for districts near military bases, and school lunches. But now we had lots of money available to the school districts to spend pretty much as they chose.

At the same time, the war on poverty began, with federal money going into the Office of Economic Opportunity for such programs as Head Start and Job Corps. The Peace Corps had been started a few years earlier. One of the basic thrusts of the war on poverty—besides helping the poor—was to involve the private sector in helping solve some of society's problems. Some of the largest corporations in the country were brought in at the request of President Johnson and Sargent Shriver, including Westinghouse, General Electric, Brunswick, Burroughs, RCA, Sylvania, Philco-Ford, and Northern Natural Gas. All these companies had been dealing with the government in other areas, such as defense and space exploration, so it seemed natural that they should expand into this newly financed field, education, where they hoped to market their technological know-how to the government.

The programs under the Elementary and Secondary Education Act, Head Start, Job Corps, and the Peace Corps, involved not only selling supplies and equipment but also the services of people. These companies got into the training field as a business venture, and it was natural for them to go into training programs at the local level when the financing came from the federal government. Of course, many new companies came into being only to get in on the action, but the money was not as large as some had thought it would be, some of the early programs received bad press, and there were other problems. Some of the larger companies were used to large overhead amounts to federal contracts (used to cover unapplied time and proposal costs). Some were more successful than others. Many of the smaller companies could compete better in the marketplace because of lower overhead costs; as a result we now find many larger companies exploring other fields, for example, ecology and home building, while smaller companies remain, competing for the educational market.

Is the notion of contracting for private educational services outlandish? To those who have such thoughts, we might point out that schools have always been involved in purchasing from the private sector, including such items as grass seed, toilet paper, buses, band instruments, telescopes, pencils, desks, light bulbs, chalk, and so on. Most if not all supplies are purchased from profit-making companies. Often these items are purchased as a result of bidding (sometimes this is required by law), but sometimes the lowest bid is not accepted, as when a school district has discovered that the lowest-priced pencil breaks often, does not sharpen well, and ends up being more expensive than one that is initially higher in price. Our basic point is that it is not new for schools to purchase supplies from a private, profit-making, concern; tax dollars have been used to buy from private companies for years.

Schools have also traditionally purchased *services* from private, profit-making, companies. Some examples are contracted bus transportation, construction of a school facility, and architectural services. These too are often purchased as a result of competitive bidding, but not always. (Architects, for instance, generally charge a percentage of construction costs, so all architects' fees would be basically the same. The school district decides on the basis of qualifications or some other criteria, such as visiting other schools designed by the architect, whether or not to use his services.)

We also find that schools contract for such services as computerized scheduling and computer time. Schools contract to use the services of private consultants to help solve school problems or to hire a new superintendent, and for the continued services of people to provide guard service, food service, groundskeeping, window washing, and, of course, teaching. We should not forget that schools contract for the services of teachers now, or that many districts contract for the professional services of others: school doctors, psychologists, athletics coaches, etc. Is it really so different to contract with a private company to provide teaching services than to provide other services to the school district? We do not equate teaching with washing windows or groundskeeping, but we do maintain that there is nothing really different about contracting for the services of people and that schools have been doing this for some time now.

Some Early Findings on How It Has Worked

We have been talking about where performance contracts now exist and how private industry got involved in providing services to school districts. We now turn to an examination of how performance contracts have worked. RAND Corporation recently published a report that examined the performance contracts in Norfolk, Texarkana, Gary, Gilroy, and Grand Rapids, covering eight programs in fifteen schools. The study discusses implications and conclusions under seven headings: instructional processes, cognitive growth, resource requirements, evaluation, program management, returns to contractors, and the major advantages and disadvantages of performance contracting.[18]

Instructional Processes

The report cites five conclusions about the influence of performance contracting on the instructional process. It was found that all the programs had individualized instruction as a goal and that there was an emphasis on basic skills. Since the programs were aimed primarily at the disadvantaged, there were some problems in providing for abler pupils. Some evidence of a humanization in the programs was found. Most of the programs were not off-the-shelf programs but were developed to meet the needs of the particular situation. Finally, the program was seen as an educational change agent within the local schools.

Cognitive Growth

Major gains in achievement were not found, but there was an increase. Attention has been focused on the problems of using standardized achievement test scores as a measurement device; it is difficult to interpret the results from present tests. We conclude that people involved in decision making must be involved in selecting appropriate testing instruments and that efforts should be made to keep these instruments "secure" (in the sense that the temptation of persons to give students special word lists and other coaching devices geared to a knowledge of the test items is negated by keeping the test secured before use).

Resource Requirements

The RAND study found that the performance contract programs cost more than conventional programs, but this may be due to the fact that all special programs for the educationally disadvantaged seem to cost more than regular programs. The performance programs were found to cost about the same as, or even less than, comparable programs under Title I. It is not yet possible to determine the cost effectiveness of these programs because they use such different staffing patterns from conventional programs.

Evaluation

Learning on the part of the individual student is focused on in performance contracts to an extent not usually found in other programs. The problem of "teaching for the test"[19] makes it difficult to evaluate achievement gains. Since the emphasis for the contractor was on dollar return, there was not as much concern for evaluation as the researchers would have liked to see, and data was often inaccessible or unavailable. We repeat our concern for test security.

Program Management

The RAND study found that performance contracts enabled people to make changes more quickly than regular teachers had been able to. The cooperation and support of the local school system is very important for the success and continuation of the program. Flexibility was possible and desired in the programs to an extent not found in traditional classes. Multiyear programs seem to have some advantages over shorter programs. There are two potential areas for serious conflict: teacher opposition to merit pay based on student performance and the requirement for public control of all school programs. RAND believes that teachers must be involved in the program design. Interestingly, parents generally were uninformed about the programs.

Returns to Contractors

In general there do not seem to be large profits from performance contracts. Contractors have been able to get some additional business in the districts, but usually this is not related to a performance-type contract. Some contractors are getting out of the business, while others are attempting to convert their contracts to other types of programs or consultantships. There has been some good publicity for a few companies, which may have helped them in other market areas.

Major Advantages and Disadvantages

The RAND study finds three major advantages and three major disadvantages to performance contracts. The advantages are that change is facilitated, increased emphasis is placed on accountability, and new businesses were generated. The disadvantages are that some of the costs have been very high, the focus has been on only a few skill areas, and problems (usually opposition from teacher organizations) have been regenerated because of the new arrangements.

Types of Performance Contracts

There are several types of performance contracts about which one might want to know before considering this means to develop an educationally accountable program. There are two major categories of contracts: *internal* and *external.* Internal performance contracts are those in which the school district contracts with a subunit of its own system, e.g., a school, department, or a group of teachers. It usually involves some form of incentive payment to school personnel based on agreed-on criteria. External performance contracting involves an outside group or company or institution that agrees to a contractual relationship requiring it to perform some service for the school system. External performance contracting is the most prevalent, but it is the internal type that is supported by the National Education Association.

Internal contracts

There are many possible variations of internal performance contracts, depending on the needs and desires of the school district. One consideration is whether to have competition for the contract, or to award it on a sole source basis.[20] When a contract is awarded as the result of competition, it is necessary to develop some specifications for the prospective bidders. This is called a *request for proposal,* and will be discussed later in this chapter. When the contract is awarded on a sole source basis the district negotiates with only one group to provide the service. If they cannot agree, there is no contract, and the district may chose to discuss the proposed project with another group.

There are many possible ways to make payment under an internal contract, but the two most commonly discussed are the "baseline" and "nonbaseline." A baseline is simply some dollar amount (usually per child since most school costs have traditionally been computed on this basis) from which the amount of expenditures are negotiated. For example, a district may be spending $850 per child at the elementary level. The negotiations might revolve around this figure in terms of how much per child would be paid for certain achievement. If over a year's time a child improved one year or one grade level, based on some testing mechanism, the group would receive $850; but if the achievement were 10 percent higher, the payment might be an additional 10 percent, or an additional $85 per child. Conversely, if the child achieved less than one grade level, say only half a grade level, the payment might be 50 percent less, or $425. Under such a contract the points that would have to be negotiated include (1) how much would be paid above or below the baseline figure, and (2) on what basis this would be paid. It should be remembered that the group wanting the contract will seek the highest possible return for students who achieve well, but may want to minimize liability for those who do not do as well.

The group may also want to negotiate the payments on a monthly basis during the course of the contract, to reduce its investment. That is, it may want to be paid some amount each month throughout the contract, perhaps 10 percent of the baseline figure, so the teachers can be paid and other obligations met. The group may even attempt to negotiate an initial payment before the contract starts, perhaps on signing, to further reduce its investment; otherwise it may have to borrow money to meet its obligations until the first payment is received. Exactly this point—the investment, or rather the *return on investment*—makes a performance contract relatively attractive. If the type of advance, or pay-as-you-go, payments that we have discussed can be negotiated, the group has made almost no investment of dollars before it starts receiving a dollar return. This same factor makes these contracts attractive to private industry. Ordinarily in private business the company must build up an inventory of products before starting to get a return. This buildup includes the operation of the manufacturing plant and its related costs of raw materials, salaries, utilities, amortization of the building, warehousing, advertising, sales expense, shipping, and so forth. Only when the customer purchases the product at the retail store, or when it is wholesaled to a distributor, does the company get its return on the initial investment. Under a performance contract there are some initial costs, such as the preparation of the proposal, but they are nowhere near the magnitude of what business is accustomed to. If the project is successful the company's return on the investment can be very high, and it can usually recover minimum costs even if the project does not go as well as planned. Most private companies will not contract unless they feel they can recover at least their minimum costs. This is primarily due to the fact that the manager of the company is responsible for the profit and loss of his group, and he has much to lose if he does not make a profit—sometimes including his job. Public school people may be willing to take some risks that the businessman will not, simply because if the project does not work out the chances are they will still have a job.

There are other variables that can be considered in an internal performance contract, including who is going to regulate the project. The possibilities here include the teachers, the administration, the school board, an outside agency, or some combination of these. Of course, the usual procedure is for the administration to regulate the schools. In chapter 8, we recommended using a project manager.

External Contracts

The external performance contract is by far the most common. This may be due to the reason for having the performance contract in the first place, i.e., there may be some dissatisfaction with the manner in which the schools are performing, so an outside group is considered. Even so, there are two basic kinds of external contract, the *competitive* and the *noncompetitive*.

When a district seeks a competitive contract, a request for proposal must be developed, which is then distributed to all who are interested in bidding on the contract. Sometimes a prebidding conference is held to permit prospective bidders to ask questions. The district may request interested bidders to submit a *statement of capability* (i.e., a statement of their credentials and supporting data to indicate that they can be considered as serious bidders). This allows the district to screen the bidders before giving them the request for proposal. Once the bids are received, they are evaluated and a contract is negotiated.

The noncompetitive contract, sometimes called a *sole source contract,* can also be used in external performance contracting. This is usually done after evaluating statements of capability, or because the district is familiar with the group's work, or because the proposal was received on an unsolicited basis (i.e., it was presented to a district without the district having asked for proposals).

The competitive contract has several advantages. There is little danger that the district can be accused of playing favorites with certain bidders, and the district may receive a more favorable price as a result of the competition. Receiving bids from a number of groups may present the district with some innovative ideas and approaches that it may not have considered—almost like free consultation. However, there are disadvantages to the external competitive bidding procedure. Since the bidding is usually in response to a statement of the work required, a lot of time may have to be spent in developing the request for proposal. The district may not have knowledgeable people to do this, and may need to secure the services of an outside consultant. Also, the whole bidding procedure is very time consuming, sometimes taking as long as several months. There may be difficulty too in evaluating the proposals, since they may not be easily compared. Then too, a careful balance must be struck between making the request for proposal so restrictive that the responders feel they cannot be creative in their proposals, and letting them be so creative and innovative that it is difficult to compare the various bids. We recommend an approach in which the outcomes, or performance objectives, that are expected are rather carefully stipulated, but the methods of achieving them are relatively flexible. For instance, the district may require that the performance contract improve the reading level of the students by a certain amount, e.g., at least one grade level per year, but the bidders might be free to select the teaching methods and staffing patterns to accomplish this.

Noncompetitive contracts have advantages and disadvantages, too. Since there is only one proposal to consider, the district does not have to develop a detailed request for proposal and does not have to evaluate one proposal against another. However, there may be some question whether or not the best "deal" has been obtained. It is more difficult in some respects to negotiate this kind of contract because there are only two alternatives: to award the contract or not. The district will not have the advantages of having several solutions suggested, and thus may not have a choice of a variety of materials and approaches.

In sum, there are two basic types of performance contract, internal and external. Either of these may be awarded after competitive bidding, or may be given on a sole source basis. Internal contracts have the advantages of being able to become a normal part of the school's operation since they already involve school personnel. They are less threatening to people in the district than external contracts, which bring in "outsiders." Internal contracts ordinarily do not require expensive outside consultants. They may stimulate some competition within the district for better performance. Among the disadvantages of internal contracts is the cost of providing training to the staff, since they will probably be trying new approaches. There is some danger of procrastination due to a lack of commitment or to internal political maneuvering. There may be some problems in coordinating new approaches with current programs in use in the district.

External contracts have the advantage of probably being a better vehicle for an innovative approach to the task. There is a more immediate start to the project since the district does not have to train the staff (although the contractor may need to), and a better chance that the lowest price will be obtained. If the project does not work out as well as expected, there is no staff that must be retained since they are on the contractor's payroll. Among the disadvantages of external contracts are that it may be more difficult for the district eventually to take over the project because of teacher resistance, and that the administration may not be accustomed to dealing with an outside contractor. Negotiation for an external contract is also more difficult, and its legal ramifications need to be carefully examined.

If you are considering a performance contract you would be well advised to read as widely as possible in the field. We also recommend visiting a performance contracting district similar to yours to find out firsthand how well it might work in your district. Finally, if you feel the need for reassurance we suggest that you seek outside assistance before making a final decision.

Steps to Developing a Performance Contract

Once you have decided to use a performance contract, a number of steps must be taken before it can be implemented. Let us consider some of these steps.

Assess Needs

Before deciding in favor of a performance contract it is absolutely necessary that the district determine its needs. Chapter 3 describes in greater detail how this might be done. This step should not be omitted. To contract successfully, you will need to know the current educational state of affairs in your district (or building) and have a fairly clear concept of what they ought to be. It may be determined that there are several things in the district that need doing, in which case an order of priority will have to be established. Care should be exercised to determine if some of the problems are interrelated.

Evaluate Alternatives

Once needs have been determined and an order of priority established, there may be several alternatives that can be considered. For instance, the district may determine that improving the reading instruction in the primary grades is needed and that this has high priority over other needs in the district. Among alternative solutions might be: hiring additional staff, getting new books, reducing class size, establishing a nongraded program, using paraprofessionals, lengthening the school day, or seeking outside assistance. Any of these may be used, and have been used, to attempt to improve reading instruction. However, the district may decide to try a performance contract.

Select a Plan of Action

A plan of action should emerge as a result of evaluating the alternatives. In this case, it will be to try a performance contract. The district should be ready to justify this plan over other plans that could have been selected. A team of people from the district, which might include administrators, board members, teachers, and students, may be used at this point. It probably would be a good idea to have such a group involved from the very beginning. Often this is not done, however, until the project assumes some definite shape.

Develop a Strategy for Change

Whether or not a performance contract is the chosen means to reach the particular ends, change is bound to come about in the district as a result of all of this work. (Chapter 4 discusses some things that should be considered in developing a strategy for change.) The major elements of change in this case will probably be the resistance of the teachers to the proposal because they may view it as threatening to them. Community groups, taxpayers (if it appears to reduce costs), and administrators are likely to favor the proposed change. Perhaps at this point serious consideration might be given to the possibility of an internal rather than an external performance contract. We suggest holding this idea open as a possibility, but proceed with plans for developing the other steps in this process; they will not be wasted since they are needed for an internal contract as well.

Of course, it may be that the attention given to improving reading may be sufficient to impress on the staff the seriousness of the reading problem in the district.

Outside Assistance

At this point it might be useful to you to pay a visit to a site where a performance contract is in operation, and also consider the use of some outside assistance. While no one in the district is likely to have had previous experience with this type of contract or its preparation, it can be done with a little study and effort. Naturally, technical assistance is reassuring. There are many good booklets, pamphlets, and magazine articles dealing with the subject that should be consulted.[21]

Legal Review

Many authorities believe a review should take place on the legal feasibility of a performance contract so that any legal problems may be identified and corrected before the project proceeds. If they appear insurmountable, or very time consuming to resolve, it may become necessary to return to the stage where alternatives were evaluated and select another alternative. However, since performance contracting is already relatively widespread geographically, legal problems in its operation should not be insurmountable. With all due respect to local school district attorneys, most may not be familiar with performance contracting, and may themselves require help. As a source of legal assistance, the state education department should not be overlooked.

Identify Student Population

At first this may appear to be an easy step, but it is crucial, especially as far as the potential contractors are concerned. In addition to a statement of how many students are to be involved, the grade levels, educational deficiencies, test scores, socioeconomic status, racial composition, class size, geographic distribution within the district, and any attitudinal and motivational data will all be helpful. In other words, the prospective bidders will want to know as much about the students as possible.

Determine Program Objectives

What do you want to accomplish? The answer to that question is your program objective (or objectives). This should not be stated in general terms, such as "improved reading ability," because there are too many variables. What is "improved," what is "reading," and what is "ability"? It is better to describe your desires in terms of an increase in a score on a certain achievement test, or a combination of scores. You may be after improved reading ability, but you should specify how you want your learners to behave *after* they have improved their reading ability. What should they be able to demonstrate on the basis of improvement? The answer may be a higher test score (you specify how high) on the items you want to see improved (e.g., reading comprehension, reading speed, word attack skills, etc.).

Of course, the program objectives may be more complicated. The important thing to remember is to describe them in a way that leaves no doubt what learning outcomes you want achieved. You would not ask a contractor to "build me a house" without being specific about the number and size of the rooms, whether or not you want a fireplace, what kind of heating is required, and so on. Similarly, you would not ask a contractor to operate a portion of your school system without telling him what it is you want done.

On the other hand, you may want to give the bidders some latitude in how they approach your problem. Some districts prefer to state what the *problem* is and let the contractor present his ideas on how to overcome it. This procedure makes evaluating proposals more difficult, but has the advantage of encouraging new approaches to the problem. If the program objectives are stated in terms of desired outcomes, the contractors will be able to provide a variety of approaches. This is a procedure we encourage.

Evaluate Local Resources

A careful statement of what local resources are available should be prepared. One of these resources is what funds are available for the project. In some cases this will be local money, but many performance contracts have used federal funds, commonly from Title I of the Elementary and Secondary Education Act. It should be indicated clearly if the project is to be funded from a proposal to be developed after the contract is awarded. This last type is the least desirable for an external contract, but may be quite acceptable for an internal contract.

Other local resources to be listed include the facilities and equipment to be provided. Ordinarily the district will furnish the classroom, desks, and utilities to the contractor, but there may be some items, such as teaching machines, motion picture projectors, cassette recorders, etc., that may be legitimate items for negotiation. In any case, it should be clearly understood what is to be furnished by the district and what items the contractor must provide. (If the facilities, utilities, and some furniture are furnished by the district, the value of these items should be *deducted* from the usual per pupil cost, if that is the baseline for cost comparison.)

The teaching staff or a teachers' group are also among resources to be considered. This may be a good point at which to decide whether to use an internal contract or an external one (or ask both groups to submit bids). We have already observed that it is possible to get both inside and outside groups to bid, and then select the most attractive proposition.

The potential involvement of community groups, both

favorable and unfavorable, is another local resource. This may be
crucial if the project has to deal with students from a minority
group. If their involvement is to be part of the contract, it should be
stated how and under what conditions.

Determine Measurement Instrument

It is usually necessary to specify what measurement instruments
will be used to judge results. The district may want to specify which
instruments will be used. There are advantages and disadvantages in
doing this. The major advantage is that all bidders will have similar
criteria on which to bid, and the district can specify devices with
which they are familiar. A disadvantage is that specifying the tests
may reduce the creativity of the bidders, and the district may lose a
chance to discover some new measurement devices. One method of
getting the best of both is to specify that a certain measurement
device be used for the basic bid, but indicate that alternative proposals will be accepted in addition to the one requested. In this way
bids can be compared, and the district will have the advantage of
learning about possible new devices.

A more serious question, however, is that of what is really being
measured. In chapter 2 we noted that there is frequently a poor fit
between the objectives of the school and those of the standardized
test (if this sort of test is used), sometimes a problem inherent in the
measurement design and test instrument format for a particular
school populations, poor administration of the measurement instruments, and a problem with a measurement instrument that does not
measure what it claims to measure.[22]

There is also the question whether to use individual or group
scores as the basis for payment. The average, or mean, increase may
be a better indicator of achievement than individual scores. In either
case it is also worth considering the possibility of teaching for the
test (see note 19). One way around this problem is to have an outside
group provide the evaluation for the students' achievement. It is also
possible to have this outside group select the testing instruments to
be used in accordance with the particular objectives of the program,
and for these instruments to be kept unknown from the contractor
(the "test security" discussed in chapter 8).

It has been suggested that the most satisfactory solution may be
to extend the contract over several years. This way, the contractor
would be judged on how well students retained what they had

learned.[23] There are obviously some disadvantages to this procedure (for example, what happens if the project does not go as well as expected), but some of these same problems are present now.

Payment Method Chosen

The contractor's incentive in winning a performance contract is usually to make money. There may be other reasons, such as to sell his product, or in the hope of continued business, or to cover some staff costs until something better comes along, but basically the contractor will attempt to negotiate the best possible financial arrangement for himself.

The method usually suggested is to tie the payments to the increase in student achievement with more money paid for students who achieve very well, and less money paid for students who do not achieve so well. A wide variety of payment plans could be suggested. It makes sense to examine the possible consequences of any payment plan. Ask yourself, What would happen if . . . ? It may be well to place a limit on the maximum payment that could be received under the contract.

Another approach is to ask the prospective bidders to suggest a payment plan in their proposal. Not only may this lead to some ideas that had not been considered, but the contractor will then be working under a plan he "owns." Any payment plan should be clear to all parties, be specific about the conditions of payment, and provide for a maximum as well as minimum payment.

Develop the Request for Proposal

Once you have gone through the steps discussed above, it is time to develop the request for proposal (RFP).[24] Put simply, this is a description of the work that is to be done. The RFP should provide enough information to the bidders so they can bid intelligently on the project. At the same time, it should not be so restrictive that the bidders will not be able to innovate. The RFP will usually ask for bids to be submitted in two parts: first, a technical proposal from the bidder stating what he will do and, second, a cost proposal. This will enable the evaluators to choose the best proposals separately from the lowest cost proposal.

The RFP should contain a definition of the *problem* to be solved. This would include how many children are involved and at what grade levels, what subject matter, etc. Any specific information, e.g., socioeconomic status, previous test results, etc., will also be helpful to the bidders.

The next section is often called the *scope of the work*. It is here that the performance objectives, discussed earlier, are included. The facilities to be provided should be listed in this section, along with any services that will be available.

A third section might contain the *calendar,* which describes the time during which the contract will take place. It also tells when and where a bid should be submitted, when the decision will be made, and when the contractor is expected to begin work. It might also indicate at what periods throughout the contract certain reports are due, when testing is to occur, and information about the school calendar during which the contract will take place.

Another section of the RFP deals with the *financial arrangements,* indicating what type of contract is anticipated,[25] whether or not funds are available, how the funds will be paid, some statement about maximum dollar amounts to be paid, and whether or not alternative methods of payment will be considered.

While some contractors may be reluctant to submit a budget along with their proposal, it is not unreasonable to ask them to indicate how they plan to spend the money. You should have some idea of how many people they plan to hire, what amount will be spent on equipment, and what services the contractor will provide.

It is also helpful to give prospective bidders a copy of the district's current salary schedules, as well as any information from groups like the Chamber of Commerce about salaries in the general area.

There should be a section on *restrictions* and *policy guidelines.* This will include a copy of the school district policies, or the appropriate applicable sections. Any requirements in regard to sub-contractors should be clearly stated. Any unusual items about the district are covered here, such as a court order to desegregate, the liability of the contractor, insurance requirements, an equal employment clause requirement (most federally funded projects require this), contractor rights to material developed during the contract, and so on. Some contracts will require a statement that local school officials cannot benefit from the contract.

Another section is on *evaluation* procedures, including a description of the measurement instruments to be used and a time schedule of when the testing will occur. If an outside third party is to be involved in the evaluation, this should be made clear. The district may wish to let the contractors suggest the means of evaluating the program, but the general parameters are shown in this section.

The RFP should also contain a section on *reporting procedures,* which will include what reports will be required from the contractor during the course of the project. It should indicate whether the forms for these will be provided by or to the contractor. The kind of reports that may be required could include attendance, materials used, number of minutes or hours of instruction, a form to request payment, and certification of the payment of various insurance and other required fees.

A very important section is the *contractor's operation plans.* The contractor is asked to describe in some detail how the project will be organized and operated, to specify what books, materials, machines, and techniques will be used. A proposed staffing plan should be required, along with résumés of some of the key staff. (This last item will vary depending on the size of the contract.) If the contractor is required to use some of the personnel presently employed by the district he should be asked to indicate how these people will be trained and what benefits they will have. In general, this section is where the contractor is asked to "put his best foot forward." It should be clear in the RFP how much freedom the contractor has in developing a program or how closely he must adhere to a predetermined outline.

The final section of the RFP usually contains the *format* for the proposal. It is most desirable to ask all bidders to present their proposals in the same format, making it much easier to read, compare, and evaluate them. There should be a statement to the effect that the proposals need not contain a lot of artwork, expensive covers, and fancy printing. There are two reasons for this; first, this only increases the cost to the district and, second, some smaller companies that might be able to perform very well could be excluded. How many copies of the proposal are required should also be indicated. Usually one copy is needed for each member of the team that reads and evaluates the proposals. Generally contractors are used to submitting fifteen or twenty copies of a proposal, but more than this seems to be too many.

Included in the final section in many RFPs is a section describing how the proposals will be evaluated. Generally this is done by weighting the various sections of the proposal according to their relative importance. It is only fair for a bidder to know on what he will be evaluated.

We have attempted to present above *some* of the items that

might be included in a request for proposal for a performance contract. Obviously, no list can be complete or can be applicable equally to all types of contracts. Perhaps our basic point is that the RFP is a very important document, and should be prepared with great care. It is not enough to copy an RFP from another district, since the conditions may not be similar in both cases.

Develop Evaluation Criteria for Proposals

The RFP contains an outline of how the proposals will be evaluated, and this must be done before the proposals are submitted. Some of the items that might be included in an evaluation scheme would be the technical soundness of the approach, the cost, the past performance and reputation of the company, the type and quality of equipment, copyright provisions, size and quality of the staff, the presentation and organization of the proposal, and the responsiveness of the proposal. Not all of these items need be included, and they may have different weights. The intention is to enable the district to assess adequately the proposals they have received, and to justify the decision that is made.

Develop a List of Potential Bidders

All the preceding work will have gone for naught if several responsible bids are not received. The district must plan to inform prospective bidders about the RFP, and we urge that some effort be expended in compiling a list of reputable bidders for your project.

The district can also get names of prospective bidders from other performance contracts. If the prospective contract has received some newspaper publicity a few bidders may write asking to be placed on a bidding list. Another idea is to contact some bidders and ask for a statement of capability and/or interest. This will give an idea of the level of interest, and can serve as a screening device. However, this should be used with care since many companies get asked every day to present such statements, and they tend to be rather general since it is expensive to prepare a separate statement for each district.

Hold a Prebidding Conference

We think it is a good idea to hold a conference for prospective bidders before the final date for submission of the bids. It is usually a good idea to hold this after advertising for bids, but it can also be held before.

There are several advantages to holding such a conference. It provides an opportunity for bidders to see the facilities and to ask questions. The district has the opportunity to update the RFP, if that is appropriate. And it gives everyone the same access to information.

Districts in out-of-the-way locations should be mindful that some contractors may be traveling by air to reach the conference. If possible, airline schedules and other travel arrangements should be considered. For instance, it might be convenient for the district to open the conference at nine o'clock in the morning, but if the only flight into the community is at nine-fifteen in the morning it would require all those traveling by air to be in the community an extra day. Remember that time is money to most contractors.

Advertise for Bids

People need to know that you have a contract to award. Newspaper articles and advertisements can be of some help, but not everyone reads the *Daily Bugle*. It may be a good idea to send copies of the RFP to the prospective bidders you have already identified. There are several knowledge industry newsletters that are read by contractors; ads can be placed in these.

The advertisement should briefly outline the project, indicate where copies of the RFP are available, when and where the pre-bidding conference will be held, and the date bids are due.

Evaluate Proposals

The process of evaluating the proposals should begin as soon as they are received. Evaluation should be finished and the best proposals selected in about two weeks. It is not a good idea to let too much time elapse between the submission of the proposals and the start of negotiations. Some contractors may even have a statement in their proposal indicating that the price is good only for a sixty-day period.

We recommend selecting the best proposals by the use of the evaluation criteria, already described. It is a good idea to select more than one proposal in case one of the contractors decides to back out, or in case the negotiations do not go well.

Negotiate Contract

The final stage in the process is the negotiation of the contract. This is a very important step, especially when the dollar portion is discussed.

Negotiation usually takes place in two stages. First is the technical part of the discussions, during which time the contractor answers any questions about his operational plan. There may be some modifications desired, which may or may not affect the cost. The second part of the negotiation concerns the costs after agreement has been reached on the program portion.

At the first meeting it should be determined whether or not both parties can in fact negotiate. If not, the negotiations should stop until it is determined why, and until both parties are satisfied. It can be very frustrating for both sides if one group must constantly check back with the "home office" or with "the board."

Turn-key Contracts

An interesting variation of a performance contract is the *turn-key contract*. In simple terms, this is a performance contract that at some point is turned over to the local district to operate. A turn-key contract may at its inception either be an internal or external performance contract. In the case of an internal performance contract, the turn-key idea is a natural outgrowth of the contract, and poses many fewer problems than may be found in an external turn-key contract. However, both are possible, and should be considered by the district.

The basic question is, will the contractor—be it an internal group or external company—always operate the project? The answer is usually, No. The next concern is how the transition from one operation to the other will be accomplished. Who owns the materials and equipment? Who trains the district's staff so they can continue in the project? What, if any, responsibilities in following up does the contractor have? The question of follow-up is probably most crucial in a vocational training project, where job placement and counseling are important factors. It may be less important in a primary grade reading program, but should be considered nonetheless.

Consideration should be given to the turn-key question in developing the request for proposal. Part of the responsibility of the contract, as outlined in the RFP, may be to provide training for the personnel who will operate the program when the contractor leaves.

The major advantage of a turn-key contract is that there is more likelihood of the benefits of the contract being continued once the contractor completes his obligations. It also provides a convenient means to terminate the contract if it is not working out too well.

Summary

In this chapter we have tried to present only an overview of the field of performance contracting. It is not possible to treat all aspects of this very complicated subject in a short chapter. Discussed were internal, external, and turn-key contracts and their variations; some advantages and disadvantages of each were presented. The steps in developing a performance contract were outlined, along with a discussion of preparing a request for proposal.

In conclusion, how do *we* see the issue of performance contracting? We find agreement in the words of Campbell and Lorion:

In our view, performance contracts are but one expression of the larger accountability concept. We are not sure whether performance contracts in education, as we now know them, will remain or disappear. On the other hand, we are convinced that the accountability emphasis in education will be with us for some time.[26]

Performance contracting—particularly its internal application—remains for us an intriguing concept.

Notes for Chapter 9

1. Seth S. King, "Pupils Improve in School Run by Private Company," *New York Times,* September 28, 1971, p. 1.

2. "Learning-Plan Test Is Called a Failure," *New York Times,* February 1, 1972, p. 1.

3. Albert Shanker, "Where We Stand," *New York Times,* December 5, 1971, p. E7 (advertisement).

4. George Gallup, "Third Annual Survey of the Public's Attitudes Toward the Public Schools, 1971," *Phi Delta Kappan* (September 1971): 36.

5. J. P. Stucker and George R. Hall, *The Performance Contracting Concept in Education* (Santa Monica, Calif.: RAND Corp., May 1971), p. 1.

6. See for example John R. Miles, "A School Where Kids Can't Fail," *Saturday Evening Post,* spring 1972.

7. "Accountability, Vouchers, and Performance Contracting," *Today's Education* (December 1971): 13.

8. Ibid.

9. Ibid.

10. "NEA and AFT Positions on Performance Contracting," in *Performance Contracting: A Guide for School Board Members and Community Leaders* (Evanston, Ill.: National School Boards Association, 1971), p. 66.

11. Ibid., p. 67.

12. Charles Blaschke, "Performance Contracting Costs, Management Reform, and John Q. Citizen," *Phi Delta Kappan* (December 1971): 246-47.

13. "NEA and AFT Positions on Performance Contracting," p. 65.

14. "1972 Resolutions," *The School Administrator* (December 1971): 15.

15. *Accountability* (White Plains, N.Y.: Knowledge Industry Publications, January 1971), p. 4.

See also James R. Forsberg, "Accountability and Performance Contracting," no. EA-003-680 (Eugene, Ore.: University of Oregon, ERIC Clearinghouse, October 1971).

16. John W. Adams and Karen H. Kitchak, *A Guide to Performance Contracting* (Madison, Wis.: Wisconsin Department of Public Instruction, 1971), p. 29.

17. For an extended evaluation of performance contracting, see Stucker and Hall, *The Performance Contracting Concept in Education;* and Charles Blaschke, *Performance Contracting in Education* (Chicago: Education Turnkey Systems, Research Press, 1970).

18. Polly Carpenter and George W. Hall, *Case Studies in Educational Performance Contracting* (Santa Monica, Calif.: RAND Corporation, December 1971). This report was prepared for the Department of Health, Education and Welfare.

19. In Texarkana, the Dorsett Corporation was accused of "teaching for the test" by including some items in instructional material that were quite similar to those on the standardized test. This caused some initial speculation about performance contracting, but later contracts have usually contained safeguards to prevent this from occurring.

20. A complete discussion of all the ramifications of contracting is beyond the scope of this chapter. We suggest consulting an attorney who is familiar with contracting; a good reference is Stucker and Hall, *The Performance Contracting Concept in Education.*

21. Particularly recommended is Roald Campbell and James Lorion, *Performance Contracting in School Systems* (Columbus, Ohio: Charles E. Merrill Publishing Co., 1972).

22. Robert A. Feldmesser, "Measurement Problems in Performance Contracting," *NCME Measurement News* (July 1971): 6-7; Stephen Klein, "The Use and Limitations of Standardized Tests in Meeting the Demands for Accountability," *Evaluation Comment* 2, no. 4 (January 1971): 1-7.

23. Ibid., p. 7.

24. Excellent discussions about preparing RFPs are to be found in Marilyn Grayboff, "Tools for Building Accountability: The Performance Contract," in *Emerging Patterns of Administrative Accountability*, ed. Lesley Browder, Jr. (Berkeley: McCutchan Publishing Corp., 1971), pp. 414-31; Adams and Kitchak, *A Guide to Performance Contracting;* and the RAND documents. Sample RFPs may be found in the works listed above in note 17.

See also Leon Lessinger, *Every Kid a Winner: Accountability in Education* (Palo Alto, Calif.: Science Research Associates, 1970), pp. 141-231.

25. A variety of contracts exists, including Cost Plus Fixed Fee, Fixed Fee, Fixed Payment, Time and Materials, etc. Stucker and Hall, in *The Performance Contracting Concept in Education*, have a good discussion of the advantages and disadvantages of some of these.

26. Campbell and Lorion, *Performance Contracting in School Systems*, pp. 8-9.

10. Program Evaluation

The Controversy over Program Evaluation

Evaluation is one of the most controversial issues in education. Attitudes range from a total acceptance of Thorndike's assumption that if anything exists, it can, to some degree, be measured, to a complete rejection of evaluation as being discriminatory, harmful to individual integrity or technological development in a mechanistic society, and impossible to carry out anyway. At one extreme the proponents of evaluation view the "humanists" as soft-headed and insecure, unable to submit themselves to any kind of scrutiny, and at the other the "humanists" view the evaluators as technological mutants, behaving like robots as alien to the populace of education as Martians would be on earth. These extremes are somewhat tempered when the proponents of each are forced to meet and work together by the requirements of state and federal programs, where funding is contingent upon "cooperation" and an accompanying evaluation.

On a federal level, Title I and III evaluations have created as many problems as they have solved. The need to meet the evaluation requirements of these programs has led the educator to obtain the services of evaluators without at the same time considering the nature and scope of the process. The evaluators, on the other hand, have assessed products—specified either by the educator or by themselves—without a clear understanding of the process. Some of these evaluations have followed the canons of good evaluation design with sufficient evidence of reliability and validity. Others have been pseudo or "symbolic" evaluations, hastily designed and conducted, more to show evidence of an activity called evaluation than to assess anything.

These differences in the quality of evaluations, added to the already existing differences in attitudes toward evaluation, have contributed to widespread controversy, which can be observed nationally as well as at the level of the local school district.

A close look at State Educational Assessment Programs[1] indicates a number of problems threatening assessment efforts. A majority of the states have comprehensive assessment programs, but more and more states are discovering that their existing testing programs of pupil achievement are too narrowly conceived. Attempts to formulate broader goals on which to build assessment programs are often arduous and time consuming. The Educational Testing Service survey shows that not only is this a complex and difficult task, but it also gets bogged down by conflicting political and economic interests related to education.

There are clear indications, however, of increasing application of program evaluation to educational endeavors. Some examples are the existence of educational needs assessment programs in every state, as required by ESEA, Title III (the "Belmont Project," a system for consolidating evaluation reporting for several federally funded programs), the growing application of cost-benefit analysis found in some forms of PPBS (planning, programming, budgeting systems).

At the local level, the administrator who is faced with accountability cannot escape evaluation. The total process of assessing needs, specifying desired outcomes, and applying systems analysis approaches contributes to the process of program evaluation and facilitates its instrumentation. At this point, however, the administrator should have a clear understanding of what program evaluation is and is not, in order to apply it usefully within the concept of accountability.

Program Evaluation: What It Is and Is Not

Evaluation is often comprised of two components: measurement and the value judgment connected with (a) the selection of what is to be measured or (b) the interpretation of the results. It is a systematic process having several stages: (1) operational definition of the variables to be measured, (2) designing the measurement to be conducted, (3) the instrumentation and data collection, (4) the analysis of results, (5) the interpretation of results and conclusions to be drawn concerning the value or success of the program, and (6) reporting and feedback for further improvement.

Evaluation is concerned with measuring changes both in the program and in the product to be achieved, since its main purpose is to determine whether or not designated changes in the program bring about desired changes resulting from the program. This purpose is universal whether the relationship is only of local interest or can be generalized to other situations. The process of evaluation is itself subject to evaluation, through what has recently been called program auditing (more on this topic in chapter 11). In the following sections, each of the stages in the evaluation process is described in detail. The measurement and value-judgment components are identified where relevant, criteria with which the appropriateness or quality of the evaluation may be judged are given at each stage, and the evaluation activities described are related to the purposes of the evaluation.

Stage I

Operational Definition of Variables to Be Assessed

In any educational program something is done or changed or manipulated, resulting hopefully in a desired product. What is done or changed or manipulated is usually called the program and the desired outcome resulting from it is called the product. For example, increasing the time children spend studying arithmetic from forty to eighty minutes each day would be the program; if this increase in time brings about twice as much achievement in math as measured by some math test, the increased achievement is the product. In most educational endeavor one neither expects nor finds such simply stated single variable programs and products. More often, the program consists of a complex set of variables that are presumed to lead to one or more product variables. In research or evaluation terminology, the program variables are called independent variables and the product variables are called dependent variables.

In the context of accountability, or in any other evaluation context, *it is extremely important that both the program and the product variables be specified operationally.* Earlier in this book the reader was cued to specifying behavioral objectives, performance criteria, and the like. In these earlier chapters, as in actual current practice, much emphasis was placed on the operational or behavioral specification of the product. At first glance, accountability may be equated with proving, through measurement, that the desired increments of change in the product have in fact been achieved. To some extent this view is reinforced by the performance contracting approach, in which desired outcomes are well specified in advance and measures are then obtained to show whether or not these changes have taken place.

Specifying desired outcomes is certainly an improvement over the vagueness that has characterized educational efforts in the past, but it is not sufficient. For example, there is something to be said for the ability to determine how many graduating seniors of a given high school can read and answer correctly 90 percent of the questions on a driver's training test (mastery on a criterion-referenced exam). In accountability, the tendency is to credit or blame the teachers or the school. But without prior specification and a concurrent assessment of the program, there is no real reason to attribute the outcome to either. Normally, if the achievement is positive and within an expected and valued range, neither the school administrator nor the community are really concerned with what led to the achievement. It is out of the negative context that the administrator and community begin to ask more questions about what may have caused the result. In fact, the move towards accountability encompasses not only what results are being obtained by the schools, but also asks what the school is doing that effects these results. Thus, program evaluation for accountability must be concerned not only with measurement of the product, but also with the systematic assessment of the variables presumed to result in the product.

We mentioned earlier that evaluation has a measurement and a value-judgment component. Measurement is broadly defined as the systematic assignment of numerals to objects, people, or events according to some prescribed rule. Thus, labeling occurrences, objects, and people is considered a form of measurement as long as it is done systematically, i.e., according to a prescribed rule. For example, if a good teacher is defined operationally as one who listens and responds to the children rather than one who continually talks and tells them what to do, observers can classify teachers as belonging to one or the other category. If this definition is extended to include the *frequency* with which a teacher behaved in the stated manner, the operational definition would include some degree of quantification since frequency of an occurrence can be counted. Through scaling techniques the definition could be extended to still more refined levels of quantification. All these definitions imply measurement regardless of the type or level of quantification.

At this stage of the evaluation, value-judgment plays a part in the selection of (1) the variables to be measured and (2) the operational definition that is accepted. For example, selecting a particular program to be tried out and its desired objectives depends mostly on the educator's knowledge of what is available, his ingenuity in innovative approaches, and the value system of the community and school. The selection of the appropriate operational definitions also depends on factors of knowledge, experience, ingenuity, and value system. Even though techniques exist for determining the relevance of the operational definition to the concept to be assessed (constant validity), frequently the school administrator is satisfied with a rather informally determined consensus among his colleagues and himself that the definition is acceptable; i.e., to a large extent, the value-judgment of the decision makers is reflected in the operational definition chosen.

To sum up, the administrator should be sure that:

1. Both the product and program variables are defined operationally so that desired change in the product can be attributed to the aspects of the program;

2. Operational definitions be given in observable and/or measurable terms;

3. Value-judgments are made in the selection of variables and operational definitions, but not in the statement of the definitions;

4. When possible, the consensus among knowledgeable people with similar values should be checked to assure that the operational definition have some degree of relevance to the concept it defines.

Stage II

Design of the Evaluation

The primary purpose of evaluating a program is to identify the effects on various educational outcomes of certain educational practices, organizational patterns, or personnel characteristics. A second purpose is to generalize from the findings so that future decisions and practices can build on the results obtained. Inability to relate outcomes to the specific features of a program leads to false generalizations, such as, "Open education and individualization was tried years ago in the little red school house," or "It doesn't matter what plan you try; if you have good teachers, you'll get good results." Such comments usually reflect emotional commitments to a particular program or idea rather than reliance on evidence. Legitimate conclusions based on research always specify the features of the program that was implemented, the conditions under which it was tested, and the outcomes of the program.

It is not unusual to hear teachers complain about the accountability movement. In part these complaints arise from the fear that student outcomes will be attributed to teacher competence (or incompetence) when home and school conditions that affect outcomes are beyond the teacher's control. Since these conditions are also likely to be beyond the evaluator's control, inadequate control in the evaluation design is quite serious. When the possibility of false generalization, resulting from inadequate control, appears to threaten a whole profession, the problem extends beyond the mere satisfaction of an evaluator's ivory tower scientific discipline; it becomes urgent for the administrator to concern himself with problems of scientific control in the design of an evaluation.

Briefly, there are three main ways of assuring adequate control of variables in evaluating educational programs: (1) through sampling techniques; (2) through experimental manipulation of variables; and (3) through statistical manipulation.

The notion that all evaluations of educational programs require control groups that are matched with the experimental groups is rather sophomoric. When feasible, of course, controlled field experiments are desirable, and they may be feasible when one or two variables (e.g., increased time of study in mathematics taught by highly specialized groups of mathematicians) constitute the program, and when a school district is large enough to provide the kind of sampling needed. The probability of finding students with matching characteristics for assignment to experimental and control groups is greater in a large school system.

When the program to be evaluated is a comprehensive one and involves many variables, control through experimental manipulation is virtually impossible. Rather than providing control, matching of groups may be misleading. Often schools are matched on the basis of teacher salary schedules, social and economic composition of communities, or ratings obtained from state surveys. These variables may serve as general indicators of some important characteristics of schools, but they are not sufficient bases for matching groups in a well-controlled study. So many uncontrolled variables remain that the similarities on which the groups were "matched" become more misleading than helpful in drawing conclusions from the study. For example, whether or not a program succeeds in a given school may hinge merely on the presence of an assertive teacher. It would be difficult to predict, let alone control, variables of this type in matching school systems, yet such specific variables may prove to be more crucial determinants of the success of a program than the socioeconomic level of two respective communities.

When programs are comprehensive and the determinants affecting the outcomes are unpredictable from the start, the best alternative is to use the process evaluation approach. This approach calls for the systematic recording of events during the course of the program, usually by full-time evaluators. Recording takes place at regular, predetermined time intervals, throughout the duration of the program. For example, if the program has to do with new techniques to be employed in an instructional space, the process evaluator conducts periodic observations based on time-sampling techniques, to record what techniques are in fact employed during that time. The precision teaching technique of determining a teacher's behavior on a regular time-interval basis is another method that can be applied in process evaluation.[2] The computerized achievement monitoring[3] yields useful process data on children's achievement over a period of time.

Another means of controlling unpredictable or extraneous variables in a complex program is through the use of both random sampling and random assignment of students and others to various groups. Random does not mean haphazard. A class of children is not randomly selected because no pattern of selection can be discerned. Random selection requires that every individual in the population from which the sample is selected have an equal chance of being selected into the sample. Children may be placed into a particular class for many reasons, and rarely are the reasons the same for two individuals. To place children in this seemingly haphazard manner (i.e., a different rule applied to every child) is very different from selecting children from a total group solely on the basis of chance. Theoretically, randomly selected groups from the same total population should not differ from one another.

The suggested randomization provides the evaluator with groups that, at least initially, can be considered comparable. However, for the compulsive evaluator who is not satisfied with random sampling followed by random assignment to groups, the use of a pre and postprogram test is recommended. In this approach baseline measures are obtained on the product variables before the program starts. Then, if differences between experimental and control groups exist, (1) new samples can be drawn or (2) the initial differences may be used statistically to adjust the differences after the program has been implemented. For example, suppose that at the end of a program the experimental group is found to be a whole year ahead of the control group in expected achievement. However, pretest information indicated that the experimental group started out one year ahead of the control group. Adjusting the differences observed at the end of the program on the basis of the pretest data yields no differences between the experimental and control groups as a result of the program.

While this kind of statistical manipulation provides a degree of control, it is typically still used in experimental designs. There are actual situations that make an experimental design of any kind virtually impossible. In these situations probably the best alternative is to apply multivariate analysis techniques, which, through the use of large numbers of measurable variables with additional statistical manipulations, allow the evaluator to draw conclusions about the relationships among the measured features of the program (e.g., teacher characteristics and classroom processes), the characteristics of the conditions within which the program is implemented (e.g., school, community, family, peer-group influences), and the measured products resulting from the implementation (e.g., student growth in the five categories of outcomes discussed in chapter 6).[4]

In evaluating open education programs through the use of multivariate techniques, we could, for example, find the answer to the question, What are the features of "open education" that are associated with growth in the five categories of pupil outcomes discussed in chapter 6, and what personal, social, and educational characteristics of teachers are related to these associations? Paraphrasing a metaphor from Chronbach, Messick explains the role of the multivariate approach in evaluating a realistic setting with few if any controls:[5]

The experimentalist is an expert puppeteer, able to keep untangled the strands to a half-dozen independent variables. But in real life we are mere observers of a play in which Nature pulls a thousand strings and all the puppets are part Pinocchio. Multivariate analysis gives us a basis for figuring out where to look for the hidden strings—including those controlled by the puppets themselves—that animate the dance.[6]

To sum up, the administrator should make sure that:

1. The evaluation design that observed changes in the product variables may be accounted for by the variables included in the design;

2. Adequate control of variables is built into the design, and

have to do with (a) the program, (b) the conditions that affect the program as well as the results, and (c) the results themselves;

3. Adequate control[7] is achieved through (a) sampling, (b) experimental manipulation, (c) statistical manipulation, or (d) all of these.

Stage III

Instrumentation and Data Collection

In program evaluation the measurement and data collection procedures are dictated by (1) the operational definition of the variables of concern and (2) the evaluation design, and both are derived from the statement of the problem. Unlike most research studies, the problem is not a question derived from a theoretical frame of reference and is not intended to test a theory; it emerges out of the specific needs of a school. The evaluation design and the operational definition of the variables should reflect the program needs and in turn dictate the type of measure to be used in the assessment. Even when the program is widespread, such as team-teaching or alternative school programs, the schools putting it into effect differ in institutional variables, in the characteristics of programs already in effect, and in the traits the staff and students bring with them.

Not only do the actual programs differ from school to school, even though they have the same label, but the expected outcomes may also differ. Thus, a set of measures used to evaluate a program in one setting may not be applicable in a different setting. Given this specificity of an evaluation design, the administrator is well advised to know the general types of measurements that are available to him. He can then make his selections of specific measures, using validity and reliability indices as his criteria.

There are four general types of measures:

1. Demographic, purely descriptive information (e.g., numbers of students in a grade, numbers of graduates accepted to colleges, absenteeism and illness records, teacher and administrator salaries, per capita income and per pupil expenditure, teacher-student ratio, time individuals spend in given subjects) is available in most school records.

2. Judgmental measures refer to value-judgments concerning other people or materials, made through the use (a) of structured

instruments, such as rating scales, interview schedules, or observation instruments, or (b) inferences made from nonstructured observations and review of materials. The validity and reliability of judgmental information must be established before conclusions are drawn from it. In other words, an evaluation plan should provide for checking both the accuracy of the judgments, and their consistency from judge to judge, as well as over a time period. Since value-judgments may be highly subjective, especially in unstructured situations, it is advisable to use several judges and through establishing agreement among them to objectify what might otherwise have little measurement value.

3. Ordinarily, measurement refers to any set of structured items to which a response must be made, and paper-and-pencil testing is the method most commonly associated with measurement. Questionnaires and attitude scales do not necessarily have a right-or-wrong response, but aptitude and achievement test items have predetermined answers that the respondent is expected to supply. Tests may be either norm-referenced or criterion-referenced. Norm-referenced tests compare the individual with others taking the same test or with himself upon repeated measurements; they yield averages, standard scores, percentiles, grade-level scores, and the like, based on the total distribution of scores in groups. In norm-referenced tests, the value judgments are relative to the group performance. Criterion-referenced tests, on the other hand, are designed to determine whether an individual has mastered a topic to the level of proficiency desired; for example, those who answer correctly 90 percent of the items on an achievement test pass it, others continue to study the same material until they meet the predetermined criterion of mastery. In criterion-referenced tests, the value-judgments are reflected in the selection of the criterion of mastery. Indices of validity and reliability must always accompany norm-referenced *and* criterion-referenced tests, to ensure relevant, accurate, and consistent measurement.

4. The fourth category of measurement is direct measurement of performance through the use of simulation techniques, for example, having a law student actually defend a case in a mock trial, a medical student apply anesthetics to a dummy tied to a computer, and using micro-teaching techniques as evaluative devices. If the simulation is presented in the form of a written description, or requires a written response from the observed individual, it is called a situational test. The in-basket technique of testing administrative performance is an example of a situational test. The main difficulty

facing the evaluator in direct measurement of performance is specification of what would be desired or acceptable performance. When applied to evaluating teacher performance, the criterion of successful performance is the increment of change produced in the learner. However, without sufficient understanding of how change in the learner comes about or within what expected optimum time such change is to occur, this criterion is justifiably subject to criticism for its lack of validity. The problem of determining the criterion for directly evaluating performance has not yet been satisfactorily solved in education.

One might ask what is the responsibility of the administrator to these four types of measurement? Says Henry Dyer: "There are four groups of variables in the school as a social system that must be recognized and measured if one is to develop acceptable criteria of staff accountability. These four groups of variables I call *input, educational process, surrounding conditions,* and *output.* Taken together they form the pupil-change model of a school."[8] Ideally, the administrator should see to it that all four types of measures are applied to gathering continuous information on the four groups of variables, regardless of what program is being evaluated. This ideal data collection program would facilitate the evaluation of any program change, and would not disrupt the whole educational process by the threat to the persons being evaluated and by the introduction of rigor in an evaluation program that is otherwise alien to the normal life of the school.

The discussion of design (Stage II) indicated that in evaluating complex programs perhaps the most fruitful design utilized multivariate techniques. It is clear that for the administrator to make rational and sound value-judgments he must be aware of the interactions among the variables in the system and have sufficient information to cope with them. This level of information may be possible if all variables within the four groups (input, educational process, surrounding conditions, and output) are measured, appropriately interrelated, and combined to produce readily interpretable indices. Through this multivariate approach, with comprehensive application of measurement techniques for data collection, the school staff can identify how much of the expected changes in pupils is due to its own efforts, making adequate allowance for those variables over which it has no control. Dyer has proposed such an approach to measurement which leads to obtaining "school effectiveness indices (SEIs)."[9]

Stages IV and V

Analysis and Interpretation of Results

Anything that is measured lends itself to an analysis which is appropriate for it. Given the availability of statisticians and computer services, the administrator does not need to be an expert in either statistics or computerized data-processing to obtain adequate statistical analyses. The main point to remember is that in the context of accountability the purpose of evaluation is to determine what accounts for the desired change in the product, as well as the degree of that change. The statistician translates this purpose into technical terminology and asks what proportion of the variance observed in the product is accounted for by change in the variables associated with Dyer's categories of inputs, educational process, and surrounding conditions.

To answer these broadly stated questions the evaluator applies variance analysis techniques, which range from a simple t-test to an F-test, to the use of partial or multiple regression techniques and application of analysis of covariance and factor analysis.[10] In order to judge the appropriateness of the technique to be applied, the administrator should ask for information concerning: (1) what assumptions underlie the technique being used, (2) in what format will output of data analysis appear, and (3) what specific questions will be answered by the results of the analysis. The answers should match his own expectations from the data analysis.

Interpretation of the results is usually given in probabilistic statements. Statistical analyses will indicate the level of confidence one can place in the obtained relationships. In educational evaluation, nothing is proven; only relationships among variables are confirmed at a level of probability high enough to attribute the relationship to something other than pure chance. For example, a "significant" difference between two groups' achievement scores in mathematics occurs after the experimental group has had increased instruction time in a math program. Let us assume that the difference shows higher math scores for the experimental group. This only means that the probability of the experimental group achieving higher math scores through lengthened instruction is high enough for the increased achievement to be attributed to the lengthened instruction rather than to chance alone.

Once again value judgment plays a role in determining what

probability level should be accepted as "high enough." Conventionally, .05 or .01 or .001 levels are used, depending on the reliability of
the measurement tools and the expectations concerning the program
results. Statistical significance at these levels of probability, however,
should not be equated with educational significance of a program. It
is common to find the following type of claim: Because the intelligence of children in experimental groups increased by eight IQ points
as a result of a program when the same increase was not observed in
the control groups, and because the difference was statistically significant at the .05 level of confidence, the program is educationally
significant. Eight IQ points equal only half a standard deviation in
the total population, and given the errors in IQ measurement this is
hardly an educationally significant increase. The statistical significance obtained may tell us that with the given sample size the eight
points could not have occurred by chance; it does not tell us that the
eight points are worth the expense and effort put into implementing
a program which on the whole increases IQ scores by an average of
half a standard deviation. Whether or not a statistically significant
result is also educationally significant must be decided on the basis of
educational expectations and criteria, not statistical ones. Once again
the administrator is faced with a value-judgment that must be considered in determining accountability.

Stage VI

Reportings and Feedback for Further Improvement

There is nothing final in evaluating educational programs. Unlike rigorous and well-controlled research studies whose results contribute to theoretical relations and establishment of scientific laws,
program evaluation is designed to provide information to the practitioner who needs to find ways of matching his program variables
with the desired educational outcomes. In fact, if program evaluation
includes obtaining process data, as suggested earlier, these data may
well be used to alter some program features in the course of the
try-out. Thus, when program evalution is conducted as it should be,
it provides the kind of information that is useful in needs assessment
(see chapter 3). The ideal type of ongoing program evaluation in a
school setting provides the framework for completing the circle of
accountability from the specification of objectives, to the assessment
of needs, implementing agreed-on program changes, evaluating the
relationship among program variables, product variables and existing

conditions, and utilizing the evaluation results to identify further needs and objectives.

The following table is an attempt to summarize what evaluation is and is not, in the hope of giving the school administrator a set of criteria against which to quickly check an evaluation program.

Desired characteristics of a program evaluation plan	What program evaluation is not
1. It deals with systematic assessment of operationally defined variables that are derived in the context of a school problem or need.	1. It is not an attempt to test theoretical knowledge through rigorous research.
2. It has a measurement and a value-judgment component which should be identified at all stages of the evaluation process.	2. It is not void of value judgments.
3. It purports to relate measurable changes in the product to the program variables and conditions leading to it.	3. It is not concerned with product only.
4. It is a systematic process which should be continuous.	4. It is not a single shot assessment, nor is it a haphazard quantification technique.
5. It provides a feedback mechanism for continuing improvement.	5. It does not provide a final answer.
6. It utilizes subjective judgements with an aim to objectify through consensus.	6. It is not a mechanistic detached process run by technology.
7. It utilizes and attempts to approximate the scientific canons of validity and reliability.	7. It is not an attempt to quantify by any means that may be available.
8. It leads to legitimate generalizations regarding what accounts for change or lack of it.	8. It is not an excuse to hold someone accountable through false generalizations.

Program Auditing: Evaluation of the Evaluation

"The general purpose of a program audit is to verify the results of the project evaluation and to assess the appropriateness of the evaluation procedure."[11] Program auditing is done by an independent outside agency whose job it is to review the evaluation procedures, tools used, the results obtained, to verify these results, and to determine the appropriateness of the procedures used.

Since the auditing agency is independent of the local educational institution being audited, the relationship and the auditing process are specified in a contract between the two agencies. This relationship is spelled out in brief detail in chapter 11.

The USOE guidelines are available for the auditor's critique of the evaluation design and processes. These guidelines raise a number of questions that the school administrator may find valuable in judging the evaluation program in his school. Discussed further in chapter 11 and partially offered in appendixes B and C, these questions deal with such categories as (a) selection of instruments, (b) data collection procedures, (c) data analysis procedures, (d) data analysis presentation. The concerns of a program auditor may well provide a set of criteria for educational evaluation plans in general. It should be pointed out, however, that if the points covered in this chapter are followed, they would not only meet these criteria but also additional ones not covered by the usual program auditing guidelines. Furthermore, the evaluation model presented by Stufflebeam[12] and the PPBS model also provide general frameworks similar to that presented here and covered by the guidelines for program auditing.

Notes for Chapter 10

1. Education Commission of the States and ERIC, *State Educational Assessment Programs* (Princeton, N.J.: Educational Testing Service, 1969).

2. Grant L. Martin, *Precision Teaching in the Classroom*, mimeographed paper (Bellingham, Wash.: University of Washington Experimental Education Unit, 1971).

3. Computerized achievement monitoring is a process developed at Stanford University. It has been sponsored in Long Island public schools by the New York State Education Department.

4. For a clear and relatively brief explanation of the multivariate approach, listen to Fred Kerlinger's tape, *Multivariate Analysis*, distributed by AERA.

5. Lee J. Chronbach, "The Two Disciplines of Scientific Psychology," *American Psychologist* 12 (1957): 671-84; Samuel Messick, "Can You Do Real Research in a Real World?" in *Untangling the Tangled Web of Education*, a special symposium sponsored by the National Council on Measurement in Education (Princeton, N.J.: Educational Testing Service, April 1969).

6. Messick, "Can You Do Real Research in a Real World?" p. 26.

7. For an excellent detailed discussion of prototypes of designs, see Fred Kerlinger, *Foundations of Behavioral Research* (New York: Holt, Rinehart & Winston, 1964), chapters 16 and 17.

See also Richard Light and Paul Smith, "Choosing a Future: Strategies for Designing and Evaluating New Programs," *Harvard Educational Review* 40, no. 1 (February 1970): 1-28.

8. Henry S. Dyer, "Toward Objective Criteria of Professional Accountabil-

ity in the Schools of New York City," *Phi Delta Kappan* (December 1970): 207; also in *Emerging Patterns of Administrative Accountability*, ed. Lesley Browder, Jr. (Berkeley: McCutchan Publishing Corp., 1971), pp. 441-55.

9. For a full explanation of the "school effectiveness indices" and their uses, see Dyer's article in *Emerging Patterns*, pp. 441-55.

10. The reader interested in further conceptual knowledge on the statistical techniques mentioned should study Fred Kerlinger's *Foundations of Behavioral Research* (New York: Holt, Rinehart & Winston, 1964).

11. Robert Kraner, "Educational Program Audit," in *Educational Accountability Through Evaluation*, ed. E. W. Roberson (Englewood Cliffs, N.J.: Educational Technology Publications, 1971), p. 94.

12. David Stufflebeam, "The Relevance of the CIPP Evaluation Model for Educational Accountability," *Journal of Research and Development in Education* 5 (fall 1971): 19-23.

11. Rendering the Account: A Conclusion

Like the Day of Judgment, a final point arrives in the process of developing an educationally accountable program: rendering the account. When this part of the process is completed, critical decisions await. For the program, it is the determination of its future (what shall it be?). For the stewards, it is the passing of judgment upon the stewardship (should the reviewers maintain their level of confidence in the stewards?). What factors might be kept in mind as the steward prepares to offer his account?

To review, we have held certain notions about educationally accountable programs. The first set of these ideas concern the emerging accountability concept itself, viewed as having four aspects:

1. Accountability is a process that occurs in a relationship between those entrusted with the accomplishment of specific tasks (stewards), and those having power of review (reviewers);

2. The heart of the process is for the party "standing to account" (i.e., the requirement on the occupant of a role, by those who authorize that role, to answer for the results of work expected from him in the role), the steward, to explain as rationally as possible the results of efforts to achieve the specific task objectives of his stewardship;

3. Of major concern to the parties reviewing the stewardship of the tasks performed is matching performance and attainment levels against their expectations as expressed in the task specifications, and making a determination of their level of confidence in the steward and his efforts;

4. Of major concern to the steward standing to account is his

ability to accomplish the specific tasks as well to explain attainment levels in a manner that maintains or builds the reviewer's confidence in his stewardship.

Secondly, in the translation of the emerging accountability concept into educationally accountable programs, we have maintained that: (1) there are multiple ways to make the translation; (2) the rigor of application of the theoretical concept to practice is expected to vary with specific circumstances; and (3) governed by the climate of opinion today, it may be well to heed six imperatives as preliminary guides to the steward before he commits himself and/or others to the task of designing an educationally accountable program. The program design must:

1. Have knowledgeable designers;
2. Lead to improved education;
3. Recognize and accommodate diverse forms of participation;
4. Train personnel before and during implementation;
5. Fulfill the conditions of the accountability concept;
6. Be judged politically attainable.

Third, from among the variety of educationally accountable programs that we might chose to develop, a four-phase model was proposed (with several options as embellishments toward increasing program effectiveness). A summary of the critical elements in our proposed model consisted of:

Phase 1: Preliminary planning
• Assess needs.
• Develop a preliminary change strategy.
• "Go-no go" decision to move to Phase 2.

Phase 2: Formal planning
• Involve community and staff.
• Develop goal consensus and performance objectives.
• "Go-no go" decision to move the recommended program design to Phase 3.

Phase 3: Program implementation
• Develop program staff.
• Implement program procedures.
• Reach predetermined reporting points on program.

Phase 4: Rendering the account
• Evaluate program.
• Report the program results.
• Determine level of confidence.
• Certify the nature of the results.

In this, we have assumed a great deal:

· That the schools exist primarily to produce publicly endorsed changes in the learning behavior of their major clients, the students;

· That learning behaviors, expressed as outcomes, can be achieved in multiple ways, some more effective than others;

· Because the resources (time, money, staff, etc.) available in any school district are customarily less than the demands made upon them, the administrative staff must seek an optimum balance between the available resources and the most effective means of expending them in the attainment of those publicly endorsed goals and objectives;

· Without some form of accountability process, it is difficult or impossible to gauge well learner progress—either individual or group—or instructional effectiveness for purposes of decision making;

· Programs carrying the conditions of the accountability process lend themselves to better, more informed kinds of decision making toward seeking the optimum balance between resource expenditures and learning achievement;

· Given sufficient time and operation, programs identified by the accountability process as "ineffective" (i.e., failing to pass the level-of-confidence review of results) should be modified, eliminated, or replaced by more effective ones;

· The accountability process is a vehicle that holds promise for improving learning outcomes, decision making, and rational adjustments to change pressures.

Finally, we have reached the point in the process where we consider the formal rendering of the account. For our purposes, four components are given attention in rendering an account of an educational program: (1) who will make the report, (2) to whom it will be made, (3) what it should contain, and (4) how it will be made. These components receive attention in the steward's account, reviewed first from a theoretical position and then as applied to educationally accountable programs.

The Steward's Account: Some Theoretical Underpinnings

Who will make the report (and to whom), what it contains, and how it will be made are all items that, under normal circumstances, are resolved at the time of initial approval of the program or project. Under an accountability system, however, a close look at who reports to whom carries implications that go beyond being merely a reporting procedure. It delineates who the accountable stewards and the judging reviewers are. In this context, standing-to-account procedures have a sense of definition frequently less specific in the common practices of public education. Because the relationships among terms and parties, attitudes and procedures, seem important to us, we will explore them, theoretically, further.

As we indicated in chapter 1, the terms *responsibility* and *accountability* are popularly equated with each other. In ordinary school operation, it is not necessary to make close distinctions. The stewards (at various times teachers, but usually administrators) are more or less generally responsible. But in creating an educationally accountable program we are attempting to develop a sharpened idea of responsibility—accountability for a specific program or project under a different set of conditions—and accordingly have drawn a tighter distinction for the term *accountable*. The individuals or group holding a role are obligated *to answer for the results of work expected from that role*.

Misunderstanding, however, frequently arises in the shift (a shift as much in attitude and outlook as in degree and design) from generalized responsibility to more specific accountability. Two points may be made in this connection. First, if a person is to be genuinely accountable for the results of work required of him, he is, within certain boundaries, accorded some minimal authority or rights that accrue to his position. We believe the degree of that authority must be greater when people are held specifically accountable rather than generally responsible.

Second, if he is to be held rigorously answerable for the work of others, his authority should permit him to make (or at least veto) decisions on who these others will be, the work to be done, the conditions of work, and how the work is to be assessed and rewarded.

An illustration of these two points applied to generalized responsibility and specific accountability might be useful. Illustrating our first point (and moving the setting purposely away from education) are two woodcutters, Ames (generalized responsibility) and Brown (specific accountability). Woodcutter Ames agrees to chop wood for a day's pay. Maybe Mr. Cole, the man who pays Ames' hire, is happy with the results of Ames' work—and maybe he is not. Mr. Cole thinks that the next time he hires Ames he will have someone check on Ames to see that he is doing a fair day's work. At the same time, Ames feels upset. Mr. Cole did not seem to appreciate the amount of wood that was chopped. When Mr. Cole sends his foreman around the next day to "see how Ames is getting along", Ames feels threatened, insecure, and mad. He feels it is necessary to be "respectful" to Mr. Cole's foreman so that he will report favorably on Ames and how hard he is working. Ames does not feel trusted and finds himself devoting as much time to figuring ways to curry the foreman's favor for a good report as to figuring wood chopping problems.

Mr. Brown also chops wood occasionally for Mr. Cole. He works under a different arrangement; before any work is done, Brown and Cole come to an agreement on a work order form. The number of cords of wood, the size and shape of the pieces, the kind of wood to be cut, the date by which it is to be completed, and the amount to be paid for the completed task are recorded. It took Cole longer to reach this agreement with Brown than the easier "day's hire" agreement with Ames, and at times this agreement-making was unpleasant. Brown and Cole clashed on some points in the agreement over what were "fair" terms. But once the agreement has been reached, Mr. Cole leaves Brown alone. If he does send his foreman around to check on progress, Brown has a number of response options (e.g., he can stop work until the foreman leaves, tell the foreman to get lost, or have a cup of coffee with him). Brown has control over the elements of his job. Within the framework of the agreement he is answerable to Cole only for completed achievements. He is also paid for the results he achieves according to the agreement. If Brown feels frustrations, they are more likely to be related to his diagnosis of wood problems (e.g., can he chop a particular kind of wood fast enough to finish a cord in the allotted time period or is he going to have to put in a few extra hours of chopping oak instead of pine to get the desired result?). When next he agrees to cut wood for Cole, Brown figures, there will be a different set of terms for handling the chopping of oak.

And when they do meet next, Cole learns something from Brown about the problems of chopping oak as opposed to pine (no wonder, ponders Cole, so little oak ever appears in Ames' efforts). Under the agreement with Brown, attention usually focuses on wood and its cutting. With Ames, it seems to focus on his performance of the day's work—that is, whether it *appears* as if enough wood was chopped or a sufficient amount of sweat was shed in the process.

Extending the illustration now to embrace our second point— answering for the work of others—we find that time and fortune have added more business for Mr. Cole to handle; he needs much more wood cut. He continues his arrangements of general responsibility with Ames and of specific accountability with Brown, but with some differences. Mr. Cole hires other woodcutters on the basis of a day's pay to work with Ames. Because of the size of the investment, Cole hires a foreman with the general responsibility of watching over this group. The frustrations of general responsibility that Ames originally had are now easier to bear with the addition of other woodcutters. On the job, they quickly establish their own ideas on what a fair day's effort should be. Because they are paid on the same scale for the aggregate time they work (the only important difference being length of service to Mr. Cole), there is not much concern among the men about what the others do as long as it does not too grossly violate their sense of their general responsibilities to Cole. When Cole's foreman (who answers primarily to Cole and accordingly has a sharper sense of what a fair day's work entails than do the less answerable woodcutters) reprimands some of Ames' group for failing to do their job adequately, feelings of mistrust quickly surface among the woodcutters. They go to Mr. Cole and complain that his foreman does not "understand" them; he "communicates" poorly; he pushes them too hard; he lacks "leadership" and should be replaced. Cole acts on these complaints and removes his foreman for failing in his general responsibilities, and selects a man from Ames' work group to act as foreman.

Mr. Cole finds that things continue much as before, only fewer complaints are made. This seems an improvement; he had grown tired of all the complaints made about his other foreman. But one day Mr. Cole visits the woodcutting area, and is deeply disturbed. Many of the harder woods are untouched or so poorly cut as to be unusable; much of the more easily cut white pine has diminished and some of it is poorly cut, too. Mr. Cole's foreman explains that the men do not have proper tools to cut the tougher wood, Mr. Cole expects too much from them, handling the harder wood requires special training, wood "specialists" are needed, and many other reasons that seem plausible to the foreman but sound like excuses to Mr. Cole. Mr. Cole can see that some woodcutters are more conscientious than others in clearing their assigned areas, and when he asks one of these individuals why his work area is so well cleared, the man says with pride that he is a "professional" woodcutter. When Mr. Cole questions one of the individuals whose area is poorly cleared, the man replies sharply that he is a "professional" and that Mr. Cole, knowing nothing about woodcutting, should leave such matters to professionals. Angry and confused, Cole returns to his office, fires the foreman for failing in his general responsibilities, and hires an ambitious young man from another company.

The young man, hoping to impress Mr. Cole and to clear up

some of the former foreman's problems, assumes more authority than did his predecessor and makes changes in the work styles of the men. A union organizer appears, and a woodcutters' union grows with Ames as its leader. Some of the changes that were made are reversed. For example, the union rejects the young foreman's decision to have the more experienced woodcutters work with the tougher wood. The older pattern of allowing woodcutters with seniority the right to select their own work areas is restored. This means that, with few exceptions, the experienced woodcutters cut white pine and leave less experienced men to work in the least desirable areas. Some of the "extras" that Mr. Cole had come to expect—like clearing underbrush—are now excluded from the woodcutters' work. Their job is to cut wood. Brush clearing, stump removal, and other such activities are nonprofessional and are classified at a different pay rate and require new "nonprofessionals" to be hired, or that the woodcutters be paid overtime to do this work after hours.

Mr. Cole now spends much of his time working with Ames, who is still "generally responsible" to Cole but is the union leader. They argue about working conditions, fringe benefits, the size of work areas, and the compensation to be paid woodcutters for their "general responsibilities." Very little is said about actually cutting wood, but a lot is said about regulating the foreman's activities. The men insist on a voice in any change the foreman makes; he must now consult (i.e., get approval from) Ames first. While Ames acknowledges a general responsibility to chop wood for a day's hire, he insists that how much, what kind, and how well the wood is cut are matters of professional discretion. He also warns Mr. Cole that the men will not work if Mr. Cole does not comply with their contract.

Cole now feels that perhaps he should not have asked the woodcutters to have done so many non-wood cutting jobs before, but he nevertheless worries about production: only portions of the wood are being cut, and not all of that is cut properly. Much potentially good wood is going to waste.

Mr. Cole reminds his young foreman about his responsibility for getting the wood cut. The foreman tries hard to make changes (he now uses in-service workshops and sensitivity training programs for volunteer woodcutters to help them to perceive the hard woods with more "understanding"), but things remain much the same. After all, the woodcutters are only responsible for "a fair day's work."

Mr. Cole finally decides to call on Brown again to handle some special assignments. The harder wood Ames' group seemed unable to cut in sufficient quantity is important to Cole; for his purposes, *all* the wood must be cut. However, Brown is so independent that Cole does not like to go to him; he cannot wheedle Brown to do "special" things (the way he can coax his own "generally responsible" foreman). Brown insists on full and specific descriptions of what Cole wants, and Cole finds it tiresome to be specific about the cuts, sizes, lengths, etc., of wood. Brown is such a stickler that it seems easier just to tell Ames to do it. But then Cole remembers that Ames somehow never seems to get the results he wants.

To some of the expectations Cole specifies Brown replies that he cannot be certain of attaining the desired results; his tools cannot cut with enough precision, the wood has individual peculiarities (Brown spells out some of these in detail), the particular terrain influences the cutting in ways Brown cannot control, etc. However, he feels that his experience and approach to this kind of woodcutting is good enough to succeed with 85 percent of the area designated to be cut. Cole wants *all* the wood cut, and insists that Brown make the effort. Brown explains that, to cut the last 15 percent, the costs will be as high as cutting the first 50 percent, and Cole's foreman studies the estimate and agrees with it. Cole cannot afford that cost, and while he remains committed to getting all the wood cut he realizes that 85 percent is reasonable. He contracts with Brown, and they agree that Brown will try to cut the final 15 percent for special additional fees (Brown also is paid proportionately less if he cuts less than the 85 percent). Cole's foreman will periodically check the progress of the work.

To handle the task Brown collects a group of woodcutters, mostly from among those of Ames' woodcutters who volunteer, and several others from "outside." Each man is briefed on the nature of the contract with Cole and the terms Brown is willing to offer; some accept, some do not. Some return to woodcutting in Ames' group.

Because some of the men work particularly well together, Brown forms them into a separate group and provides them with a mutually acceptable subcontract that outlines the results Brown expects from them for their assigned area. He then leaves them to work out among themselves how they will divide their work loads, etc. This more independent group knows that Brown and Cole's foreman will periodically check on the work, and also knows specifically what they expect to see.

Brown chooses to assume a more assertive role with his other group of woodcutters. He lets them know the framework of his expectations and tells them that within that framework they are free to use their own discretion. Two men disagree with Brown's framework of expectations; Brown reconsiders and modifies the framework. This satisfies one man but not the other, who wants the other woodcutters to vote on Brown's decisions. Brown tells the discontented woodcutter that he may be excused from the group if he cannot accept Brown's decision-making style. Within the framework Brown established, which the workers accepted when they were hired, Brown reserves the right to make his own decisions. He also recognizes the authority—more limited than his—that belongs to his men. Whenever he wishes to change any conditions of this basic framework, or seeks to have the men work outside it (such as the time Mr. Cole asked if Brown's group would work elsewhere on a Saturday), Brown goes to these men and seeks their opinions and/or agreement to the change.

Both of Brown's groups have some authority over their own work. The independent group is provided with a mutually agreeable subcontract, and autonomously determines within the boundaries of the contract the work to be done, the working conditions, and how the group members will assess and reward their own efforts. The independent group is accountable as a group to Brown, not to Cole.

The members of Brown's immediate group are accountable to him on an individual basis. Surprisingly, both groups get nearly similar results for their efforts. At first Brown's immediate group is troubled at his close supervision (having been accustomed to working in self-contained areas), but they eventually adjust to having him work directly with them, and come to function as a team with Brown as leader. Brown keeps Mr. Cole posted on the progress of both of his groups, and Cole's foreman corroborates the periodic progress reports.

The deadline finally arrives. Brown reviews the report of his independent group and sees that they are pleased with their efforts. They have managed to exceed the expected 85 percent by a few percentage points and know they will receive extra pay from Brown. His immediate group is less successful, falling short by a few percentage points. In standing to account before Mr. Cole, Brown is able to report an 84 percent achievement of the stated expectations and accepts a slightly reduced compensation from Cole. He pays the extra amount due the independent group (who divide it among themselves as they had previously determined), and separately pays the members of his immediate group according to their individual agreements with him. Some men receive more than others, according to their individual achievements.

Two men, however, receive considerably less. One of these men, on the basis of Brown's almost daily observation, is an inferior woodcutter. Brown determines not to hire him again and pays him what he has earned. The other man worked hard and well but was given what developed into an unforeseeably difficult assignment. Brown felt this man did a remarkable job with the assignment, even if it did not meet original expectations. The man is paid what he earned, but to his surprise, he receives an additional amount, taken from Brown's own earnings. Brown gives this bonus payment, although the man did not achieve the results expected, as an indication that he retains a high level of confidence in the man's work and would like to employ him in the future.

The inferior woodcutter complains that Brown is unfair not to pay him extra, too, and Brown lets him know that he is under no obligation to do so and that he retains the right to reward additionally (i.e., beyond the stipulated agreement) those whom he chooses, since it comes from his own pocket.

In dealing with the men accountable to him, Brown acts as a reviewer. In dealing with Mr. Cole, Brown acts as a steward in Cole's service, and sustains the small loss in expected earnings based on the results of his groups' efforts.

Looking back over the year's work, Cole reflects on Ames and Brown. He sees many similarities: both Ames and Brown do assigned tasks; both have degrees of authority over their tasks; both are accountable; both work under contracts; and both have a sense of responsibility.

Cole also notes differences: whereas Ames was hired and then was assigned tasks, Brown agreed to highly defined tasks *before* he agreed to be hired; Ames' authority over his tasks could be expanded or contracted as Cole desired (until Ames' union curbed Cole's ability to do this), while Brown's authority was made clear at the outset of the agreement and could be adjusted only with Brown's consent; whereas Ames was accountable (for getting to work on time, giving a "fair day's work," etc.), it was for the *means* of doing his task, while Brown's accountability focused on the *results* of doing the task; whereas Ames' contract with Cole focused on the conditions surrounding the means, Brown's contract centered on the results expected and the conditions necessary to achieve those results; and whereas Ames' sense of responsibility seemed to be ambivalently directed personally toward Cole and the union members, Brown's appeared singularly directed at honoring his agreements with Cole and with Brown's own crew.

Wondering why Brown always seemed more committed to his tasks than did Ames, Cole believes it is possible because Brown: (1) knows more explicitly what is expected of him (both Cole and Ames tended to avoid that issue); (2) had an opportunity to study carefully and appraise the feasibility of the task before he accepted it (Cole merely assigned tasks to Ames); and, (3) on the basis of being able to take a free hand in the work where he feels it is needed, Brown is willing to commit himself personally to pursuing agreed-upon goals (Ames perhaps has reservations about the goals he is required to pursue or, finding them vague, tends to move forward with undue caution).

Thus Cole concludes his thoughts, and we our illustration.

Steward's Account of Educationally Accountable Programs

The basis for the steward's account of an educationally accountable program is identifying the specific task or work to be done. We call the identification of the task a "needs assessment." Mr. Cole simply needed to get wood cut and went ahead with hiring people to get it done. In chapter 3, however, we indicated ways of identifying educational needs. It is possible for anyone familiar with educational practice not to have first to identify a "need"; one may easily assume the Jeffersonian view, that any currently operating educational program is infinitely perfectable, and determine educational needs by subjective goal preferences.

However, this latitude in operation is not typically afforded school administrators, who are expected to be able to make a public case for any significant educational undertaking. To the extent that they can use objective data or otherwise rationally explain their basis for determining needs, we believe they will be more able to accomplish two things: (1) to win the support of their superiors (the board of education) and others (the community, staff, and students); and (2) ultimately to help shape the identified need into an educationally accountable program with goals, objectives, and performance prescriptions.

As the assessed need is processed through the participation of others into a program, other things also happen. Added to the assessed need are the views of others toward the need and its general place in education. Priorities, goals, and objectives are welded into a consensus that specific tasks need to be done.

But this alone does not provide the accountability we seek. The tasks must be further shaped into a program that embodies goals or target-type standards (generalized ideals), objectives (directions to be taken toward realizing the goals), and—most important for accountability purposes—performance objectives or prescriptions (statements of standards by which criteria are used to make decisions and by which results may later be measured).

In moving from generalized goals to program prescriptions, the degree of accountability increases. If the expected results of work are not defined beyond generalized goals and objectives, the quality of accountability is highly diffuse. Without standards of quantity, quality, time, and expenditure, it is "impossible to ensure that the occupant's work will be relevant to that of the rest of the . . . system."[1] We believe this condition is too often permitted in public education (to the detriment of all parties involved—students, teachers, administrators, board members, parents, and the community).

Where does this discussion lead us? Perhaps the following guidelines might frame the steward's account of educationally accountable programs:

· *Who reports?* The steward(s) report(s).

· *Who is the steward?* He is any individual or group that agrees to be held answerable for the results of specified tasks and possesses commensurate authority and resources to do the tasks.

· *What is being "held answerable"?* It means agreeing to accept a range of rewards and/or penalties offered by the reviewer(s) in exchange for degrees of accomplishment of the specified tasks. These rewards and penalties may be predetermined and/or postdetermined. At the heart of the issue of answerability is the notion expressed by John Stuart Mill that "responsibility is null when nobody knows who is responsible."[2] A modern corollary to Mill's insight is suggested by James Thompson: "Individuals exercise discretion whenever they believe it is to their advantage to do so and seek to evade discretion on other occasions."[3] The spirit of the emerging patterns of accountability moves counter to such actions by stewards. Degrees of responsibility and discretion are pinned down in the specification of tasks. *But* the reviewer's responsibilities and discretions are also fixed. In his agreement with the steward, the reviewer acknowledges areas of discretion and authority in which the steward may operate free from the reviewer's arbitrary hand. At the same time, as the reviewer agrees to commit resources to the steward for the operation of the program, he accepts that he too is answerable for his part of the agreement. It is a form of negotiated accountability.

· *How are the tasks to be specified?* To the extent that it is possible and deemed appropriate by the stewards and reviewers, the tasks should specify: (1) quantity, (2) quality, (3) time, and (4) expenditure. A sample might be:

The major intent of this special program is that every child identified by the state-administered reading test as reading two grade levels below his class and who is provided 200 hours of instructional time (but not less than 150 hours nor more than 250 hours) according to the steward's plan, at the least cost (but not more than $X budgeted for this program), between the annually administered state tests (but not less than eleven months nor more than thirteen), improves his reading performance on the state reading test by 1.5 grade levels or better, and by at least 1.25 grade levels over his previous performance.

To agree on terms as specific as these is considered a high degree of accountability.

It is argued by many that such terms are not possible for educational programs, are inappropriate, or are too limited in scope, and under specific circumstances these critics can be right. It is, however, the *intent* of the specification that we are pointing out. It may be neither possible nor desirable to specify closely every task. But if not all tasks, how many? most? half? a few? If not specified closely, then within a looser-but-still-measurable framework?

Here is another task sample, in which the student is the steward:

The purpose of this year's independent honor study program is that each qualified student who volunteers and is accepted by an adviser of the social studies department shall, as a learning experience, identify, research, and submit an appropriately documented report (according to the guidelines of the department) yielding an analysis and evaluation of some major social, political, and/or economic event occurring in our county not more than twenty-five nor less than ten years ago, including analysis and evaluation of its impact up to the present time. The student shall be excused from social study classes, submit weekly a descriptive log of his research efforts to his adviser (who will respond to each report with written "advisory" comments), report at mutually agreeable intervals to his faculty adviser to discuss progress and problems, and conduct this research at least expense (but not to exceed $X budgeted for him). It is expected that these efforts will reflect a work of 200 hours of time (but not more than 300 nor less than 180 hours) and involve a dozen contact hours of the adviser's time (but not more than fifteen nor less than ten hours). The acceptability of the study will be determined by a three-member review team consisting of a student from last year's honors program, a member of the social studies department (other than the adviser), and a community leader familiar with the subject. On unanimous acceptance of the report, it will be filed in the public library.

If Thompson is correct in assuming that "uncertainty appears as *the* fundamental problem for complex organizations, and coping with uncertainty, as the essence of the administrative process,"[4] we would contend that accountability is a process that works to remove uncertainty in the relationship between steward and reviewer, a major aspect of any organization's operation. We would like to think this frank approach can yield results in line with Woodrow Wilson's observation that "the highest and best form of efficiency is the spontaneous cooperation of a free people," and that the possibility for cooperation is enhanced when people know clearly what is expected of them; what discretion, authority and resources they have at hand; and what certainty of behavior can be expected from significant others. Such task specification, arrived at beforehand, establishes between steward and reviewer boundaries of terminal responsibility, terminal authority, and terminal decision-making power over allocated resources. It represents the conjoining of freedom with responsibility, whether largely or narrowly defined, but agreeable to the parties of the covenant.[5]

• *What does "commensurate authority" mean?* We use this term to mean that once the tasks have been specified and the boundaries of the steward's freedoms and responsibilities delineated, he has both adequate discretion and resources to do the work prescribed. If he is also to be held answerable for the work of others, his authority may include at maximum control, and at minimum veto power, over: (1) who the people are for whom he is answerable; (2) removal or transfer of persons he judges to be inadequate to the tasks; (3) work assignments and conditions; and (4) the right to review their performance, determining his own level of confidence in their performance and distributing rewards and penalties. All these activities usually take place within the framework of the institution employing the steward, but (as in the case of Brown) need not be under the control of the reviewers except where agreed.

Under our approach and within the educational setting, the steward will probably want to establish with these others (in this case "subordinates," a term not popular in educational circles, which prefer to maintain an image of egalitarianism even when responsibility is unevenly distributed) a chart of expectations similar to his own but with correspondingly smaller latitudes. Using a management-by-objectives approach, the steward jointly plans with his subordinate what action the subordinate is to undertake. Because the steward's task is usually of longer duration, the subordinate typically reports his progress at periodically shorter intervals. The degree of the steward's answerability with his reviewers is greater, so we expect the steward's authority to extend over his subordinate's work in this manner: when the steward reviews his subordinate's work, he will be searching to see if it is at variance with the expectations they jointly established; and, if it is, the steward may exercise his discretion to modify his subordinate's task and/or resources. Within this framework and between reviews, the subordinate is free to do his own tasks. Because the variety of accountability suggested here is new to American public education, it is our hope that wherever an educationally accountable program is contemplated, those involved—stewards and subordinates—are free agents, i.e., in a position to decline entering into an educationally accountable program.

• *Who will assume reviewer and stewardship roles in the educational setting?* The process requires two parties. It is not expected that the roles of steward and reviewer will be played by the same party (although some might argue that this sort of self-contained autonomous accountability is implied in the tenuring of professionals). A commonplace sampling of educational role possibilities might include:

If the program reviewer is:	The program stewards might be any or all of these:
Teacher(s)	Student(s) Teacher aide(s)
Program manager(s) (special project manager, head teacher, department chairman, etc.)	Student(s) Teacher aide(s) Teacher(s) Externally contracted personnel
Building administrator(s)	Student(s) Teacher aide(s) Teacher(s) Externally contracted personnel
District administrator(s)	Student(s) Teacher aide(s) Teacher(s) Externally contracted personnel Subordinate administrator(s)
Mixed review team (e.g., students, teachers, administrators, parents)	Student(s) Teacher aide(s) Teacher(s) Externally contracted personnel Administrator(s)

Superintendent of schools	Student(s)
	Teacher aide(s)
	Teacher(s)
	Externally contracted personnel
	Subordinate administrator(s)
	Mixed task team(s)
Board of education	Superintendent of schools
State department of education	Local board of education
U.S. Office of Education/	Local board of education
Office of Economic	Local educational agency
Opportunity	State department of education

Two more questions remain to be asked: (1) what will the steward's report contain? and (2) how will his report be made? We defer the answers to these questions to the next section, on the educational program audit (mentioned briefly in chapter 1). If the educational program audit is correctly done and if the steward's account is accurate, the two reports should yield identical pictures to the reviewers.

Corroborating the Steward's Account: The Option of the Educational Program Audit

One of the new arrivals on the educational scene is the educational program auditor (EPA). In part a product of the current accountability movement, the EPA was created by the U.S. Office of Education under the influence of W. Stanley Kruger and Leon Lessinger, to audit—much like the certified public accountant—a series of projects funded under Title VII (bilingual education) and VIII (dropout prevention) of the Elementary and Secondary Education Act. The EPA makes an educational audit instead of a financial one. Why?

If one considers several circumstances in public education, it is not hard to imagine why the use of an educational program auditor might have growing appeal. The phrase that most quickly comes to mind to justify the EPA's existence is "lack of public trust," that is, a deficient degree of assurance that certain expectations of public officials can be depended on. As a recent book title, *In God We Trust, All Others Pay Cash,* suggests, public officials are not a uniquely untrusted group; untrustworthiness is a condition of our times. But that knowledge hardly helps the school administrator. Officials in Washington, state legislators, taxpayers, community groups, parents, and boards of education—all want assurance that what is reported to them about the quality of children's education is to be trusted; that the public funds are yielding positive educational gains; and that what their stewards' report is accurate. The educational program auditor's arrival is a natural outgrowth of this state of affairs.

What does the EPA do? He makes educational program audits. As influenced by the U.S. Office of Education, acting as a reviewer of the "local educational agency's" stewardship (the LEA or federal parlance for what is usually the local board of education), an educational program audit might serve the following purposes, suggested by Alfred Morin:[6]

· A performance-control procedure;
· A verification of evaluation findings;
· A form of program management tool;
· A form of quality assurance;
· A report of program validation;
· An objective process free from personal or group vested interests.

Whereas the certified public accountant (CPA) generally restricts himself to a validation of the client's fiscal procedures and statements, the federal version of the EPA moves beyond this. Figure 11.1 illustrates these two views of auditing procedures.

Versions of the educational program audit, as might be imagined, can become quite complicated. Most, however, seem to recognize four distinct stages: (1) seeking out an appropriate auditor; (2) preaudit activity culminating in a contract with the EPA; (3) audit procedures as the specific program moves into operation, including interim reporting; and (4) the final audit report.[7]

Stage I: Finding an EPA

This task is not too easily accomplished, especially where federal programs are involved. Where external educational experts are used (e.g., professional accrediting associations, the occasional university professor, and/or an educational consulting firm), they are not usually expected to provide an empirical audit-like report on the outcomes of a specific program as much as they are to render an authoritative opinion on the client's progress in relation to the field.

Figure 11.1. Two views of auditing procedures

Fiscal audit by certified public accountant

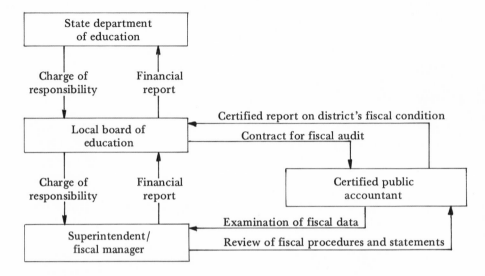

Educational program audit by educational program auditor (federal version)

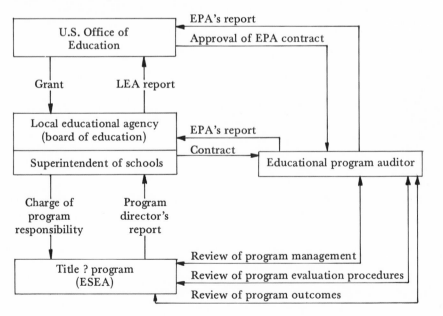

In the case of the federal programs, the LEA selects the EPA, and the USOE approves. Federal approval is provisional; and the provisions include:

(1) The prospective auditor must be clearly independent from or otherwise unattached to the program and the LEA (it is important that he be recognized as a disinterested third party);

(2) He must be able to get to the project site conveniently and at reasonable cost (it is disappointing to have major auditing costs reflected in travel, room, and board);

(3) While the qualifications of the EPA are still in the process of definition, the rule of thumb is that his background (or their background, if you are hiring a team) and record of performance should at least equal his opposite number, the "inside" person (or team) responsible for evaluating the program under the steward's direction (these qualifications range from expertise in measurement, research, and evaluation techniques to management systems design, data processing, and the various systems-based technologies);

(4) There should be abundant evidence that the EPA (group or individual) is "organizationally capable"—that is, reputable, of solid character, can be expected to perform the functions required, will stay with the contract to completion, and is capable of remaining a reasonably unobtrusive, independent observer (rather than an organizational problem for the steward);

(5) The U.S. Office of Education has formerly requested that EPAs register themselves with USOE by attending USOE's annually offered Education Audit Institute.

Stage II: Preaudit and contract

Assuming a potential EPA can be located,[8] he is then expected to study all materials related to the program. These may include federal regulations, Office of Education guidelines, the community advisory committee's recommendations and program design, the board of education's accountability policy, the agreement between reviewer and steward, and numerous similar documents and materials related to the planning of the program. Of particular interest will be the program's plans for development, operation, and evaluation.

After this review, the EPA offers a critique of the proposed evaluation design. That is, he tries to determine if it will be possible for him, given the program's direction and how the steward proposes to evaluate and operate it, to make a legitimate audit. For example: Is the baseline data sufficient? Will the proposed evaluation instruments and the way they are to be used yield appropriate data? Will there be enough and correct kinds of information available to assess the operational and management areas? And so on.

Assuming he finds the new program reasonably feasible for a program audit, the EPA will make recommendations concerning variances, omissions, etc., that he notes in his analysis of the plan. He will look particularly for discrepancies between the performance objectives and task prescriptions with the procedures and instruments used to measure their attainment. If he discovers problems that cannot be easily remedied, he will offer some alternative solutions. These solutions changes must be approved by the steward and reviewer. Appendix B contains an "Evaluation Review Instrument" developed by the U.S. Office of Education.

Having critiqued the plan of the reviewer and steward, the EPA presents his plan for auditing the program. In the audit plan he makes his case for what duties he will perform, when he will perform them, how (i.e., techniques, instruments, sampling procedures, etc.), and the kinds of data and other information he hopes to deliver to the LEA at designated times. Like the steward's task prescription, the EPA presents a statement of work to be done, specifying the quantity, quality, time, and resources. Accordingly, it now becomes necessary for the program steward and reviewer to critique the auditor's plan: is it possible?

At the same time, the EPA will have drawn up a related document, the "audit contract." Essentially, the audit contract states the purpose of the audit; a display of the professional pedigree of the auditor and his associates (if any); specifications of documents, services, schedules, sampling techniques, procedures, reports, and related details; a budget and payment schedule; and probably has a few special clauses to fit the local situation. Again, is the audit contract feasible? Usually the LEA's own evaluation expert or team will check the technical aspects of the audit plan, and the steward-reviewer will check the total plan and contract. If the Office of Education is a partner in the program, it must be consulted before the audit contract is signed and give its blessing to the transaction.

Stage III: Interim audit activities

Once the contract is signed, the auditor begins to put into operation his own program, governed by the pace and scheduling of the LEAs. Figure 11.2 suggests roughly a hypothetical schedule that might be employed by the auditor in relation to the ongoing program. Avoiding the intricate technical aspects of the auditor's work,

Figure 11.2. Hypothetical schedule for auditing an educationally
accountable program

Activities for educational program auditor	Time line	Activities of local educational agency
	December	Community advisory committee presents program design and recommendations to board
	January	Board approves new program, adopts accountability policy
	February	Board reaches agreement with program steward
LEA tentatively selects an auditor		
	March	
EPA critiques evaluation design, reviews relevant materials		
	April	
EPA submits audit plan for review		
LEA and EPA complete audit contract		
	May	
		Revised evaluation design approved
EPA visits site to observe data collection procedures and verify revised evaluation plan procedures being used	June	Staff development program started
	July	
EPA reviews appropriateness of instruments	August	
EPA observes (on-site) testing and data collecting procedures	September	Pretesting students
		Formal instructional program implementation
	October	
EPA reviews methods of analyzing data, verifies evaluation plan according to procedures, does evaluation sampling		
	November	
EPA reviews methods of analyzing data, verifies evaluation procedures according to plan, does evaluation replications	December	
	January	Interim testing (midterm)
EPA observes (on-site testing and data collecting procedures		
	February	Interim evaluation report
EPA observes (on-site) testing and data collecting procedures		
	March	Complete any program adjustments
EPA reviews methods of analyzing data, verifies evaluation procedures according to plan, does evaluation replication and samplings	April	

Activities for educational program auditors	Time line	Activities of local educational agency
	May	
		Final testing and program evaluation
EPA submits draft on final audit report, verifies product outcomes	June	
		Rendering of the steward's account
	July	
EPA submits final audit report		
	August	Reviewer's determination of level of confidence
	September	Reviewer's certification of program results to the public

he generally seeks to verify that the steward and the program are doing what, according to plans and agreements, they are expected to do. To determine this, the auditor visits classes, looks at materials, talks to people, sample tests, and generally pokes around according to the authority the audit contract has given him. He also thinks a lot about what is happening and what it means. The results of his pokings and thoughts, he shares with the program steward as reports. At some point in the program's operation (usually at midpoint), the auditor will follow up the steward's formal interim report to the reviewer with an interim report of his own. The auditor's report verifies or questions the steward's report regarding the operation, management, and evaluation procedures and results. If discrepancies in the interim reports arise, questions follow. Based on the information in the interim reports, consideration is given by the reviewer, steward, and auditor to making any necessary adjustments in the program. If the data warrants it, changes are made, and the program moves toward its final stage.

Stage IV: The final audit report

The interim report dealt with the effectiveness of the program's evaluation process in regulating its implementation, documentating its functioning, and calling attention to areas needing trouble shooting. The final audit report either certifies or takes exception to the evaluation findings submitted by the steward to the reviewer; the auditor in effect certifies—or does not—the account rendered by the steward. The U.S. Office of Education suggests that the auditor's final report contain: (1) some introductory summary comments; (2)

a close critique of the evaluation process and the total results; (3) descriptions of the on-site visits and their findings; (4) recommendations made for revisions in the evaluation design; and (5) confirmation or questioning of the program results reported by the steward. Appendix C offers a "Program Audit Review Instrument," developed by the U.S. Office of Education, that should be useful to both auditors and stewards in suggesting material for the contents of their individual accounts.

The steward and the auditor

It has probably become clear to the reader that the steward and the auditor are linked in terms of what accounts they present to the reviewer. While the contents, general format, results, and other information contained in each man's final account to the reviewer may have strong similarities, the vantage point and perspective of each individual will be different. It is difficult to assess how happy this pairing is likely to be in operation. Optimistically, the steward should welcome the auditor as another pair of eyes and a finely trained mind brought to bear upon the problems of the steward's program. Given the right blending of personalities and approaches, it might yield solid contributions beyond merely confirming or not confirming the steward's account. But do they really share similar goals? It takes little imagination to guess at the possible unhappiness for all if the wrong people have to work together. Given open, positive stewards and auditors, we prefer to be optimistic.

Determining the Level of Confidence: An Act of Judgment

The time arrives in every organizational enterprise when there is a significant pause for reflection. In our presentation, this moment comes at the end of the reviewer's examination of the steward's account (and the auditor's, if one is used), when the reviewer comes to his own conclusions about the steward and the product of his labors. This determination of the level of confidence represents a review of the past in the present with portents for the future. It focuses on the outcomes, the program, and the steward, asking simply: Are they acceptable? The answer requires an act of judgment.

Judgment making is a curious blend. It is broader in size and scope than decision making, an expression often substituted for it. Judgment is the ability of persons to fit the pattern of reality into a larger framework; the bits and pieces of data that form an incomplete mosaic in the mind evolve into a collection of impulses that say now or later, good or bad, this way or that. Sometimes these impulses are strong and firm; at other times, weak and tenuous. They motivate decision making toward action or delay it, determine whether the decisions made are to be valued "good" or "bad," and represent a quality of the mind we describe as "judgment," whose value can be assessed only after the fact. Technically correct "good" decisions have lost wars, bankrupted companies, and performed intellectual lobotomies on children; "poor" judgments have had the same effects, but such experiences seldom get attached to "good" judgments, defined in retrospect. Judgment making is one of the higher acts of man and, because of its partially intuitive nature and the need for historical assessment, defies being clearly accounted for in its exercise.

Among the virtues offered by the process of educational accountability is its tendency to provide the reviewer with a basis for exercising "informed judgment." We neither take lightly nor disregard the intuitive quality of judgment making; we do assume that the quality of judgments made in situations of uncertainty of critical information is likely to be inferior to that of judgments made with higher certainty of critical information. Given more exact information on areas believed to be significant, the incidence of superior judgment increases. Accordingly, judgments made on the basis of significant information (as opposed to those lacking data and based largely on conjecture) are considered informed judgments.

The availability of significant information does not guarantee that the process of forming a judgment will be any easier, but the information provided should permit resolution of many imponderables in making judgments. Several elements were deliberately built into the process of developing an educationally accountable program to assure the presence of significant factors believed necessary for informed judgment.

First, the reviewer's initial intentions and expectations had to be thought through, clarified, and presented in written form beforehand. This action was necessary at the point of reviewing the program design and everything related to it (e.g., the board's accountability policy, the negotiated agreement between the reviewer and steward, and—if used—the agreement with the educational program auditor). The general direction of the program was never dim nor doubtful. The standards of desirability were articulated.

Secondly, as the program's goals and objectives were translated and negotiated into educational performance objectives and task prescriptions, understandings grew between the steward and the reviewer about what seemed possible or likely to result from certain approaches, and what approaches seemed unfruitful. This established a second precondition for later judgment making. Both the reviewers and the steward refined what they separately desired to happen and believed might be possible into what they were now willing to commit themselves to as criteria for acceptable performance. Thus, the broad standard of desirability yielded a tighter, narrower second standard: the standard of acceptability.

For example, both the publisher and authors of this book, as a broad standard of desirability, hope it will be well received (with each of us having his own further particularized thoughts on what that term means). But, confronted with the task of creating a "well-received" book on this topic, we settled on an agreement that converted this standard of desirability into a standard of acceptability through task prescriptions on the quantity, quality, time, and resources to be involved in the publication effort. The authors worked as stewards, the publisher (also accepting obligations) as reviewer. The book's sales, reviews, consumer use, and other unanticipated outcomes will render the long-term judgment related to our standard of desirability. But the immediate necessary judgment for the publisher/reviewer is whether to accept for publication the manuscript results offered by the author/stewards. If you are reading these words, you know what judgment our publisher exercised regarding the standards of acceptability. Presumably having read through our effort to this point, you should be in a position (on completion) to make a judgment, based on your own perceptions, of how likely we are to achieve our broader standard of desirability, a "well-received" publication. In a sense, the steward/authors labored to produce an outcome, a manuscript; the reviewer/publisher (after submitting it to his own auditor, his editor, for an opinion) exercised his judgment and expressed his level of confidence by accepting the manuscript outcome, modifying the program (in this case, book) by making some changes, and rewarded the steward/authors by publishing the manuscript. Now, like a board of education that has passed judgment on an educationally accountable program and publicly released this news (i.e., certified the results), we await the larger public's reaction. Will there be any, or will the people "out there" only yawn indifferently? Did we offend someone? Will the results be ridiculed or praised; declared "good" or "bad"? In short, will the future render a kind judgment? We hope so. And so will the board of education, administrators, and all others who in the present must generally defer to the judgment of the future on efforts they made in the past.

In sum, the accountability process is structured so that at the point of determining a level of confidence for the outcomes, the program, and the steward, the reviewer has gathered before him:

· Statements of what was desired;

· Statements of what was to be done to accomplish the desired ends;

· Statements of what was considered acceptable for the results of work done;

· An account of what the steward did and did not achieve and an explanation why;

· An account (if used) of whether the steward and others did what was expected of them and whether the results offered in the steward's account were certified correct;

· And, most importantly, an implied record of the reviewer's previous judgments and commitment to the standards, tasks, goals, and objectives of the program.

All these items should operate to produce an informed judgment coming to fruition on the acceptability of the outcomes, the program itself, and the stewardship.

Regarding this last determination, where predetermined levels of confidence have been made in the initial agreement between steward and reviewer, it follows that the judgment will yield its determination of rewards or penalties (usually monetary) in accordance with the actual results that trigger it. Whether pre or post-determined, there is normally a sort of karma form of future reward or penalty for the steward based on the reviewer's level of confidence in his performance. It might be expressed in the reviewer permitting or not permitting the steward to undertake similar responsibilities in the future. In case of severe loss of confidence in the steward, the relationship might be forever terminated. Conversely, great confidence in the steward's ability to achieve desired results may increase the size and scope of his authority, responsibility, and rewards.

The exercise of judgment itself remains never wholly predictable. Our accountability process, once the inputs have been accepted, has been generally presented as a closed system in that if there are problems, they are presumed contained within the system and its operation. The big world, however, try as we might to avoid it, has a way of intruding into the ordered affairs of men at times and places and with consequences unforeseen. The extent to which outside influences affect the operation of the program must also be weighed and considered by the reviewers in making their judgment.

In the end, the level of confidence is made. It is conveyed first to the appropriate immediate parties and then publicly to the community. This public statement acts as the reviewer's "certification of results." Normally, the board of education makes a news release and prepares a formal report on the program. In recent years, "school profiles" have been used, for example, in districts in Columbus, Ohio, and New Rochelle, New York, as expressions of the local board's accountability policy. Prepared by the board's professional staff, these profiles contain enormous amounts of data on the local learning environment. Starting with facts and figures about the community itself, they include data on pupil absence, mobility rates, racial makeup; staff preparation, assignment turnover rates, and amounts of experience; and then focus heavily on evaluation of educational ability and academic achievement by district, school, and grade level. Compared with the more traditional forms of educational progress reporting, these accountability profiles (as they are sometimes called) tell a more direct tale to the community: what learning results their children have achieved over the past year.[9] With this certification of results recorded by the reviewer, he now finds himself the subject of review.

Concluding Thoughts

Because of the nature of public institutions, we believe educational progress is more likely to result from rationally designed programs whose purposes and intentions are measurably and publicly clear, and that seek some form of accountability for the results obtained under a covenant that conjoins freedom and responsibility. Loosely understood educational programs producing unnoted outcomes for partially delineated purposes, developed and influenced by unanswerable parties—even when seemingly successful—make the form and direction of progress unclear. Cause-and-effect relationships remain clouded, the latitudes of freedom and responsibility blurred. "To err is human," yet without greater accountability within education, there seems to be little hope of redressing error or of even locating it for attention and redirection. Rather, both progress and error remain fixed like the needle of a recording disc caught in a groove, repeating and repeating, until someone accepts responsibility for noting it and uses his freedom to do something about it.

Again, we do not see the accountability process as a great panacea for public education. The road we have marked out is not an easy one to travel (as the imperatives of chapter 2 should indicate). There still remains much skepticism about education's technical ability (let alone other considerations) to produce educationally accountable programs. Many readers may still question the desirability of such programs.

But the concept itself has value. It offers promise and potential, worth trying at least at the level of a pilot program or two in the local district, working out technical problems, locating errors, and accounting for results. Given positive people, willing to give and accept defined freedoms and responsibilities, with the authority that attends them for achieving specified tasks, and answering for the results of their efforts, we think such educationally accountable programs possible. As the combination of experience, research, and development of such programs increases (perhaps urged on by external pressures for more visible educational results), a future for educationally accountable programs is probable.

If significant progress in public education is to be made over the final quarter of the twentieth century, we believe its route lies along the path made by accountable programs. We fully expect and hope superior forms of program development will emerge with the passing of time. If and when they do, our guess is that accountability will be part of their foundation.

We opened our work suggesting that mankind faces an uncertain future of accelerating changes. We have the choice of picking our way through the changes with forethought, planning, and deliberate choices of direction, charted with provisions of accountability to monitor and modify the course; or simply being swept along indifferently on the currents of change. We value accountability as a way to increase public education's fitness to respond. It can be expected to shape the manner in which our children will stand to account as adults in that strangest of places, the future. If our work has been successful, it should be helpful today for that voyage into tomorrow. Ignazio Silone remarks: "On a group of theories one can found a school; but on a group of values one can found a culture, a civilization, a new way of living together among men."[10] Moving toward that uncertain future, the qualities of educationally accountable programs have something of value.

Notes for Chapter 11

1. A. D. Newman and R. W. Rowbottom, *Organizational Analysis* (Carbondale, Ill.: Southern Illinois University Press, 1968), p. 82.

2. This quote and several others related to the accountability topic appear "A Thought Collage," in *Emerging Patterns of Administrative Accountability*,

ed. Lesley Browder, Jr. (Berkeley: McCutchan Publishing Corp., 1971), pp. 567-71.

3. James D. Thompson, *Organizations in Action* (New York: McGraw-Hill, 1967), p. 118.

4. Ibid., p. 159.

5. For a classic statement of conjoined freedom and responsibility, see Carl L. Becker, *Freedom and Responsibility in the American Way of Life* (New York: Alfred A. Knopf, 1945).

6. Alfred J. Morin, "Handbook for Educational Program Audit," USOE Contract no. OEC-0-70-5047 (Washington, D.C.: Alfred J. Morin Associates, June 1971), p. 18.

7. In addition to Morin's work, there are several related sources worth checking on this topic: W. Stanley Kruger, "Outline of Educational Program Auditing Procedures" (Washington, D.C.: USOE, April 3, 1970); Robert Kraner, "Educational Program Audit," in *Educational Accountability Through Evaluation,* ed. E. Wayne Roberson (Englewood Cliffs, N.J.: Educational Technology, Inc., 1971), pp. 92-107; EPIC, *Educational Program Audit* (Tucson, Ariz.: Educational Innovators Press, 1971); A. Jackson Stenner and William J. Webster, *Educational Program Audit Handbook* (preliminary edition developed for Alabama State Department of Education Workshop, May 1971); Leon Lessinger, "The Independent Educational Accomplishment Audit," in *Every Kid a Winner* (Palo Alto, Calif.: Science Research Associates, 1970), chapter 5.

8. If uncertain where to look, try:
> Division of Plans and Supplementary Centers
> Bureau of Elementary and Secondary Education
> United States Office of Education
> 400 Maryland Avenue
> Washington, D.C. 20202

Several private consulting companies have been involved in educational program auditing also (e.g., Booz, Allen, and Hamilton; Dunlop Associates). Nonprofit groups like Educational Testing Service of Princeton, N.J., and Evaluative Programs for Innovative Curriculums (EPIC) of Tucson, Ariz., have representatives over most of the country.

Some universities also train program auditors directly or otherwise do considerable work in that area. Florida State University, University of California at Riverside, Georgia State University, and the Bureau of Educational Evaluation at Hofstra University are examples.

9. An informative article on the efforts by several school districts to report publicly their students' achievement test results appears in Gene R. Hawes, "Releasing Test Scores: Urgent or Unthinkable?" *Nation's Schools* 89, no. 4 (April 1972): 41-55.

10. Quoted from *The Saturday Evening Post* (spring 1972), p. 134.

Appendixes

Appendix A. A Sample Board Policy

District policy re: **Basic Reading Competence**

I. A Recognized Educational Need

We recognize a need in basic reading competency. This year's state-administered standardized tests for grades three and six, our own tests for grades two and five, and the applied standardized commercial achievement tests for grades one and four, *all* confirm the same trend: by the third grade, 24 percent of our 1,857 third graders read below minimum competence and, instead of decreasing, the percentage increases to 31 percent of the 1,763 sixth graders. In addition, this trend roughly parallels the perceptions of pupils (and their parents) on their own abilities to read; 32 percent of third graders and 38 percent of sixth graders state that they read considerably less well than their classmates (40 percent of third-grader parents and 22 percent of sixth-grader parents hold a similar opinion about their children's reading ability). In a close analysis of the sixth grade student group, 55 percent of them report they do not like reading and 70 percent of sixth grader parents claim that they have not observed or been aware of their child's doing more than the minimum required reading in the last six months. Nearly 40 percent of the sixth-grader parents recall having bought reading material in the last six months that they believed had special appeal to their child's interest, yet only one in five of these parents report that the child made any effort to read this material. In a review of this year's 20 percent dropout rate at the high school level, four out of every five dropouts had sub-sixth grade level reading competency skills.

Yet it is the cardinal goal of this district's philosophy that *every child shall learn,* and 95 percent of our community regard the assurance of basic reading competency as the school's first priority.

II. District Policy for Basic Reading Competency

• *Policy rationale.* In our search for guidelines to meet this educational need and to ensure that every child shall learn, this board subscribes to the notion that:

If students are normally distributed with respect to aptitude, but the kind and quality of instruction and the amount of time available for learning are made appropriate to the characteristics and needs of *each* student, the majority of students may be expected to achieve mastery of the subject. And, the relationship between aptitude and achievement should approach zero. (Bloom, 1968, p. 3)

• *Policy goal.* From this notion, developed by Carroll (1963) and supported by the works of Morrison (1926), Bruner (1966), Skinner (1954), Suppes (1966), Goodlad and Anderson (1959), Glaser (1968), and best stated by Bloom (1968), this board states as a curriculum policy goal that *every child shall learn mastery of basic reading competency.*

• *Policy objectives.* The following objectives we believe to be related to the rationale offered and support our policy goal. This board holds that:

1. Because of the vital importance of reading and our serious commitment to the goal for "mastery of basic reading competency," we interpret this term to mean that: (a) at the elementary level (K-6), mastery is grade reading level (within standard scoring deviations) as determined by standardized tests; and, (b) before high school graduation, all graduating students shall be required to demonstrate an adult survival reading capacity of 90 percent proficiency on such reading materials as the local newspaper, the United States Constitution, the state driver's manual, state and federal income tax forms, standard health insurance policies, and similar items.

2. In keeping with the rationale of our policy, we offer special attention to the variables of mastery learning (Bloom, 1968):

    a. *Aptitude for learning.* This board believes that, where basic reading is concerned, aptitude is the amount of time required by the learner to attain mastery of the learning task (Carroll, 1963). Implicit in this belief is the assumption that given enough time, all pupils can conceivably attain mastery of the learning task (Bloom, 1968; Glaser, 1968; Atkinson, 1967). It is an objective of this district that each child shall be given sufficient instructional time according to his need to attain basic reading mastery as a first instructional priority. At the elementary level (K-6), this means that reading instruction will be geared to each child and an estimation made and followed of the amount of time necessary to bring each child up to grade level performance. In no case, however, is the amount of time expected to exceed 50 percent of the child's instructional day. At the secondary level (7-12), all seventh and eighth grade students falling two reading grade levels below shall attend special reading classes. Above the eighth grade, students not meeting sixth grade reading competency will participate in a special "adult literacy program."

b. *Quality of instruction.* This board believes that individual students need different types and qualities of instruction to achieve mastery, and recognizes that the same goals and objectives can be achieved by different students following different types of instruction. Therefore, quality of instruction is the degree to which the presentation and ordering of elements of the task to be learned approaches the optimum for a given learner (Carroll, 1963; Bloom, 1968). Accordingly, it is an objective of this district that the basic reading abilities of each child be diagnosed as well as the child's characteristic learning style. A *Monthly Learning Profile,* that is, a monthly record of each elementary and specially identified secondary student's reading efforts shall be kept, to include: (a) the learning diagnosis; (b) a description of the resulting individualized learning prescription; (c) the degree to which the student fulfilled these prescribed tasks; (d) the level of success attained; (e) when, where, and how this progress was reported to the student and his parents; and (f) the nature of the prescription for the month ahead. Until the optimum learning conditions for each child can be recognized, the learning prescriptions in the Monthly Learning Profile should reflect a range of alternative approaches.

c. *Ability to understand instruction.* It is our belief that the student should be able to understand what is expected of him both from the teacher and the learning materials. Where understanding is uncertain, difficulty frequently arises. The ability to understand instructions is the ability of the learner to understand the nature of the task he is to learn and the procedures he is to follow in learning the task (Bloom, 1968). Toward this understanding, it is the objective of this board that each child shall interpret to his teacher (who shall write down this interpretation if the child cannot) what he is expected to do in his individually prescribed reading program prior to the undertaking. This interpretation will become part of Monthly Learning Profile. Other things being in order, we contend that learning defeats can be countered with clear understanding of the learning tasks and the plentiful use of alternative instructional strategies.

d. *Learning perseverance.* Vital to a successful learning effort is perseverance—the time the learner is willing to spend in learning (Carroll, 1963). We make a distinction between spending time on learning and the time actively utilized by the student in learning; there is a vast difference between an hour spent watching a book gather dust and one spent avidly reading its contents. In part, perseverance is related to attitudes toward and interest in learning. At the risk of overgeneralizing, a learner experiencing some success, some earned recognition of that success, and some well-defined reasonably difficult further learning tasks (judged to be significant by the parties concerned) will usually respond favorably in terms of learning perseverance. When the learner experiences only frustration, receives no recognition for success or failure (or is overrewarded by attention for failure), has only a foggy notion of what he should be doing, and sees little advantage in making the effort to learn, he is not likely to persevere long and *is* likely to seek some escape from the task. As a strategy to increase student perseverance, an objective of this district is that the teacher review each month with the student, in a positive manner, the Monthly Learning Profile, tracing its successes and failures, contrasting it with the previous month, and attempting (within the framework of the teacher's instructional strategy) to solicit from the student his interest in and choice of learning materials as well as his estimate of his own ability to handle the upcoming learning tasks. The outcomes of this discussion should be recorded and kept with the Monthly Learning Profile.

Future meetings can repeat this process, starting with a review of the student's own estimation of what he could do. At least three times during the school year, parents will be formally invited (they are welcome by appointment at any other time also) to review the Monthly Learning Profiles (and other items). At these times, teachers will solicit from the parents their own observations of their child's progress and degree of perseverance in reading. These observations shall be added to the Monthly Learning Profile.

e. *Fondness for reading.* The board realizes that it is impossible to engineer directly the fondness for any learning task in a student. We believe that the degree to which a student likes a task is in large measure governed by his success in that task and the attitudes toward it of persons significant to the student. If we have been successful in our varied instructional approaches and student-teacher conferring efforts, as well as in our attempts to involve parents in triad situations, we believe that we have done as well as we can. It is an objective, however, to poll annually and independently our students on their academic work. We expect this poll and other items (e.g., independent library usage) to provide us with a significant indication of our progress.

III. Procedures for Implementing Policy

The superintendent shall implement the plan design submitted with this policy statement by the Advisory Planning Committee on [date]. This plan, with modifications made by the board, is hereby attached as part of this district's curriculum policy.

IV. Rendering an Account of Progress

The superintendent shall annually render an account of progress achieved on this board's policy. The guidelines and form of this report are contained in the reviewer-steward agreement of [date] and are considered a binding part of this policy.

In addition, the board shall retain an independent educational program auditor to certify the superintendent's account of the educational results stipulated in this policy and render an opinion on how the reviewer-steward agreement was adhered to by both parties.

After its review of the steward's and educational program auditor's separate accounts, the board shall certify annually the achievements toward fulfillment of this policy in its *School Profile: A Report on Educational Outcomes to the Community.*

Policy Attachments

• Advisory Planning Committee, Report: *Goals, Objectives and Educationally Accountable Program Plan Design* [date].
• Board of Education and Superintendent of Schools, *Reviewer-Steward Agreement for Basic Reading Competence* [date].
• *Reviewer-Steward—Educational Program Auditor Agreement* [date].
• Board of Education, *School Profile: A Report on Educational Outcomes to the Community* [tentative date of publication].
Date of policy approval: _____
Board of Education for _____

References

Atkinson, R. C., "Computerized Instruction and the Learning Process," Technical Report no. 122. Stanford, Calif.: Institute for Mathematical Studies in the Social Sciences, 1967.

Bloom, Benjamin, "Learning for Mastery." *Evaluation Comment* 1, no. 2 (May 1968).

Bruner, Jerome, *Toward a Theory of Instruction.* Cambridge, Mass.: Harvard University Press, 1966.

Carroll, John, "A Model of School Learning." *Teachers College Record* 6 (1963): 723-33.

Goodlad, John, and Anderson, Robert H., *The Nongraded Elementary School.* New York: Harcourt, Brace and World, 1959.

Glaser, Robert, "Adapting the Elementary School Curriculum to Individual Performance," *Proceedings: The 1967 Invitational Conference on Testing Problems.* Princeton, N.J.: Educational Testing Service, 1968.

Morrison, H. C., *The Practice of Teaching in the Secondary School.* Chicago: University of Chicago Press, 1926.

Related Board Accountability Policies

• Basic learning policies—writing, arithmetic [dates of adoption].
• Optimized learning policy [date of adoption].
• Subject area policies [listed and dated by adoption].

Appendix B. Evaluation Review Instrument

Instructions

The Evaluation Review Instrument has been designed for use in reviewing a variety of documents related to the evaluation process. Primarily, the instrument is intended as a guide for the examination of evaluation reports, in determining the quality of an evaluation that has been performed. However, the first two sections of the instrument—General Information and Critique of the Evaluation Design—can also be used in examining an evaluation plan.

Many of the items contained in the instrument call for responses on an *all—many—few—none* scale (all of the possible cases, many of the possible cases, few of the possible cases, none of the possible cases). Since we are focusing on the quality of the process, credit should be given only when evaluation activities have been adequately performed (or planned). If an evaluation report indicates that an evaluation has considered *many* of the possible cases but that his consideration has been adequate (scope, depth, accuracy, clarity, etc.) in only a *few*, the item should be marked X: *few*.

An alternate marking procedure would be the use of a checkmark to indicate the extent of consideration (e.g., *many*); with an X to indicate the extent of *adequate* consideration (e.g., *few*). In using this procedure, both indicators should always be used, even if in some cases they would both be in the same response blank.

Every short-response item should be checked on the scale provided. This will permit summarization of a group of review instruments, or quick initial comparison of several appraisals of performance on a given item. However, throughout the instrument

335

spaces are provided for comments on items within the major instrument categories. These spaces (or additional blank sheets) may be used for elaboration on specific responses whenever the reviewer wishes to do so.

Evaluation Review Instrument

Part I. General Information
Project number | Local education agency (name and address)

Evaluator (name, title, and address)

Dollar amount and percentage of budget (budget period covering academic year)
  Total budget $ _____
  Evaluation $ _____   _____%
  Audit $ _____   _____%

Type of arrangement (check *one* in *each line* below)
  Part-time evaluator ____   Full-time evaluator ____
  Outside evaluator ____   Staff evaluator ____
  Paid by project funds ____   Paid by non-project LEA funds ____
  Letter of agreement ____   Contract ____ Consultant ____ Payroll ____
  Other project duties ____   No other project duties ____

Type of evaluation document (check appropriate item)
  Evaluation plan ____
  Interim report ____
  End of budget-year report ____

Comments on Part I

Part II. Critique of the Evaluation Design

	All	Many	Few	None
A. Objectives were written in measurable terms by applying the five criteria for adequate performance objectives.	☐	☐	☐	☐

B. Adequate performance objectives for *product* existed for every component of the project.

Operation:	Yes	No	No answer
Instructional	____	____	____
Staff development	____	____	____
Materials development	____	____	____
Community involvement	____	____	____
Pupil personnel services	____	____	____
Other: _____	____	____	____
Management: General	____	____	____
	____	____	____
	____	____	____

C. Adequate performance objectives for *process* existed for every component of the project:

Operation:	Yes	No	No answer
Instructional	____	____	____
Staff development	____	____	____
Materials development	____	____	____
Community involvement	____	____	____
Pupil personnel services	____	____	____
Other: _____	____	____	____
Management: General	____	____	____
	____	____	____
	____	____	____

D. The following were part of the general evaluation design:

	All	Many	Few	None
1. Selection of appropriate evaluation techniques for determining the achievement of objectives selected for evaluation.	☐	☐	☐	☐
2. Comparability (matching or statistical treatment) of control and experimental groups (if used) in terms of relevant variables.	☐	☐	☐	☐
3. Comparability (matching or statistical treatment) of pre- and posttest populations in terms of relevant variables.	☐	☐	☐	☐
4. Determination of appropriate baselines for data-collection.	☐	☐	☐	☐

E. The instruments selected for operation and management evaluation met the following conditions:

	All	Many	Few	None
1. Appropriateness of range of instruments as related to range of objectives selected for evaluation.	☐	☐	☐	☐
2. Validity of instruments.	☐	☐	☐	☐
3. Reliability of instruments.	☐	☐	☐	☐
4. Suitability of both pre- and posttest instruments for repetition.	☐	☐	☐	☐

F. Procedures for the development of evaluation instruments included provisions for the following:

	All	Many	Few	None
1. Criterion measures for assessing attainment of objectives or groups of related objectives selected for evaluation.	☐	☐	☐	☐
2. Logistical arrangements for instrument development (personnel, schedule, budget, etc.)	☐	☐	☐	☐
3. Determination of the validity of instruments.	☐	☐	☐	☐
4. Determination of the reliability of instruments.	☐	☐	☐	☐

G. Data-collection procedures were appropriate for the following:

	All	Many	Few	None
1. Scheduling of data-collection activities.	☐	☐	☐	☐
2. Ethnic/language or other group differentiation for data-collection purposes.	☐	☐	☐	☐
3. Specifications for selection and training of testers, observers, or interviewers for the administration of each evaluation instrument.	☐	☐	☐	☐

H. Data-analysis procedures were appropriate for the following:

	All	Many	Few	None
1. Data tabulation and summarization arrangements.	☐	☐	☐	☐
2. Descriptive statistics for data-analysis.	☐	☐	☐	☐
3. Tests of significance for data-analysis.	☐	☐	☐	☐

I. Data-analysis presentations were appropriate for the following:

	All	Many	Few	None
1. Time schedules for the submission of evaluation reports in relation to evaluation activities.	☐	☐	☐	☐
2. Reporting time schedule in terms of relationship to key decision-making points within project, LEA, and OE requirements.	☐	☐	☐	☐
3. Establishment of person(s) responsible for report preparation and submission.	☐	☐	☐	☐
4. Provisions for transmitting reports to decision makers.	☐	☐	☐	☐

Comments on Part II

Part III. Assessment of the Project Evaluation Process

A. The evaluation design (techniques and procedures) was implemented as planned for each project component:

Operation:	Product			Process		
	Yes	No	No answer	Yes	No	No answer
Instructional	___	___	___	___	___	___
Staff development	___	___	___	___	___	___
Materials development	___	___	___	___	___	___
Community involvement	___	___	___	___	___	___
Pupil personnel services	___	___	___	___	___	___
Other: _____	___	___	___	___	___	___
Management: General	___	___	___	___	___	___
	___	___	___	___	___	___
	___	___	___	___	___	___

B. The evaluation design was implemented on schedule (time) for each component:

Operation:	Product			Process		
	Yes	No	No answer	Yes	No	No answer
Instructional	___	___	___	___	___	___
Staff development	___	___	___	___	___	___
Materials development	___	___	___	___	___	___
Community involvement	___	___	___	___	___	___
Pupil personnel services	___	___	___	___	___	___
Other: _____	___	___	___	___	___	___
Management: General	___	___	___	___	___	___
	___	___	___	___	___	___
	___	___	___	___	___	___

C. Measurement instruments to be developed for the project were:

	All	Many	Few	None
1. Actually developed	☐	☐	☐	☐
2. Developed on time	☐	☐	☐	☐
3. Developed in accordance with established criteria	☐	☐	☐	☐
4. Checked for reliability	☐	☐	☐	☐
5. Validated	☐	☐	☐	☐

D. The implementation of data-collection procedures considered:

	All	Many	Few	None
1. Completion of scheduled data-collection activities.	☐	☐	☐	☐
2. Conditions and circumstances of evaluation instrument administration.	☐	☐	☐	☐
3. Training of data-collection personnel.	☐	☐	☐	☐

E. The implementation of data-analysis procedures considered the following:

	All	Many	Few	None
1. Data tabulations and summarization activities.	☐	☐	☐	☐
2. Descriptive statistics for data analysis.	☐	☐	☐	☐
3. Tests of significance for data analysis.	☐	☐	☐	☐
4. Cognizance of factors not provided for in evaluation design but affecting experimental and/or control groups.	☐	☐	☐	☐

F. The implementation of data-analysis presentation procedures considered the following:

	All	Many	Few	None
1. Time schedules for submission of evaluation reports in relation to completed evaluation activities.	☐	☐	☐	☐
2. Time schedules for reporting related to key decision-making points within project, LEA, and OE requirements.	☐	☐	☐	☐
3. Format (content) of evaluation reports.	☐	☐	☐	☐
4. Identification of person(s) responsible for evaluation reports.	☐	☐	☐	☐

5. Provisions for transmitting evaluation reports to:

	All	Many	Few	None
Project management	☐	☐	☐	☐
Project staff	☐	☐	☐	☐
LEA officials	☐	☐	☐	☐
Parents	☐	☐	☐	☐
Community groups	☐	☐	☐	☐

Comments on Part III

Part IV. Evaluator Recommendations

	All	Many	Few	None
A. The evaluator made recommendations for program modifications based on project evaluation.	☐	☐	☐	☐
B. Rationales were provided for the recommendations.	☐	☐	☐	☐
C. Recommendations were phrased in terms of:				
1. Alternative actions or possible sources of assistance.	☐	☐	☐	☐
2. Specific corrective actions.	☐	☐	☐	☐

Comments on Part IV

Part V. General Assessment of Evaluation by Reviewer

Reviewer

Date

Appendix C. Program Audit Review Instrument

Instructions

The Program Audit Review Instrument has been designed for use in reviewing a variety of documents related to the educational program audit process. Primarily, the instrument is intended as a guide for the examination of audit reports, in determining the quality of an educational program audit that has been performed. However, with proper adjustments in reading an item (e.g., instead of "the auditor assessed . . . ," read, "the auditor plans to assess . . ."), the instrument can also be used in the examination of an educational program audit plan.

Many of the items contained in the instrument call for responses on an *all–many–few–none* scale (all of the possible cases, many of the possible cases, few of the possible cases, none of the possible cases). Since we are focusing on the quality of the educational program audit process, credit should be given only when audit activities have been adequately performed (or planned). If an audit report indicates that an auditor has considered many of the possible cases, but that his consideration has been adequate in only a few of the possible cases (scope, depth, accuracy, clarity, etc.), the item should be marked X: *few.*

An alternate marking procedure would be the use of a checkmark to indicate the extent of consideration (e.g., *many*), with an X to indicate the extent of *adequate* consideration (e.g., *few*). In using this procedure, both indicators should always be used even if in some cases they would both be in the same response blank.

Program Audit Review Instrument

Part I. General Information

Project number	Local education agency (name and address)	Dollar amount and percentage of budget (budget period covering academic year)	
		Audit	Evaluation
Auditor (name, title, and address)		$_____	$_____
		_____ %	_____ %
		Total budget $ _____	

Person/team primarily responsible for evaluation and his/its relationship to project (on staff, full- or part-time, under contract, etc.)

Type of audit document(s) received (check appropriate items)
1. Audit plan (contract/letter of agreement) _____
2. Critique of evaluation design—preaudit report _____
3. Critique and interim audit report combined _____
4. Interim audit report(s) _____
5. End of budget-year report _____
6. All audit reports combined _____

Type of audit arrangement (check *one* in *each line* below)
Letter of agreement _____   Contract _____
Paid auditor _____   Unpaid auditor _____
Approved by OE _____   Not approved by OE (paid on consultant basis) _____

Comments on Part I

Part II. Functions of the Auditor
A. In his plan/report the auditor focused attention on the assessment of (check appropriate items):

Program design _____   Evaluation process _____
Program operations _____   Evaluative data _____
Evaluation design _____   Program management _____

Comments on Part II

Part III. Critique of the Evaluation Design

A. The auditor submitted a written critique of the evaluation designs to the LEA. (If the answer is No, proceed to Part IV.)

Yes ☐   No ☐

B. The auditor assessed the degree to which ob-   All   Many   Few   None
   jectives were written in measurable terms by
   applying the five criteria for adequate per-
   formance objectives.   ☐   ☐   ☐   ☐

C. The auditor assessed the degree to which adequate performance objectives for
   product existed for every component of the project.

   Operation: Yes   No   No answer
     Instructional   ____   ____   ____
     Staff development   ____   ____   ____
     Materials development   ____   ____   ____
     Community involvement   ____   ____   ____
     Pupil personnel services   ____   ____   ____
     Other: _____   ____   ____   ____

D. The auditor assessed the degree to which adequate performance objectives for
   process existed for every component of the project.

   Operation: Yes   No   No answer
     Instructional   ____   ____   ____
     Staff development   ____   ____   ____
     Materials development   ____   ____   ____
     Community involvement   ____   ____   ____
     Pupil personnel services   ____   ____   ____
     Other: _____   ____   ____   ____
   Management: General   ____   ____   ____
                                                ____   ____   ____
                                                ____   ____   ____

E. The auditor considered the following in his critique of the general evaluation
   design:

                                                   All   Many   Few   None
   1. Selection of appropriate evaluation tech-
      niques for determining the achievement of
      objectives selected for evaluation.   ☐   ☐   ☐   ☐
   2. Comparability (matching or statistical
      treatment) of control and experimental
      groups (if used) in terms of relevant vari-
      ables.   ☐   ☐   ☐   ☐
   3. Comparability (matching or statistical
      treatment) of pre and posttest population
      in terms of relevant variables.   ☐   ☐   ☐   ☐
   4. Determination of appropriate baselines for
      data-collection.   ☐   ☐   ☐   ☐

F. The auditor considered the following in his critique of instruments selected
   for operation and management evaluation:

                                                   All   Many   Few   None
   1. Appropriateness of range of instruments as
      related to range of objectives selected for
      evaluation.   ☐   ☐   ☐   ☐
   2. Validity of instruments.   ☐   ☐   ☐   ☐
   3. Reliability of instruments.   ☐   ☐   ☐   ☐
   4. Suitability of both pre and postinstruments
      for repetition.   ☐   ☐   ☐   ☐

G. The auditor determined that procedures for the *development* of evaluation instruments included provisions for the following:

	All	Many	Few	None
1. Criterion measures for assessing attainment of objectives or groups of related objectives selected for evaluation.	☐	☐	☐	☐
2. Logistical arrangements for instrument development (personnel, schedule, budget, etc.)	☐	☐	☐	☐
3. Determination of the validity of instruments.	☐	☐	☐	☐
4. Determination of the reliability of instruments.	☐	☐	☐	☐

H. The auditor considered the following in assessing data-collection procedures:

	All	Many	Few	None
1. Scheduling of data-collection activities.	☐	☐	☐	☐
2. Ethnic/language or other group differentiation for data-collection purposes.	☐	☐	☐	☐
3. Specifications for selection and training of testers, observers, or interviewers for the administration of each evaluation instrument.	☐	☐	☐	☐

I. The auditor considered the following in assessing data-analysis procedures:

	All	Many	Few	None
1. Data tabulation and summarization arrangements.	☐	☐	☐	☐
2. Descriptive statistics for data-analysis.	☐	☐	☐	☐
3. Tests of significance for data-analysis.	☐	☐	☐	☐

J. The auditor considered the following in assessing data-analysis presentations:

	All	Many	Few	None
1. Time schedules for the submission of evaluation reports in relation to evaluation activities.	☐	☐	☐	☐
2. Reporting time schedule in terms of relationship to key decision-making points within project, LEA, and OE requirements.	☐	☐	☐	☐
3. Establishment of person(s) responsible for report preparation and submission.	☐	☐	☐	☐
4. Provisions for transmitting reports to decision makers.	☐	☐	☐	☐

K. The auditor made recommendations for revisions in the evaluation design.

	All	Many	Few	None
	☐	☐	☐	☐

Rationales were provided for the recommendations.

	All	Many	Few	None
1. Alternative actions or possible sources of assistance.	☐	☐	☐	☐
2. Specific corrective actions.	☐	☐	☐	☐

Comments on Part III

Part IV. Assessment of the Project Evaluation Process

A. The auditor assessed the degree to which the evaluation design (techniques and procedures) was implemented *as planned* for each project component.

	Product			Process		
Operation:	Yes	No	No answer	Yes	No	No answer
Instructional	___ ___		___	___ ___		___
Staff development	___ ___		___	___ ___		___
Materials development	___ ___		___	___ ___		___
Community involvement	___ ___		___	___ ___		___
Pupil personnel services	___ ___		___	___ ___		___
Other: _____	___ ___		___	___ ___		___
Management: General	___ ___		___	___ ___		___
	___ ___		___	___ ___		___
	___ ___		___	___ ___		___

B. The auditor assessed the degree to which the evaluation design was implemented *on schedule* (time) for each component.

	Product			Process		
Operation:	Yes	No	No answer	Yes	No	No answer
Instructional	___ ___		___	___ ___		___
Staff development	___ ___		___	___ ___		___
Materials development	___ ___		___	___ ___		___
Community involvement	___ ___		___	___ ___		___
Pupil personnel services	___ ___		___	___ ___		___
Other: _____	___ ___		___	___ ___		___
Management: General	___ ___		___	___ ___		___
	___ ___		___	___ ___		___
	___ ___		___	___ ___		___

C. The auditor assessed the degree to which measurement instruments to be developed for the project were:

	All	Many	Few	None
1. Actually developed.	☐	☐	☐	☐
2. Developed on time.	☐	☐	☐	☐
3. Developed in accordance with established criteria.	☐	☐	☐	☐
4. Checked for reliability.	☐	☐	☐	☐
5. Validated.	☐	☐	☐	☐

D. The auditor assessed the implementation of data-collection procedures in terms of:

	All	Many	Few	None
1. Completion of scheduled data-collection activities.	☐	☐	☐	☐
2. Conditions and circumstances of evaluation instrument administration.	☐	☐	☐	☐
3. Training of data-collection personnel.	☐	☐	☐	☐

E. The auditor assessed the implementation of data-analysis procedures in relation to the following:

	All	Many	Few	None
1. Data tabulation and summarization activities.	☐	☐	☐	☐
2. Descriptive statistics for data-analysis.	☐	☐	☐	☐
3. Tests of significance for data-analysis.	☐	☐	☐	☐

	All	Many	Few	None
4. Cognizance of factors not provided for in evaluation design but affecting experimental and/or control groups.	☐	☐	☐	☐

F. The auditor assessed the implementation of data-analysis presentation procedures in terms of the following:

	All	Many	Few	None
1. Time schedules for submission of evaluation reports in relation to completed evaluation activities.	☐	☐	☐	☐
2. Time schedules for reporting related to key decision-making points within project, LEA, and OE requirements.	☐	☐	☐	☐
3. Format (content) of evaluation reports.	☐	☐	☐	☐
4. Identification of person(s) responsible for evaluation reports.	☐	☐	☐	☐

5. Provisions for transmitting evaluation reports to:

	All	Many	Few	None
Project management	☐	☐	☐	☐
Project staff	☐	☐	☐	☐
LEA officials	☐	☐	☐	☐
Parents	☐	☐	☐	☐
Community groups	☐	☐	☐	☐

Comments on Part IV

Part V. Verification of Project Evaluation Results

A. The auditor presented a summary of consistencies and discrepancies between evaluation and audit findings for each program component:

Operation:	Yes	No	No answer
Instructional	___	___	___
Staff development	___	___	___
Materials development	___	___	___
Community involvement	___	___	___
Pupil personnel services	___	___	___
Other: _____	___	___	___
Management: General	___	___	___
	___	___	___
	___	___	___

	All	Many	Few	None
B. The auditor assessed the evaluator's recommendations for program modifications based on project evaluation.	☐	☐	☐	☐

Comments on Part V

Part VI. Audit Report Feedback to Project

	All	Many	Few	None
A. The auditor provided feedback in sufficient detail to be useful to project.	☐	☐	☐	☐
B. The auditor provided feedback in time to influence the planning and/or implementation of the evaluation.	☐	☐	☐	☐

If not, why not?

Comments on Part VI

Part VII. General Assessment of Audit Reports by Reviewer of Reports

Reviewer

Date

Index

Names

Adams, John W., 280
Aikin, Wilford, 193
Alexander, William, 170
Alioto, Robert, 223
Alkin, Marvin C., 239, 245, 246, 253
Alpha Learning Systems, 259
American Association of Colleges for Teacher Education (AACTE), 230
American Association of School Administrators (AASA), 258
American Education Research Association (AERA), 173
American Federation of Teachers (AFT), 119, 257
Amidon, J., 194
Anderson, D. P., 173
Anderson, Scarvia, 103
Anton, Todd, 223
Archibald, Russell, 253
Armstrong, Robert, 194
Association of School Business Officials (ASBO), 174, 196, 222
Association for Supervision and Curriculum Development (ASCD), 170
Atkin, Myron J., 176, 193
Atkins, William A., Jr., iii-iv
Ausubel, D. P., 69

Bailey, Stephen K., 141, 171, 194
Baker, Bruce, 253
Baker, N. R., 69
Ballachey, Egerton, 30, 69, 138, 171
Banathy, B. H., 103
Barnard, Chester, 24, 30
Barro, Stephen, 12, 27, 28, 240, 245, 253
Baumgartner, John, 237, 252
Baynham, Doresy, 127
Becker, Carl L., 325
Beer, C. R., 254
Behavioral Outcomes Project (Norwalk, Conn.), 176
Behavioral Research Laboratories, 255, 259
Bell, Daniel, 26
Bell, Terrell H., 20, 29, 146, 172
Bellack, Arnold, 194
Belmont Project, 282
Benne, Kenneth, 126
Bennis, Warren, 126, 253
Bernabei, Raymond, 28, 54, 70, 195
Bessent, Wailand, 251
Billings, Charles, 170
Blake, Robert, 108, 126
Blaschke, Charles, 71, 280
Bloom, Benjamin, 15, 27, 69, 70, 92, 104, 176, 179, 193, 194

Topics